ANNUAL EDITIONS

Education

Thirty-fourth Edition

07/08

EDITOR

Fred Schultz

University of Akron (Retired)

Fred Schultz, former professor of education at the University of Akron, attended Indiana University to earn a B.S. in social science education in 1962, an M.S. in the history and philosophy of education in 1966, and a Ph.D. in the history and philosophy of education and American studies in 1969. His B.A. in Spanish was conferred from the University of Akron in May 1985. He is actively involved in researching the development and history of American education with a primary focus on the history of ideas and social philosophy of education. He also likes to study languages.

 **Contemporary Learning Series**

2460 Kerper Blvd., Dubuque, IA 52001

Visit us on the Internet
http://www.mhcls.com

Credits

Copyright

Cataloging in Publication Data
Main entry under title: Annual Editions: Education. 2007/2008.
1. Education—Periodicals. I. Schultz, Fred, *comp*. II. Title: Education.
ISBN-13: 978–0–07–351625–7   ISBN-10: 0–07–351625–2   658'.05   ISSN 0272–5010

Thirty-fourth Edition

Cover image © Comstock Images/Juniper Images and Digital Vison/PunchStock
Printed in the United States of America   1234567890QPDQPD987   Printed on Recycled Paper

Editors/Advisory Board

Members of the Advisory Board are instrumental in the final selection of articles for each edition of ANNUAL EDITIONS. Their review of articles for content, level, currentness, and appropriateness provides critical direction to the editor and staff. We think that you will find their careful consideration well reflected in this volume.

Preface

In publishing ANNUAL EDITIONS we recognize the enormous role played by the magazines, newspapers, and journals of the public press in providing current, first-rate educational information in a broad spectrum of interest areas. Many of these articles are appropriate for students, researchers, and professionals seeking accurate, current material to help bridge the gap between principles and theories and the real world. These articles, however, become more useful for study when those of lasting value are carefully collected, organized, indexed, and reproduced in a low-cost format, which provides easy and permanent access when the material is needed. That is the role played by ANNUAL EDITIONS.

As we approach the final years of this first decade in this new century, it is amazing to see the great advances in our technologically powered ability to find alternative paths to information from which develop our "education" as persons. This is a good time to reflect on our educational heritage and to act for the betterment of all.

We face a situation with reference to our educational policy priorities that is divided and not easily resolved. On the one hand, we are to have "highly qualified teachers"; on the other hand, we leave it to state politicians and the local school authority as to what constitutes "highly qualified teachers." This is a typical enigmatic dilemma in the history of American education. If we are not to leave any student behind, really and sincerely, can we come to grips with what it means to have a "highly qualified teacher?"

Issues regarding the purposes of education as well as the appropriate methods of educating have been debated throughout all generations of literate human culture. This is because the meaning of the word "educated" shifts within ideological realms of thought and cultural belief systems. There will always be debates over the purposes and the ends of "education" as it is understood in any time or place. This is because each generation must continuously reconstruct the definition of "education" based upon its understanding of "justice," "fairness," and "equity" in human relations, and each generation must locate and position their understanding of social and personal reality.

We must decide what knowledge is of most worth and what basic skills and information each child needs to know. We must face this question once and for all; it is a duty, if we are disciplined persons interested in the well-being of our children and adolescents. We have before us a great qualitative challenge, our response to which may determine the fate of future generations of our society.

The technological breakthroughs now developing in the information sciences are having an amazing impact on how people learn. The rates of change in how we learn and how we obtain information are already increasing at a very rapid pace that will assuredly continue.

The public conversation on the purposes and future directions of education is as lively as ever. Alternative visions and voices regarding the broad social aims of schools and the preparation of teachers continue to be presented. *Annual Editions: Education 07/08* attempts to reflect current mainstream as well as alternative visions as to what education ought to be. Equity issues regarding

what constitutes equal treatment of students in the schools continue to be addressed. This year's edition contains articles on gender issues in the field and on the application of research in multicultural education to the areas of teacher preparation and the staff development of teachers already in the schools. The debate over whether all public monies for education should go to the public schools or whether these funds should follow the student into either public or private schools has again intensified.

Communities are deeply interested in local school politics and school funding issues. There continues to be healthy dialogue about and competition for the support of the various "publics" involved in public schooling. The articles reflect a spirited critique of our public schools. There are competing, and very differing, school reform agendas being discussed. All of this occurs as the United States continues to experience fundamentally important demographic shifts in its cultural makeup.

In assembling this volume, we make every effort to stay in touch with movements in educational studies and with the social forces at work in schools. Members of the advisory board contribute valuable insights, and the production and editorial staffs at the publisher, McGraw-Hill Contemporary Learning Series, coordinate our efforts. Through this process we collect a wide range of articles on a variety of topics relevant to education in North America.

The readings in *Annual Editions: Education 07/08* explore the social and academic goals of education, the current conditions of the nation's educational systems, the teaching profession, and the future of American education. In addition, these selections address the issues of change and the moral and ethical foundations of schooling. As always, we would like you to help us improve this volume. Please rate the material in this edition on the postage-paid *article rating form* provided at the back of this book and send it to us. We care about what you think. Give us the public feedback that we need.

Fred Schultz

Fred Schultz

Editor

Contents

UNIT 1
How Others See Us and How We See Ourselves

The concepts in bold italics are developed in the article. For further expansion, please refer to the Topic Guide and the Index.

UNIT 2
Rethinking and Changing the Educative Effort

UNIT 3
Striving for Excellence: The Drive for Quality

The concepts in bold italics are developed in the article. For further expansion, please refer to the Topic Guide and the Index.

UNIT 4
Values, Society, and Education

The concepts in bold italics are developed in the article. For further expansion, please refer to the Topic Guide and the Index.

UNIT 5
Managing Life in Classrooms

UNIT 6
Cultural Diversity and Schooling

The concepts in bold italics are developed in the article. For further expansion, please refer to the Topic Guide and the Index.

UNIT 7
Serving Special Needs and Concerns

The concepts in bold italics are developed in the article. For further expansion, please refer to the Topic Guide and the Index.

UNIT 8
The Profession of Teaching Today

The concepts in bold italics are developed in the article. For further expansion, please refer to the Topic Guide and the Index.

UNIT 9
For Vision and Hope: Alternative Visions of Reality

The concepts in bold italics are developed in the article. For further expansion, please refer to the Topic Guide and the Index.

Topic Guide

This topic guide suggests how the selections in this book relate to the subjects covered in your course. You may want to use the topics listed on these pages to search the Web more easily.

On the following pages a number of Web sites have been gathered specifically for this book. They are arranged to reflect the units of this *Annual Edition*. You can link to these sites by going to the student online support site at *http://www.mhcls.com/online/*.

ALL THE ARTICLES THAT RELATE TO EACH TOPIC ARE LISTED BELOW THE BOLD-FACED TERM.

Internet References

The following Internet sites have been carefully researched and selected to support the articles found in this reader. The easiest way to access these selected sites is to go to our student online support site at *http://www.mhcls.com/online/*.

AE: Education 07/08

The following sites were available at the time of publication. Visit our Web site—we update our student online support site regularly to reflect any changes.

General Sources

Education Week on the Web
http://www.edweek.org

At this *Education Week* home page, you will be able to open its archives, read special reports on education, keep up on current events in education, look at job opportunities, and access articles relevant to educators today.

Educational Resources Information Center
http://www.eric.ed.gov

This invaluable site provides links to all ERIC sites: clearinghouses, support components, and publishers of ERIC materials. You can search the ERIC database, find out what is new, and ask questions about ERIC.

National Education Association
http://www.nea.org

Something about virtually every education-related topic can be accessed via this site of the 2.3-million-strong National Education Association.

National Parent Information Network/ERIC
http://npin.org

This is a clearinghouse of information on elementary and early childhood education as well as urban education. Browse through its links for information for parents and for people who work with parents.

U.S. Department of Education
http://www.ed.gov

Explore this government site for examination of institutional aspects of multicultural education. National goals, projects, grants, and other educational programs are listed here as well as many links to teacher services and resources.

UNIT 1: How Others See Us and How We See Ourselves

Charter Schools
http://www.edexcellence.net/topics/charters.html

Open this site for news about charter schools. It provides information about charter school research and issues, links to the U.S. Charter Schools Web site, and Best on the Web charter school sites.

Pathways to School Improvement
http://www.ncrel.org/sdrs/pathwayg.htm

This site of the North Central Regional Educational Laboratory leads to discussions and links about education, including the current state of education, reform issues, and goals and standards. Technology, professional development, and integrated services are a few of the subjects also discussed.

UNIT 2: Rethinking and Changing the Educative Effort

The Center for Innovation in Education
http://www.center.edu

The Center for Innovation in Education, self-described as a "not-for-profit, nonpartisan research organization" focuses on K–12 education reform strategies. Click on its links for information about and varying perspectives on school privatization and other reform initiatives.

Colorado Department of Education
http://www.cde.state.co.us/index_home.htm

This site's links will lead you to information about education-reform efforts, technology in education initiatives, and many documents of interest to educators, parents, and students.

National Council for Accreditation of Teacher Education
http://www.ncate.org

The NCATE is the professional accrediting organization for schools, colleges, and departments of education in the United States. Accessing this page will lead to information about teacher and school standards, state relations, and developmental projects.

Phi Delta Kappa International
http://www.pdkintl.org

This important organization publishes articles about all facets of education—from school vouchers and charter schools to "new dimensions" in learning.

UNIT 3: Striving for Excellence: The Drive for Quality

Awesome Library for Teachers
http://www.awesomelibrary.org

Open this page for links and access to teacher information on everything from educational assessment to general child development topics.

Education World
http://www.education-world.com

Education World provides a database of literally thousands of sites that can be searched by grade level, plus education news, lesson plans, and professional-development resources.

EdWeb/Andy Carvin
http://edwebproject.org

The purpose of EdWeb is to explore the worlds of educational reform and information technology. Access educational resources around the world, learn about trends in education policy and information infrastructure development, examine success stories of computers in the classroom, and much more.

Kathy Schrock's Guide for Educators
http://www.discoveryschool.com/schrockguide/

This is a classified list of sites on the Internet found to be useful for enhancing curriculum and teacher professional growth. It is updated daily.

Teacher's Guide to the U.S. Department of Education
http://www.ed.gov/pubs/TeachersGuide/

Government goals, projects, grants, and other educational programs are listed here as well as many links to teacher services and resources.

UNIT 4: Values, Society, and Education

Association for Moral Education
http://www.amenetwork.org/

AME is dedicated to fostering communication, cooperation, training, curriculum development, and research that links moral theory with educational practices. From here it is possible to connect to several sites on ethics, character building, and moral development.

Child Welfare League of America
http://www.cwla.org

The CWLA is the United States' oldest and largest organization devoted entirely to the well-being of vulnerable children and their families. This site provides links to information about issues related to morality and values in education.

Ethics Updates/Lawrence Hinman
http://ethics.acusd.edu

This site provides both simple concept definition and complex analysis of ethics, original treatises, and sophisticated search engine capability. Subject matter covers the gamut from ethical theory to applied ethical venues. There are many opportunities for user input.

The National Academy for Child Development
http://www.nacd.org

This international organization is dedicated to helping children and adults reach their full potential. Its home page presents links to various programs, research, and resources into such topics as ADD.

UNIT 5: Managing Life in Classrooms

Classroom Connect
http://www.classroom.com

This is a major Web site for K–12 teachers and students, with links to schools, teachers, and resources online. It includes discussion of the use of technology in the classroom.

Global SchoolNet Foundation
http://www.gsn.org

Access this site for multicultural educational information. The site includes news for teachers, students, and parents, as well as chat rooms, links to educational resources, programs, and contests and competitions.

Teacher Talk Forum
http://education.indiana.edu/cas/tt/tthmpg.html

Visit this site for access to a variety of articles discussing life in the classroom. Clicking on the various links will lead you to electronic lesson plans covering a variety of topic areas from Indiana University's Center for Adolescent Studies.

UNIT 6: Cultural Diversity and Schooling

American Scientist
http://www.amsci.org/amsci/amsci.html

Investigate this site to access a variety of articles and to explore issues and concepts related to race and gender.

American Studies Web
http://www.georgetown.edu/crossroads/asw/

This site provides links to a wealth of resources on the Internet related to American studies, from gender studies to race and ethnicity. It is of great help when doing research in demography and population studies.

National Institute on the Education of At-Risk Students
http://www.ed.gov/offices/OERI/At-Risk/

The At-Risk Institute supports research and development activities designed to improve the education of students at risk of educational failure due to limited English proficiency, race, geographic location, or economic disadvantage.

Prospects: The Congressionally Mandated Study of Educational Growth and Opportunity
http://www.ed.gov/pubs/Prospects/index.html

This report analyzes cross-sectional data on language-minority and LEP students in the United States and outlines what actions are needed to improve their educational performance. Family and economic situations are addressed. Information on related reports and sites is provided.

UNIT 7: Serving Special Needs and Concerns

Constructivism: From Philosophy to Practice
http://www.stemnet.nf.ca/~elmurphy/emurphy/cle.html

Here is a thorough description of the history, philosophy, and practice of constructivism, including quotations from Socrates and others, epistemology, learning theory, characteristics, and a checklist.

National Association for Gifted Children
http://www.nagc.org/home00.htm

NAGC, a national nonprofit organization for gifted children, is dedicated to developing their high potential.

National Information Center for Children and Youth with Disabilities (NICHCY)
http://www.nichcy.org/index.html

NICHCY provides information and makes referrals in areas related to specific disabilities, early intervention, special education and related services, individualized education programs, and much more. The site also connects to a listing of Parent's Guides to resources for children and youth with disabilities.

UNIT 8: The Profession of Teaching Today

Canada's SchoolNet Staff Room
http://www.schoolnet.ca/home/e/

Here is a resource and link site for anyone involved in education, including special-needs educators, teachers, parents, volunteers, and administrators.

Teachers Helping Teachers
http://www.pacificnet.net/~mandel/

This site provides basic teaching tips, new teaching methodology ideas, and forums for teachers to share their experiences. Download software and participate in chat sessions. It features educational resources on the Web, and new ones are added each week.

The Teachers' Network
http://www.teachers.net

Bulletin boards, classroom projects, online forums, and Web mentors are featured on this site, as well as the book *Teachers' Guide to Cyberspace* and an online, 4-week course on how to use the Internet.

Teaching with Electronic Technology

http://www.wam.umd.edu/~mlhall/teaching.html

Michael Hall's Web site leads to many resources of value to those contemplating the future of education, particularly regarding the role of technology in the classroom and beyond.

UNIT 9: For Vision and Hope: Alternative Visions of Reality

Goals 2000: A Progress Report

http://www.ed.gov/pubs/goals/progrpt/index.html

Open this site to survey a progress report by the U.S. Department of Education on the Goals 2000 reform initiative. It provides a sense of what goals educators are reaching for as they look toward the future.

Mighty Media

http://www.mightymedia.com

The mission of this privately funded consortium is to empower youth, teachers, and organizations through the use of interactive communications technology. The site provides links to teacher talk forums, educator resources, networks for students, and more.

Online Internet Institute

http://www.oii.org

A collaborative project among Internet-using educators, proponents of systemic reform, content-area experts, and teachers who desire professional growth, this site provides a learning environment for integrating the Internet into educators' individual teaching styles.

We highly recommend that you review our Web site for expanded information and our other product lines. We are continually updating and adding links to our Web site in order to offer you the most usable and useful information that will support and expand the value of your Annual Editions. You can reach us at: *http://www.mhcls.com/annualeditions/*.

UNIT 1

How Others See Us and How We See Ourselves

Unit Selections

1. **The Biology of Risk Taking**, Lisa F. Price
2. **Squeeze Play**, Glenn Cook
3. **Democracy's First Step**, Kathleen Vail
4. **Social Science and the Citizen**, *Society*
5. **Parents Behaving Badly**, Nancy Gibbs
6. **Sobriety Tests Are Becoming Part of the School Day**, Patrick O'Gilfoil Healy
7. **The 37th Annual Phi Delta Kappa/Gallup Poll of the Public's Attitudes Toward the Public Schools**, Lowell C. Rose and Alec M. Gallup

Key Points to Consider

- Describe the change in American population statistics between 1950 and the present. How have these changes affected education?

- What can teachers do about the unhealthy dietary practices of children and adolescents?

- How can we most accurately assess public perceptions of the educational system?

- What is the fundamental effect of public opinion on national public policy regarding educational development?

Student Website
www.mhcls.com/online

Internet References
Further information regarding these websites may be found in this book's preface or online.

Charter Schools
   http://www.edexcellence.net/topics/charters.html
Pathways to School Improvement
   http://www.ncrel.org/sdrs/pathwayg.htm

There are many ways in which children and youth are educated. The social, racial, and cultural landscape in the United States is becoming more and more diverse and multifaceted. How youth respond to current issues is a reflection of their perceptions as to how older citizens respond to social reality. How to improve the quality of educational services remains a concern of the general public. Public perceptions of the nation's efforts in the education of its youth are of great importance to those who work with children and youth. We must be attentive to the peoples' concerns; we cannot ignore them.

How the people served by a nation's schools perceive the quality of the education they received is of great interest, because public perceptions can translate into either increased or decreased levels of support for a nation's educational system. Achieving a public consensus as to what the aims or purposes of education ought to be can be difficult. Americans in every generation debate what the purposes of education should be. Many different sorts of schools exist at both the elementary and the secondary levels. Many different forms of "charter" schools are attracting the interest of parents; some of these charter schools are within public school systems and some are private ones. Parents wish to have choices as to the types of schools their children attend.

Schools need to be places where students and teachers feel safe, places that provide hope and that instill confidence in the prospects for a happier and better future for all. The safety of students and teachers in schools is a matter of concern to many persons due to tragic events in the recent past. Schools also need to be places where students can dream and hope and work to inform themselves in the process of building their futures. Schools need to help students learn to be inquiring persons.

There are several major policy issues regarding the content and form of schooling that are being debated. We are anticipating greater ranges of choice in the types and forms of schooling that will become available to our children and youth. The United States has great interest in policy issues related to increased accountability to the public for what goes on in schools. Also, we are possibly the most culturally pluralistic nation in the world, and we are becoming even more diverse.

We may be approaching a historic moment in our national history regarding the public funding of education and the options parents might be given for the education of their children. Some of these options and the lines of reasoning for them are explored in this volume. Financial as well as qualitative options are being debated. Scholars in many fields of study as well as journalists and legislators are asking how we can make our nation's schools more effective as well as how we might optimize parents' sense of control over how their children are to be educated.

Young people "read" certain adult behaviors well; they see it as hypocrisy when the adult community wants certain standards and values to be taught in schools but rewards other, often opposite behaviors in society. Dialogue regarding what it means to speak of "literacy" in democratic communities continues. Our students read much from our daily activities and our many information sources, and they form their own shrewd analyses of what social values actually do prevail in society. How to help young people develop their intellectual potential and become

perceptive students of and participants in democratic traditions are major public concerns.

There is serious business yet to be attended to by the social service and educational agencies that try to serve youth. People are impatient to see some fundamental efforts made to meet the basic educational needs of young people. The problems are the greatest in major cities and in more isolated rural areas. Public perceptions of the schools are affected by high levels of economic deprivation among large sectors of the population and by the economic pressures that our interdependent world economy produces as a result of international competition for the world's markets.

Studies conducted in the past few years, particularly the Carnegie Corporation's studies of adolescents in the United States, document the plight of millions of young persons in the United States. Some authors point out that although there was much talk about educational change in the 1990s, those changes were only marginal and cosmetic at best. States responded by demanding more course work and tougher exit standards from schools. With still more than 25 percent of schoolchildren in the United States living at or below the poverty level, and almost a third of them in more economically and socially vulnerable nontraditional family settings, the overall social situation for many young people continues to be difficult. The public wants more effective responses to public needs.

So, in the face of major demographic shifts and of the persistence of many long-term social problems, the public watches how schools respond to new as well as old challenges. In recent years, these challenges have aggravated rather than allayed much public concern about the efficacy of public schooling. Various political, cultural, corporate, and philanthropic interests continue to articulate alternative educational agendas. At the same time the incumbents in the system respond with their own educational agendas, which reflect their views from the inside.

The Biology of Risk Taking

For help in guiding adolescents into healthy adulthood, educators can look to new findings in the fields of neuroscience and developmental psychology.

LISA F. PRICE

I celebrate myself,
And what I assume you shall assume,
For every atom belonging to me as good belongs to you.

—Walt Whitman, *Leaves of Grass*

A dolescence is a time of excitement, growth, and change. Whitman's words capture the enthusiasm and passion with which teenagers approach the world. Sometimes adolescents direct this passion toward a positive goal, such as a creative essay, an art project, after-school sports, or a healthy romance. At other times, they divert their passions to problematic activities, such as drug experimentation, reckless driving, shoplifting, fights, or school truancy.

Why do adolescents take risks? Why are teens so passionate? Are adolescents just young adults, or are they fundamentally different? Advances in developmental psychology and neuroscience have provided us with some answers. We now understand that adolescent turmoil, which we used to view as an expression of raging hormones, is actually the result of a complex interplay of body chemistry, brain development, and cognitive growth (Buchanan, Eccles, & Becker, 1992). Moreover, the changes that teenagers experience occur in the context of multiple systems—such as individual relationships, family, school, and community—that support and influence change.

Educators are in a pivotal position to promote healthy adolescent growth. Understanding the biological changes that adolescents undergo and the behaviors that result can provide the foundation for realistic expectations and effective interventions.

The Impact of Puberty

The hormonal changes of adolescence are often considered synonymous with puberty. The word *puberty* comes from the Latin term *pubertas*, meaning "age of maturity." As implied by the word's etymology, the changes of puberty have long been understood to usher in adulthood; in many cultures, puberty and the capacity to conceive continue to mark entry into adulthood. In contrast, puberty in modern Western culture has become a multistep entry process into a much longer period of adolescence (King, 2002).

Hormonal changes of adolescence include adrenarche, gonadarche, and menarche (Dahl, 2004; King, 2002). Adrenarche refers to the increased production of adrenal hormones and occurs as early as age 6-8. These hormones influence skeletal growth, hair production, and skin changes. Gonadarche refers to the pulsatile production of a cascade of hormones and contributes to driving the growth spurt and genital, breast, and pubic hair development. Menarche refers to the beginning of girls' menses, which generally occurs late in girls' pubertal development.

The Stages and Ages of Puberty

The clinician J. M. Tanner developed a system for classifying male and female pubertal growth into five stages (Tanner I-V). In the 1960s, he identified a trend of progressively earlier age at menarche across cultures (1968). Since then, investigators have identified similar trends of earlier arrival of other markers of puberty, such as breast and pubic hair development (Herman-Giddens et al., 1997). These trends have diverged across race in the United States, with proportionately more African American girls experiencing earlier-onset puberty than white girls. The implications of these trends have ranged from debates over the threshold for premature puberty to investigations into factors that contribute to earlier-onset puberty (Kaplowitz & Oberfield, 1999).

Boys who enter puberty at an earlier age experience certain advantages, including higher self-esteem, greater popularity, and some advances in cognitive capabilities (King, 2002). These same boys may also be more likely to engage in risk-taking behavior, possibly because they often socialize with older boys (Steinberg & Morris, 2001). Girls, on the other hand, often have more problems associated with earlier entry into puberty, including lower self-esteem and elevated risk for anxiety, depression, and eating disorders. These girls are also more likely to engage in risk-taking behaviors, including earlier sexual intercourse.

Don't Blame It On Hormones

In the past, hormones were believed to be in a state of great flux, which presumably caused adolescents to be dramatic, erratic, intense, and risk-prone. Evidence suggests, however, that only minimal association exists between adolescent hormone levels and emotional/behavioral problems (Buchanan et al., 1992; King, 2002). Youth with higher levels of hormones do not appear to be at higher risk for emotional or behavioral problems (Dahl, 2004).

Adolescence is a time of excitement, growth, and change.

Today, adolescent specialists view emotional intensity and sensation-seeking as normative behaviors of adolescence that are more broadly linked to pubertal maturation than to hormone levels. Pubertal stage rather than chronological age is linked to romantic and sexual pursuits, increased appetite, changes in sleep patterns, and risk for emotional disorders in girls. One group of investigators studying teen smoking and substance use found that increased age had no correlation with increased sensation-seeking or risky behavior (Martin et al., 2002). Instead, they determined that pubertal maturation was correlated with sensation-seeking in boys and girls, which, in turn, led to a greater likelihood of cigarette smoking and substance use.

Pubertal stage was clearly linked to difficulties that Derek began experiencing in school. He had been a solid student in 6th grade who scored in the average range and generally turned his homework in on time. He socialized with a group of same-age friends and was teased occasionally because he was skinnier and shorter than his peers. By 7th grade, however, he had begun his growth spurt. He was now a few inches taller and had developed facial hair. Although he appeared more confident, he also seemed more aggressive and was involved in several fights at school. He began to spend part of his time with a few 8th grade boys who were suspected of writing graffiti on a school wall.

A teacher who had a good relationship with Derek took him aside and spoke with him about the change in his behavior from 6th to 7th grade. Derek was able to talk about his own surprise at the changes, his wish for more respect, and his ambivalence about entering high school—he was worried about what teachers would expect of him. Derek and the teacher agreed to talk periodically, and the teacher arranged for Derek to meet with the school counselor.

The Adolescent Brain

Neuroscientists used to believe that by the time they reached puberty, youth had undergone the crucial transformations in brain development and circuitry. Data obtained through available technology supported this view, identifying similar brain structures in children and adults. The adolescent brain seemed entirely comparable to the adult brain.

This view of adolescent brain development has undergone a radical shift during the last decade, with the identification of ongoing brain changes throughout adolescence, such as synaptic pruning and myelination. People have the mature capacity to consistently control behavior in both low-stress and high-stress environments only after these neurobiological developments are complete. This maturation does not take place until the early 20s.

Synaptic pruning refers to the elimination of connections between neurons in the brain's cortex, or gray matter. In the 1990s, researchers determined that during adolescence, up to 30,000 synapses are eliminated each second (Bourgeois & Rakic, 1993; Rakic, Bourgeois, & Goldman-Rakic, 1994). The removal of these redundant synaptic links increases the computational ability of brain circuits, which, in turn, enhances a function intricately connected to risk taking: the capacity to regulate and rapidly stop activity. Myelination, which refers to the wrapping of glial cell membranes around the axon of neurons, results in increased speed of signal transmission along the axon (Luna & Sweeney, 2004). This facilitates more rapid and integrated communication among diverse brain regions.

Synaptic pruning and myelination, along with other neurobiological changes, facilitate enhanced cognitive capacity as well as behavioral control, also known as *executive function*. Executive function is the ability to interact in a self-directed, appropriate, organized, and purposeful manner. The prefrontal cortex plays a vital role in guiding executive function, which is also influenced by such areas of the brain as the hippocampus (which coordinates memory), the amygdala (which coordinates emotional processing), and the ventral striatum (which coordinates reward-processing). The prefrontal cortex is less mature, however, in young adolescents than in adults.

Given these three factors—an inability to completely regulate and refrain from certain activities, an absence of fully integrated communication among the various regions of the brain, and a less developed prefrontal cortex—it is not surprising that adolescents biologically do not have the same capacities as adults to inhibit their impulses in a timely manner.

Biology and Thrill-Seeking

By their mid-teens, adolescents appear to have achieved many decision-making abilities seen in adults (Steinberg & Cauffman, 1996). In fact, studies have found that teens can identify the same degree of danger in risky activities that adults can—driving while intoxicated, for example (Cauffman, Steinberg, & Woolard, 2002). However, certain methodological flaws in studies of adolescents may have prevented investigators from accurately assessing adolescent risk taking (Steinberg, 2004). These flaws include evaluating teens individually rather than in the context of a group, within which most risk-taking behavior occurs; asking teens to evaluate theoretical situations, which may not sufficiently represent the challenges of actual situations; and evaluating teens in settings that reduce the influence of emotion or induce anxiety rather than generate the exhilaration associated with risk taking.

One result of these flaws may be that measures of adolescents' cognitive abilities—particularly their evaluation of risk—do not adequately reflect their actual cognitive and emotional processes in real time. Consequently, teens *appear* to have the cognitive capacities of adults yet continue to engage in more risky behaviors.

The emotional lives of adolescents also appear to shift during these years. Adolescents seek more intense emotional experiences than children and adults do. They appear to need higher degrees of stimulation to obtain the same experience of pleasure (Steinberg, 2004). Developments in an area of the brain called the limbic system may explain this shift in pursuit and experience of pleasure (Spear, 2000).

Teenagers generally thrive in reasonable, supportive environments that have a predictable, enforced structure.

Ongoing cognitive development and emotional shifts result in a biologically based drive for thrill-seeking, which may account for adolescents' continued risk taking despite knowledge of the accompanying hazards. Some interventions attempt to reduce the potential for risky behavior through external means—laws and rules, for example—rather than placing sole emphasis on the practice of educating teens in risk assessment (Steinberg, 2004). Others have considered teens' ability to reason well in "cool" circumstances but their failure to do so when in "hot" situations that arouse the emotions. Providing adolescents with sufficient scaffolding, or a good balance of support and autonomy, may be particularly important (Dahl, 2004).

This kind of scaffolding would be especially effective with a student like Shauna. Shauna raised the concerns of school faculty soon after she started 9th grade. Her attendance, class participation, and assignment completion were erratic. She had also run away from home during the summer and received a warning for shoplifting. The school counselor learned that Shauna's parents had separated over the summer and that her mother was struggling to set limits in the absence of Shauna's father. The school counselor, several teachers, and the vice principal decided to meet with both of Shauna's parents.

Although tension between the parents was evident, both parents agreed that Shauna should come home immediately after school instead of going to the mall, which she had recently started to do. Both parents also felt strongly that she needed to regularly attend school and complete assignments. The parents arranged to meet with Shauna together to discuss their shared expectations for her. The parents and teachers agreed to stay in contact with one another regarding Shauna's attendance and homework. The group also decided that a home-based reward system might encourage Shauna's success at school. The reward system would involve outings to the mall and to friends' homes, with incrementally less adult supervision and more autonomy as she continued to succeed.

The Role of Educators

These new findings suggest some beneficial approaches that educators might follow to guide adolescents into healthy adulthood.

- *Ensure that schools provide adolescents with vital support.* School bonding provides a protective influence for youth. The mentorship of a teacher can make the difference in a teen's course.

- *Keep a long view.* Researchers have found that the benefits of successful interventions may disappear for a few years in adolescence to reappear in later adolescence (Masten, 2004). Other teens are late bloomers whose troubled earlier years are followed by success.

- *Prioritize your concern.* The junior who has never been a problem and gets into trouble once is at a different level of risk than the 7th grader who has a long history of worrisome behaviors, such as fights, school truancy, mental illness, exposure to trauma, loss of important adult figures, or absence of stable supports. Act early for adolescents with long histories of risk taking.

- *Remember that puberty is not the same for all teens.* Some adolescents enter puberty earlier than others, giving them a perceived social advantage as well as possible disadvantages. There may be a biological drive to risk taking in teens, which is expressed by individual teens at different ages.

- *Remember that teens are not adults.* Having the scientific evidence to support the view that teens are not adults can be helpful to educators working with families, adolescents, or other professionals who may have unrealistic expectations for adolescents.

- *Take advantage of adolescent passion.* Direct adolescents' enthusiasm toward productive ends. A teen's passion can become a bridge to learning about such topics as music theory, history, politics, race relations, or marketing.

- *Reduce risk with firm structure.* Although teenagers dislike rules, they generally thrive in reasonable, supportive environments that have a predictable, enforced structure. For example, an authoritative stance in parenting—which reflects firmness coupled with caring—has repeatedly been found to be the most effective parenting strategy. Continue to maintain school rules and expectations, even when an adolescent continues to break the rules.

- *Collaborate to solve problems.* Working with risk-taking adolescents can be demanding, taxing, and worrisome. Talk regularly with colleagues for support. Contact appropriate consultants when your concern grows. Teens who see teachers collaborate with other adults benefit from these healthy models of problem solving.

It's important for educators to keep in mind that up to 80 percent of adolescents have few or no major problems during this period (Dahl, 2004). Remembering that most adolescents do well can encourage the positive outlook that educators need to effectively work with youth during this exciting and challenging time in their lives.

References

Bourgeois, J-P., & Rakic, P. (1993). Changes of synaptic density in the primary visual cortex of the macaque monkey from fetal to adult stage. *Journal of Neuroscience, 13*, 2801–2820.

Buchanan, C. M., Eccles, J. S., & Becker, J. B. (1992). Are adolescents the victims of raging hormones? *Psychological Bulletin, 111*, 62–107.

Cauffman, E., Steinberg, L., & Woolard, J. (2002, April 13). *Age differences in capacities underlying competence to stand trial.* Presentation at the Biennial Meeting of the Society for Research for Adolescence, New Orleans, Louisiana.

Dahl, R. E. (2004). Adolescent brain development: A period of vulnerabilities and opportunities. *Annals of the New York Academy of Science, 1021*, 1–22.

Herman-Giddens, M. E., Slora, E. J., Wasserman, R. C., Bourdony, C.J., Bhapkar, M. V., Koch, G. G., et al. (1997). Secondary sexual characteristics and menses in young girls seen in office practice. *Pediatrics, 99*, 505–512.

Kaplowitz, P. B., & Oberfield, S. E. (1999). Reexamination of the age limit for defining when puberty is precocious in girls in the United States. *Pediatrics, 104*, 936–941.

King, R. A. (2002). Adolescence. In M. Lewis (Ed.), *Child and adolescent psychiatry* (pp. 332–342). Philadelphia: Lippincott Williams & Wilkins.

Luna, B., & Sweeney, J. A. (2004). The emergence of collaborative brain function: fMRI studies of the development of response inhibition. *Annals of the New York Academy of Science, 1021*, 296–309.

Martin, C. A., Kelly, T. H., Rayens, M. K., Brogli, B. R., Brenzel, A., Smith, W. J., et al. (2002). Sensation seeking, puberty, and nicotine, alcohol, and marijuana use in adolescence. *Journal of the American Academy of Child and Adolescent Psychiatry, 41*, 1495–1502.

Masten, A. S. (2004). Regulatory processes, risk, and resilience in adolescent development. *Annals of the New York Academy of Science, 1021*, 310–319.

Rakic, P., Bourgeois, J-P., & Goldman- Rakic, P. S. (1994). Synaptic development of the cerebral cortex. *Progress in Brain Research, 102*, 227–243.

Spear, P. (2000). The adolescent brain and age-related behavioral manifestations. *Neuroscience and Biobehavioral Reviews, 24*, 417–463.

Steinberg, L. (2004). Risk taking in adolescence: What changes, and why? *Annals of the New York Academy of Science, 1021*, 51–58.

Steinberg, L., & Cauffman, E. (1996). Maturity of judgment in adolescence. *Law and Human Behavior, 20*, 249–272.

Steinberg, L., & Morris, A. S. (2001). Adolescent development. *Annual Review of Psychology, 52*, 83–110.

Tanner, J. M. (1968). Early maturation in man. *Scientific American, 218*, 21–27.

LISA F. PRICE, M.D., is the Assistant Director of the School Psychiatry Program in the Department of Psychiatry at Massachusetts General Hospital, 55 Fruit St., YAW 6900, Boston, MA 02114. She is also an Instructor in Psychiatry at Harvard Medical School.

Squeeze Play

Glenn Cook

Rae Waters had no reason to believe things would turn out like this. The Kyrene Elementary District, located in an affluent suburb in the Phoenix-Tempe area, was growing rapidly when she ran for the school board seven years ago. Buoyed by its proximity to Intel and Motorola, the 17,000-student district had a reputation as "the go-to place" for good schools.

But enrollment has dropped by almost 7 percent in the K-8 district over the past five years, and the number of Title I schools has climbed from two to five. The No Child Left Behind Act has brought attention to a growing achievement gap. Still, even as enrollment declined, expectations didn't—on the part of the schools or the parents.

When those expectations are different, as Waters has learned, the board feels the squeeze. In her case, the dispute was over schedule changes and cutbacks in electives at Kyrene's six middle schools, part of an effort to add more concentrated time in reading, writing, and math. In March—just three months after taking office as president of the Arizona School Boards Association—Waters faces a recall board election, and she remains perplexed by the entire affair.

"On our school board, we have five people who are not supposed to represent one group. We're supposed to be doing what's best for all kids," Waters says. "That's a conundrum for school boards: How do you meet the state and federal laws doing?"

For boards and administrators, the long-term stakes are higher as well, perhaps more so than at any time since the school reform movement started. Over the past two-plus decades, the tradition of local control has been shaken to its core, beset by a rash of state and federal mandates, battles over consolidation and choice, and the growth of well-funded national organizations that have placed schools at the center of the political and culture wars. And parents, chafed by the loss of control, are taking out their frustrations on board members.

This constant friction, played out amid local politics, contributes to the belief that boards are unable or unwilling to do their job, when in all but isolated—and highly publicized—instances that's not the case.

"One of the dilemmas school boards face is that they have become the focal point of every single person with the latest fix for how to save children, and these fixes take on a million different forms," says William Howell, a Harvard University professor and editor of the book *Besieged: School Boards and the Future of Education Politics.* "There is a strong push for top-down control. At the same time, people want bottom-up accountability through parent choice, so everything is in flux."

Crossing Muddy Waters

Local control was based on the premise that the school board has the last word on curriculum, funding, staffing, and policy in district schools. But as times have changed, political battles for control have moved largely to state legislatures and increasingly to Congress, limiting the ability and authority of individual boards to take action.

From politicians to parents to advocacy groups, school boards are being pressured on all sides. Are the battles for control distracting boards from doing what's best for children?

"School boards are seen as the lowest rung on the political hierarchy, especially by other elected officials," says Pedro Noguera, executive director of the Metropolitan Center for Urban Education at New York University. "But what that means is they are closer to the electorate than most elected officials. That to me is a position of influence, and it's not being used sufficiently to advocate policies and programs that schools need."

As a result, Noguera and others say, "local control" no longer means what it once did. Legislators and public interest groups use the term to drum up support for a particular issue, but the authority to make decisions usually rests with state or federal lawmakers. And school boards are left to implement mandates from above, many of which are underfunded or not funded at all, further crippling local authority to decide what's best for children.

"Everyone in my state says we should have site-based management, and that our schools are the best decision makers in terms of what needs to happen in that building," says Betty Baitland, superintendent of Texas' Fort Bend Independent School District. "However, in reality, more and more of their ability to make decisions is being taken away."

And the squeeze on local boards shows no signs of slowing soon. Talk of a national curriculum and national standards continues, although more in whispers and sound bites than in policy. Diane Ravitch, a former assistant secretary of education under the first President Bush, said in November that scores on the National Assessment of Educational Progress exam will remain flat as long as states retain their own curriculum and standards. Arizona Gov. Janet Napolitano, a Democrat with a strong education record, co-chaired a national task force that announced support in August for the creation of voluntary national standards.

"If you look back to the 2000 elections, both President Bush and Al Gore talked about testing kids," Howell says. "The whole notion that presidents would have strongly held views about testing and what it would look like was new and extraordinary. But it shows how everyone is weighing in and trying to get a handle on education policy, and at the same time trying to push boards to the side."

"Whether it's legislators or the business community, everyone wants to tell us how to do our job."

—Linda Lopez

Linda Lopez sees the issue from both sides—as a board member in the Sunnyside Unified School District and as the assistant minority leader in the Arizona House. While she supports Napolitano's efforts to improve education through more funding for all-day kindergarten and other programs, Lopez says other legislative actions—such as requiring districts to teach sun safety—prevent boards from serving their local communities.

"Everybody is an expert when it comes to education," Lopez says. "Whether it's legislators or the business community, everyone wants to tell us how to do our job. At the federal and state level, they say they want local control. Then, they say, 'We're going to tell you how you have to do it, and you have to do it our way.' That's not local control, that's a power grab."

The Money War

Nowhere is the struggle for power more pronounced than in the area of school finance. Anti-tax groups have pushed for caps on state spending to limit government growth, while districts in 45 of 50 states have filed court challenges over how schools are funded. Meanwhile, national initiatives such as the "65 cent solution," which would require districts to spend almost two-thirds of every dollar in the classroom, also are gaining traction in some regions.

"I'm not typically a guy who wakes up every morning worried about black helicopters looming overhead, but I believe this is all about finding reasons not to fund public schools," says Winston Brooks, superintendent of Kansas' Wichita Public Schools. "If it's not one strategy, it's another strategy someone has uncovered. And it's all with the belief that if they can prove that schools are not spending money correctly, then we won't have to spend more money on them."

Arizona and Kansas are at the forefront of numerous education battles—political, financial, and ideological—that districts across the country face. Each has a Democratic governor and a Republican-controlled legislature with different agendas on how to resolve those battles.

"There is an ideological push to treat the public sector one way and the private sector another," says Becky Hill, Napolitano's education policy adviser. "You need to decide that education should be publicly funded and that there's a public expectation or there isn't. If you decide to fund the district and set goals, then you need to give local school districts the support and flexibility to achieve that goal."

In both states, consolidation and unification plans are being floated as a way to conserve resources and improve efficiency. Choice—in the form of open enrollment, charters, and vouchers—is being pushed, debated, or implemented at the state level. Arizona's legislature is expected to consider the 65 cent solution; Kansas lawmakers, who already have passed bills encouraging districts to use the model, are considering broader limits on government spending with the Taxpayer's Bill of Rights, similar to the Colorado initiative better known as TABOR.

"No Child Left Behind has, in many ways, circumvented school boards' authority, but governors are faced with the same problem," Noguera says. "It's not just local government. State government also lost authority under NCLB, and now what you're seeing are state legislatures reacting to the loss of control over the schools."

Roger Pfeuffer, superintendent in the Tucson Unified School District, says the power shift squeezing school boards is not a surprise, given what is taking place across the country.

"We don't have a concept of local anymore. It's state. It's national. It's global," Pfeuffer says. "People are not as altruistic about their neighbors. They want vouchers. They want open enrollment. They want all of these educational shopping options. For school boards, it means they have to deal with the whole concept of not being a monopoly anymore. It's a sad commentary, but community does not seem to matter as much as it once did."

The Rise of National Advocacy

Propelling these debates are a growing number of well-funded national advocacy groups, such as First Class Education, which touts the 65 cent solution as a way to inject nearly $14 billion into classrooms nationwide. Like other organizations that have sprouted up since the choice movement began, First Class Education relies on a simple message ("Money is wasted in education"), a simpler solution ("You have the power to stop it"), and few details on how it will actually work.

Anne L. Bryant, executive director of the National School Boards Association, says advocacy groups such as First Class Education "are far removed from local school districts" and are not concerned with the challenges educators face. Instead, she says, the rhetoric these groups generate "distracts school board members and educators from their real work, which is focusing on student achievement."

An analysis by Standard & Poor's, released in late November, supported Bryant's comments, concluding that "no minimum spending allocation is a 'silver bullet' solution for raising student achievement." The analysis, available on the www.schoolmatters.com website, found "no significant positive correlation between the percentage of funds that districts spend on instruction, and the percentage of students who score proficient or higher on state reading and math tests."

"These state and nationwide initiatives really have nothing to do with educating students," Bryant says. "On the surface, the 65 percent formula appears to be harmless, but as school board members know, there are many things that make up a student's experience in school that go far beyond what happens in the classroom."

Failing to recognize such nuances, critics of the 65 cent solution say, could be disastrous for public education, especially if states use a strict formula in developing the model. Under Kansas' current definitions, elementary art and music would not be defined as classroom instruction under the 65 cent rule. Librarians, counselors, psychologists, peer coaches, and mentor teachers also would not qualify.

"It's about the way you define it," says Brooks, whose district spends about 59 cents of every dollar on classroom instruction. "My argument is that if we are spending taxpayer dollars wisely, getting good results, and are still under 65 percent, then why should the state pull some arbitrary figure out of the air?"

One reason appears to be politics. Tim Mooney, a Republican political consultant in Arizona, founded First Class Education with $250,000 in seed money from Patrick Byrne, CEO of Overstock.com and a contributor to pro-voucher efforts. Mooney has told lawmakers that his initiative will improve Republicans' credibility on education issues in the mid-term election. At the same time, he claims, "This doesn't hurt local control."

Under the group's plan, voters would decide whether each state should require that 65 cents of every dollar spent for education go directly to the classroom. Formulas on what "in the classroom" means vary from state to state, but First Class Education says only four—Maine, New York, Tennessee, and Utah—currently meet its standard.

Mooney's message appears to have resonated with Republican lawmakers. In Kansas and Louisiana, legislators have passed bills encouraging school districts to follow the formula. After Texas legislators rejected the 65 percent rule, Gov. Rick Perry—a Republican who faces re-election in 2006—issued an executive order requiring schools to meet the goal starting in 2006-07.

"This is as local as you can possibly get," says Mooney, who is trying to have the initiative placed on ballots in up to 10 states this year and in all 50 states by 2008. "It says the local school board gets to decide how to spend 65 percent of every dollar in the classroom. You can increase teacher pay. You can pay for new textbooks and computers. You can bring back arts and music. How is that not local?"

Changing Priorities

Returning to daily arts and music classes in Kyrene is important to McKell Keeney, spokeswoman for the Kyrene Community Leadership. The group, which formed after the board approved the curriculum changes last April, spent six months gathering more than 9,000 signatures in an attempt to force a recall vote against Rae Waters.

Keeney, a jazz musician whose four children have attended the Kyrene schools, is angry about the process the district used in switching the middle school schedule from seven to five periods a day. Daily music and arts classes, as well as P.E. and Spanish, were cut back to provide more time for reading, math, and writing.

"There was a large group of parents and community members who felt they had no voice," says Keeney, whose slogan is Electives Count! "We had more than 50 different parents who went to board meetings and e-mailed board members about the cutbacks and we did not receive any response back from them. They had already made up their minds."

Waters, the board president, admits the district could have done a better job of communicating Kyrene's issues sooner. Still, she maintains, a group of 50 parents does not represent the majority of families in the district.

"We've been very complacent. We've been very good at resting on our laurels, promoting ourselves as a good district, but we weren't sending all kids to high school with the skills they needed," Waters says. "I think that's something the community doesn't want to face, that we're not as good as we think we are. It's a control issue for them, too."

Waters, who ran for the school board after serving as a PTO president and band booster officer, says she understands why parents don't want to lose what they have. She says the Kyrene Community Leadership is filled with parents who are "well-educated people, very intelligent people who have drawn a different conclusion."

"Parents are focused on what's good for their child," she says. "Teachers look out for their class. Principals and administrators look out for the schools. As board members, we have to look out for the entire district, not just a single group of people who are interested in getting their way because it's best for their children."

What Can Be Done?

The question is: Will the outside groups vying for control let school boards do their job? Not if board members remain complacent or continue to have ill-defined roles as community leaders, observers say.

"Boards need to realize they have much more power than they know," Noguera says. "They should be more engaged in pushing back on state government. A lot of times decisions are being made at the state level that have a negative impact on schools and the boards just take it. Their budgets are being cut. There are new policies regarding assessments being written, and the boards just sit there. You can't just sit there."

Francis X. Shen, a Harvard University professor who has conducted extensive research on school takeovers, says boards can and should unite when they face outside threats from parents, anti-public education advocates, or other forms of government.

"I think school boards that demonstrate an ability to work constructively with each other, to overcome narrowly interested motives, and to work for overall district improvement will find themselves gaining respect and power," Shen says. "This can be difficult when boards are made up of many diverse members, but if they can come to consensus on core values, perhaps they can present a unified front. The multiple voices on a board must bring diversity, not discontent."

Bryant acknowledges that it's difficult for board members to be objective when they are being assaulted from all sides. "It's very hard to be moderate in these times of extremism," she says. "It's hard to be calm when you have to listen to the shouting and yelling of these issue-focused people. But that's what school boards have to be. They have to be the calm voice, the focused governor of their public schools, and they have to articulate for the general public why these distracting issues have to be defeated."

Brooks, who witnessed discontent first hand as Kansas waged a bitter battle over intelligent design and evolution, believes that extremists ultimately will not prevail. As examples, he points to two events in November: The repeal of TABOR in Colorado, and the defeat of Dover, Pa., board members who ran on a pro-intelligent-design platform.

"I think it's the nature of politics," he says. "What has a tendency to happen, both on the Republican and the Democratic side, is that the moderates are the silent majority. Oftentimes we are being represented by the vocal minority. The American people are very smart, and eventually they are going to see through all of this at the polls."

With two months to go until the recall election, Waters is working to explain her side of the story to voters. The past several months, she says, have provided her with valuable lessons about her community and society as a whole.

"In general, we don't have common values or common ideals right now. We think about ourselves," she says. "My family has been that way. We want what we want, and we do what we need to do to get it.

"But we need to start looking at that. We've got to start looking beyond our lives and our needs. And we've got to do it sooner than later."

GLENN COOK (gcook@nsba.org) is managing editor of *American School Board Journal*.

Democracy's First Step

Some of the nation's most respected public servants began their political careers on the school board

KATHLEEN VAIL

Jimmy Carter began his political career on his local school board. So did U.S. Sens. Richard Lugar and Patty Murray, former Arkansas Gov. Dale Bumpers, and hundreds of other state and national politicians who got their first taste of public life by serving on their local school boards. During their board tenure, they decided they could make wider reforms and better serve the public by going on to higher office.

Serving on a school board for some is a vocation; for others, it's the genesis of a political career that could—as was true with President Carter—take them all the way to the top. Some who've gone on to higher office say they've used their school board skills and their knowledge of public education in making decisions in their current positions as lawmakers.

"They run for the board with all the same intentions; they care about school and community; they want to make a difference," says Anne L. Bryant, executive director of the National School Boards Association. "That's why they ran and continue to serve. They have that local experience; it motivates them to serve a broader public good. There's nothing better than having them take their experience and knowledge to another public office."

The Roots of Service

Lugar, a Republican, is probably the most powerful and prominent current politician to have held school board office. Although he has been in the U.S. Senate for nearly 30 years, and before that served a memorable stint as mayor of Indianapolis, Lugar considers his days on the city's school board as seminal to his political career.

He was trying to get his family's struggling business in order when, in 1963, some prominent city residents asked him to run for the school board. Lugar says he knew little about the board or its issues at the time. However, the months after President Kennedy's assassination found him pondering public service. "Conscience spoke, and I said I would run," he said. "We were on the cusp of a civil rights revolution and an educational revolution."

Lugar joined a board and a school system roiling with tension over desegregation. He supported a voluntary desegregation program that was met with much resistance by his opponents. "It was an extraordinarily formative period, a great deal of political action," Lugar says of his school board tenure. One of the most volatile meetings he ever attended was one at which the desegregation plan was discussed. "Police had to break it up, it was so violent," he recalls.

Lugar says he ran for mayor in part because of his frustrations on the school board and the fact that other board members blocked his becoming board president. "It seemed a way out of the box," he says. "I saw it as a way to make some changes I couldn't on the board."

Political Paradox

You could argue that the issues school boards regularly struggle with—local control, unfunded mandates, more money for schools—might be eased if more state and national legislators had school board experience. But despite the old stereotype of opportunists using the school board as an easy entry to political office, the opposite turns out to be true. Very few of the thousands of past and current school board members actually go on to serve in higher office. And while many decry the increase of politics in school board elections, particularly in large urban and suburban districts, the process remains nearly free of political trappings.

It's a paradox, to say the least, and a long-standing one. While school boards regularly are accused of being used as political stepping-stones, century-old changes by Progressive Movement reformers purposely divorced partisan politics from school board elections.

Evidence of this reform is in full force today. According to NSBA's 2002 survey of school boards, *School Boards at the Dawn of the 21st Century*, nearly 90 percent of school board elections are nonpartisan. Even the timing of board elections reveals an effort to distance them from partisan politics. Fewer than half (46.5 percent) are always held on the same day as national or state elections, while 34.7 percent are never held on the same day. Approximately a third of districts (34.2 percent) always hold board elections on the same day as mayoral or city council elections, while another third (35.7 percent) never do.

Indeed, some school board members are uncomfortable with the idea that they are politicians, considering the political process unworthy of people who want to serve children and education. The specter of board members putting their political futures ahead of the good of children and schools rests uneasily in their minds—and in the minds of many citizens.

Sue Huhn, a member of the Franklin School Board in Franklin, Wis., says she's been asked to run for higher office but always refuses, in part because she does not want to join a political party. "I could not make decisions based on a party platform," she says. "I believe that political parties are why bad decisions are made. Everyone is afraid to take a stand against their party's position even when they know the position is wrong."

But North Carolina State Rep. Rick Glazier, D-Cumberland County, a lawyer who served on the Cumberland County School Board for two terms, wishes board members would get over the perception that politics is tainted. "Politics is the art of governing," he says. "Politics is not a dirty word. It's an important part of public service. It is the running of government in the service of people."

In fact, says Linda Lopez, a member of the Sunnyside School Board and a sitting Arizona state representative, board members can benefit their district and education as a whole by attaining state and federal offices. "They can be important advocates," says Lopez, a Democrat who serves as assistant minority leader. "School board members who think they are not politicians are living in a fantasy."

Why They Ran

The motivation for board service can spring from a variety of sources. At least two politicians ran for their school boards because they wanted to increase the representation of minorities. Alaska State Sen. Bettye Davis, D-Anchorage, was appointed to the Anchorage School Board in 1981 to replace an African-American man who had won a seat in the state house of representatives. When he left, there were no other minorities on the board, says Davis, a social worker with many district connections. She asked for the appointment. "I didn't know that I would stay for nine years," she says.

Similarly, U.S. Rep. Raul Grijalva, D-Ariz., ran and won a seat on the Tucson School Board in 1974 and served for 12 years. He decided to run, in part, because there was no Latino representation on the board. Another reason, he says, was "having come up through the public school system, realizing how important public school was, my own desire to be part of the system."

The desire to make changes on their boards and in their districts also motivated these politicians to run for higher office. For Davis, the first African-American woman to be elected to the Alaska state senate, the frustration of asking the legislature every year for more money for her schools—money that usually wasn't forthcoming—drove her to become a state lawmaker.

"I figured I had a lot to bring to the table. I'd been begging for money all these years," she says. "I went to get funding for public education and pushed for new buildings, smaller class sizes. I did pretty well on some of those issues."

Funding education was also behind Sen. Patty Murray's jump from the Shoreline School Board to the Washington state Senate in 1989. "I knew that if I really wanted to help schools, I had to be at the state capitol in Olympia, where the funding decisions were made," says Murray, D-Wash. She ran for the U. S. Senate in 1992 because, she says, "I felt that working families did not have a voice in the United States. I wanted to be their voice." She ended up serving on Senate committees that fund education and set federal education policy.

"You know, it's funny," says Murray. "Before I was a member of the state legislature, I went to visit Olympia to lobby for funding for our schools. I sat in the gallery watching the legislature in session, and I remember that all I saw were a lot of shiny, bald heads. That experience showed me there were very few young parents making the crucial decisions about their children's future, and that was something I felt needed to change."

For her part, Lopez ran for higher office because, as a board member, she saw that many things were out of the district's control. "We can't be parochial," says Lopez, who won her seat in the Arizona state House in 2001. "Decisions at the state and federal level impact what we do at the district level. I started thinking, I need to put my voice there. I have a unique perspective to offer at the state level."

Advantages of Membership

The politicians interviewed for this article all said they have found their school board experience invaluable as they've navigated other political offices. Practical knowledge of education and experience dealing with a vocal and ever-present constituency give these public servants an expertise they can use to their advantage in their current offices.

As a member of the Agriculture, Nutrition, and Forestry Committee, for example, Lugar championed the federal school lunch program in 1994 when there was talk of making it a state block grant program. He was under great pressure from fellow Republicans to do so, but he held fast. "It's difficult for progress to occur if children are hungry," Lugar says. He also created programs for students in summer school to receive federal school lunches.

Lugar's experience with the federal school lunch program dates from his school board tenure. The Indianapolis School Board was not taking any federal money, which meant the district's children were not getting federal school lunches. The issue was controversial, and the board narrowly voted to participate in the program. "We did get the money," says Lugar. "Children got the food."

Murray says her time on the school board gave her a perspective on how decisions made at the federal level affect local schools. That experience has guided her when she's written legislation.

"For example, I wrote a bill called the PASS Act—Pathways for All Students to Succeed," says Murray. "This bill helps our high school students get the help they need—like literacy coaches and career counselors—to get a diploma and go on to college or a good career."

Lawmakers with hands-on policy experience, like the kind you get on the school board, have an essential perspective when it comes to making federal school policy, says Grijalva, who asked to serve on the Committee on Education and the Workforce, as well as on the School Reform Subcommittee. "It'd be good to rely on someone with practical experience," he says.

"The relationships I built with educators have served me well," Grijalva adds. "Those are strengths that I have brought to the committee. People respect the fact that you are at the real level of democracy." School board service, he says, "teaches organizational and survival skills that Washington, D.C., can use."

U.S. Rep. John Boozman, R-Ark., an optometrist who served on the Rogers School Board, says, "I tell my friends and colleagues, the issues we are dealing with here are nothing like dealing with the cheerleading problems and redistricting. Those decisions affect people directly. I would see my constituents everyplace. People aren't bashful at all."

Boozman has relied on his school board experience to inform him when voting on major legislation such as No Child Left Behind. "I understand teacher, administrator, and school board concerns about testing special groups and about how schools end up being tagged with 'needs improvement' although they're on the excellence list. I've worked hard to try to remedy some of those things."

In Raleigh, Glazier is the chairman of the elementary and secondary education subcommittee and vice chair of the education committee. He says he's used his training and knowledge of public education in the North Carolina legislature.

"The school board was incredible education and experience," he says. "I couldn't do my job as well without my experience on the board."

The Most Important Job

Clearly, these experienced politicians don't believe school board members should shy away from further political life. The advantages to schools outweigh any potential disadvantages, they say.

"It's totally person dependent," says Glazier. "Some people are incredibly effective board members for dozens of years, and that is the best use of their talents. Others don't want to be there long term."

If he hadn't gotten the opportunity to run for state office, Glazier says, he'd still be on the school board. "It is the most important job in elected service," he says. "We deal with the most important things people have, their children and their money. Nothing is more local and important than being a school board member."

It's a reality, of course, that some people whose real interest isn't education will try to use the board as a first step in a political career. And that's not necessarily a disaster, says Lopez. "We have people who run for school board just to put it on the resume. You can tell by the service they provide. If they are just marking time until they get to the legislature, that's fine," she says. "They learn about local control, and they don't forget that when they get elected."

The best board members base their decisions solely on the welfare of the children. But a board member who wants to run for higher office has nothing to apologize for, says Thomas Hutton, a staff attorney for NSBA. "It's good for American democracy itself that local people have the opportunity to participate firsthand in government and gain important experience," he says. "That strengthens democracy."

And a board member with political ambitions can add energy to a school board, says Hutton. "That drive can be an advantage to the board. In order to push change, it takes a certain amount of drive, energy, and personal initiative."

KATHLEEN VAIL (kvail@nsba.org) is a senior editor of *American School Board Journal*.

Social Science and the Citizen

Leaning to the Left

American professors are overwhelmingly liberal, according to a new report on faculty political attitudes.

Previous surveys have reached similar conclusions, but this one suggests that the ideological divide on campuses may be greater than has previously been thought. And the authors of this survey say that their evidence suggests say that conservatives, practicing Christians and women are less likely than others to get faculty jobs at top colleges.

The research, published in *The Forum,* is being praised as path-breaking by some scholars and as garbage by others. But since the study is being released at a time of heightened debate over charges of classroom bias, the report is likely to be closely examined and critiqued.

The findings are based on a survey of 1,643 faculty members at 183 four-year colleges and universities, and the results were analyzed by three political scientists: Stanley Rothman of Smith College, S. Robert Lichter of George Mason University and Neil Nevitte of the University of Toronto. In the abstract to their report, they say that the research "suggests that complaints of ideologically based discrimination in academic advancement deserve serious consideration and further study."

Rosemary G. Feal, executive director of the Modern Language Association, said that the implication that liberal faculty members were keeping conservative scholars out was "rubbish," and said that anyone who has been on dozens of search committees, as she has, knows that. "It boggles my mind the degree to which this is rubbish."

Faculty members in the study were asked to place themselves on the political spectrum, and 72 percent identified as liberal while only 15 percent identified as conservative, with the remainder in the middle. The professors were also asked about party affiliation, and here the breakdown was 50 percent Democrats, 11 percent Republicans, and the rest independent and third parties.

The study also broke down the findings by academic discipline, and found that humanities faculty members were the most likely (81 percent) to be liberal. The liberal percentage was at its highest in English literature (88 percent), followed by performing arts and psychology (both 84 percent), fine arts (83 percent), political science (81 percent).

Other fields have more balance. The liberal-conservative split is 61-29 in education, 55-39 in economics, 53-47 in nursing, 51-19 in engineering, and 49-39 in business.

Beyond general political identification, the professors were asked for views on specific issues, and here too, the authors find faculty backing for positions associated with liberal politics. Of professors, 84 percent somewhat or strongly agree that women should have the right to have abortions, and 88 percent agree that policies should favor environmental protection even if those policies result in higher prices and fewer jobs.

The report's authors say that their findings suggest a "sharp shift to the left" from earlier studies, which found more ideological balance. But in fact numerous studies have made similar findings (although in many cases less detailed) in recent years.

"The American College Teacher" is a major study by the Higher Education Research Institute at the University of California at Los Angeles that features some questions on politics. The last survey, in 2001, found that 5.3 percent of faculty members were far left, 42.3 percent were liberal, 34.3 percent were middle of the road, 17.7 percent were conservative, and 0.3 percent were far right. Those figures are only marginally different from the previous survey, in 1998.

Unlike the survey released this week, the UCLA survey includes faculty members at community colleges, and those faculty members are more evenly split than their four-year counterparts, with 33.3 percent identifying as liberal, 41.1 percent as middle of the road, and 22 percent as conservative.

The new study published in *The Forum* also attempts to look at the impact of the ideological split on college faculties.

So the authors devised an "academic achievement index" of faculty members by looking at such factors as books written, journal articles and service on editorial boards. Then the authors looked at certain factors, such as political views, whether someone was religious (defined as attending services "at least once or twice a month"), and gender. The authors then tracked where scholars ended up to see whether there was a relationship between various factors in their backgrounds and whether they ended up at top colleges.

The authors report that among scholars with equivalent academic achievements, liberals are more likely than conservatives to be at top colleges. The scholars also found a negative correlation for being a practicing Christian to getting positions at top colleges (but not for observant Jews) and for women.

In the conclusion to the report, the authors acknowledge that their findings on possible discrimination against conservatives, Christians and women are "preliminary." But they go on to say that "these results suggest that conservative complaints of the presence and effects of liberal homogeneity in academia deserve to be taken seriously, despite their self-interested quality and the anecdotal nature of the evidence previously presented."

Stephen H. Balch, president of the National Association of Scholars, said that "the big news here is the first social science confirmation of the existence of discrimination in hiring and the personnel process." While previous studies have demonstrated the breadth of liberal support in the academy, he said, they have not made as direct a link to hiring and advancement.

Balch said there is now "very strong evidence" that there is bias in the hiring process against conservatives, whereas before this study, there was just "an enormous amount of anecdotal evidence."

College faculty members and presidents, "given their interest in diversity of all other kinds, and their professed desire to overcome discrimination, need to grapple with this." Many academic leaders, however, say that the lopsided political identification totals are entirely predictable, and do not indicate discrimination of any kind. Feal, the MLA executive director, said that when humanities professors say that they are liberals, "the majority of us understand it to be not a narrow political ideology, but a conception of the world."

"We profess the liberal arts," she said. "That comes from freedom that we hold as a high value, from the pursuit of the truth, the pursuit of academic freedom, the belief that the learning and teaching of values will make us better citizens."

Prior to coming to the MLA, Feal was a professor and department chair in modern languages at the State University of New York at Buffalo, and she says that searches never focused on questions of religion or politics. "These things are irrelevant in a search."

"When all was said and done, we had conservative Christians, we had liberal atheists, we had everyone," Feal said.

The study is part of a broader campaign, she said, to question the qualifications and rights of faculty members, especially in the humanities. "This is such a dangerous moment," she said. "We are facing the kind of scrutiny on politics and religion that truly signals danger."

Cary Nelson, author of *Manifesto of a Tenured Radical*, said that he wasn't surprised that some disciplines were largely liberal. Nelson, an English professor at the University of Illinois at Urbana-Champaign, said that in his field, "which has devoted itself significantly to expanding the canon over the last 25 years, it's most likely that the people who are coming into the disciplines are going to have a liberal sentiment rather than a reactionary sentiment."

Nelson said, however, that even if most professors in some fields are liberal, you wouldn't know it from what goes on in classrooms, where he said most scholars are "bloody cowards about letting their politics out." Nelson said that he always tells his students that he is a liberal, and that conservative students will do well in his class as long as they speak up and challenge him.

When it comes to hiring, he says that some departments do engage in "PC hiring," which he defined as the kind of hiring "where a search committee will say, 'We need more women so we're going to give this slot to a woman' or 'We don't have enough gay people so we've got to hire a gay person.'" Nelson said this kind of hiring was wrong—and foolish in the humanities—where there is enough diversity in the total pool that "if you go for the very best people, you'll still end up with diversity."

In his department, he said, hiring is quality based, and even though many of his colleagues focus on issues of race and gender, "we hire people who work only on traditional authors, most of whom are dead white men." The question in hiring, he says, is are you excited by a person's work and its potential, not do you agree with it.

Not all scholars accept the premise that the ideological split is necessarily hurting higher education—or at least not in a black-and-white way. Joel Carpenter, provost of Calvin College, said that many faculty members he hires are committed Christians who welcome the opportunity to work in an environment where they will not stand out. "People are always saying that they have finally found a place where they can be true to their beliefs," he said. While some people assume that a religious college like his is "less free" than other places, many of the scholars feel "more free" to talk about faith, he said, than they would at a secular university.

Carpenter said he would worry if religious faculty members felt that "they had been defined out of the realms of what's worth considering" at secular institutions. But he said he doesn't feel that is the situation yet. "I see a lot of strong, articulate, interesting voices at those institutions—people who don't mind being in a minority, who have the courage of their convictions."

He speaks from some experience, having earned his Ph.D. in history from Johns Hopkins University, where he said he probably did stand out to his fellow students and to professors for his faith and views on some issues. "I think the fact that I really needed to defend my views to people who were originally skeptical helped make me stronger as a scholar," said Carpenter. But he also said that he saw "everyone have their ideas challenged—no one got a pass."

"My own personal experience would say that yes, there is bias, but I haven't seen it to be a 'shut you down' kind of bias," he said. "I'm sure there were some who thought I was a little special, but I come from a Christian tradition that doesn't mind having a beer, so when the library closed, I went down to the grad club like everyone else."

From *Society*, January/February 2006, pp. 3-4. Copyright © 2006 by Transaction Publishers. Reprinted by permission of Transaction Publishers via the Copyright Clearance Center.

Parents Behaving Badly

**Inside the new classroom power struggle:
what teachers say about pushy moms and dads who drive them crazy**

NANCY GIBBS

If you could walk past the teachers' lounge and listen in, what sorts of stories would you hear?

An Iowa high school counselor gets a call from a parent protesting the C her child received on an assignment. "The parent argued every point in the essay," recalls the counselor, who soon realized why the mother was so upset about the grade. "It became apparent that she'd written it."

A sixth-grade teacher in California tells a girl in her class that she needs to work on her reading at home, not just in school. "Her mom came in the next day," the teacher says, "and started yelling at me that I had emotionally upset her child."

A science teacher in Baltimore, Md., was offering lessons in anatomy when one of the boys in class declared, "There's one less rib in a man than in a woman." The teacher pulled out two skeletons—one male, the other female—and asked the student to count the ribs in each. "The next day," the teacher recalls, "the boy claimed he told his priest what happened and his priest said I was a heretic."

A teacher at a Tennessee elementary school slips on her kid gloves each morning as she contends with parents who insist, in writing, that their children are never to be reprimanded or even corrected. When she started teaching 31 years ago, she says, "I could make objective observations about my kids without parents getting offended. But now we handle parents a lot more delicately. We handle children a lot more delicately. They feel good about themselves for no reason. We've given them this cotton-candy sense of self with no basis in reality. We don't emphasize what's best for the greater good of society or even the classroom."

When our children are born, we study their every eyelash and marvel at the perfection of their toes, and in no time become experts in all that they do. But then the day comes when we are expected to hand them over to a stranger standing at the head of a room full of bright colors and small chairs. Well aware of the difference a great teacher can make—and the damage a bad teacher can do—parents turn over their kids and hope. Please handle with care. Please don't let my children get lost. They're breakable. And precious. Oh, but push them hard and don't let up, and make sure they get into Harvard.

But if parents are searching for the perfect teacher, teachers are looking for the ideal parent, a partner but not a pest, engaged but not obsessed, with a sense of perspective and patience. And somehow just at the moment when the experts all say the parent-teacher alliance is more important than ever, it is also becoming harder to manage. At a time when competition is rising and resources are strained, when battles over testing and accountability force schools to adjust their priorities, when cell phones and e-mail speed up the information flow and all kinds of private ghosts and public quarrels creep into the parent-teacher conference, it's harder for both sides to step back and breathe deeply and look at the goals they share.

> **"The parent doesn't know what you're giving and accepts what the child says. Parents are trusting children before they trust us. They have lost faith in teachers."**

Ask teachers about the best part of their job, and most will say how much they love working with kids. Ask them about the most demanding part, and they will say dealing with parents. In fact, a new study finds that of all the challenges they face, new teachers rank handling parents at the top. According to preliminary results from the MetLife Survey of the American Teacher, made available exclusively to TIME, parent management was a bigger struggle than finding enough funding or maintaining discipline or enduring the toils of testing. It's one reason, say the Consortium for Policy Research in Education and the Center for the Study of Teaching and Policy, that 40% to 50% of new teachers leave the profession within five years. Even master teachers who love their work, says Harvard education professor Sara Lawrence-Lightfoot, call this "the most treacherous part of their jobs."

"Everyone says the parent-teacher conference should be pleasant, civilized, a kind of dialogue where parents and teachers build alliances," Lawrence-Lightfoot observes. "But what most teachers feel, and certainly what all parents feel, is anxiety, panic and vulnerability." While teachers worry most about the parents they never see, the ones who show up faithfully pose a whole different set of challenges. Leaving aside the monster parents who seem to have been born to torment the teacher, even "good" parents can have bad days when their virtues exceed their boundaries: the eager parent who pushes too hard, the protective parent who defends the cheater, the homework helper who takes over, the tireless advocate who loses sight of the fact that there are other kids in the class too. "I could summarize in one sentence what teachers hate about parents," says the head of a private school. "We hate it when parents undermine the education and growth of their children. That's it, plain and simple." A taxonomy of parents behaving badly:

> **"You get so angry that you don't care what the school's perspective is. This is my child. And you did something that negatively impacted my child. I don't want to hear that you have 300 kids."**

The Hovering Parent

It was a beautiful late morning last May when Richard Hawley, headmaster at University School in Cleveland, Ohio, saw the flock of mothers entering the building, eager and beaming. "I ask what brings them to our halls," he recalls. "They tell me that this is the last day the seniors will be eating lunch together at school and they have come to watch. To watch their boys eat lunch? I ask. Yes, they tell me emphatically. At that moment, a group of lounging seniors spot their mothers coming their way. One of them approaches his mother, his hands forming an approximation of a crucifix. 'No,' he says firmly to his mother. 'You can't do this. You've got to go home.' As his mother draws near, he hisses in embarrassment, 'Mother, you have no life!' His mother's smile broadens. 'You are my life, dear.'"

Parents are passionate, protective creatures when it comes to their children, as nature designed them to be. Teachers strive to be dispassionate, objective professionals, as their training requires them to be. Throw in all the suspicions born of class and race and personal experience, a culture that praises teachers freely but pays them poorly, a generation taught to question authority and a political climate that argues for holding schools ever more accountable for how kids perform, and it is a miracle that parents and teachers get along as well as they do. "There's more parent involvement that's good—and bad," notes Kirk Daddow, a 38-year veteran who teaches Advanced Placement history in Ames, Iowa. "The good kind is the 'Make yourself known to the teacher; ask what you could do.' The bad kind is the 'Wait until something happens, then complain about it and try to get a grade changed.'" Overall, he figures, "we're seeing more of the bad."

Long gone are the days when the school was a fortress, opened a couple of times a year for parents' night and gradua-

tion but generally off limits to parents unless their kids got into trouble. Now you can't walk into schools, public or private, without tripping over parents in the halls. They volunteer as library aides and reading coaches and Mentor Moms, supplement the physical-education offerings with yoga and kickboxing, sponsor faculty-appreciation lunches and fund-raising barbecues, supervise field trips and road games and father-daughter service projects. Even the heads of boarding schools report that some parents are moving to live closer to their child's school so that they can be on hand and go to all the games. As budgets shrink and educational demands grow, that extra army of helpers can be a godsend to strapped schools.

> **In a survey, 90% of new teachers agreed that involving parents in their children's education is a priority at their school, but only 25% described their experience working with parents as "very satisfying." When asked to choose the biggest challenge they face, 31% of them cited involving parents and communicating with them as their top choice. 73% of new teachers said too many parents treat schools and teachers as adversaries.**

But parents, it turns out, have a learning curve of their own. Parents who are a welcome presence in elementary school as library helpers need to learn a different role for junior high and another for high school as their children's needs evolve. Teachers talk about "helicopter parents," who hover over the school at all times, waiting to drop in at the least sign of trouble. Given these unsettled times, if parents feel less in control of their own lives, they try to control what they can, which means everything from swooping down at the first bad grade to demanding a good 12 inches of squishy rubber under the jungle gym so that anyone who falls will bounce right back. "The parents are not the bad guys," says Nancy McGill, a teacher in Johnston, Iowa, who learned a lot about handling parents from being one herself. "They're mama grizzly bears. They're going to defend that cub no matter what, and they don't always think rationally. If I can remember that, it defuses the situation. It's not about me. It's not about attacking our system. It's about a parent trying to do the best for their child. That helps keep the personal junk out of the way. I don't get so emotional."

While it's in the nature of parents to want to smooth out the bumps in the road, it's in the nature of teachers to toss in a few more: sometimes kids have to fail in order to learn. As children get older, the parents may need to pull back. "I believe that the umbilical cord needs to be severed when children are at school," argues Eric Paul, a fourth- and fifth-grade teacher at Roosevelt Elementary School in Santa Monica, Calif. He goes to weekend ball games and piano recitals in an effort to bond with families but also tries to show parents that there is a line that shouldn't be crossed. "Kids need to operate on their own at school, advocate on their own and learn from each other. So in my class, parents' involvement is limited," he says.

High schools, meanwhile, find themselves fending off parents who expect instant responses to every e-mail; who request a change of teacher because of "poor chemistry" when the real issue is that the child is getting a poor grade; who seek out a doctor who will proclaim their child "exceptionally bright but with a learning difference" that requires extra time for testing; who insist that their child take five Advanced Placement classes, play three varsity sports, perform in the school orchestra and be in student government—and then complain that kids are stressed out because the school doesn't do enough to prevent scheduling conflicts. Teachers just shake their heads as they see parents so obsessed with getting their child into a good college that they don't ask whether it's the right one for the child's particular interests and needs.

"They'll misbehave in front of you. You see very little of that 'I don't want to get in trouble' attitude because they know Mom or Dad will come to their defense."

And what if kids grow so accustomed to these interventions that they miss out on lessons in self-reliance? Mara Sapon-Shevin, an education professor at Syracuse University, has had college students tell her they were late for class because their mothers didn't call to wake them up that morning. She has had students call their parents from the classroom on a cell phone to complain about a low grade and then pass the phone over to her, in the middle of class, because the parent wanted to intervene. And she has had parents say they are paying a lot of money for their child's education and imply that anything but an A is an unacceptable return on their investment.

These parents are not serving their children well, Sapon-Shevin argues. "You want them to learn lessons that are powerful but benign. Your kid gets drunk, they throw up, feel like crap—that's a good lesson. They don't study for an exam, fail it and learn that next time they should study. Or not return the library book and have to pay the fine. But when you have a kid leave their bike out, it gets run over and rusty, and you say, 'O.K., honey, we'll buy you a new one,' they never learn to put their bike away."

The Aggressive Advocate

Marguerite Damata, a mother of two in Silver Spring, Md., wonders whether she is too involved in her 10-year-old son's school life. "Because he's not in the gifted and talented group, he's almost nowhere," she says. "If I stopped paying attention, where would he be?" Every week she spends two hours sitting in his math class, making sure she knows the assignments and the right vocabulary so that she can help him at home. And despite all she sees and all she does, she says, "I feel powerless there."

Parents understandably argue that there is a good reason to keep a close watch if their child is one of 500 kids in a grade level. Teachers freely admit it's impossible to create individual

teaching programs for 30 children in a class. "There aren't enough minutes in the day," says Tom Loveless, who taught in California for nine years and is now director of the Brown Center on Education Policy at the Brookings Institution. "You have to have kids tackling subject matter together as a group. That's a shoe that will pinch for someone." Since the passage of the No Child Left Behind Act, which requires schools to show progress in reading and math test scores in Grades 3 through 8 across all racial and demographic groups, parents are worried that teachers will naturally focus on getting as many students as possible over the base line and not have as much time to spur the strongest kids or save the weakest. Some educators argue that you can agree on the goals of accountability and achievement, but given the inequalities in the system, not all schools have the means to achieve them. "A really cynical person who didn't want to spend any more money on an educational system might get parents and teachers to blame each other and deflect attention away from other imperfect parts of the system," observes Jeannie Oakes, director of the Institute for Democracy, Education and Access at UCLA.

"With the oldest, I think I micromanaged things. I had to come to a point where I said, These are his projects. They're not my projects. I'm not helping him."

Families feel they have to work the system. Attentive parents study the faculty like stock tables, looking for the best performer and then lobbying to get their kids into that teacher's class. "You have a lot of mothers who have been in the work force, supervising other people, who have a different sense of empowerment and professionalism about them," notes Amy Stuart Wells, professor of sociology and education at Columbia University's Teachers College. "When they drop out of the work force to raise their kids, they see being part of the school as part of their job." Monica Stutzman, a mother of two in Johnston, Iowa, believes her efforts helped ensure that her daughter wound up with the best teacher in each grade. "We know what's going on. We e-mail, volunteer on a weekly basis. I ask a lot of questions," she says. "I'm not there to push my children into things they're not ready for. The teachers are the experts. We've had such great experiences with the teacher because we create that experience, because we're involved. We don't just get something home and say, 'What's this?'"

"Most teachers will do what they need to, but there are teachers who are uncomfortable, who turn their backs or close their eyes or ears because they do not want what they perceive might be a confrontation."

Parents seeking to stay on top of what's happening in class don't have to wait for the report card to arrive. "Now it's so easy for the parents through the Internet to get ahold of us, and they expect an immediate response," notes Michael Schaffer, a classroom veteran who teaches AP courses at Central Academy in Des Moines, Iowa. "This e-mail—'How's my kid doing?'—could fill my day. That's hyperbole. But it's a two-edged sword here, and unfortunately it's cutting to the other side, and parents are making demands on us that are unreasonable. Yeah, they're concerned about their kids. But I'm concerned about 150 kids. I don't have time during the day to let the parent know when the kid got the first B." As more districts make assignments and test scores available online, it may cut down on the "How's he doing" e-mails but increase the "Why did she get a B?" queries.

Beneath the ferocious jostling there is the brutal fact that outside of Lake Wobegon, not all children are above average. Teachers must choose their words carefully. They can't just say, "I'm sorry your child's not as smart as X," and no parent wants to hear that there are five other kids in the class who are a lot smarter than his or hers. Younger teachers especially can be overwhelmed by parents who announce on the first day of school that their child is going to be the smartest in the class and on the second day that he is already bored. Veteran teachers have learned to come back with data in hand to show parents who boast that their child scored in the 99th percentile on some aptitude test that 40 other students in the class did just as well.

It would be nice if parents and teachers could work together to improve the system for everyone, but human nature can get in the way. Both sides know that resources are limited, and all kinds of factors play into how they are allocated—including whose elbows are sharpest. Many schools, fearful of "bright flight," the mass departure of high-achieving kids, feel they have no choice but to appease the most outspoken parents. "I understand, having been a parent, the attitude that 'I don't have time to fix the whole system; I don't have time and energy to get rid of systemic injustice, racism, poverty and violence; I have to get what's right for my kid,'" says Syracuse's Sapon-Shevin. "But then the schools do educational triage. They basically attend to the most vocal, powerful people with more resources. They say, 'Don't get angry. We'll take care of this issue.' And they mean, 'We'll take care of it for your child. We'll get your kid out of the class with the bad teacher and leave the other kids in there.'"

At the deepest level, teachers fear that all this parental anxiety is not always aimed at the stuff that matters. Parents who instantly call about a grade or score seldom ask about what is being taught or how. When a teacher has spent the whole summer brightening and deepening the history curriculum for her ninth-graders, finding new ways to surprise and engage them, it is frustrating to encounter parents whose only focus is on test scores. "If these parents were pushing for richer, more meaningful instruction, you could almost forgive them their obnoxiousness and inattention to the interests of all the other children," says Alfie Kohn, a Boston-based education commentator and author of *Unconditional Parenting*. But "we have pushy parents pushing for the wrong thing." He argues that test scores often measure what matters least—and that even high test scores should invite parents to wonder what was cut from the curriculum to make room for more test prep.

"It's a challenge to be a good parent of a high school student. You want to help our kids without putting too much pressure on."

Kohn knows a college counselor hired by parents to help "package" their child, who had perfect board scores and a wonderful grade-point average. When it was time to work on the college essay, the counselor said, "Let's start with a book you read outside of school that really made a difference in your life." There was a moment of silence. Then the child responded, "Why would I read a book if I didn't have to?" If parents focus only on the transcript—drive out of children their natural curiosity, discourage their trying anything at which they might fail—their definition of success will get a failing grade from any teacher watching.

The Public Defenders

By the time children turn 18, they have spent only 13% of their waking lives in the classroom. Their habits of mind, motivation and muscles have much more to do with that other 87%. But try telling that to an Ivy-educated mom and dad whose kids aren't doing well. It can't be the genes, Mom and Dad conclude, so it must be the school. "It's the bright children who aren't motivated who are most frustrating for parents and teachers," says Nancy McGill, a past president of the Iowa Talented and Gifted Association. "Parents don't know how to fix the kid, to get the kid going. They want us to do it, and discover we can't either." Sometimes bright kids intentionally work just hard enough to get a B because they are trying to make a point about what should be demanded of them, observes Jennifer Loh, a math teacher at Ursuline Academy in Dallas. "It's their way of saying to Mom and Dad, 'I'm not perfect.'" Though the best teachers work hard to inspire even the most alienated kids, they can't carry the full burden of the parents' expectations. In his dreams, admits Daddow, the Iowa history teacher, what he would like to say is "Your son or daughter is very, very lazy." Instead, he shows the parents the student's work and says, "I'm not sure I'm getting Jim's best effort."

When a teacher asks parents to be partners, he or she doesn't necessarily mean Mom or Dad should be camping in the classroom. Research shows that though students benefit modestly from having parents involved at school, what happens at home matters much more. According to research based on the National Education Longitudinal Study, a sample of nearly 25,000 eighth-graders, among four main areas of parental involvement (home discussion, home supervision, school communication and school participation), home discussion was the most strongly related to academic achievement.

Any partnership requires that both sides do their part. Teachers say that here again, parents can have double standards: Push hard, but not too hard; maintain discipline, but don't punish my child. When teachers tell a parent that a child needs to be reprimanded at home, teachers say they often get the response, "I don't reprimand, and don't tell me how to raise my child."

Older teachers say they are seeing in children as young as 6 and 7 a level of disdain for adults that was once the reserve of adolescents. Some talk about the "dry-cleaner parents" who drop their rambunctious kids off in the morning and expect them to be returned at the end of the day all clean and proper and practically sealed in plastic.

At the most disturbing extreme are the parents who like to talk about values but routinely undermine them. "You get savvier children who know how to get out of things," says a second-grade teacher in Murfreesboro, Tenn. "Their parents actually teach them to lie to dodge their responsibilities." Didn't get your homework done? That's O.K. Mom will take the fall. Late for class? Blame it on Dad. Parents have sued schools that expelled kids for cheating, on the grounds that teachers had left the exams out on a desk and made them too easy to steal. "Cheating is rampant," says Steve Taylor, a history teacher at Beverly Hills High School in California. "If you're not cheating, then you're not trying. A C means you're a loser." Every principal can tell a story about some ambitious student, Ivy bound, who cheats on an exam. Teacher flunks her. Parents protest: She made a mistake, and you're going to ruin her life. Teachers try to explain that good kids can make bad decisions; the challenge is to make sure the kids learn from them. "I think some parents confuse advocating on behalf of their student with defending everything that the student does," says Scott Peoples, a history teacher at Skyview High School outside Denver.

"I called the parents on a discipline issue with their daughter. Her father called me a total jerk. Then he said, "Well, do you want to meet someplace and take care of this man to man?"

Student-teacher disputes can quickly escalate into legal challenges or the threat of them. The fear of litigation that has given rise to the practice of defensive medicine prompts educators to practice defensive teaching. According to Forrest T. Jones Inc., a large insurer of teachers, the number of teachers buying liability insurance has jumped 25% in the past five years. "A lot of teachers are very fearful and don't want to deal with it," says Roxsana Jaber-Ansari, who teaches sixth grade at Hale Middle School in Woodland Hills, Calif. She has learned that everything must be documented. She does not dare accuse a student of cheating, for instance, without evidence, including eyewitness accounts or a paper trail. When a teacher meets with a student alone, the door always has to be open to avoid any suspicion of inappropriate behavior on the teacher's part. "If you become angry and let it get to you, you will quit your job," says Jaber-Ansari. "You will hate what you do and hate the kids."

Teacher's Pests

Some parents ask too much of the school or too little of their kids

Helicopter Parents

In order to grow, kids need room to fail; the always hovering parent gets in the way of self-reliance

Monster Parents

The lurking moms and dads always looking for reasons to disagree are a teacher's worst nightmare

Dry-cleaner Parents

They drop their rambunctious kids off and want them all cleaned up and proper by the end of the day

The Culture Warriors

Teachers in schools with economically and ethnically diverse populations face a different set of challenges in working with parents. In less affluent districts, many parents don't have computers at home, so schools go to some lengths to make contact easier. Even 20 minutes twice a year for a conference can be hard for families if parents are working long hours at multiple jobs or have to take three buses to get to the school. Some teachers visit a parent's workplace on a Saturday or help arrange language classes for parents to help with communication. Particularly since a great goal of education is to level the playing field, teachers are worried that the families that need the most support are least able to ask for it. "The standards about what makes a good parent are always changing," notes Annette Lareau, a professor of sociology at Temple University, who views all the demand for parent involvement as a relatively recent phenomenon. "And it's middle-class parents who keep pace."

Lareau also sees cultural barriers getting in the way of the strong parent-teacher alliance. When parents don't get involved at school, teachers may see it as a sign of indifference, of not valuing education—when it may signal the reverse. Some cultures believe strongly that school and home should be separate spheres; parents would no more interfere with the way a teacher teaches than with the way a surgeon operates. "Working-class and poor families don't have a college education," says Lareau. "They are looking up to teachers; they respect teachers as professionals. Middle-class parents are far less respectful. They're not a teacher, but they could have been a teacher, and often their profession has a higher status than teachers'. So they are much more likely to criticize teachers on professional grounds."

And while she views social class as a major factor in shaping the dynamic, Lareau finds that race continues to play a role. Middle-class black parents, especially those who attended segregated schools, often approach the teacher with caution. Roughly 90% of teachers are white and middle class, and, says

Lareau, many black parents are "worried that teachers will have lowered expectations of black children, that black boys will be punished more than white boys. Since teachers want parents to be positive and supportive, when African-American parents express concerns about racial insensitivity, it can create problems in their relationship."

Finally, as church-state arguments boil over and principals agonize over what kids can sing at the Winter Concert, teachers need to be eternally sensitive to religious issues as well. This is an arena where parents are often as concerned about content as grades, as in the debate over creationism vs. evolution vs. intelligent design, for instance. Teachers say they have to become legal scholars to protect themselves in a climate where students have "rights." Jaber-Ansari was challenged for hanging Bible quotes on her classroom walls. But she had studied her legal standing, and when she was confronted, "the principal supported me 100%," she says.

Perhaps the most complicated part OF the conversation—beyond all the issues of race and class and culture, the growing pressures to succeed and arguments over how success should be defined—is the problem of memory. When they meet in that conference, parent and teacher bring their own school experiences with them—what went right and wrong, what they missed. They are determined for it to be different for the child they both care about. They go into that first-grade room and sit in the small chairs and can easily be small again themselves. It is so tempting to use the child's prospects to address their own regrets. So teachers learn to choose their words with care and hope that they can build a partnership with parents that works to everyone's advantage and comes at no one's expense. And parents over time may realize that when it comes to their children, they still have much to learn. "I think that we love our children so much that they make us a little loony at times," says Arch Montgomery, head of the Asheville School in North Carolina. He winces at parents who treat their child as a cocktail-party trophy or a vanity sticker for the window of their SUV, but he also understands their behavior. "I think most parents desperately want to do what is right for their kids. This does not bring out the better angels of our natures, but it is understandable, and it is forgivable."

—With reporting by Amanda Bower, New York, Melissa August, Washington, Anne Berryman, Athens, Cathy Booth Thomas, Dallas, Rita Healy, Denver, Elizabeth Kauffman, Nashville, Jeanne McDowell, Los Angeles and Betsy Rubiner, Des Moines

Sobriety Tests Are Becoming Part of the School Day

PATRICK O'GILFOIL HEALY

EAST HAMPTON, N.Y.— For years, schools across the country have deployed breath analyzers at proms, pep rallies and other after-school events to catch students who arrived drunk or smuggled in alcohol.

After some resistance and fevered debate, student advocates and even lawyers gradually came to accept that schools were within their rights to use every means to ensure that students were not toting six-packs and liquor bottles to after-school, night and weekend events.

Quietly though, a few districts around the country, from Indiana to Connecticut to Long Island, have begun to integrate breath-testing devices into the regular school day, a move that adds a new wrinkle to the ongoing struggle between students' privacy rights and a school's duty to limit drug and alcohol abuse.

Schools say they need to ensure that no students are drinking in class. Civil rights lawyers worry that high school students pulled out of class and forced to take a breath-alcohol test could be unfairly stigmatized for goofy or strange behavior.

Manufacturers of breath analyzers say they have sold their devices to thousands of schools across the country, but it is impossible to say how many districts have started using breath-alcohol tests during the school day. Officials with the Office of National Drug Control Policy and the National School Boards Association said they knew of no statistics tracking schools' use of breath analyzers. But lawyers who argue cases involving students' civil liberties said that tests during the school day are rare, and represent untested ground for most districts.

On the East End of Long Island, the East Hampton School District is venturing into this terrain with a proposal to use breath analyzers on students suspected of being intoxicated in high school.

District officials said they grew concerned after hearing of rampant student drinking. Teenagers were caught drinking on school trips to Costa Rica and Italy. A drunk student vomited on a bus on the way to a field trip. Then there were students showing up in class drunk, sometimes after having alcohol at lunch.

Things seemed to be getting out of hand, even for East Hampton, a summer oasis for wealthy New Yorkers that reverts to a rural small town in the off-season where teenagers can get away with holding beach bonfire parties where alcohol flows freely, and year-round residents describe 16 as the de facto drinking age.

So, to stop what seemed like a swell of student drinking, school administrators this winter proposed administering breath analyzers to students while high school is in session. Any student suspected of being drunk in class would be tested by a trained staff member, and not a police officer, board officials said. Results showing alcohol consumption would mean suspension. Refusing to take a test would be seen as an admission of guilt.

In central Connecticut, officials in the Avon School District are writing a plan similar to East Hampton's. A school district near South Bend, Ind. has had the policy in place for several years. Other districts around the country may well use their breath analyzers during the school day, even if their policies were originally intended for events outside of school.

But on Long Island, only one other school district—the Sayville School District—already has an in-school breath-alcohol test policy, and in that case administrators say they have not tested a single student in the seven years it has been in effect. Still, they say it has merit. "It's really preventative," said Geri Sullivan-Keck, Sayville's assistant superintendent for curriculum.

Prof. Bernard James of Pepperdine University, who specializes in constitutional law, said such policies easily survive legal challenges, but often crumple under community opposition. "In policy, it's an extraordinarily controversial issue," he said.

News of the plan has roiled East Hampton. Last month, parents and teachers crowded a school board meeting to cheer the proposal. The op-ed pages of The East Hampton Star overflowed with letters, many of them calling the plan heavy-handed and invasive.

Wendy Hall, the school board president, said the seven-member board would probably approve the plan at a meeting in early April. She called the plan gutsy and said it was one of several efforts the district had undertaken to restrict student drinking.

The proposal has forced students, teachers and parents to focus on drinking in East Hampton. The high school is a drab, boxy building set among the town's cedar-shingled homes. It spends $16,000 per student per year, and 80 percent of its 1,000 students graduate with a Regents diploma. Right now, students are preparing for spring break and Advanced Placement Tests, but the breath analyzer plan is what really drives conversation, residents said.

Daniel Otto, a senior at East Hampton High, mulled it over one night in his kitchen, as he sipped Coors Light. It was Thirsty Thursday, the night he and a few friends play poker and drink. Mr. Otto said the plan was ridiculous.

"I think they're trying to fix a problem they can't fix," he said. "Everybody drinks. It's the way East Hampton kids are."

Claudia Pilato Maietta, the president of the Parent Teacher Student Association, said the breath analyzer proposal had come after a rash of complaints about student drinking. In addition to complaints about drinking at pep rallies and at a beach at lunch, there was one complaint in October from a parent who e-mailed the principal photos of East Hampton students drinking at parties. Officials alerted the students' parents, and suspended some of the students from extracurricular activities.

Kevin Flaherty, a senior in the pictures who was not among those drinking, said that the incident had helped pave the way for the testing, which he called an over-reaction. "I know the whole senior class," he said, "and no one drinks at school."

He and other students expressed concern that students with past problems would be targeted and those who were zany, tired or rowdy would be misjudged as being drunk.

In Indiana, at Penn High School in Mishawaka, which has a similar policy, the principal was forced to apologize to a student who had been pulled out of class by a police officer last year and given three breath tests, all of which were negative.

But school officials in East Hampton insist they would use the tests fairly and discreetly. Scott Farina, the principal, said the school would call parents before giving the test, and would make sure students were safe if the results came out positive.

"This is just one way that we're trying to be proactive," he said.

One of the few students unfazed by the proposal was James Westfall, a senior, who said he had smuggled alcohol to school in a Gatorade bottle just before Christmas vacation. He was caught that day by school officials, he said, even without a breath analyzer, and said the school should have carte blanche to keep students from drinking.

"They're trying to keep it out of school," he said. "They're right to do that."

The 37th Annual Phi Delta Kappa/ Gallup Poll of the Public's Attitudes Toward the Public Schools

This is the 37th consecutive year for this poll. Its early success can be credited to George Gallup, Sr. Gallup considered it his poll, picked the panel to select the questions, oversaw the surveying, analyzed the results, and wrote the report. The close relationship between Phi Delta Kappa and the Gallup Organization continued after the death of George Gallup, Sr., with his son, Alec Gallup, representing that organization. Since 1992, I have had the privilege of directing the poll for PDK. Alec and I share the beliefs that the procedures used minimize the possibility of bias in the poll and present the results in user-friendly fashion. The Gallup Organization has absolute authority over the phrasing of the questions and certifies that the data support the findings and conclusions. Alec and I use the executive summary to state our best judgment as to what the data mean. Each conclusion cites the table or tables containing the data on which it is based. Some readers tell us that they read the tables first, draw their own conclusions, and then compare those with the ones we have drawn. Alec and I believe the information in this poll is unusually significant and commend it to your use. —LCR

LOWELL C. ROSE AND ALEC M. GALLUP

Executive Summary

In this Executive Summary we present a number of findings and conclusions of this, the 37th Annual Phi Delta Kappa/Gallup Poll of the Public's Attitudes Toward the Public Schools. Some conclusions strike us as more significant than others. Conclusions 10 and 11, for example, regarding the achievement gap, and conclusions 12 through 16, dealing with the No Child Left Behind (NCLB) Act, seem worthy of special notice. That the public is so strong in its support for closing the achievement gap should send a clear message to policy makers. There is also a message in the conclusions related to NCLB in that they note the public's disagreement with the law's strategies and, at the same time, suggest that there is still time for midcourse corrections. Again, we feel that policy makers would do well to heed the message.

Another important contribution of the poll results is that they should help to destroy one of the myths surrounding the public schools: that the public schools are losing public support. The trend lines in this poll suggest the exact opposite. The grades the public assigns the schools remain as high as ever and are truly impressive when public school parents give their evaluation; the public continues to express a strong preference for change through the existing public schools; support for choice shows no sign of increasing and could be said to be lagging; and it is the public schools to which the public turns for closing the achievement gap.

Finally, before we move to the specific conclusions, it seems necessary to comment on the important distinction between the nation's schools and schools in the community. These polls have repeatedly documented that the public has a low opinion of the nation's schools and a high opinion of schools in the local community. The media, some education experts, and some government leaders base their comments on the nation's schools and are then surprised when they do not resonate with a public that is concerned primarily with the schools in the community, schools that generally draw approval. As long as those seeking to improve the public schools make their case on the supposed inadequacy of the schools in the community, support for improvement will be hard to build.

We turn now to the 20 conclusions that we believe summarize the most significant findings of this year's poll. The data supporting each conclusion are provided, and the tables in which additional supporting data will be found are cited by number.

1. Lack of financial support is solidly entrenched in the public mind as the major problem facing the nation's public schools. Responding to an open-ended question, 20% of those surveyed mention lack of financial support. This problem has been among the top problems mentioned for 15 straight years and has been the top problem for six years running. This year, it attracts almost twice the number of mentions of any other problem. (See Table 1.)

PDK/Gallup Poll Advisory Panel

The following individuals worked with Alec Gallup and the Gallup Organization to select and frame the questions asked in the 37th Annual Phi Delta Kappa/Gallup Poll of the Public's Attitudes Toward the Public Schools.

G. Thomas Houlihan, Executive Director, Council of Chief State School Officers, Washington, D.C.

Jack Jennings, President and CEO, Center on Education Policy, Washington, D.C.

Rossi Ray-Taylor, Executive Director, Minority Student Achievement Network, Evanston, Ill.

Ted Sanders, Executive Chairman, Cardean Learning Group, Chicago.

William J. Bushaw, Executive Director, Phi Delta Kappa International.

Sherry G. Morgan, Past President, Phi Delta Kappa International, and Superintendent of Catholic Schools, Diocese of Knoxville.

Lowell C. Rose, Executive Director Emeritus, Phi Delta Kappa International.

Bruce Smith, Editor, *Phi Delta Kappan.*

Sandra Weith, Associate Executive Director, Phi Delta Kappa International.

2. The high level of support Americans give to schools in their community is unchanged, and support for the public schools grows in direct proportion to the closeness of respondents to those schools. In this poll, 24% assign an A or a B to the nation's schools; 48% award an A or a B to schools in the community. This figure rises to 57% when public school parents grade the schools in the community and to 69% when parents grade the school their oldest child attends. (See Tables 2, 3, and 4.)

3. The public's strong preference is for improvement that comes by reforming the current public schools rather than by finding an alternative system. Asked to choose between the two options, the public has, since this question was first asked, consistently chosen reform through the existing system. (See Table 6.)

4. The public opposes permitting parents and students to choose to attend private schools at public expense. Fifty-seven percent of respondents oppose making this choice available as compared to 38% who favor it. The percentage in favor peaked at 46% in 2002 and has declined by 8% since that time. (See Table 7.)

5. The major reason cited for supporting private school attendance at public expense is the belief that achievement is better in private schools. Forty-nine percent of those supporting this alternative point to better achievement, 18% cite safety, and 25% mention receptivity to religious practices. (See Table 8.)

6. A plurality of respondents support the idea of charter schools. However, strong majorities say that such schools should be accountable to the state in the same way as regular public schools and should not be created if doing so means less funding for regular public schools. While 49% favor charter schools, 80% say they should be accountable to the

state just as regular public schools are accountable. In addition, 65% of respondents oppose having charter schools in their community if it means reducing regular public school funding. (See Tables 9, 10, and 11.)

7. The public believes that the amount of achievement testing in schools is just about right, and a majority of respondents support additional testing in three grades at the high school level. The 40% saying there is about the right amount of testing and the 17% saying there is not enough constitute a majority in support of testing at least at current levels, while 67% support testing in high school at grades 9, 10, and 11. (See Tables 12 and 13.)

8. The public is divided regarding the use of student scores on standardized tests for the purpose of evaluating teachers and principals. Fifty-two percent believe student performance on standardized tests should be one measurement used in determining a teacher's ability; 44% say it should not. As for evaluating principals, 50% endorse taking student test scores into consideration, while 46% disapprove. It is important to note that the question asks if standardized test results should be "one measure." (See Tables 14 and 15.)

9. The public believes that the current emphasis on standardized tests will lead teachers to teach to the test and does not regard this as a positive outcome. Fifty-eight percent say that teaching to the test will be encouraged, and 54% say that this is a bad thing. (See Tables 16 and 17.)

10. The public approaches consensus on the importance of closing the achievement gap, attributes the gap to factors other than schooling, believes parents and students have more to do with whether students learn than teachers, but still believes that it is the responsibility of the schools to close the gap.

- Ninety percent say it is either very important or somewhat important to close the gap.
- Seventy-five percent relate the gap to factors other than the quality of schooling received.
- Sixty-three percent say that parents or students themselves determine student performance.
- Nevertheless, 58% say that it is the responsibility of the public schools to close the gap. (See Tables 18, 19, 20, and 21.)

11. The public believes that the achievement gap can be substantially narrowed while maintaining high standards for all students. Eighty-one percent of respondents hold the view that the gap can be narrowed without sacrificing high standards. (See Table 22.)

12. The fact that so much of the public still considers itself uninformed regarding No Child Left Behind (NCLB) can be taken as reason to regard current opinions as preliminary. The public's final judgment of NCLB is presumably yet to be made. While the number saying they know a great deal or fair amount about NCLB has grown from 24% in 2003 to 40% in this year's survey, 59% say they know very little or nothing at all. (See Table 23.)

13. We drew the conclusion in 2003 that the public's dissatisfaction with the strategies used in NCLB gave reason to believe that greater familiarity with the act was unlikely to

bring approval. Based on the findings in this year's poll, that conclusion is even more valid today. Forty-five percent in the current poll still say that they do not know enough about NCLB to express an opinion. Twenty-eight percent of respondents say that their view is either very favorable or somewhat favorable, while 27% say that it is somewhat unfavorable or very unfavorable. More significant is the fact that among those professing a "great deal" of knowledge about NCLB, 57% view it unfavorably, while 36% view it favorably. (See Table 24.)

14. The NCLB strategies are frequently out of step with approaches favored by the public.

- NCLB uses a single test to determine if a school is in need of improvement. Sixty-eight percent say that a single test cannot give a fair picture. (See Table 25.)
- NCLB tests only English and math to determine if a school is in need of improvement. Eighty percent say testing English and math only will not give a fair picture. This rises to 87% within the "great deal" of knowledge group. (See Table 26.)
- NCLB gives parents of a child attending a school found to be in need of improvement the chance to transfer their child to a school making "adequate yearly progress" (AYP). Seventy-nine percent say they would prefer to have additional help given to their child in his or her own school. (See Table 28.)
- NCLB requires that test scores be broken out into eight groups based on ethnicity, English-speaking ability, poverty level, and disability status and reported separately by each group. A plurality of 48% opposes this requirement, with most of that group saying that they do so because they believe all students are equal—and presumably should be treated in the same way. Support for reporting scores separately, however, is strong among those claiming knowledge of NCLB. (See Tables 29 and 30.)
- With limited exceptions, NCLB requires students enrolled in special education to meet the same standards as other students. Sixty-eight percent say these students should not be held to the same standards. (See Table 31.)
- NCLB includes the scores of special education students in determining whether a school is or is not in need of improvement. Sixty-two percent say these scores should not be included. (See Table 32.)
- NCLB designates a school in need of improvement if one group fails to make AYP for two consecutive years. The public is evenly split on whether this should happen if the special education group is the only one failing. However, a majority of the "great deal" of knowledge group says that scores of the special education group alone should not determine the designation. (See Table 33.)
- NCLB determines whether a school has made AYP based on the percentage of students meeting fixed goals in passing English and math. Eighty-five percent believe that it would be better to base AYP on *improvement* shown during the year. (See Table 35.)
- NCLB requires that all of the groups meet the same fixed goals regardless of how far a given group starts from the

goals. Sixty-three percent say the goals should vary according to where the school starts. (See Table 36.)

15. The public is split as to whether teachers and principals will be less willing to accept special education students at their schools knowing that doing so could reduce their chances of making AYP. However, those professing knowledge of NCLB are more likely to say that teachers and principals will be less willing to accept these students. The public splits on this question, with 47% saying that teachers and principals will be less willing to accept special education students and 45% saying that it will make no difference. Sixty-two percent of those in the "great deal" of knowledge group and 56% of those in the "fair amount" of knowledge group say that teachers and principals will be less willing to accept these students. (See Table 34.)

16. The public is equally divided on whether a large number of school failures would reflect shortcomings of the schools or of the law. Forty-five percent believe that the public schools should be blamed if a large number of schools fail to meet requirements. Forty-three percent say it is the law that should be blamed. (See Table 37.)

17. The public's concerns regarding NCLB are consistent with the facts that the public favors a curriculum that offers a wide variety of courses and would prefer to see a child of theirs be active in extracurricular activities and earn average grades in school as compared to earning A grades but not participating in activities. Asked to choose between a wide variety of courses and a concentration of courses, 61% of respondents opt for a wide variety of courses. Given a choice between having a child of theirs earn A grades and having a child earn average grades but be active in extracurricular activities, 64% choose average grades and extracurricular activities. (See Tables 38 and 39.)

18. The public does not believe that the increasingly common practice of pursuing postsecondary education online should lead to a requirement that each high school student take at least one course online. Fifty-six percent of respondents say they would not require each high school student to take one course online. (See Table 40.)

19. The public believes that students who do not speak English should learn to do so in public school classes before enrolling in regular classes. Sixty-one percent of respondents support requiring non-English-speaking students to learn English in public school classes before enrolling in regular classes. (See Table 41.)

20. Almost two-thirds of those surveyed would like to see a child of theirs take up teaching as a career. Sixty-two percent of respondents endorse teaching as a career for their child. (See Table 42.)

Problems and Assessment
The Biggest Problem

The question asked in every year since 1969 gives those surveyed the chance to mention the biggest problem the schools in their communities face. The public is consistent and slow to change. Discipline topped the list for the first 16 years of the poll. Use of drugs then occupied the top by itself until 1991, when lack of financial support drew into a tie. Lack of financial support has been unchallenged as the top problem since 2000.

Grading the Public Schools

Three questions dealing directly with the public's assessment of its schools trace back to the 1980s. The data are reported in Tables 2, 3, and 4. This year's responses vary little from recent years. Twenty-four percent give the nation's schools an A or a B. The percentage rises to 48% for schools in the community, to 57% when public school parents grade their community's schools, and to 69% when parents grade the school their oldest child attends. The long-term trend line for community schools shows the percentage assigning an A or a B at 41% in 1990, 49% in 1999, and 48% in 2005. In addition to the three longtime questions, respondents to this year's poll were asked a new question regarding the effectiveness of community schools in preparing students for employment after graduation. The data in Table 5 show that 41% assign the schools an A or a B in preparing students for employment.

School Improvement and School Choice

Source of School Improvement

Taking as a given the public's desire to see improvement, the 1997 poll queried respondents as to whether they wanted that improvement to come by reforming the existing public schools or by finding an alternative system. Seventy-one percent said in 1997 that reform should come through the existing schools. That percentage has changed little in the intervening years and now stands at 68%. The fact that over two-thirds of Americans want change to come through the existing schools provides a benchmark against which proposals for change can be assessed.

Table 1 What do you think are the biggest problems the public schools of your community must deal with?

	National Totals			No Children In School			Public School Parents		
	'05 %	'04 %	'03 %	'05 %	'04 %	'03 %	'05 %	'04 %	'03 %
Lack of financial support/funding/money	20	21	25	19	22	26	21	20	24
Overcrowded schools	11	10	14	9	9	12	15	13	16
Lack of discipline, more control	10	10	16	12	10	17	8	8	13
Use of drugs/dope	9	7	9	9	7	10	8	7	7

Table 2 Students are often given the grades of A, B, C, D, and FAIL to denote the quality of their work. Suppose the public schools themselves, in your community, were graded in the same way. What grade would you give the public schools here—A, B, C, D, or FAIL?

	National Totals		No Children In School		Public School Parents	
	'05 %	'04 %	'05 %	'04 %	'05 %	'04 %
A & B	48	47	45	42	57	61
A	12	13	9	11	20	17
B	36	34	36	31	37	44
C	29	33	29	37	29	24
D	9	10	9	9	8	10
FAIL	5	4	4	3	5	5
Don't know	9	6	13	9	1	*

*Less than one-half of 1%.

Table 3 How about the public schools in the nation as a whole? What grade would you give the public schools nationally—A, B, C, D, or FAIL?

	National Totals		No Children In School		Public School Parents	
	'05 %	'04 %	'05 %	'04 %	'05 %	'04 %
A & B	24	26	24	28	26	22
A	2	2	2	2	3	3
B	22	24	22	26	23	19
C	46	45	47	45	42	44
D	13	13	14	13	8	13
FAIL	4	4	3	3	6	6
Don't know	13	12	12	11	18	15

Table 4 Using the A, B, C, D, or FAIL scale again, what grade would you give the school your oldest child attends?

	Public School Parents	
	'05 %	'04 %
A & B	69	70
A	31	24
B	38	46
C	21	16
D	6	8
FAIL	4	4
Don't know	*	2

*Less than one-half of 1%.

Commentary:
An Important Message

Since its inception, state education policy makers have looked to the annual PDK/Gallup poll to garner a clear picture of the public's attitudes toward public education. As in years past, the findings of the 2005 poll communicate an important message. The findings affirm the approaches to school reform that many states have adopted, including high standards and meaningful accountability for all students. The poll results reflect an understanding on the part of the public of the challenges our nation's schools face. And the results send an unmistakable signal to education leaders and policy makers at the local, state, and national level that the public believes in the institution of public schools and that we as a nation have the capacity and responsibility to transform them from within.

Members of the public articulate the conviction that the achievement gap can be closed and that it can be closed within the current system of public schooling. They understand that it takes resources to provide a high-quality education to every student, and they believe that a comprehensive public school experience includes subject matter beyond mathematics and English and provides for co-curricular activities. Clearly the public is not interested in policies that divide, but in policies and practices that get results. —*Brenda Lilienthal Welburn,* executive director, National Association of State Boards of Education, Alexandria, Va.

Table 5 What grade would you give the public schools in your community for preparing students for employment following graduation from high school?

	National Totals %	No Children In School %	Public School Parents %
A & B	41	39	43
A	9	8	12
B	32	31	31
C	32	33	29
D	10	10	10
FAIL	7	6	11
Don't know	10	12	7

Private School at Public Expense

Two possible alternatives to regular public schools—private school choice and charter schools—are covered in Tables 7 through 11. Table 7 reports on this poll's trend question related to choice. Respondents are asked whether they favor or oppose permitting parents to have their child attend a private school at public expense. This year's percentage in support is the lowest since 2001, 38%. The percentage opposed is up to 57% from

Table 6 In order to improve public education in America, some people think the focus should be on reforming the existing public school system. Others believe the focus should be on finding an alternative to the existing public school system. Which approach do you think is preferable—reforming the existing public school system or finding an alternative to the existing public school system?

	National Totals					No Children In School					Public School Parents				
	'05 %	'04 %	'03 %	'02 %	'01 %	'05 %	'04 %	'03 %	'02 %	'01 %	'05 %	'04 %	'03 %	'02 %	'01 %
Reforming existing system	68	66	73	69	72	67	63	73	69	73	72	72	73	69	73
Finding alternative system	23	26	25	27	24	23	28	24	26	23	22	21	25	27	25
Don't know	9	8	2	4	4	10	9	3	5	4	6	7	2	4	2

Table 7 Do you favor or oppose allowing students and parents to choose a private school to attend at public expense?

	National Totals							
	'05 %	'04 %	'03 %	'02 %	'01 %	'00 %	'99 %	'98 %
Favor	38	42	38	46	34	39	41	44
Oppose	57	54	60	52	62	56	55	50
Don't know	5	4	2	2	4	5	4	6

Table 8 (Asked of those in favor.) Which of the following statements comes closest to indicating why you favor permitting parents to choose a private school at public expense?

	National Totals %	No Children In School %	Public School Parents %
Student achievement will be better in private schools	49	48	52
Private schools are safer	18	17	18
Private schools are more receptive to religious practices	25	24	25
Don't know	8	11	5

54% in 2004. This year's poll also explored why attendance at private schools is favored by some respondents. Forty-nine percent cite better student achievement at private schools, and 25% attribute their support to private schools' greater receptiveness to religious practices.

Charter Schools

The next three tables deal with the charter school alternative. Started in 1992, charter schools are considered public schools. Their supposed advantage is that they operate with fewer rules and more flexibility. The data in Table 9 suggest that about half of the public supports the concept of charter schools. However, 80% of respondents say that charter schools should be accountable to the

Table 9 As you may know, charter schools operate under a charter or contract that frees them from many of the state regulations imposed on public schools and permits them to operate independently. Do you favor or oppose the idea of charter schools?

	National Totals				No Children In School				Public School Parents			
	'05 %	'02 %	'01 %	'00 %	'05 %	'02 %	'01 %	'00 %	'05 %	'02 %	'01 %	'00 %
Favor	49	44	42	42	49	44	40	42	48	44	43	40
Oppose	41	43	49	47	40	43	51	47	43	44	47	47
Don't know	10	13	9	11	11	13	9	11	9	12	10	13

Table 10 Do you think that charter schools should be accountable to the state in the way regular public schools are accountable?

	National Totals				No Children In School				Public School Parents			
	'05 %	'02 %	'01 %	'00 %	'05 %	'02 %	'01 %	'00 %	'05 %	'02 %	'01 %	'00 %
Should be accountable	80	77	77	79	79	78	77	78	81	77	77	81
Should not	14	19	18	17	14	19	18	18	14	19	18	14
Don't know	6	4	5	4	7	3	5	4	5	4	5	5

Table 11 Would you favor charter schools in your community if funding them meant reducing the amount of funds for the regular public schools—or not?

	National Totals		No Children In School		Public School Parents	
	'05 %	'02 %	'05 %	'02 %	'05 %	'02 %
Favor	28	30	29	31	26	25
Oppose	65	65	63	64	69	70
Don't know	7	5	8	5	5	5

state in the same way as other public schools. This is significant in that it seems contrary to the greater flexibility that is one of the reasons for organizing such schools. The response to a final question indicates that a majority of the public would oppose operating charter schools if it meant reduced funding for regular public schools.

Testing
Amount of Testing

The testing mandated by NCLB and additional testing required by state-level initiatives have meant that the use of standardized testing to drive instruction has increased. The trend question reported in Table 12 assesses the public's opinion on the amount of testing. The percentage saying there is too much testing is up 6% since 2000, while the percentage saying there is about the

Table 12 Now, here are some questions about testing. In your opinion, is there too much emphasis on achievement testing in the public schools in your community, not enough emphasis on testing, or about the right amount?

	National Totals					No Children In School					Public School Parents				
	'05 %	'04 %	'02 %	'01 %	'00 %	'05 %	'04 %	'02 %	'01 %	'00 %	'05 %	'04 %	'02 %	'01 %	'00 %
Too much	36	32	31	31	30	35	30	30	29	28	39	36	32	36	34
Not enough	17	22	19	22	23	17	23	20	22	26	17	20	14	20	19
About the right amount	40	40	47	44	43	39	40	46	45	41	43	43	54	43	46
Don't know	7	6	3	3	4	9	7	4	4	5	1	1	*	1	1

*Less than one-half of 1%.

Table 13 The No Child Left Behind law currently requires testing in one grade in high school. A proposal has been made to expand the testing to include grades 9, 10, and 11. Do you favor or oppose this proposal?

	National Totals %	No Children In School %	Public School Parents %
Favor	67	66	68
Oppose	28	28	30
Don't know	5	6	2

right amount is down by 3%. That suggests a slight movement in the direction of concern about too much testing. That concern, however, is countered by the fact that two-thirds support President Bush's proposal for testing in grades 9, 10, and 11.

Testing and High-Stakes Decisions

One result of the growing emphasis on accountability has been an increase in the use of standardized tests for making high-stakes decisions involving schools and students. Several instances of this practice will be dealt with in the subsequent section on NCLB. The four tables that follow relate to the use of standardized test results in evaluating teachers and principals and the extent to which high-stakes uses encourage teaching to the test. Table 14 deals with the public's view of using standardized test data to assess teacher performance. Fifty-two percent support such use. Similarly, 50% of the public supports using student test results for evaluating principals. Tables 16 and 17 summarize the responses on the issues of teaching to the tests. A majority of respondents believe that the emphasis on standardized test results will cause teachers to teach to the test, and 54% say this is a bad thing.

Table 14 In your opinion, should one of the measurements of a teacher's quality be based on how well his or her students perform on standardized tests or not?

	National Totals		No Children In School		Public School Parents	
	'05 %	'04 %	'05 %	'04 %	'05 %	'04 %
Yes, should	52	49	53	50	52	49
No, should not	44	47	43	45	46	49
Don't know	4	4	4	5	2	2

Table 15 How about school principals? In your opinion, should one of the measurements of a principal's quality be based on how well the students in his or her school perform on standardized tests?

	National Totals		No Children In School		Public School Parents	
	'05 %	'04 %	'05 %	'04 %	'05 %	'04 %
Yes, should	50	47	51	47	47	48
No, should not	46	50	44	50	51	51
Don't know	4	3	5	3	2	1

Table 16 In your opinion, will the current emphasis on standardized tests encourage teachers to "teach to the tests," that is, concentrate on teaching their students to pass the tests rather than teaching the subject, or don't you think it will have this effect?

	National Totals		No Children In School		Public School Parents	
	'05 %	'03 %	'05 %	'03 %	'05 %	'03 %
Will encourage teachers to teach to the tests	58	66	57	64	60	68
Will not have this effect	33	30	32	32	35	27
Don't know	9	4	11	4	5	5

Table 17 If the current emphasis on results is encouraging teaches to "teach to the tests," do you think this will be a good thing or a bad thing?

	National Totals		No Children In School		Public School Parents	
	'05 %	'03 %	'05 %	'03 %	'05 %	'03 %
Good thing	39	39	36	38	45	40
Bad thing	54	60	55	61	51	58
Don't know	7	1	9	1	4	2

Commentary:
Facing a Messy Reality

The American public doesn't know a lot about No Child Left Behind (NCLB), has mixed feelings about the law itself, and is dubious about the statute's machinery. These results aren't shocking. The implications could be another story.

While the public embraces educational accountability in principle, it always hesitates when faced with the messy reality. The poll results depict antipathy toward key NCLB components, including the emphasis on math and English assessment, use of subgroups, and uniform state performance standards for schools and students. Suggesting discomfort with the most basic tenets of performance-based accountability, respondents were evenly split on whether student achievement should be one measure of teacher or principal quality.

Most respondents think their schools are fine and that schools have a pretty limited ability to close the achievement gap. Meanwhile, the most commonly cited educational problem is insufficient funding. Cumulatively, these beliefs undermine the case for performance-based accountability—which presumes that schools are underperforming, that they can address achievement gaps, and that the key problems are institutional and organizational.

This skepticism isn't about to melt away. Respondents who know "a great deal" about NCLB are no more supportive of its provisions—aside from the requirement to disaggregate performance data by student subgroups—than anyone else. Whether proponents can find a way to persuade the public that NCLB is necessary, effective, and sensibly designed will likely determine the fate of this landmark legislation. —*Frederick M. Hess,* **director of education policy studies, American Enterprise Institute, Washington, D.C.**

The Achievement Gap

The achievement gap—white students outperforming black and Hispanic students and non-poverty-level students outperforming those from poverty-level homes—is present in all states. This poll has consistently delved into the public's views on what causes the gap and who is responsible for closing it. Table 18 deals with a trend question on the importance of closing the gap. For four years running, some 9 of 10 respondents indicate that it is very important or somewhat important to close the gap. The results reported in Tables 19 and 20 make it clear that the public does not see the schools as responsible for the gap. On the contrary, the percentage blaming the gap on the quality of schooling is down 12 points since 2002. Data in Table 20 may explain this belief, with 63% of respondents saying parents or students are responsible for what students learn and only 33% saying teachers. But the majority of the public nonetheless believes that schools are responsible for closing the gap, and 81% believe substantial progress in doing so can be made while maintaining high standards.

Table 18 Black and Hispanic students generally score lower on standardized tests than white students. In your opinion, how important do you think it is to close this academic achievement gap between these groups of students?

	National Totals				No Children In School				Public School Parents			
	'05 %	'04 %	'03 %	'02 %	'05 %	'04 %	'03 %	'02 %	'05 %	'04 %	'03 %	'02 %
Very + somewhat important	90	88	90	94	89	89	91	93	89	89	88	96
Very important	63	64	71	80	3	65	70	80	62	63	73	80
Somewhat important	27	24	19	14	26	24	21	13	27	26	15	16
Not too important	3	5	5	2	2	4	5	2	5	3	4	2
Not at all important	5	5	4	3	6	5	3	4	4	7	7	1
Don't know	2	2	1	1	3	2	1	1	2	1	1	1

Table 19 In your opinion, is the achievement gap between white students and black and Hispanic students mostly related to the quality of schooling received or mostly related to other factors?

	National Totals				No Children In School				Public School Parents			
	'05 %	'04 %	'03 %	'02 %	'05 %	'04 %	'03 %	'02 %	'05 %	'04 %	'03 %	'02 %
Mostly related to quality of schooling received	17	19	16	29	17	19	15	31	17	20	18	22
Mostly related to other factors	75	74	80	66	75	73	80	64	75	76	80	75
Don't know	8	7	4	5	8	8	5	5	8	4	2	3

Table 20 In your opinion, who is most important in determining how well or how poorly students perform in school—the students themselves, the students' teachers, or the students' parents?

	National Totals		No Children In School		Public School Parents	
	'05 %	'04 %	'05 %	'04 %	'05 %	'04 %
Students themselves	20	22	20	23	20	21
Students' teachers	33	30	32	31	35	29
Students' parents	43	45	44	42	41	48
Don't know	4	3	4	4	4	2

Table 21 In your opinion, is it the responsibility of the public schools to close the achievement gap between white students and black and Hispanic students or not?

	National Totals			No Children In School			Public School Parents		
	'05 %	'04 %	'01 %	'05 %	'04 %	'01 %	'05 %	'04 %	'01 %
Yes, it is	58	56	55	58	56	56	56	56	53
No, it is not	37	40	41	36	39	39	42	41	45
Don't know	5	4	4	6	5	5	2	3	2

Commentary: Listening to the Public

This year's PDK/Gallup poll, like so many polls before it, reaffirms that the vast majority of the American people support our public schools. Critics of public education need to listen hard to what the American people are saying: help us improve the system, don't walk away from it.

The public also recognizes the direct link between maintaining high standards, investing in public education, and closing the achievement gap. For almost a decade, there has been an intense national focus on making sure that all children can read by the end of the third grade. This bipartisan commitment of extra resources, focus, and expertise spans two Administrations. As a result, reading scores for the National Assessment of Educational Progress are up for 9-year-olds. Funding matters in education, especially if we want to close the achievement gap for older students.

Testing is necessary, the public tells us, but an over-emphasis on standardized tests is a growing concern. Teaching to the test is not the answer. The public senses that this narrow focus is causing America's students to lose out on music, art, civics, foreign language, and other learning opportunities that help them grow to be well-rounded individuals and better citizens.

The public, of course, is correct. We should respond by shifting our focus away from standardized testing and placing a greater emphasis on quality teaching and making our schools exciting community learning centers. This will require some midcourse corrections in NCLB. —**Richard W. Riley, former U.S. secretary of education**.

Table 22 Do you believe that the achievement gap can be narrowed substantially while maintaining high standards for all children or not?

	National Totals %	No Children In School %	Public School Parents %
Can be narrowed	81	83	78
Cannot be narrowed	15	13	19
Don't know	4	4	3

No Child Left Behind

NCLB was signed into law on 8 January 2002 and was explored in depth for the first time in this poll later that year. The results then led to the conclusion that the public knew little about the law. In the 2003 poll, the public's attitudes toward the strategies the law employs led us to conclude that greater familiarity with the law was unlikely to bring approval. Developments to date have given no cause to change that assessment.

Table 23 Now, here are a few questions about the No Child Left Behind Act. How much, if anything, would you say you know about the No Child Left Behind Act—the federal education bill that was passed by Congress in 2001—a great deal, a fair amount, very little, or nothing at all?

	National Totals			No Children In School			Public School Parents		
	'05 %	'04 %	'03 %	'05 %	'04 %	'03 %	'05 %	'04 %	'03 %
Great deal + fair amount	**40**	**31**	**24**	**39**	**28**	**25**	**45**	**37**	**22**
A great deal	8	7	6	8	6	5	10	8	7
A fair amount	32	24	18	31	22	20	35	29	15
Very little	43	40	40	44	41	37	40	38	44
Nothing at all	16	28	36	16	30	38	14	24	34
Don't know	1	1	*	1	1	*	1	1	*
Very little + nothing at all	**59**	**68**	**76**	**60**	**71**	**75**	**54**	**62**	**78**

*Less than one-half of 1%.

Table 24 From what you know or have heard or read about the No Child Left Behind Act, do you have a very favorable, somewhat favorable, somewhat unfavorable, or very unfavorable opinion of the act—or don't you know enough about it to say?

				Knowledge of NCLB			
	National Totals			Great Deal	Fair Amount	Very Little	None At All
	'05 %	'04 %	'03 %	'05 %	'05 %	'05 %	'05 %
Very favorable + somewhat favorable	**28**	**24**	**18**	**36**	**44**	**21**	**11**
Very favorable	7	7	5	19	9	5	6
Somewhat favorable	21	17	13	17	35	16	5
Somewhat unfavorable	15	12	7	21	20	15	4
Very unfavorable	12	8	6	36	18	4	7
Don't know enough to say	45	55	69	7	18	60	77
Don't know	*	1	*	*	*	*	1
Somewhat unfavorable + very unfavorable	**27**	**20**	**13**	**57**	**38**	**19**	**11**

*Less than one-half of 1%.

Knowledge and Approval

The data in Table 23 show that, while the percentage claiming some level of knowledge about NCLB has climbed, 59% still say they know little or nothing at all. Surprisingly, a majority of public school parents say they are in the uninformed group. Meanwhile, the percentage saying they do not know enough to say whether their view is favorable or unfavorable is down from 69% in 2003 to 45% this year. Twenty-eight percent say their view is favorable while 27% say it is unfavorable.

NCLB Strategies

The following tables reflect the public's views with regard to the strategies used in NCLB. Each table summarizes the responses to a particular strategy. Preceding each table is a statement of the strategy and the public's position in relation to the strategy.

Strategy. NCLB requires each state to decide if a school is in need of improvement based on the percentage of students showing proficiency in English and math on a state-selected test.

Public position. Sixty-eight percent of respondents say that a single test cannot give a fair picture of whether a school is in need of improvement.

Table 25 According to the NCLB Act, determining whether a public school is or is not in need of improvement will be based on the performance of its students on a single statewide test. In your opinion, will a single test provide a fair picture of whether or not a school needs improvement?

				Knowledge of NCLB			
	National Totals			Great Deal	Fair Amount	Very Little	None At All
	'05 %	'04 %	'03 %	'05 %	'05 %	'05 %	'05 %
Yes	29	31	32	37	28	27	32
No	68	67	66	63	70	71	64
Don't know	3	2	2	*	2	2	4

*Less than one-half of 1%.

Strategy. NCLB bases its system of determining a school's status on student performance in English and math only.

Public position. Eighty percent of respondents say that a test of English and math only cannot give a fair picture of whether a school is in need of improvement.

Table 26 According to the NCLB Act, the statewide tests of student performance will be devoted to English and math only. Do you think a test covering only English and math would provide a fair picture of whether a school in your community is or is not in need of improvement, or should the test be based on other subjects?

				Knowledge of NCLB			
	National Totals			Great Deal	Fair Amount	Very Little	None At All
	'05 %	'04 %	'03 %	'05 %	'05 %	'05 %	'05 %
Yes, would provide fair picture	17	16	15	13	19	18	14
No, test should be based on other subjects also	80	83	83	87	77	80	83
Don't know	3	1	2	*	4	2	3

*Less than one-half of 1%.

Strategy. The subjects NCLB uses in determining if a school is in need of improvement are English and math.

Public position. Eighty-two percent of respondents are concerned that the reliance on English and math will mean less emphasis on art, music, history, and other subjects.

Table 27 How much, if at all, are you concerned that relying on testing for English and math only to judge a school's performance will mean less emphasis on art, music, history, and other subjects? Would you say you are concerned a great deal, a fair amount, not much, or not at all?

	National Totals			Knowledge of NCLB			
				Great Deal	Fair Amount	Very Little	None At All
	'05 %	'04 %	'03 %	'05 %	'05 %	'05 %	'05 %
A great deal + a fair amount	82	81	80	92	82	82	79
A great deal	39	37	40	66	39	33	36
A fair amount	43	44	40	26	43	49	43
Not much	12	13	14	4	11	14	11
Not at all	5	4	6	4	7	3	9
Don't know	1	2	*	*	*	1	1

*Less than one-half of 1%.

Strategy. NCLB provides that parents of a child attending a school that fails to make "adequate yearly progress" (AYP) for two consecutive years must be offered the opportunity to transfer their child to a school making AYP.

Public position. Seventy-nine percent of respondents say they would prefer to have additional help given to their child in the school he or she attends rather than transferring their child to another school.

Table 28 Assume you had a child attending a school identified as in need of improvement by the NCLB Act. Which would you prefer, to transfer your child to a school identified as NOT in need of improvement or to have additional efforts made in your child's present school to help him or her achieve?

	National Totals			Knowledge of NCLB			
				Great Deal	Fair Amount	Very Little	None At All
	'05 %	'04 %	'03 %	'05 %	'05 %	'05 %	'05 %
To transfer child to school identified as not in need of improvement	16	16	25	20	17	16	15
To have additional efforts made in the child's present school	79	80	74	76	81	79	80
Don't know	5	4	1	4	2	5	5

Commentary: Good News and Bad

This latest PDK/Gallup poll offers good news and bad news for public school educators. Despite the efforts of those who seek to undermine public education, there is still strong support for public schools, particularly at the local level. The closer people are to schools, the better they feel about them. Members of the public believe in personal experience more than in the words of reformers from afar. They are also able to parse what is important and what is not. Tests are important but not to the exclusion of a broader curriculum, and they should not determine the future of a child or school.

The bad news is embedded in the best of the news. Members of the public want to see the achievement gap closed and understand that the gap is created outside the schools, but they believe schools can overcome the ravages of social and economic conditions. While this belief is a vote of confidence for schools, when coupled with the recognition that money is the biggest challenge facing schools and is increasingly difficult to find, these expectations could set the schools up for failure if they cannot do what society will not do. —**Paul D. Houston, executive director, American Association of School Administrators, Arlington, Va.**

Strategy. NCLB requires that test scores be reported separately for American Indians, Asians, blacks, Hispanics, whites, limited-English-proficient students, economically disadvantaged students, and special education students.

Public position. Forty-eight percent of respondents oppose reporting scores separately. However, separate reporting is supported by two-thirds of the "great deal" of knowledge group. A follow-up question indicates that 60% of those opposing this method of reporting scores do so based on the belief that all students are equal—and presumably should be treated in the same way.

Table 29 The No Child Left Behind Act requires that test scores be reported separately by students' race and ethnicity, disability status, English-speaking ability, and poverty level. Do you favor or oppose reporting test scores in this way in your community?

	National Totals		Knowledge of NCLB			
			Great Deal	Fair Amount	Very Little	None At All
	'05 %	'04 %	'05 %	'05 %	'05 %	'05 %
Favor	44	42	67	45	39	44
Oppose	48	52	31	48	53	45
Don't know	8	6	2	7	8	11

Table 30   (Asked of those opposed.) Why do you oppose reporting test scores separately?

	National Totals %	Knowledge of NCLB			
		Great Deal %	Fair Amount %	Very Little %	None At All %
All students are equal	60	46	60	61	67
Should judge by individuality	8	5	12	7	2
Unfair	7	9	9	6	2
Will cause differences between children	6	5	6	7	6
Will make no difference	3	7	1	4	2
Should apply only to disabled	2	1	4	2	*
Scores are a private issue	2	*	2	2	*

*Less than one-half of 1%.

NCLB and Special Education

Students in special education are the one demographic group whose designation for separate reporting of scores is based on cognitive ability. When NCLB rules were issued, special education scores were treated like other scores. Even before the rules were ever enforced, changes were made allowing a small percentage of those with the most severe disabilities to be tested at other than grade-level standards. This percentage has recently been expanded. Still, special education scores are among the most frequent reasons that schools fail to make AYP.

Strategy. NCLB requires that all special education students except those with the most severe cognitive handicaps be tested against grade-level standards.

Public position. Just over two-thirds of respondents say that these students should not be held to the same standards as other students.

Table 31   In your opinion, should students enrolled in special education in a public school be required to meet the same academic standards as all other students in that school?

	National Totals %	No Children In School %	Public School Parents %
Yes	28	28	29
No	68	67	68
Don't know	4	5	3

Strategy. NCLB includes special education students with all other students in determining whether a school is in need of improvement.

Public position. Sixty-two percent of respondents say special education students should not be included in determining whether a school is in need of improvement; 34% say they should be in-

cluded. The percentage saying these students should not be included is 12% higher for the "great deal" of knowledge group.

Table 32   In your opinion, should the standardized test scores of special education students be included with the test scores of all other students in determining whether a school is in need of improvement under NCLB or not?

	National Totals		Knowledge of NCLB			
			Great Deal	Fair Amount	Very Little	None At All
	'05 %	'04 %	'05 %	'05 %	'05 %	'05 %
Yes, should	34	39	25	29	35	46
No, should not	62	57	74	69	60	48
Don't know	4	4	1	2	5	6

Strategy. NCLB provides that if any demographic group fails to make AYP, the entire school fails to make AYP. The result is that the special education group causes a disproportionate number of AYP failures.

Public position. The public is split on whether a school should be designated as in need of improvement if the special education group is the only failure. However, majorities of those claiming a "great deal" or a "fair amount" of knowledge of NCLB are against that designation.

TABLE 33   How about if the special education students are the only group in a school whose test scores fail to meet NCLB requirements? Should that school be designated as in need of improvement or not?

	National Totals %	Knowledge of NCLB			
		Great Deal %	Fair Amount %	Very Little %	None At All %
Yes, should	47	7	44	50	50
No, should not	48	55	54	44	44
Don't know	5	8	2	6	6

Respondents were asked whether a situation in which a large number of schools fail to make AYP because special education students alone fail to make AYP would make teachers and principals less willing to have special education students assigned to their schools. The public is also split on that possibility. Again, the two groups professing knowledge of NCLB differ from respondents overall, with majorities saying that teachers and principals will be less willing to accept these students. The data are shown in Table 34.

Table 34 NCLB results have shown that schools with special education students are less likely to make adequate yearly progress than schools with no special education students. Do you think this will make principals and teachers less willing to have special education students assigned to their schools, or will it make no difference?

	National Totals %	Knowledge of NCLB			
		Great Deal %	Fair Amount %	Very Little %	None At All %
Less willing	47	62	56	47	26
Make no difference	45	38	38	44	65
Don't know	8	*	6	9	9

*Less than one-half of 1%.

Measuring School Performance Under NCLB

Fixed Goals Versus Improvement

NCLB measures school performance based on the percentage of students who meet specific goals in English and in math. Many believe that the amount of improvement made during the school year is a more appropriate measure than the percentage meeting fixed goals. The data in Table 35 reflect responses to a question in which the public was asked which method it preferred. Eighty-five percent prefer the improvement approach and reject the fixed-goals approach NCLB uses. A second question (reported in Table 36) sought to find out if the amount of improvement required should vary for schools starting far from the goals and schools starting close to the goals. Sixty-three percent say that the improvement required should vary. It does not under NCLB.

The Significance of Failure to Make AYP

Under NCLB the number of school failures is expected to grow with each passing year as the goals for students passing increase at the rate needed to reach 100% proficiency by 2013–14. Anticipating this steady increase in failing schools, the poll sought to find out how the public will react. The public splits on this question, with 45% saying they would blame the schools and 43% saying they would blame the law. Those claiming to know a "great deal" about NCLB differ from respondents overall, with a majority of 61% saying the law would be to blame. The data are found in Table 37.

Table 35 One way to measure a school's performance is to base it on the percentage of students passing the test mandated by the state at the end of the school year. Another way is to measure the improvement students in the school make during the year. In your opinion, which is the best way to measure the school's performance—the percentage passing the test or the improvement shown by the students?

	National Totals %	Knowledge of NCLB			
		Great Deal %	Fair Amount %	Very Little %	None At All %
Percentage passing the test	13	16	13	13	9
Improvement shown by the students	85	84	86	85	88
Don't know	2	*	1	2	3

*Less than one-half of 1%.

Table 36 Let's assume that one school starts a year with 35% of its students passing the NCLB test, while another school starts with 65% passing the test. In your opinion, should the amount of improvement required be the same for both schools or should it vary according to where the school started?

	National Totals %	Knowledge of NCLB			
		Great Deal %	Fair Amount %	Very Little %	None At All %
Should be the same for both schools	32	27	30	30	46
Should vary according to where the school started	63	70	67	64	48
Don't know	5	3	3	6	6

Table 37 Let's say that large numbers of public schools fail to meet the requirements established by the NCLB law. In your opinion, which would be more to blame for this—the public schools themselves or the NCLB law?

	National Totals %	Knowledge of NCLB			
		Great Deal %	Fair Amount %	Very Little %	None At All %
The public schools	45	36	44	48	44
The NCLB law	43	61	47	37	40
Don't know	12	3	9	15	16

Curriculum and Instruction

Curriculum

A frequent criticism of NCLB is that its focus on English and math will lead to a narrowing of the curriculum and mean less attention to the differing needs of students. This concern was addressed in two questions. The data in Table 38 come from a question first asked in 1979, in which respondents were asked to express their preference for a curriculum with a wide variety of courses or one emphasizing basic courses. A plurality of the 1979 respondents chose a concentration on basic courses, and a majority did so in 1993. However, the 2001 repeat found that the public had reversed its position, with 54% favoring a wide variety of courses. That majority reaches 61% with this poll. This preference seems to be confirmed by the data in Table 39, in which 64% of respondents choose the option of having their child earn average grades and participate in a broad range of extracurricular activities, compared to 29% who choose having their child get straight A's.

Instruction

In a question new to the poll, respondents were asked if the greater use of computers in postsecondary education translated into the need for an online experience in high school. The data in Table 40 indicate that a majority of respondents do not think so. In a question repeated from 1993, this poll sought to determine the public preference for helping students who come to school lacking the ability to speak English. The data in Table 41 indicate that 61% believe such students should learn English in public school classes before enrolling in regular classes.

Miscellaneous

Two poll questions did not fit into any particular grouping. Table 42 reports responses to a trend question asking parents whether they would like to see their child take up teaching as a career. While the 62% saying yes is down 5% from 1993, it is still the fourth-highest percentage in the nine times that the question has been asked. Table 43 shows that a majority, 59% of those surveyed, are seeing more children from other countries in their community than they did in the past.

Table 38 Public high schools can offer students a wide variety of courses, or they can concentrate on fewer basic courses, such as English, mathematics, history, and science. Which of these two policies do you think the local high schools should follow in planning their curricula—a wide variety of courses or fewer but more basic courses?

	National Totals					No Children In School					Public School Parents				
	'05 %	'02 %	'01 %	'93 %	'79 %	'05 %	'02 %	'01 %	'93 %	'79 %	'05 %	'02 %	'01 %	'93 %	'79 %
Wide variety of courses	61	57	54	48	44	59	57	50	44	44	66	57	64	55	44
Basic courses	37	41	44	51	49	39	41	48	54	47	31	42	35	44	53
Don't know	2	2	2	1	7	2	2	2	2	9	3	1	1	1	3

Table 39 Which one of the following would you prefer of an oldest child—that the child get A grades or that he or she make average grades and be active in extracurricular activities?

	National Totals		No Children In School		Public School Parents	
	'05 %	'96 %	'05 %	'96 %	'05 %	'96 %
Get A grades	29	28	26	26	35	33
Average grades and extracurricular activities	64	60	67	63	60	56
Both (volunteered)	*	9	*	8	*	9
Don't know	7	3	7	3	5	2

*Less than one-half of 1%.

Table 40 It is becoming common for education courses after high school to be taken online. Should the high school in your community require every student to take at least one course online while in high school?

	National Totals %	No Children In School %	Public School Parents %
Yes, should	39	43	34
No, should not	56	52	64
Don't know	5	5	2

Table 41 Many families who come from other countries have school-age children who cannot speak English. Which one of the following three approaches do you think is the best way for the public schools to deal with non-English-speaking students? Require students to learn English in special classes at the parents' expense, require public schools to provide instruction in the students' native language, or require students to learn English in public school classes before enrolling in regular classes?

	National Totals		No Children In School		Public School Parents	
	'05 %	'93 %	'05 %	'93 %	'05 %	'93 %
Require students to learn English in special classes at the parents' expense	19	25	18	27	19	23
Require public schools to provide instruction in the students' native language	16	27	15	26	18	30
Require students to learn English in public school classes before enrolling in regular classes	61	46	62	45	59	45
Don't know	4	2	5	2	4	2

Table 42 Would you like to have a child of yours take up teaching in the public schools as a career?

	National Totals								
	'05 %	'93 %	'90 %	'88 %	'83 %	'81 %	'80 %	'72 %	'69 %
Yes	62	67	51	58	45	46	48	67	75
No	33	29	38	31	33	43	40	22	15
Don't know	5	4	11	11	22	11	12	11	10

Table 43 Just your impression, do there seem to be more children from other countries attending the public schools in your community today than in the past, fewer than in the past, or about the same number?

	National Totals %	No Children In School %	Public School Parents %
More than in the past	59	60	56
Fewer than in the past	3	3	3
About the same number	31	28	38
Don't know	7	9	3

Closing Statement

Polling has become an important player in most aspects of American life, and the effort to improve the public schools is no exception. The issues explored in this poll are shaping the daily decisions made in K–12 schools. Moreover, given the variability of data interpretation, it is not surprising that this report and the interpretations provided by the authors are always subject to a critical review. That is as it should be. The poll is intended to contribute to the ongoing debate regarding the public schools, and disagreement fuels that debate. However, we continue to believe that the public has a way of getting it right with issues that are both complex and puzzling. And, whether the public is right or wrong, its attitudes determine, over the long haul, how those issues can be addressed. We believe that this poll and the one last year send an important message regarding NCLB. Agree or disagree, policy makers shaping any revisions to NCLB would find it profitable to study the results carefully and consider their implications for the ultimate success of that law.

Research Procedure

The Sample. The sample used in this survey embraced a total of 1,000 adults (18 years of age and older). A description of the sample and methodology can be found at the end of this report.

Time of Interviewing. The fieldwork for this study was conducted during the period of 9 June through 26 June 2005.

Due allowance must be made for statistical variation, especially in the case of findings for groups consisting of relatively few respondents.

The findings of this report apply only to the United States as a whole and not to individual communities. Local surveys, using the same questions, can be conducted to determine how local areas compare with the national norm.

Sampling Tolerances

In interpreting survey results, it should be borne in mind that all sample surveys are subject to sampling error, i.e., the extent to which the results may differ from what would be obtained if the whole population surveyed had been interviewed. The size of such sampling error depends largely on the number of interviews. For details and tables showing the confidence intervals for the data cited in this poll, please visit the Phi Delta Kappa website at **http://www.pdkintl.org/kappan/kpoll0509sample.htm.**

Design of the Sample

For the 2005 survey the Gallup Organization used its standard national telephone sample, i.e., an unclustered, directory-assisted, random-digit telephone sample, based on a proportionate stratified sampling design.

The random-digit aspect of the sample was used to avoid "listing" bias. Numerous studies have shown that households with unlisted telephone numbers are different in important ways from listed households. "Unlistedness" is due to household mobility or to customer requests to prevent publication of the telephone number.

To avoid this source of bias, a random-digit procedure designed to provide representation of both listed and unlisted (including not-yet-listed) numbers was used.

Telephone numbers for the continental United States were stratified into four regions of the country and, within each region, further stratified into three size-of-community strata.

Only working banks of telephone numbers were selected. Eliminating non-working banks from the sample increased the likelihood that any sample telephone number would be associated with a residence.

The sample of telephone numbers produced by the described method is representative of all telephone households within the continental United States.

Within each contacted household, an interview was sought with the household member who had the most recent birthday. This frequently used method of respondent selection provides an excellent approximation of statistical randomness in that it gives all members of the household an opportunity to be selected.

Up to three calls were made to each selected telephone number to complete an interview. The time of day and the day of the week for callbacks were varied so as to maximize the chances of finding a respondent at home. All interviews were conducted on weekends or weekday evenings in order to contact potential respondents among the working population.

The final sample was weighted so that the distribution of the sample matched current estimates derived from the U.S. Census Bureau's Current Population Survey (CPS) for the adult population living in telephone households in the continental United States.

Composition of Sample

Adults	%	Income	%
No children in school	67	$50,000 and over	35
Public school parents	30	$40,000 and over	44
Nonpublic school parents	3	$30,000–$39,999	13
		$20,000–$29,999	12
Gender	**%**	Under $20,000	16
Men	44	Undesignated	15
Women	56	**Region**	**%**
Race	**%**	East	22
White	81	Midwest	23
Nonwhite	15	South	32
Black	12	West	23
Undesignated	1	**Community Size**	**%**
Age	**%**	Urban	32
18–29 years	18	Suburban	47
30–49 years	40	Rural	21
50 and over	40		
Undesignated	1		
Education	**%**		
Total college	58		
College graduate	24		
College incomplete	34		
Total high school	40		
High school graduate	32		
High school incomplete	8		

LOWELL C. ROSE is executive director emeritus of Phi Delta Kappa International. **ALEC M. GALLUP** is co-chairman, with George Gallup, Jr., of the Gallup Organization, Princeton, N.J.

UNIT 2
Rethinking and Changing the Educative Effort

Unit Selections

Key Points to Consider

- What are some issues in the debate regarding educational reform?

- Should the focus of educational reform be on changing the ways educators are prepared, on the changing needs of students, or on both of these concerns? Defend your answer.

- Compare American concepts about alternative schooling and the uses of public funds to the views of other countries on school choice issues.

Student Website
www.mhcls.com/online

Internet References
Further information regarding these websites may be found in this book's preface or online.

The Center for Innovation in Education
http://www.center.edu

Colorado Department of Education
http://www.cde.state.co.us/index_home.htm

National Council for Accreditation of Teacher Education
http://www.ncate.org

Phi Delta Kappa International
http://www.pdkintl.org

The "No Child Left Behind" (NCLB) legislation has sparked a major debate among the educational community in the United States. What constitutes a "highly qualified teacher?" How many of them do we have? Which students get them? The questions roll on and on. We are left to decide the equity issues involved in all of this. We are also left to decide the most fundamental question of all: What constitutes a "highly qualified teacher?" What educational background should the person have? What are the motivations to do this? How are we to assess this person's ability to take this role? All of these questions need to be addressed plus the question as to how "highly qualified teachers" are to be permitted to play their professional roles in the classrooms assigned to them. We are a democratic society committed to the free education of all our citizens.

Rethinking and redirecting the educational system of a nation requires intensive reflective and analytical effort. How to best restructure educational services is a question that requires considerable contemplation and forethought as to the consequences of our decision-making processes. The dialogical processes involved among citizens as they engage in this decision-making process will shape the forms of our educational futures.

American educators could have a much better sense of their own past as a profession, and the public could better understand the history of public education. In the United States, a fundamental cycle of similar ideas and practices reappears in school curricula every so many years. The decades of the 1970s and 1980s witnessed the rise of "behavioral objectives" and "man-agement by objectives," and the 1990s brought us "outcome-based education" and "benchmarking" in educational discourse within the public school system's leadership. These are related behavioral concepts focusing on measurable ways to pinpoint and evaluate the results of educational efforts. Why do we seem to "reinvent the wheel" of educational thought and practice every so many decades? This is an important question worth addressing. Many of our ideas about change and reform in educational practice have been wrongheaded. There is a focus on more qualitative, as opposed to empirical, means of assessing the outcomes of our educative efforts; yet many state departments of education still insist on objective assessments and verifications of students' mastery of academic skills. How does this affect the development of imaginative teaching in schools? All of us in the education system are concerned, and many of us believe that there really are some new and generative ideas to help students learn basic intellectual skills and content.

Our current realities in the field of education reflect differing conceptions of how schooling ought to change. It is difficult to generalize regarding school quality across decades because of several factors; high schools, for instance, were more selective in 1900, when only 7 percent of American youths graduated from them. Today we encourage as many students as possible to graduate. The social purposes of schooling have been broadened; now we want all youths to complete some form of higher education.

We have to consider the social and ideological differences among those representing opposing school reform agendas for change. The differences over how and in what directions change is to occur in our educational systems rest on which educational values are to prevail. These values form the bases for differing conceptions of the purposes of schooling. Thus the differing agendas for change in American education have to be positioned within the context of the different ideological value systems that underpin each alternative agenda for change.

There are several currently contending (and frequently conceptually conflicting) strategies for restructuring life in schools as well as options open to parents in choosing the schools that they want their children to attend. On the one hand, we have to find ways to empower students and teachers to improve the quality of academic life in classrooms. On the other hand, there appear to be powerful forces contending over whether control of educational services should be even more centralized or more decentralized (site-based). Those who favor greater parental and teacher control of schools support greater decentralized site management and community control conceptions of school governance. Yet the ratio of teachers to nonteaching personnel (administrators, counselors, school psychologists, and others) continues to decline as public school system bureaucracies become more and more "top heavy."

In this unit, we consider the efforts to reconceive, redefine, and reconstruct existing patterns of curriculum and instruction at the elementary and secondary levels of schooling and compare them with the efforts to reconceive existing conflicting patterns of teacher education. A broad spectrum of dialogue is developing in North America, the British Commonwealth, Russia, Central Eurasia, and other areas of the world about the redirecting of learning opportunities for all citizens.

Prospective teachers here are being encouraged to question their own individual educational experiences as part of this process. We must acknowledge that our values affect our ideas about curriculum content and the purpose of educating others. This is perceived as vitally important in the developing dialogue over liberating all students' capacities to function as independent inquirers. The dramatic economic and demographic changes in our society necessitate a fundamental reconceptualization of how schools ought to respond to the many social contexts in which they are located. This effort to reassess and reconceive the education of persons is a vital part of broader reform efforts in society as well as a dynamic dialectic in its own right. How can schools, for instance, better reflect the varied communities of interest that they serve? What must they do to become better perceived as just and equitable places in which all young people can seek to achieve learning and self-fulfillment?

Each of the essays in this unit relates to the tension involved in reconceiving how educational development should proceed in response to all the dramatic social and economic changes in society.

Educating Leaders for Tomorrow

Dancing Lessons for Elephants: Reforming Ed School Leadership Programs

Although Mr. Murphy challenges the negative stereotypes commonly associated with schools of education, he agrees with the critics of programs that educate school administrators. In introducing this special section, for which he served as guest editor, he expresses his hope that the articles to follow can move us beyond the criticism and stimulate reforms in the preparation of school leaders.

JEROME T. MURPHY

DURING A dinner party in an elegant Fifth-Avenue apartment overlooking Central Park, an investment banker asked me, "Just how does it *feel* to be the dean of an Ed School?" I was attending this party, along with the president of Harvard, to raise funds from a select group of Wall Street wizards. My daunting task was to woo these potential donors with an after-dinner speech.

The banker's surprising question came after we had hit it off, swapping stories over sautéed scallops. "It feels great to be an Ed School dean," I replied. "It's such a wonderful challenge." "Yes," the banker responded hesitantly while looking a trifle sheepish, "but it is *such* a low-status job." Forging ahead, I smiled and prated on about the opportunity to make a difference.

To be sure, I was somewhat taken aback by my new friend's bluntness. But I was also moved by his awkward honesty, for he seemed to be candidly sharing with me his shattered stereotype—surprised that his tablemate could be both an Ed School dean and an interesting guy.

Let's face it, schools of education are held in low regard in many circles, and not just among titans of finance dining on Fifth Avenue. As dean I was regularly reminded during fundraising forays and even in meetings with colleagues from other parts of the university that schools of education were perceived to be part of the problem with our public schools, not part of the solution. This low regard, which runs deep and is increasingly

widespread, undermines the credibility and influence of schools of education.[1]

Do Ed Schools deserve these negative perceptions? No—and yes. As an unrepentant enthusiast of schools of education, I believe that many are a lot better than their reputation and are inhabited by outstanding individuals who do important work. To convince critics of the worth of education schools, however, is a challenge. I have learned that the most effective strategy is to avoid railing against deep-seated stereotypes and instead to keep an open mind, listen sincerely to the views of critics, and then invite them to meet with faculty members and students. If stereotypes breed contempt, familiarity can breed support, and rubbing elbows can lead to mutual respect.

However, when it comes to programs that educate school administrators, the critics are mostly on target—and they have been for a long time.[2] Unless this problem is faced squarely, I think these negative perceptions will metastasize, and, given the current climate, schools of education risk becoming progressively marginalized and deemed irrelevant.

The granddaddy of high-profile complaints about administrator preparation programs is the withering attack made 19 years ago by the National Commission on Excellence in Educational Administration, which recommended that more than 60% of these programs be closed.[3] Since then, other observers have regularly chimed in with ever louder complaints.[4] For example, the Broad Foundation and Fordham Institute issued a "manifesto" three years ago that pointed to "a leadership famine amidst a feast of 'certified' leaders" and recommended giving up on schools of education and deregulating the field.[5]

Exactly one year ago, in the latest high-decibel indictment, Arthur Levine contended that university-based leadership programs range from "inadequate to appalling." He described a "race to the bottom," with failures in admissions, curriculum, faculty, pedagogy, and more. Particularly chilling was the reported growth of university satellite operations with little regard for quality.[6]

I agree with much of the latest indictment—and Levine deserves credit for reminding us yet again of this enduring problem. While a number of programs are better than he suggests,[7] far too many are inadequate and, with the heightened pressures for high-status credentials and fast-track programs, may be getting worse. At the very least, schools of education are slow-stepping elephants when it comes to leadership education—sluggishly adjusting to today's call for new blood, stronger content, more relevance, and higher quality.

To be sure, this latest indictment is old news. But what may be a new wrinkle is today's political climate, which some believe may finally provide the external pressure needed to spur schools of education to embrace widespread reform. First, expectations for schools to perform—and the belief in the centrality of leadership to reform—have never been higher.[8] Consequently, the pressure on administrator preparation programs to turn out principals and superintendents who can ensure results has never been greater.

A second aspect of the new education environment is that the university hammer lock on administrator preparation has been broken—and that's a plus. A growing number of high-profile superintendents who came from outside the profession seem to be holding their own in a number of cities. And competition in the preparation of superintendents and principals now exists—witness, for example, the exciting work of the Broad Academy and New Schools for New Leaders. If universities don't act, some believe that alternative providers will step in to address the critical shortage of first-rate principals and superintendents.

The third new element is that higher education, which has long been spared searing analysis by outsiders, is increasingly being considered fair game and is, perhaps, more open to growing demands that it provide relevant content, not just credentials. Witness the compelling argument of Warren Bennis and James O'Toole that business schools have "lost their way" and Henry Mintzberg's blistering attack on MBAs.[9] Witness the wake-up call of Richard Hersh and John Merrow, who contend that the crown jewels of the American education system—its colleges—are in a disturbing state of decline.[10] And, of course, witness the vitriolic debate about the preparation of teachers, including a recent *New York Times* article provocatively titled "Who Needs Education Schools?"[11] Indeed, in a column appearing in the 16 January 2006 issue of *Newsweek*, George Will contends that "the surest, quickest way to add quality to primary and secondary education would be addition by subtraction: Close all the schools of education."

In this volatile new atmosphere, it is time to look forward and examine the preparation of the next generation of princi-

pals, superintendents, and other educational leaders. This special section takes a fresh look at fundamentally redesigning leadership education programs, with a particular focus on universities. The section asks, Where should schools of education place their bets? Who should be selected as students, and how should they be educated? What are the organizational structures, pedagogical techniques, and curricular models that constitute best practice for leadership education? Indeed, will universities rise to the occasion? And what will cause them to change?

Of course, there are ways other than university-initiated reform to think about fixing the leadership problem—and if universities don't act, others will. Given space limitations, however, this special section does not fully explore such important topics as regulating (or deregulating) administrator preparation, developing alternative leader education programs, and changing the conditions that leaders face.[12] While university reform alone is not the answer, it is potentially part of the solution that requires in-depth examination.

The first three of the following 14 articles in the section explore current efforts to reform administrator preparation.[13] In the first, Terry Orr maps the innovations under way within U.S. schools of education and contends that important improvements have gone largely unnoticed. Next, Lee Teitel focuses on the growth of pioneering alternative routes to administrative positions, which he believes represent a welcome shift in the preparation of educational leaders.[14] (University faculty members have much to learn from these nimble entrepreneurial efforts.) In the third article, Tony Bush spotlights the National College for School Leadership—a highly visible exemplar in England—and points to important advances it has made as well as mixed views about its accomplishments and influence.

Looking to the future, 9 commentators, including several who hail from outside the world of K-12 education, participate in a "forum" on reforming leadership education. A number of the commentaries explore areas in which universities should place their bets, while two add spice to the debate by being outspokenly skeptical about university reform. Following the forum, Henry Mintzberg offers his perspective in the format of an interview. Together, these pieces present a treasure chest of diverse suggestions on such issues as the essence of leadership and whom universities should educate, the need for schools of education to collaborate with other professional schools and to form close alliances with school districts, how nonuniversity providers should be licensed, and program structure, content, instruction, and incentives.

In the concluding article, I suggest that the new external pressures are insufficient to force major changes at most universities. However, this moment of discontent does present a rare opportunity for forward-looking schools of education to rethink the preparation of administrators—and I offer a hypothetical program that synthesizes many of the ideas presented in this special section. I also suggest that an opportunity exists to address an even bigger problem: the declining influence of schools of education. Reform will require them to take risks and exercise leadership.

In my view, schools of education should take the lead and act, rather than wait for conclusive evidence about what works or still another scolding or overwhelming political pressure to change. If these slow-stepping elephants fail to dance to today's new tune, they risk becoming irrelevant.[15] Indeed, they may just morph into dinosaurs. And there's no sautéed scallops with Wall Street wizards for "deans of dinosaurs."

Notes

1. For a detailed exploration of the lowly status of education schools, see David F. Labaree, *The Trouble with Ed Schools* (New Haven: Yale University Press, 2004).

2. This is not the only problem facing education schools. For an excellent discussion of the problems of research at education schools, see Patricia Albjerg Graham, *Schooling America: How the Public Schools Meet the Nation's Changing Needs* (New York: Oxford University Press, 2005), especially pp. 194–200. Also, see Labaree, op. cit.

3. National Commission on Excellence in Educational Administration, *Leaders for America's Schools: The Report of the National Commission on Excellence in Educational Administration* (Tempe, Ariz.: University Council for Educational Administration, 1987).

4. Fifteen years ago, for example, I added my two cents in this journal, contending that most programs were in disarray, offering watered-down courses to part-time students with virtually any applicant gaining admission. See Jerome T. Murphy, "Superintendents as Saviors: From the Terminator to Pogo," *Phi Delta Kappan*, March 1991, pp. 507–13.

5. *Better Leaders for America's Schools: A Manifesto* (Washington, D.C.: Broad Foundation and Thomas B. Fordham Institute, 1 May 2003), p. 14.

6. Arthur Levine, *Educating School Leaders* (Washington, D.C.: The Education Schools Project, March 2005), especially pp. 23–48.

7. While I applaud Levine's report, in my view he goes too far in dismissing pockets of excellence—not a single American program meets his high standards. While he cites two "strong" programs—one at the University of Wisconsin, Madison, and one at Peabody College, Vanderbilt University—in my experience there are other exemplars doing innovative work. For example, there is the Urban Superintendents Program at the Harvard Graduate School of Education and the Mid-Career Doctorate in Educational Leadership at the Penn Graduate School of Education. For a fuller critique of Levine's analysis, see Michelle D. Young et al., "An Educative Look at 'Educating School Leaders,'" University Council for Educational Administration, University of Missouri, Columbia, 18 March 2005. Available at **www.ucea.org.**

8. Kenneth Leithwood et al., *How Leadership Influences Student Learning* (New York: Wallace Foundation, September 2004).

9. Warren G. Bennis and James O'Toole, "How Business Schools Lost Their Way," *Harvard Business Review*, 1 May 2005, pp. 96–104; and Henry Mintzberg, *Managers Not MBAs: A Hard Look at the Soft Practice of Managing and Management Development* (San Francisco: Berrett-Koehler, 2004).

10. Richard H. Hersh and John Merrow, eds., *Declining by Degrees: Higher Education at Risk* (New York: Palgrave Macmillan, 2005).

11. Anemona Hartocollis, "Who Needs Education Schools?," *Education Life*, special supplement, *New York Times*, 31 July 2005, pp. 24–28. See also Frederick M. Hess, "The Predictable, but Unpredictably Personal, Politics of Teacher Licensure," *Journal of Teacher Education,* May/June 2005, pp. 192–98.

12. For a thoughtful commentary on the multiple dimensions of the problem, see Ted Sanders, "Preparing School Leaders—Shared Responsibilities," *Education Week,* 6 April 2005, pp. 48, 36–37.

13. There's scant research about the effects of most university programs, and thus, not surprisingly, there's little empirical evidence that documents what works in educational administration. See Stephen Davis et al., *School Leadership Study: Developing Successful Principals* (Stanford, Calif.: Stanford Educational Leadership Institute, 2005). However, there is a lot of informed opinion about promising practices, drawing on experience and research that suggest avenues for action.

14. I agree with Teitel's assessment and—given the magnitude of the task—also agree that it is unlikely that these alternative routes alone will solve the problem.

15. The "dancing elephants" metaphor is not new. See James A. Belasco, *Teaching the Elephant to Dance: The Manager's Guide to Empowering Change* (New York: Penguin, 1990).

JEROME T. MURPHY is Harold Howe II Professor of Education and dean emeritus at the Harvard Graduate School of Education, Cambridge, Mass. He is currently a visiting professor at the Graduate School of Education, University of Pennsylvania, Philadelphia. He wishes to thank Thomas Champion, Patricia Albjerg Graham, Carla Lillvik, Jean Murphy, Susan Murphy, Mary Grasso O'Neill, Jon Schnur, and Samantha Tan for their assistance on this project and the Spencer Foundation for its support.

Textural Perceptions of School Time and Assessment

Mr. Turley pinpoints one factor that has a tremendous effect on whether a school's handling of assessment aids or interferes with student learning.

Eric D. Turley

T HE 1994 REPORT *Prisoners of Time* refers to time as "learning's warden," the regulator of all aspects of our schools. Those who work in or are involved with schools—students, parents, teachers, administrators, and staff—"are captives of clock and calendar."[1]

More than a decade later, schools are still struggling with how they perceive time and how they use it. As teachers attempt to negotiate their workloads within the constraints of school time, an imbalance often occurs. Michael Apple refers to this imbalance as intensification, the process by which teachers' work becomes more time consuming because things are added to the curriculum but nothing is ever dropped or substituted.[2] Essentially, there is more work to do, but available time remains unchanged. Under this approach to curriculum and assessment, teachers feel burdened: they are told to accelerate their work to compensate for a lack of time in which to accomplish the extra tasks.

Prisoners of Time suggests that states and local boards "work with schools to redesign education so that time becomes a factor supporting learning, not a boundary marking its limits." A good visual representation of thinking about time in alternative ways is Salvador Dali's *Persistence of Memory*. In this oil painting, Dali depicts four clocks. In the bottom left corner is a clock similar to a pocket watch, solid and stagnant, its face not visible. It is being attacked by ants. The ants "seem to be devouring it as it devours the time of our lives."[3] Dali also includes three clocks that are melting and flowing over objects in the painting. Dali's clocks—solid or fluid—provide an image of two states of time that can occur within a school environment.

Here I want to explore how two schools in Nebraska perceive time as they teach and assess student learning. Parker School views time as fixed and sees its teaching and assessing as in perpetual conflict because there is not enough time to do both.[4] Ar-

bor School views time in a more fluid way, allowing teaching and assessment to work simultaneously. Ultimately, it is the perception of time within a school that most strongly affects how teaching, assessment, and overall school improvement are conceptualized and enacted. And that perception can radically change the way teachers and administrators view education and engage in school improvement.

The data for this article come from the comprehensive evaluation of the Nebraska STARS (School-based Teacher-led Assessment and Reporting System) program.[5] This evaluation included interviews with teachers, assessment coordinators, and administrators in 23 schools located in 15 districts, as well as two large surveys distributed through the mail. Parker and Arbor were two of the schools that took part in the evaluation.

Parker School: Fixed Time and the Slotting of Work

Thinking back to Dali's painting, we recall that the pocket watch represents stagnant, fixed time. It is a fixed and solid state that the ants must break into smaller pieces before they can make use of it. Thus stagnant time is presented as atomistic, broken into small increments that create a whole.[6] This concept is best exemplified by clocks that have second hands that tick as they move. Such clocks allow the viewer to see and hear the passage of time.

When time in education is viewed in this atomistic way, it becomes a force that works against teachers. The efficiency of their teaching and of their students' learning is judged by time-based measures. Class activities such as instruction or assessment become similar to a zero-sum game in relation to time. Every second, every minute, every hour must be used—and used efficiently—to do something, which necessarily means that other things are left out. The zero-sum nature of atomistic time further intensifies the work of teachers.

Parker Middle School is part of a consortium of 62 schools. The consortium has created a criterion-referenced test for math and language arts, which is given to students in the spring. Teachers from each school met to create the STARS tests for the consortium, but only the eighth-grade teachers at Parker Middle School participated in creating the test. Getting these STARS tests to the individual schools on time became an issue and demonstrates how the staff members experienced the intensification of their work.

Ultimately, it is the perception of time within a school that most strongly affects how teaching, assessment, and overall school improvement are conceptualized and enacted.

The Educational Service Unit, which serves as the coordinating center of the consortium, promised the language arts test to the schools by August so that the teachers could know what was to be covered throughout the year. However, the test did not arrive until February. An administrator from Parker Middle School said, "We don't have a STARS math test yet; it's not complete. We don't report on the STARS math this year, so that's a good thing, but we just got the language arts test Friday of last week.... We have been waiting until February to implement [the test], and now it's going to be a crunch. Hopefully, from now on, we'll be able to do it the way we designed it."

The frustration of not having the test on time grows out of the need to match a school's curriculum with an external assessment. Because the test was not available in August, when planning could reasonably have begun, teachers were forced to spend time during the school year reviewing material (and teaching anything they might have omitted) and then had to make time to give the assessment itself. The belated delivery of the test is one source of the time "crunch" that the administrator referred to. But the model of creating assessments outside the school also means that assessment is not a regular part of a teacher's class time or school day. The teachers are simply given a test and told to make it part of their curriculum and classroom practices so that the students will be prepared for the test in the spring.

At Parker Middle School the STARS tests add to the teachers' sense of intensification because they are seen as just one more thing for teachers to do in their classrooms. An eighth-grade language arts teacher claimed that "the biggest drawback is the amount of time it takes out of instructional time.... It takes two weeks." And this does not include time spent preparing the students for the test. The eighth-grade teachers originally planned on breaking up the STARS test into units to be given throughout the year, but, because of the test's late arrival, the teachers had to give the entire STARS test in the spring. But even if the STARS test had arrived in August, the teachers would still have felt that class time was being taken away from them and replaced by assess-

ment. "Last year we didn't feel like we had any time to teach," said a seventh-grade language arts teacher. "All we did was prepare them for that test, take the test, prepare them for the next test, take the test."[7] These comments make clear the perception of the assessments as a zero-sum game.

Adding to this burden for some teachers is the fact that teachers at the benchmark years—fourth, eighth, and 11th grades—are responsible for reporting assessment results to the state. For example, instruction takes place during second and third grade, while the formal assessment that occurs during the third quarter of fourth grade is reported to the state. Because sixth and seventh grades are not responsible for reporting to the state, time in these grades passes without a focus on assessment. However, during eighth grade, the teachers need to prepare their students for the test.

At Parker Middle School, the further a teacher is from the reporting year, the less knowledge and interest he or she has in the assessments. The sixth- and seventh-grade teachers do not play a role in the assessment and so leave it to the eighth-grade teachers to shoulder the load. When a seventh-grade math teacher was asked about the assessment process, he responded, "I'm not involved at all with the eighth-grade testing or how they keep track of it or how they report [it]." Likewise, when asked about what language arts assessments are used at Parker Middle School, a sixth-grade teacher responded, "I don't know." When asked if he had any input on the assessments, the same teacher replied, "They do it on the eighth-grade level."

The administration and teachers of Parker Middle School offer conflicting viewpoints on how assessment has affected classrooms. "We don't want to take too much of our classroom time for assessment.... We tested 61 days four years ago. Sixty-one days is almost one-third of our school year; that's too many days," the principal of Parker Middle School stated. The principal's perception that the school had spent less time testing over the past four years was in stark contrast to the claims of teachers that testing had increased during that period. Describing the amount of testing, a sixth-grade language arts teacher said, "We have a language arts test, and then they are going to have a math test and a science test and all of those take time ... so you get the state [test] on top of what the district has been doing, ... and it is lost time." Or as one seventh-grade teacher concluded, "We need to streamline [the process] so we are not doing standardized types of testing and reporting all those scores and giving all those tests to those kids because they really get tested out." Both the administrators and teachers at Parker Middle School discuss time used for assessment as separate from class and instructional time; they perceive assessment time to be in conflict with class time. Therefore, in order to do one, time must be given up for the other.

Arbor School: Fluid Time and the Embedding of Work

An alternative perception of time sees it as fluid or in flux. In this view, time is like a stream, continually flowing and never really divided.[8] Perceiving time as fluid allows teachers to view class time as flexible and malleable rather than as rigid and static. The opportunity to mold time to the needs of the class helps in reducing the anxiety that intensification brings because static moments do not exist. Instead, time is always changing. Rather than being a zero-sum game, it is something to be experienced. As Henry David Thoreau wrote, "Time is but the stream I go a-fishing in."[9]

Those at Arbor School, a K-12 school, view assessment and time very differently from those at Parker Middle School. While staff members at Parker emphasize the atomistic qualities of time, those at Arbor School view time and assessment as fluid and continuous. Assessments at Arbor School are created by the teachers in the school, for their classrooms, and so are seen as part of the teachers' days. A committee of teachers reviews these classroom assessments to check for reliability, validity, and bias. There is not a single large high-stakes assessment, or even several small tests; rather, the teachers at Arbor School have embedded assessment within their instructional and classroom practices, thereby allowing students multiple opportunities to master the standards to be tested.

The teachers at Arbor School not only assess students frequently in their classrooms but also have found ways to assess multiple standards through the structuring of assignments. "I used to do more chapter or unit tests," commented a third-grade teacher, "and now, especially at the third-grade level, if I assess more frequently and review more and throw in a couple questions over each skill, it seems that the students retain a lot more than they did before." A high school language arts teacher substituted an informative speech rather than having her students write another research paper. The speech "called for research, so I've piggybacked the two activities," she said. Assessment is part of the classroom procedure rather than something that takes time out of the typical classroom routine. In this model, instruction and assessment can flow along similar paths. The flexibility reduces feelings of intensification because the teachers do not add more to their workloads but adjust their curriculum and classroom practices to include a variety of assessments.

Arbor has created a systematized teaching philosophy composed of Introduce, Teach, Assess, and Review (ITAR). Every teacher in every department is responsible for introducing, teaching, assessing, or reviewing specified standards. The weight does not fall onto the reporting years, but is shared by all the teachers. "I don't think you can expect the fourth-grade teacher to cram it all into one year along with everything else she has to teach," stated a third-grade teacher. In order for the students to meet the standards that are assessed in fourth grade, the teachers have spread the introducing, teaching, assessing, and reviewing of standards across grade levels and years. Thus students will be exposed to the standards multiple times over a three-year period. Through the ITAR system, assessments are not stagnant tools used only in benchmark years but are ongoing and focused on the process of student learning over time. The same third-grade teacher describes her role in teaching and assessing standards: "I know what I am covering in third grade has to go in and flow with what will be taught next year in fourth grade so everybody will be getting what they need."

Arbor also encourages an interdisciplinary approach to assessment, which further helps the students experience standards and assessment as embedded in practice. For example, the art teacher might not assess math standards but might introduce some of the material that will later be assessed by a math teacher. The superintendent pointed out that "juniors may have been exposed to a particular standard multiple times ... perhaps as many as five or six times within their high school careers." A math standard, for example, might be assessed in an industrial arts class or in a business class. Or a health teacher might assess science standards, or music teachers might introduce and teach math standards.

Along with the local creation of assessments, every student in the school has an individual assessment plan. Each student has a folder that documents what standards he or she has met, when the standards were met, what kind of assessment was used, and the student's proficiency rating. Students are able to track their achievement as they move from grade to grade. This process allows students to meet standards whenever they are ready—either early in their schooling or even after the benchmark year.

This system stands in contrast to the practice at Parker, where the amount of time allotted for student learning is valued more than the actual learning. If a student does not meet the standard by the spring of eighth grade, he or she fails; however, at Arbor, a student can prove mastery of a standard in fifth grade or in ninth grade. The student's portfolio is simply readjusted to reflect his 'or her learning. The superintendent commented that "[students] are getting lots of chances. This is not a high-stakes test. The kids know that they are going to have several opportunities over the course of their career to reach mastery, and so it takes a lot of pressure off them."

Challenges for Assessment

Nebraska's system of assessment is unique in the nation in that it values local assessment rather than a single high-stakes test. The state has created a system of assessment that differs markedly from the federal mandates of No Child Left Behind.[10] This approach to standards and assessment provides the state's schools with flexibility that most schools in other states do not have. However, issues of time and the intensification of work are felt by teachers everywhere. Therefore, even in Nebraska, we must revise the way we teach and assess students if we are to improve the conditions under which students learn, teachers teach, and schools improve.

As we have seen, Parker School, like many schools across the nation, views assessment and instruction as competing forces. Arbor School, on the other hand, approaches assessment in a way that is radically different. What Arbor School teaches us is that instruction and assessment work best when: 1) space is created for teachers to design assessments that allow them to experience time differently, 2) school practices are aligned with alternative approaches to time and space, and 3) educational time is reconceptualized as an experience rather than an end.

First, space must be cleared so that teachers can be brought into the conversation on assessment. Chris Gallagher argues that, if teachers are given a seat at the table, they will gladly become assessors themselves.[11] Arbor School reflects an optimistic portrait of Gallagher's "idealistic faith." A majority of teachers at Arbor are involved in the process. Not only has space at the table been cleared for the entire faculty, but many teachers are actively participating, communicating, and sharing in the assessment experience. The collaborative effort of Arbor School allows them the space to create an embedded approach to teaching and assessing, which ultimately transforms the way assessments take place.

Second, school practices must be aligned with alternative approaches to the use of time and space. The assessment practices of Parker School mimic the industrial ideas of Taylorism and time-and-motion studies. Every task at Parker is broken into components, and labor is divided according to skill level. One outcome of this method is a "separation of conception from execution," by which the people doing a specific job lose sight of the entire process.[12] For example, the sixth- and seventh-grade teachers at Parker Middle School are concerned only with what goes on at their grade levels and have lost sight of the overall educational process. The eighth-grade teachers are required by default to become the assessment experts for the entire building.

Arbor School avoids such Taylorism by sharing among the entire staff the responsibility for teaching and assessment. Thus each teacher is committed to either introducing, teaching, assessing, or reviewing a portion of a standard, even if it crosses disciplinary boundaries and grade levels. The teachers at Arbor have created a process that allows them to teach and assess simultaneously within the school day. This process has helped reduce their feelings of intensification, by making instruction and assessment a single recursive process.

Finally, as teachers are brought into the conversation on assessment and as practices are created that help them experience time differently within their classrooms, a reconception of educational time can emerge. Parker School's model made assessments serve as "fixed ends" rather than as "ends in view." John Dewey uses the following anecdote to differentiate between these two views of "ends" in education:

> A farmer has to use plants and animals to carry on his farming activities. It certainly makes a great difference to his life whether he is fond of them, or whether he regards them as means which he has to employ to get something else in which he alone is interested. In the former case, his entire course of activity is significant; each phase of it has its own value. He has the experience of realizing his end at every stage; the postponed aim, or end in view, being merely a sight ahead by which to keep his activity going fully and freely. For if he does not look ahead, he is more likely to find himself blocked. The aim is as definitely a means of action as is any other portion of an activity.[13]

The STARS test serves as a "fixed end" for those at Parker School; it is something that must be completed. However, it does not serve as a means to carry activity further. Once the test has been completed, the results are reported, and that's it. No one reflects on the specific details revealed by the assessment in order to improve instruction or learning because the students have moved on to the next grade. One byproduct of a system such as this is summarized by a seventh-grade math teacher at Parker School: "We tried to teach them how to take tests. We didn't change our curriculum. We didn't try to do anything differently. [We] prepar[ed] them for the material on the test and the procedure of the test." But mere preparation for a test ends up being a hollow activity. The only reason for undertaking the activity is to acclimate students to the "real" test. Therefore, time is being used on activities that do not foster real learning.

In Arbor School, the reporting years and the assessments themselves do not serve as fixed ends, but as guideposts. This approach reflects Dewey's ideas of education as an "end in view." Because the superintendent understands that not all the state standards can be assessed thoroughly by a set date, the assessments are allowed to become more important than the time set for conducting them. Thus the assessments are not fixed ends, but ends in themselves, ends that lead onward. They guide the instruction, but they do not dictate the use of school time. Students are given several chances to pass the tests and are given a variety of ways to demonstrate their proficiency on a standard over time. And every activity becomes a meaningful opportunity for learning.

Notes

1. National Education Commission on Time and Learning, *Prisoners of Time* (Washington, D.C.: U.S. Government Printing Office, April 1994), **www.ed.gov/pubs/PrisonersOfTime/ Prisoners.html**.

2. Michael W. Apple, *Official Knowledge: Democratic Education in a Conservative Age* (New York: Routledge, 1993), p. 114.

3. Stephen Kern, *The Culture of Time and Space, 1880-1918* (Cambridge, Mass.: Harvard University Press, 1983), p. 23.

4. The names of the schools and educators have been changed to maintain confidentiality.

5. For more information on the study, see Chris Gallagher, "Charting STARS: Sustainability as Opportunity and Challenge," Year Two Report, STARS Comprehensive Evaluation Project, August 2003, **www.nde.state.ne.us/stars/index.html**. Unless otherwise noted, quotations presented throughout this article come from the evaluation interviews and surveys.

6. Kern, pp. 11, 20.

7. The seventh-grade language arts teachers piloted the STARS test the year before. They spent six weeks giving the various portions of the STARS test, not including preparing the students for the test. The following year, the seventh-grade teachers did not participate in the STARS test.

8. Kern, pp. 11, 24.

9. *The Writings of Henry David Thoreau*, vol. 2 (Boston: Houghton Mifflin, 1906), p. 109.

10. For more on Nebraska's approach to assessment, see Pat Roschewski, "Nebraskans Reach for the STARS," *Phi Delta Kappan*, April 2001, pp. 611–15; idem, "Nebraska STARS Line Up," *Phi Delta Kappan*, March 2003, pp. 517–20; Pat Roschewski, Jody Isernhagen, and Leon Dappen, "Nebraska STARS: Achieving Results," *Phi Delta Kappan*, February 2006, pp. 433–37; Douglas Christensen, "Building State Assessment from the Classroom Up," *School Administrator*, De-

cember 2001, p. 27; and Chris Gallagher, "Charting STARS: The State of Assessment in the State of Nebraska," August 2002, pp. 1–2, **www.nde.state.ne.us/stars/resources/execsummary0101.pdf**.

11. Chris Gallagher, "A Seat at the Table," *Phi Delta Kappan*, March 2000, p. 502–7.

12. Apple, p. 121.

13. John Dewey, *Democracy and Education* (1916; reprint, Carbondale: Southern Illinois University Press, 1980), pp. 112–13.

ERIC D. TURLEY is a doctoral candidate at the University of Nebraska, Lincoln.

From *Phi Delta Kappan,* February 2006, pp. 438–442, 447. Copyright © 2006 by Eric D. Turley. Reprinted by permission of the publisher and author.

The Father of Modern School Reform

Fifty years ago, Milton Friedman introduced the idea of school vouchers. Now he looks back on his legacy.

INTERVIEWED BY NICK GILLESPIE

IN 1955 FUTURE Nobel Prize–winning economist Milton Friedman kick-started modern education reform with an article titled "The Role of Government in Education." Bucking the "general trend in our times toward increasing intervention by the state" in virtually all economic and social activities, Friedman argued that universal vouchers for elementary and secondary schools would usher in an age of educational innovation and experimentation, not only widening the range of options for students and parents but increasing all sorts of positive outcomes.

"Government," wrote Friedman, "preferably local governmental units, would give each child, through his parents, a specified sum to be used solely in paying for his general education; the parents would be free to spend this sum at a school of their own choice, provided it met certain minimum standards laid down by the appropriate governmental unit. Such schools would be conducted under a variety of auspices: by private enterprises operated for profit, nonprofit institutions established by private endowment, religious bodies, and some even by governmental units."

Among other things, Friedman prophesied that an education system based on vouchers would minimize inefficient government spending while giving low-income Americans, who are traditionally stuck in the very worst public schools, a better chance at receiving a good education. Vouchers "would bring a healthy increase in the variety of educational institutions available and in competition among them. Private initiative and enterprise would quicken the pace of progress in this area as it has in so many others. Government would serve its proper function of improving the operation of the invisible hand without substituting the dead hand of bureaucracy."

Fifty years after Friedman's article appeared in the collection *Economics and the Public Interest*, proposals for education reform take many shapes: legally mandated performance assessments at the state and federal levels, means-tested vouchers, charter schools, homeschooling, and calls for universal vouchers or for the complete separation of school and state, to name just a few. Despite their many differences, what all proponents of radical and systemic change have in common is an emphasis on choice and competition as a means of increasing educational

performance and parental and student satisfaction. As in so many other areas of economic and social thought, Milton Friedman's ideas have carried the intellectual day. To be sure, if and when those ideas will be put into widespread practice is another question.

At 93 years, Friedman is still fiercely dedicated to increasing the range and quality of education—and to decrying what he sees as the pernicious influence of teachers unions and other forces of reaction. In 1996 Friedman and his wife and longtime collaborator, Rose, started the Milton and Rose D. Friedman Foundation, an Indianapolis-based nonprofit designed to act as "a resource for parents and community groups who want parental choice in education" The foundation is online at **www.friedmanfoundation.org**; visitors to the site can read through a wealth of information on school choice, including Friedman's collected works on the topic.

reason Editor-in-Chief Nick Gillespie caught up with Friedman by telephone in September. Comments should be sent to letters@reason.com.

reason: What inspired you to come up with the idea of vouchers?

Milton Friedman: Nothing. (*Laughs.*) I mean there was nothing going on in the real world at the time that caused me to think of vouchers. I was writing a piece on the role of government in education, and I started to think about how government intervention tends not to work very well. I didn't put it this way then, but if government wants to subsidize something, it can subsidize either the producer or the consumer. Subsidizing the producer is the wrong way to do it because it creates a top-down organization, which is very inefficient. The better way is to subsidize the consumer, which is what vouchers do.

reason: What would the biggest benefits be if vouchers were implemented in the way you originally discussed them in 1955?

Friedman: Let's be clear. There are many kinds of possible vouchers, but there are two basic varieties, which I label charity vouchers and educational vouchers. Charity vouchers are unfortunately what we've gotten mostly so far. They are intended for low-income people who are unquestionably the worst victims of our deficient school system. Charity vouchers help the poor but they will not produce any real reform of the educational system. And what we need is a real reform.

I want vouchers to be universal, to be available to everyone. They should contain few or no restrictions on how they can be used. We need a system in which the government says to every parent: "Here is a piece of paper you can use for the educational purposes of your child. It will cover the full cost per student at a government school. It is worth X dollars towards the cost of educational services that you purchase from parochial schools, private for-profit schools, private nonprofit schools, or other purveyors of educational services. You may add from your own funds to the voucher if you wish to and can afford to." (I try to avoid calling government schools *public schools* because I think that's a very misleading term.)

As to the benefits of universal vouchers, empowering parents would generate a competitive education market, which would lead to a burst of innovation and improvement, as competition has done in so many other areas. There's nothing that would do so much to avoid the danger of a two-tiered society, of a class-based society. And there's nothing that would do so much to ensure a skilled and educated work force.

reason: Do you think America has become more stratified by class during the last 50 years?

Friedman: I do. We have been going from a rural or quasi-rural society to an aristocratic society. There's no doubt that in recent years the upper end of the income scale has enjoyed a much larger increase in income and wealth than the lower end.

reason: Do you take any comfort that more graduating high school seniors go on to college now than in the past? About two-thirds go on to college now, which is up from 45 percent in 1960 and 50 percent in 1970. That would seem to indicate that more people have more access to more education.

Friedman: But about 30 percent of young people never graduate from high school. Moreover, if you look at the colleges that graduates go to, they differ enormously in quality. Many are close to glorified high schools.

reason: What explains the ability of the U.S. economy to still be productive if we have poorly educated high school graduates?

Friedman: Part of the reason is immigration, especially skilled immigration. And while our government is much too big, we haven't gone as far down the wrong path as many other countries. More fundamentally, a small fraction of well-educated citizens can have a disproportionate influence on the productivity of the society as a whole. The victims of our defective educational system are not the well-educated but the poorly educated.

> **"As to the benefits of universal vouchers … there's nothing that would do so much to avoid the danger of a two-tiered society, of a class-based society. And there's nothing that would do so much to ensure a skilled and educated work force."**

reason: You're optimistic that real change is upon us. In a recent piece for your foundation, you and Rose write: "The pace is picking up. In 1995, Ohio introduced a voucher program in Cleveland—the first such program since Wisconsin adopted a limited program for Milwaukee in 1991. In 1999, Florida enacted an educational reform that included a pilot statewide voucher program for students in failing schools. In the past decade, Minnesota, Illinois, and several other states have enacted refundable tax credits that promote parental choice. Privately financed scholarship programs have flowered from the seed … in Indianapolis in 1991, and this list is by no means complete. Change is now occurring so fast that it is hard to keep up with it. The [teachers unions'] dam is buckling and will shortly break. The resulting flood will bring life-giving innovation and change to elementary and secondary education."

Yet out of about 45 million kids in K–12 schools, there are less than 1 million kids in charter schools and around 20,000 kids with some form of vouchers. In percentage terms, there are fewer children in private schools now than there were 20 years ago. So what underwrites your optimism that vouchers or other reforms are about to sledgehammer the status quo?

Friedman: I remain optimistic for several reasons. One, there is increasing dissatisfaction with the schools on the part of parents. Two, there is widening interest in and support of greater parental choice. Third, some 20 states or more have various kinds of voucher-type proposals under consideration. Part of my optimism comes from a belief that vouchers seem like such an obvious solution—and from my belief that the basis of the National Education Association's and the American Federation of Teachers' power is crumbling.

What are the bases of the teachers unions' power? There are two. One, they have managed to persuade the intellectuals that being against vouchers is part of the basic Democratic Party mantra. By using their money and large membership, the unions have gotten control of the Democratic Party platform; a considerable fraction of the party's presidential delegates, for instance, come from the teachers unions.

The Democratic Party should be the natural supporter of vouchers. In Ted Kennedy's words, the Democrats are supposed to be the "voice of the voiceless." The voiceless would benefit the most from full-scale universal vouchers. You know, if you ask the voiceless, they are all in favor of vouchers. So I think, sooner or later, the nearly religious support for the anti-voucher position will crumble.

The other reason the teachers unions will crumble is the teachers themselves. Against the odds, the unions have been able to persuade teachers that universal vouchers would hurt them. On the contrary, teachers would be among the main beneficiaries. We know that in government schools not much more than half of the money spent goes to the classroom. Almost half goes to administrators, bureaucrats, and the like. In private schools, a much larger fraction goes to the classroom. In addition, we know that working conditions are much more attractive in private schools. Despite lower average wages, the turnover rate [among teachers] is much lower in private schools than it is in government schools.

reason: Can you describe the goal of the Milton and Rose D. Friedman Foundation?

Friedman: It's to increase the public's understanding and awareness of the need for parental choice as a way to reform the system of education. It's not a research foundation; it acts as clearinghouse for information. It's been doing very well: We have the financial support of a growing number of people, and we're reaching a widening group of people through newspaper mentions and that sort of thing. More important, the president of the foundation, Gordon St. Angelo, has been very active in all of the states that are moving in the direction of greater parental choice.

reason: In an interview with **reason** a decade ago, you said that the role you played in ending the military draft—you were on a presidential commission that recommended an all-volunteer army—was your proudest accomplishment when it came to public policy. If you succeed with universal vouchers and systemic education reform, where would that rank for you?

Friedman: It would rank first.

Friendly Competition

Does the presence of charters spur public schools to improve?

GEORGE M. HOLMES, JEFF DESIMONE, AND NICHOLAS G. RUPP

Most research on charter schools, and the most intense public debate over their desirability, has focused on the impact of these new schools on the students who attend them. But charter proponents also hope that the threat of students' leaving will spur traditional schools to higher levels of achievement. In the long run, such system-wide improvements, if positive, could even outweigh any negative effects on the individual students they enroll.

Can competition from a new kind of public school, right around the block or down the road in many cases, inspire traditional schools to improve? We address this question here by examining the link between the establishment of charter schools in North Carolina and average student proficiency rates at the traditional public schools most affected by the new source of competition.

Our use of proficiency rates, an aggregate measure of school performance, distinguishes our work from other recent studies that examine the performance gains made by individual students. However, aggregate school performance is the focus of state accountability systems, is reported in the media, and presumably is used by parents, along with their own observations of their child's progress, to evaluate the quality of their child's school. Schools intent on retaining students can be expected to concentrate their efforts on this indicator. Ironically, there could be a disjunction between that aggregate and the average performance of individuals at the school, for a variety of reasons. Schools affected by competition could encourage low-performing students not to take the test, could focus their efforts exclusively on students at the cusp of proficiency, or could use any number of strategies to achieve the appearance of improved performance without ensuring that students were actually learning more.

Our results indicate that traditional public schools in North Carolina responded to even the limited competition provided by charter schools by improving their average proficiency rates. However, a comparison of our results with those of other studies that examine the learning gains made by individual students suggests the need for caution in interpreting our results as unambiguously positive.

The Friendliest of Rivalries

In three short years, from the 1996–97 school year to that of 1999–2000, the final year of our analysis, the number of charter schools in operation in North Carolina rose from zero to 74. By 2004–05, the number had grown to 99; state law currently caps the total number of charter schools at 100. Because the effects of competition on the performance of traditional public schools can be identified best during periods in which the amount of competition is changing, these years offer a convenient way to test the effects of expanded school choice.

Of course, school choice was not altogether absent in North Carolina even before 1997–98. It was largely limited to choosing to live in a particular district, enrolling a child in a private school, or educating the child at home, all of which require a substantial investment of resources, fiscal or otherwise. Roughly 70 percent of districts also offered parents some degree of choice among public schools or the option of applying to a magnet school. Our results should therefore be interpreted as the effect of the introduction of additional competition from charter schools.

As in most states, students in North Carolina can leave a traditional public school and enroll in a charter, at will and for no monetary cost. Charter schools may not discriminate among students by ability, socioeconomic status, or eligibility for special education. Even so, there are reasons to suspect that the amount of additional competition provided by charter schools is relatively modest. Despite the rapid growth in the number of charter schools in the state, the 12,000 students enrolled in charters in 1999–2000 represented just 1 percent of North Carolina's 1.25 million public-school students. Moreover, before granting a charter, sponsors must consider local impact statements prepared by the district in which the school will be located. Perhaps for this reason, many charter schools in North Carolina target at-risk students and presumably do not pose a competitive threat to traditional public schools. Finally, research conducted by Robert Bifulco and Helen Ladd ("Results from the Tar Heel State: Charter Schools and Student Achievement," *research*, Fall 2005) indicates that North Carolina charter schools during this period may have been less effective in improving student achievement than were traditional public schools, at least for students who attended both charter and traditional public schools between grades 4 and 8. Although it is not clear that parents would have an accurate perception of charter schools' effectiveness, particularly in the early years of the state's program, all these factors, taken together, indicate that North Carolina provides an unusually stiff test of the theory that charter schools will spur improvement among traditional public schools.

Measuring Performance and Competition

The North Carolina Department of Public Instruction began testing students at the end of each school year in 1996–97 as part of its ABCs of Public Education program. These tests are taken statewide by all students in grades 3 through 8 in math and reading, and in grades 4 and 7 in writing. We take as our indicator of each school's performance its performance composite for grades 3 through 8, which the state computes as the percentage of tests taken in all three subjects that meet the state's proficiency standard. Since the performance composite is widely reported by the media, schools have strong incentives to improve their rating.

Despite the rapid growth in the number of charter schools in the state, the 12,000 students enrolled in charters in 1999–2000 represented just 1 percent of North Carolina's 1.25 million public school students.

The influence of a nearby charter school on traditional public schools in the area depends, in part, on the credibility of students' threats to switch to the charter. Those threats become more credible as the distance between the schools decreases. Since charter schools charge no tuition, travel costs are the major component of the price of attending one, especially in North Carolina, where charter schools are not required to provide transportation.

We therefore base our measures of the extent of charter competition facing each traditional public school on the school's distance from the nearest charter school. We first map the latitude and longitude of traditional public schools and charter schools throughout the state, identify the charter school closest to each traditional public school, and compute the aerial distance between the two. Then we develop separate indicators for each school of whether there is a charter school within 5 kilometers, 10 kilometers, 15 kilometers, 20 kilometers, and 25 kilometers.

We exclude from the analysis schools, mostly in rural areas, with addresses we were unable to map and schools with missing test performance measures for any year during our study period, which spans 1996–97 to 1999–2000. These exclusions represented about 7 percent of the total. We also drop schools located in three North Carolina Outer Banks counties with substantial water boundaries because straight line distance is a poor proxy for actual travel time to and from these localities. The analysis includes all of the remaining 1,307 traditional public schools in the state.

The average performance composite among traditional public schools increased from 67 percent in 1996–97 to 75 percent in 1999–2000 as the number of charter schools in the state increased from 0 to more than 70. Meanwhile, after the first charter schools opened in 1997–98, the average distance from a school to the closest charter school fell by about one-third, from 19.2 miles to 12.6 miles in 1999–2000. Is there a connection between these improvements in test-performance scores and growing competition from charter schools?

Results

To answer this question we examine whether the annual changes in performance made by traditional public schools during this period were more positive in schools with charter schools nearby than in schools not facing charter school competition. In these comparisons, we take into account changes in the characteristics of the student body including the percentage of students who are Hispanic, the percent African American, and the percent eligible for the federal free lunch program, as well as changes in the school's student teacher ratio. We also use information on the school's performance composite two years before the year to correct for measurement error in the school's previous-year performance. Finally, we perform separate comparisons using each of our distance-based indicators of charter-school competition.

These comparisons provide consistent evidence that charter-school competition raises the performance composite of traditional public schools. The effect is statistically significant for four of the seven measures of charter-school competition and falls just short of significance for the other three. In each case, the results indicate that, all else being equal (including the school's score on the performance composite the previous year), the presence of charter-school competition increases traditional school performance by about 1 percent. This represents more than one-half of the average achievement gain of 1.7 percent made by public schools statewide between 1998–99 and 1999–2000 and is, from a policy perspective, nontrivial.

Even a little bit of competition from charter schools can force schools to appear to be improving, but policymakers need to take care to ensure it translates into real gains for the average student.

How nontrivial? One indication comes from the information in our results about the gains in performance made by schools where the student-faculty ratio decreased over this same period. In 2002 the North Carolina governor's office proposed a $26 million increase in the state budget to reduce average class size by roughly 1.8 students. Although the relationship between changes in the student-teacher ratio and changes in school performance is not statistically significant, the size of the relationship suggests that the governor's plan would increase scores by roughly 0.36 percentage points. However, our data indicate that opening a charter school would increase public-school test scores by one full point (1.0). Expanding the number of charter schools therefore seems like a promising, and far more cost-effective, alternative to lowering class size. Since state funding follows the student, an increase in the charter-school system requires no increase in spending.

One possible alternative explanation for the improvements observed in traditional public schools when a charter school opened nearby is the migration of lower-performing students from the traditional public school to the charter school. However, simple tests we conducted, based on changes in the average previous-year test scores of students in schools affected and unaffected by charter-school competition, suggest that, if anything, the *opposite* phenomenon occurred: students switching from traditional public to charter schools appear to have been *above*-average performers compared with the other students in their school. The fact that traditional public schools experienced net gains in performance, despite a slight decrease in average student quality, suggests that our estimates of the effects of charter-school competition may understate the true effect of charters on traditional public schools.

A Word about Other Studies

The findings presented here differ from those of two previous studies that examine the same hypothesis for North Carolina charter schools. The research by Robert Bifulco and Helen Ladd fails to find an effect of charter schools on the effectiveness of traditional public schools, while a similar analysis by one of us conducted in 2003 reported improvements for students in traditional public schools smaller than the ones estimated here. There are several possible explanations for these differences.

Most important, each of the other studies uses student-level data, which we did not have access to when conducting this research. How could schools improve their performance composite scores without a change in the average gains in achievement made by their students? As discussed above, one possibility is that schools affected by competition would target students who score just below the proficiency cutoff. Roughly 3 percent of students in any given year fail by only one point. If a principal were, for example, to entice one-third of such students to gain a single point, the performance composite would increase by a full percentage point, but the average student-level gain would be tiny and could even be offset by losses made by students safely above or below the proficiency cutoff. Our other research indicates that students in schools affected by competition at or near the proficiency cutoff did in fact make the largest gains.

In short, our results reveal substantial improvements in traditional public-school performance due to the introduction and growth of charter-school choice. Read alongside the results of studies based on student-level data, they suggest that even a little bit of competition from charter schools can force schools to appear to be improving, but that policymakers need to take care to ensure that translates into real gains for the average student.

GEORGE M. HOLMES is a research fellow in health economics and finance at the Cecil G. Sheps Center for Health Services Research, University of North Carolina; **JEFF DESIMONE** is assistant professor of economics, University of South Florida, and faculty research fellow, National Bureau of Economic Research; **NICHOLAS G. RUPP** is assistant professor of economics, East Carolina University.

Urban and Rural Schools: Overcoming Lingering Obstacles

Rural and urban schools face many of the same challenges. But, Mr. Theobald argues, in order to join forces to solve their shared problems, they will have to bridge an urban/rural educational and cultural divide that has deep roots in history.

PAUL THEOBALD

WHICH public schools in the United States are having the toughest financial problems? Which are facing the most significant infrastructure dilemmas? Which find it most difficult to attract qualified teachers? The list of questions to which the answer is "urban and rural schools" is long and getting longer. That the two categories of schools share so many problems suggests that there may be significant advantages to collaborative efforts between them, but a substantial cultural divide works against that possibility. My aim here is to examine the historical causes of this divide on the assumption that overcoming it will be easier if it is better understood.

For a large part of America's history—the first 50 years or so—we had no formal system of public education. This is not to say that there were no schools. Quite the contrary. The nation boasted a large array of private, charity, religious, and partially public-funded schools. Most of these were in the northern states, for during the first 50 years of our nation's history the institution of slavery stood as an obstacle to the proliferation of schools in the South. When the common school concept was finally deemed to be an acceptable feature of life in the United States, it was no coincidence that it began in states with major urban centers, Massachusetts in particular. However, like most large-scale societal projects, the creation of the common school was actually tied to many sets of converging circumstances.

First, there was the removal of property qualifications and the extension of the male franchise in the early 1830s, a circumstance that worried the elites of early American society. Second, there was heavy foreign immigration, especially from Catholic Ireland, another development that worried American elites. Third, there was unprecedented growth in popular religious denominations—especially Methodists and Baptists—which alarmed members of the Calvinist religious hierarchy (Presbyterians and Congregationalists), who thereafter steadfastly embraced the common school concept. Last, growing levels of urbanization created the perception of a "crisis" of roaming, misdirected youths.

Rural residents across the northern states, by and large, were less affected by all of these circumstances and were therefore not as likely as their urban counterparts to openly embrace a system of free common schools. This was even more true if the free school system was placed in the hands of a Presbyterian or Congregationalist cleric, as it so often was, for these denominations were a distinct minority throughout the interior states, North and South. Convincing a large rural population to go along with the statewide adoption of a free school system, complete with a state department of education located in a distant state capital and governed by a Calvinist cleric, was not an easy task. Rev. Caleb Mills of Indiana, the second superintendent of public instruction in the Hoosier state, wrote concerning the selection of his successor in 1857: "Let him be elected by popular vote, or appointed by Executive authority, or chosen by a joint ballot of the Legislature, the question would be immediately asked by thousands, not is he qualified, but is he *Presbyterian*?"[1]

Despite considerable rural resistance, free school systems were put in place in virtually every northern state before the Civil War. This was accomplished in the Midwest with promises that there would be a great deal of local control regardless of the centralized appearance of the system. In contrast, southern state departments of education, created out of a centralized county government tradition, were invested with more power and were less inclined to be sensitive to the concept of local control. This historical dynamic still affects what happens in the name of education policy. Southern states like Texas and Florida were able to quickly operationalize statewide policy of dubious educational merit, while strong local-control states like Minnesota, Iowa, and Nebraska have resisted politically motivated education reforms.

But the point here is that right from the start, rural and urban educational differences were matters of significant consequence. State education departments situated in urban environments responded to perceived urban needs. The attempt to enforce policies that addressed those needs often generated consternation in outlying rural districts, as an early Wisconsin state superintendent of public instruction discovered soon after taking office in 1852. A rural school board clerk wrote to him to complain about a state requirement that teachers record instances of tardiness. According to this Rock County resident, when students "are entering [school] at all hours, which they have an *undeniable right* to do, it is certainly a severe task, and injurious to the school for the Teacher to be obliged to drop all business and betake himself to his Register, in order to enter therein, every instance of tardiness" (emphasis in original).[2]

The clerk's objection was entirely reasonable, given that rural children were more likely than urban students to be vital contributors to the economy of a household. Any number of farm-related exigencies might cause them to be late for school, and even the weather could disrupt the school-day routine—something as common as a heavy rain storm could turn a small creek into an impassable river or a dirt road into a mud trap. Clearly, the negative implications for student character that urban educators liked to connect with tardiness did not translate well to rural circumstances. One-size-fits-all policy emanating out of state departments of education, therefore, served to create a kind of cultural divide between urban and rural schools that has lasted to this day.

Making Sense of Rural/Urban Suspicions

But to really get to the bottom of the history contributing to the urban/rural educational divide, we need to go back further still. If we are to penetrate the meaning people have come to give these terms, then we have to look briefly at the world when the locus of power was completely flipped-flopped from what we know today. Now we take it for granted that power and authority lie in the nation's urban centers or in urban state capitals. But in the larger scope of history, an urban locus of power is a relatively recent phenomenon. If we take a brief glimpse at feudal Europe, England in particular, we see that power resided in a rural aristocracy, of which the king was a member. In some ways the American Revolution was a rejection of rural power, though this is probably too simplistic. Once the colonies achieved independence, however, they struggled with political questions fundamental to all societies: What constitutes legitimate authority? Where does it reside? And who wields it? As the former colonists looked for answers to these questions, they naturally considered the examples represented by England itself.

It turns out that the shift from the countryside to the city as a locus of authority began in England during the late 17th century, and it is worth a short digression to describe it in order to fully understand the lingering cultural dynamics that inhibit rural and urban school collaboration. The decade of the 1690s saw the development of at least two unprecedented and far-reaching financial devices that proved to be the death knell of feudalism and changed the nature of economics forever—along with the locus of power. Years of military struggle with France left the government of William III near financial disaster. But William was blessed with able finance ministers who conceived of a way out of trouble. Working with a small group of London's wealthiest merchants, they acquired huge loans on the understanding that taxes would be levied to pay back the loans. In return, the merchants were given a charter to create what became the Bank of England in 1694. In this way the concept of a funded public debt was created, along with a large, commercial, centralized bank that played an enormous role in the generation and management of government resources. These developments resulted in a huge variety of new investment strategies and an expanded money market, which in turn spurred the growth and development of industrial manufactures, overseas colonialism, trading, shipping, and the proliferation of banks and insurance houses. The government itself was transformed as administrative offices multiplied at every level.

The English monarchy was humbled by the English Civil War of the 1640s and the so-called Glorious Revolution of 1688, which removed one king and replaced him with another, making sure, in the process, that the new king understood there would be no French-style absolute monarch in England. By the 1720s, however, under the reign of George I, the monarchy gradually began to reassert itself, with the compliance of finance-oriented prime ministers like Robert Walpole. Each successive reign of Georges grew in terms of power and authority, only this time the power was aligned not with the rural aristocracy but with the emerging urban commercial class.

The radical transformation of culture that occurs when large numbers begin to make their living in new ways was not something that went uncontested in 18th-century England. Rural residents were particularly opposed to the new developments. The nobles and gentry had always believed that the countryside was the wellspring of the virtue required to ensure the nation's well-being. The land itself, they argued, was the true source of wealth, and there was something too ephemeral, in their minds, about profit that emerged from the mere manipulation of money.

They didn't have to search far for evidence to support their case. The filth, poverty, and misery in growing industrial centers like Manchester were prime examples of what was wrong with the new England according to its opponents. The more they used the Houses of Lords and Commons to express their concern through the introduction of rural-oriented policy measures, the more the king, prime minister, and urban Commons members rallied to push them back. Increasingly, rural members of parliament were dubbed backward or unwilling to change with the times. It was an epithet that would stick.

Right from the start, rural and urban educational differences were matters of significant consequence.

Amidst all of this, of course, was a renaissance in political philosophy known as the Enlightenment. Using phrases like the "rights of man" and "laissez faire," the rationalist philosophers charted an end to feudal arrangements and pushed to open up the halls of power to the emerging commercial class of which most of them were members.

This brings us close to the American story. Victorious in a prolonged military struggle with England, the Founders looked back at the mother country for examples of how they might create a new nation. Some saw the prosperous treasury, advanced finance, and industrial development and felt that this must be America's path. Others saw the sores of humanity in "the mobs of great cities," to quote Thomas Jefferson. In short, some envisioned an urban industrial republic while others envisioned a rural agrarian republic. From the outset, then, there existed an ethos of contest between urban and rural interests—one with long-standing cultural consequences.

The Urban/Rural Divide in the United States

This contest can probably best be described by using the careers of two of America's most famous statesmen: Alexander Hamilton and Thomas Jefferson. Hamilton was a New York lawyer and one of the chief architects of the U.S. Constitution. He also served as the nation's first secretary of the treasury. Hamilton was determined to follow the script set by England: create a funded public debt administered by a national bank. Prior to the Constitutional Convention in 1787, he even lobbied for the creation of a limited monarchy of the sort exemplified by George III.

Thomas Jefferson, on the other hand, was a planter from Virginia and author of the Declaration of Independence. He did not take part in the Constitutional Convention because he was in Paris serving as the U.S. ambassador to France. Had he been in Philadelphia that summer, it is possible that our Constitution might have looked somewhat different. Jefferson went on to become the third U.S. President, partially on a platform to abolish Hamilton's national bank. While Jefferson tried three times to pass laws to create free schools for children, Hamilton's only references to children concerned the role they could play "at a tender age" in the nation's new factories.[3]

As in England, citizens in the young United States were divided about what the country was to be. While the careers and beliefs of Hamilton and Jefferson exemplify the division, the ramifications of the ultimate choice went considerably beyond the realization of one or another's ideal vision for the nation. There were real costs and benefits associated with the ultimate choice, and they were apparent from the outset. In fact, one development that clearly highlights the division occurred before the Constitution was created—and was, in fact, a catalyst for the Constitutional Convention. It happened in western Massachusetts in the fall of 1786 and spring of 1787. When laws were passed in Boston demanding that debts be repaid in specie (gold) rather than tender (farm commodities), many farmers were put in a precarious position. The laws resulted in a wave of foreclosures and imprisonment for indebtedness until farmers began to unite under the leadership of Daniel Shays, a former captain during the Revolutionary War. The farmers took over courtrooms to stop foreclosures, and they also took over a state militia armory in Springfield.

The national government, whose powers were then defined by the Articles of Confederation, was unable to put an army in the field to oppose the rebel farmers. Consequently, Boston merchants created their own army and sent it to Springfield. The farmers were dispersed, and the crisis gradually ended. But many pointed to the inability of the national government to respond to this crisis and demanded a convention to amend the Articles or create a new government. Shays' Rebellion marks the start of a pattern in which urban commercialist interests carried the day in the policy arena at the expense of rural agrarian interests. The pattern is not without some interruptions—as when Jefferson was elected in 1800 and abolished the first national bank and Andrew Jackson was elected in 1828 and abolished the second one. But the point is that, from our first days as a nation, urban and rural interests differed, the differences created struggle, and the struggle created a culture marked by suspicion and in some cases outright antipathy.

A few additional examples may further demonstrate this dynamic. For example, the nation's earliest factories required swift-moving water as a source of power. This was particularly true of the nation's first blast furnace operations. These factories were typically constructed along the fast-moving streams of New England. Their presence had negative consequences for farmers in the area. For one, the dams blocked the spawning trips of anadromous fish and thus removed a staple from the local diet and an important commodity from the local economy. Second, the dams created severe flooding problems for low-lying farms. Despite the fact that the farmers often banded together to seek relief through the judicial system (and sometimes on their own at night with picks and axes), the rights of the blast furnace owners were upheld in each instance.[4]

Dating all the way back to the feudal past, there was a legacy of suspicion and distrust between farmers and millers. Indeed, throughout Europe laws were passed prohibiting peasant farmers from creating their own hand-powered grist mills. These laws, of course, preserved the ability of nobles to make a profit on investment in large water-powered mills. The laws also triggered an antipathy between the two occupational groups that followed them all the way to the United States. Charges that millers were using "short" bushels or "rigged" weights were abundant throughout the 19th century. In fact, it is difficult to find the story of a grain elevator fire anywhere in the Midwest that was not accompanied by speculation about which farmer, cheated by the miller, might have retaliated with arson.

Two other 19th-century economic developments went a long way toward exacerbating rural/urban and industrial/agrarian tensions. The first involved tariffs, and the second, the money supply. In keeping with Hamilton's plan for building a commercially oriented republic, the U.S. frequently imposed high tariffs on imported manufactured goods. This tax had the effect of raising the prices of foreign products to the point where America's infant industries could have an edge over the established producers of Europe. The problem with this strategy was that the nation's farmers, the largest consumers of these manufactured goods, were forced to pay higher prices than they would have if no tariffs existed. This circumstance was considered especially egregious by agricultural interests in the South, and they used it to build an argument for secession. But the larger point here is that the tariff question further exacerbated already growing tensions related to urban industrial versus rural agrarian policy.

When the South did secede, that action was followed by the bloodiest war in our nation's history. And while there was no urban/rural dynamic directly related to the Civil War, the old antagonism figured prominently in the debate about how to rebuild the nation's postwar economy. The immediate necessity was to combat war-driven inflation. Throughout the antebellum years the nation's money supply had been stabilized by available gold reserves. But the financial exigencies of the Civil War created the need to "suspend" the gold standard and issue paper bills, which came to be known as "greenbacks." The inflation that occurred by the war's end meant that greenback dollars were worth considerably less than a dollar. The drive to return to "sound money policy" was begun by the northern banking community at the war's end. Having loaned the government millions of dollars worth, say, 50 cents, the banks were eager to receive repayment in dollars worth a full dollar.

An immediate contraction of the money supply, however, though it would have been a great boon to the nation's financial interests, would have created so much instant hardship for the nation's debtors that it was deemed to be a socially dangerous policy option. In the end it was decided that the money supply would be held constant while the population and the economy grew. This had the effect of spreading out over a long period of time the pain associated with money contraction. It also ensured that the money-supply question would be the primary political issue for the remainder of the 19th century. This policy option was still very favorable to the nation's lenders, but it was a grievous burden to the nation's debtors—mostly farmers. Every year of a farmer's mortgage meant that he was paying back his debt with dollars worth more than those he had received with the original loan. This situation created great hardship not only for farmers but also for factory laborers in the nation's cities who struggled to repay home mortgages.

These circumstances became a catalyst for the growth of political parties (the Greenback party, Socialist party, Populist party, etc.) and occupational unions (the National Labor Union, the Knights of Labor, the Farmers Alliance, etc.). The intensity of the growing divide over the "money question" led to a pronounced schism between capital and labor. It was at this point that attempts were first made to join the interests of rural farmers and urban laborers, and while such attempts would continue right through the Great Depression of the 1930s, they were never very successful. There were too many long-standing cultural obstacles to overcome, and these were further complicated by such issues as race, ethnicity, and religion.

An Ethos of Contest

In terms of numbers of students, rural schools were the dominant educational experience of the 19th century—even the early

20th century. After about 1930 or so, a shift took place, and urban schools became the dominant educational experience in this country. Before the turn of the 21st century, however, another shift had taken place. Urban schools were eclipsed by suburban schools as the dominant educational experience. This history is linked to the connection between economic policy choices and the fate of schools, and it is worth taking a few moments to look back at these developments.

During the first half of the 20th century, tens of thousands of one-room schools dotted America's countryside. As high school attendance gradually became the norm, graduates of one-room schools moved on to high schools, where they interacted, often for the first time, with "city kids." The stigma attached to "farm kids" was often harsh and always memorable, as oral histories have shown.[5] Some of this type of peer labeling continues to this day.

But rural schools have gradually disappeared. Technological developments and agricultural policies, especially those related to farm subsidies, had the effect of encouraging ever larger farming operations—a circumstance that contributed to depopulating the countryside and emptying its small schools. The trend to close schools was intensified by a culturally popular assumption in state legislatures, state departments of education, and colleges of education at major universities: schools need to be big to be good. In fact, for many decades of the 20th century, school consolidation was considered synonymous with school improvement, despite the fact that there was virtually no evidence to support the assumption. While naive views related to consolidation still exist, and the practice continues to be one of the first "cost-cutting measures" examined when states face serious fiscal difficulties, we have at last reached the point where consolidation advocates are forced to submit evidence for claims of greater efficiency and improved instruction.

The urban story is not so very different. During the first half of the 20th century, cities invested a great deal—and took a great deal of pride—in the construction of beautiful, sometimes grandiose, schools. But as the century progressed, a series of developments worked against the initial promise of a prosperous urban future in the United States. Among them was a clear policy choice to make the city hospitable to the automobile—a condition created in part by a corporate buy-out of electric trolleys and other early means of mass transportation.[6] The huge investments in highways that followed the corporate attack on mass transit systems had the effect of speeding up "white flight" as civil rights legislation, including school desegregation, brought the races closer together within the city.

White flight created a decrease in property values, which was troublesome from a school finance perspective, but it also had the effect of concentrating the residents with the fewest economic means. In other words, ghettos were created in metropolitan areas all across the country. The ghettos continued to grow, a trend strengthened by post-1980 developments sometimes collectively referred to as "deindustrialization." These changes included 1) the decline in mass-production factories throughout the U.S., much of which was due to favorable overseas trade policies that allowed foreign producers—with lower labor costs and fewer environmental restrictions—to undermine long-standing American industries; 2) the replacement of manufacturing jobs with so-called service economy jobs, such as clerical, telemarketing, and retail sales work; 3) the trend toward "globalizing" the U.S. economy, a fancy name for exporting low-skill jobs by moving production plants abroad; 4) technological innovations that reduced the number of jobs; 5) the decline of labor unions or their inability to compete with the freedom of capital to move operations away from the threat of union activity; and 6) heavy immigration that dramatically increased the availability of low-cost labor. To complicate matters still further, the gains the country has witnessed in the manufacturing sector in the past 10 years have predominantly occurred in the suburbs, exacerbating already significant levels of inner-city unemployment.[7]

Policy choices have resulted in diminished tax bases in both urban and rural America. The fact that school finance has relied heavily on the taxation of local property, still clinging to the system created early in the 19th century, has meant that urban and rural schools have had to struggle to deliver even, in the legal language of the moment, an "adequate" education to all of their students. This is simply an ill-fitting mechanism for current circumstances, a time when local property is no longer the locus of the largest share of the nation's wealth. Given the so-called shift to a service economy, the trend in overseas job exportation via "free trade" initiatives, and rising poverty levels, rural and urban schools are shouldering the lion's share of the misery. Prosperity has moved to the suburbs. Recognizing this, urban and rural schools in a few states have joined forces to collectively challenge the constitutionality of state funding formulas that deny them both sufficient resources to do their jobs. More such collaborative efforts need to take place.

Overcoming Obstacles

It is important to thoroughly interrogate the meaning the larger culture assigns to the terms "urban" and "rural." In this article I have tried to provide a glimpse of the long pejorative history that has accompanied the status of being rural: hicks, bumpkins, crackers—you name the epithet, there are many. It is this long history that makes shows like "The Beverly Hillbillies" funny, and it is this kind of culturally accepted degradation that legitimates policy with adverse effects on rural schools and communities.

By contrast, the meaning we have attached to the term "urban" has changed quickly. At the midpoint of the 20th century, urban aspirations were practically synonymous with what was often called the "American dream"—a two-story house with a garage. Today, half a century later, "urban," like "rural," carries negative connotations. The speed with which we have come to understand urban schools and urban life generally as trouble-filled, overcrowded, and uncontrollable is largely due to the media revolution of the last half of the 20th century. Inundated with news coverage focusing on street crime—to the near exclusion of coverage of white-collar crime—Americans have learned to fear urban centers. Watching television news, it is not difficult to believe that there is a Willie Horton in every urban neighborhood. Television shows and Hollywood movies featuring car chases, drug dealers, drive-by shootings, crime scene investigations, even crime-riddled urban high schools have all

been a part of the public curriculum that has made such associations automatic. Once again, the meaning the larger culture gives to these terms—rural equals backward, urban equals crime—plays a role in the thinking that goes into creating the policies that affect urban and rural schools and communities.

The truth of the matter is that these sectors have long harbored suspicions about each other. Many urban educators suspect that small rural schools unfairly skew the distribution of state resources, while many rural educators suspect that large urban districts do the same in reverse. This ethos of contest needs to be overcome, for it is clear from a 21st-century vantage point that the circumstances faced by each group have become increasingly similar. Recognizing this, Buffalo State College has created the Center for Excellence in Urban and Rural Education, dedicated to working with urban and rural schools to help ease the burden of implementing high-quality instructional programs and to preparing excellent teachers who are unencumbered by naive stereotypes about teaching in urban and rural schools. More of these efforts are needed across America's universities if we are to make good on the nation's commitment to its young people.

The alternative is not particularly appealing. Even conservative scholars agree that in terms of economics, we have created two Americas: one prospering, the other suffering. Unless we work to overcome obstacles to collaboration between urban and rural schools, we may see the same trend in education. If this happens it will take the shape of a two-tiered system—one suburban and high quality, the other urban and rural and barely adequate.

Notes

1. Quoted in Andrew A. Sherockman, "Caleb Mills: Pioneer Educator in Indiana" (Doctoral dissertation, University of Pittsburgh, 1955), p. 118. The emphasis on "Presbyterian" belongs to Mills. Sherockman noted further that Mills believed "a man of sterling worth and religious principle could not be obtained for the state superintendency without awakening denominational prejudices and sectarian bigotry to such an extent as to preclude success" (p. 119).
2. Paul Theobald, *Call School: Rural Education in the Midwest to 1918* (Carbondale: Southern Illinois University Press, 1995), p. 119.
3. Jacob Cooke, ed., *The Reports of Alexander Hamilton* (New York: Harper & Row, 1964), p. 131.
4. Gary Kulik, "Dams, Fish, and Farmers: Defense of Public Rights in Eighteenth Century Rhode Island," in Steven Hahn and Jonathan Prude, eds., *The Countryside in the Age of Capitalist Transformation* (Chapel Hill: University of North Carolina Press, 1985), pp. 25–50.
5. See, for example, Diane Manning, *Hill Country Teacher: Oral Histories from the One-Room School and Beyond* (New York: Twayne Publishers, 1990).
6. Jane Jacobs, *Dark Age Ahead* (New York: Random House, 2004), pp. 38–41.
7. William Julius Wilson, *When Work Disappears: The World of the New Urban Poor* (New York: Vintage Books, 1996), p. 37.

PAUL THEOBALD holds the Woods-Beals Chair for Excellence in Urban and Rural Education at Buffalo College, Buffalo, N.Y.

From *Phi Delta Kappan*, October 2005, pp. 116-122. Copyright © 2005 by Phi Delta Kappan. Reprinted by permission of the publisher and author.

UNIT 3

Striving for Excellence: The Drive for Quality

Unit Selections

Key Points to Consider

- Identify some of the different points of view on achieving excellence in education. What value conflicts can be defined?

- What are some assumptions about achieving excellence in student achievement that you would challenge? Why?

- What can educators do to improve the quality of student learning?

- Have there been flaws in American school reform efforts in the past 20 years? If so, what are they?

- Has the Internet affected the critical thinking skills of students? Defend your answer.

Student Website

www.mhcls.com/online

Internet References

Further information regarding these websites may be found in this book's preface or online.

Awesome Library for Teachers
   http://www.awesomelibrary.org
Education World
   http://www.education-world.com
EdWeb/Andy Carvin
   http://edwebproject.org
Kathy Schrock's Guide for Educators
   http://www.discoveryschool.com/schrockguide/
Teacher's Guide to the U.S. Department of Education
   http://www.ed.gov/pubs/TeachersGuide/

The debate continues over which academic standards are most appropriate for elementary and secondary school students. Discussion regarding the impact on students and teachers of state proficiency examinations goes on in those states or provinces where such examinations are mandated. We are still dealing with how best to assess student academic performance. Some very interesting proposals on how to do this have emerged.

There are several incisive analyses of why American educators' efforts to achieve excellence in schooling have frequently failed. Today, some interesting proposals are being offered as to how we might improve the academic achievement of students. The current debate regarding excellence in education clearly reflects parents' concerns for more choices in how they school their children.

Many authors of recent essays and reports believe that excellence can be achieved best by creating new models of schooling that give both parents and students more control over the types of school environments available to them. Many believe that more money is not a guarantor of quality in schooling. Imaginative academic programming and greater citizen choice can guarantee at least a greater variety of options open to parents who are concerned about their children's academic progress in school.

We each wish the best quality of life that we can attain, and we each desire the opportunity for an education that will optimize our chances to achieve our objectives. The rhetoric on excellence and quality in schooling has been heated, and numerous opposing concepts of how schools can reach these goals have been presented for public consideration in recent years. Some progress has been realized on the part of students as well as some major changes in how teacher education programs are structured.

In the decades of the 1980s and 1990s, those reforms instituted to encourage qualitative growth in the conduct of schooling tended to be what education historian David Tyack once referred to as "structural" reforms. Structural reforms consist of demands for standardized testing of students and teaching, reorganization of teacher education programs, legalized actions to provide alternative routes into the teaching profession, efforts to recruit more people into teaching, and laws to enable greater parental choice as to where their children may attend school. These structural reforms cannot, however, in and of themselves produce higher levels of student achievement. We need to explore a broader range of the essential purposes of schooling, which will require our redefining what it means to be a literate person. We need also to reconsider what we mean by the "quality" of education and to reassess the essential purposes of schooling.

When we speak of quality and excellence as aims of education, we must remember that these terms encompass aesthetic and affective as well as cognitive processes. Young people cannot achieve the full range of intellectual capacity to solve problems on their own simply by being obedient and by memorizing data. How students encounter their teachers in classrooms and how teachers interact with their students are concerns that encompass both aesthetic and cognitive dimensions.

There is a real need to enforce intellectual standards and yet also to make schools more creative places in which to learn, places where students will yearn to explore, to imagine, and to hope.

Compared to those in the United States, students in European nations appear to score higher in assessments of skills in mathematics and the sciences, in written essay examinations in the humanities and social sciences, and in the routine oral examinations given by committees of teachers to students as they exit secondary schools.

What forms of teacher education and in-service reeducation are needed? Who pays for these programmatic options? Where and how will funds be raised or redirected from other priorities to pay for this? Will the "streaming and tracking" model of secondary school student placement that exists in Europe be adopted? How can we best assess academic performance? Can we commit to a more heterogeneous grouping of students and to full inclusion of handicapped students in our schools? Many individual, private, and governmental reform efforts did not address these questions.

Other industrialized nations champion the need for alternative secondary schools to prepare their young people for varied life goals and civic work. The American dream of the common school translated into what has become the comprehensive high school of the twentieth century. But does it provide all the people with alternative diploma options? If not, what is the next step? What must be changed? For one, concepts related to our educational goals must be clarified and political motivation must be separated from the realities of student performance.

Policy development for schooling needs to be tempered by even more "bottom-up," grassroots efforts to improve the quality of schools that are now under way in many communities in North America. New and imaginative inquiry and assessment strategies need to be developed by teachers working in their classrooms, and they must nurture the support of professional colleagues and parents.

Excellence is the goal: the means to achieve it is what is in dispute. There is a new dimension to the debate over assessment of academic achievement of elementary and secondary school students. In addition, the struggle continues of conflicting academic (as well as political) interests in the quest to improve the quality of preparation of our future teachers, and we also need to sort these issues out.

No conscientious educator would oppose the idea of excellence in education. The problem in gaining consensus over how to attain it is that the assessment of excellence of both teacher and student performance is always based on some preset standards. Which standards of assessment should prevail?

Alternative Approaches to High-Stakes Testing

Mr. Lederman and Mr. Burnstein propose a novel way to increase student engagement and counter the pressures of high-stakes testing.

Leon M. Lederman and Ray A. Burnstein

UNDER No Child Left Behind (NCLB), the federal government requires state governors, superintendents, and school principals, through a regime of annual testing, to demonstrate to the taxpaying public that education dollars are being used effectively to improve student achievement. Developing, administering, and scoring the required assessments call for highly specialized skills and experience that states often lack, leading them to hire outside testing companies and consultants.

Student performance on these tests—given at the end of the year to all students in grades 3 through 8—determines rewards and sanctions for schools, teachers, and students. But these standardized tests were not designed for accountability purposes, and experience in isolating and measuring the effects that schools have on student learning is rare. This test-based accountability system is being controlled by people who may know how to develop standardized achievement tests but know very little about the institutional realities of accountability—and even less about how to improve instruction in schools. For the most part, the assessments currently in use are not capable of accounting for the many nonschool factors that influence test scores, including student background, home environment, poverty level, and English-language proficiency. Such standardized tests are not always reliable measures of what is learned in the classroom, according to assessment expert James Popham.[1] And now NCLB has established these single, end-of-year tests as the dominant measures of school success or failure.

High-Stakes Testing

Tests used to make high-stakes decisions, especially in light of the fact that they are given only once or twice a year, necessarily have to meet a set of strict requirements. High-stakes tests must be "instructionally sensitive"—that is, they must be capable of determining changes in achievement related to instructional improvements. The validity of an accountability system depends on designing the right tests. These tests should meet the following criteria:[2]

1. Assessments used to measure student mastery of specific content must include clear descriptions—brief, jargon-free, and teacher-friendly—of what is going to be assessed. Classroom teachers need these descriptions to understand in detail what is expected of their students.

2. Effective assessments focus on a modest number of significant curricular aims, drawn from content standards. The selected content standards clearly must be of major importance.

3. An instructionally sensitive test to be used for accountability purposes must report student performance in a way that enables teachers to know what aspects of their instruction need to be improved and what aspects are working well.

The tests currently being used to satisfy NCLB have been judged by the majority of teachers to be instructionally insensitive—incapable of measuring the effects of instruction on student performance. This can lead to tragic results because high-stakes tests can distort instruction and may encourage teachers to "teach to the test." Teaching to a bad test and spending months on drill and skill may boost scores but surely ends up turning off students. The NCLB mandates for AYP (adequate yearly progress) and public reporting of results put enormous pressure on students, teachers, principals, and superintendents to raise test scores. This pressure can lead, in extreme cases, to cheating. The more general response is for teachers to practice on past (and even future) versions of the tests and to restrict instruction to just those subjects that will be tested; this is known as item teaching.

These outcomes of high-stakes testing distort the traditional ideal of the teacher as one who makes every effort to achieve the goals of the curricula without regard to any particular test. The real blame for inappropriate forms of teaching in response to testing lies not with teachers but with state and national policy makers who create accountability systems centered on ever-higher test scores (AYP) with little regard for how these scores relate to better learning.

Accountability based on high-stakes standardized testing ignores the vast differences students bring into the schools. As teachers, we know how genius and creativity in students may be hidden from us by so many factors, including language, motivation, boredom, gender, and, perhaps most crucially, thinking that diverges from the textbook and from typical classroom instruction. High-stakes testing may not only turn off students but may also totally disconnect them from the learning process.

Classroom Assessment and New Educational Technology

The American Psychological Association's guidelines for test use specifically prohibit basing any judgment on a single test score.[3] This position recognizes margins of error and the need for multiple measures of a student's performance before making critical decisions. It seems that a much more productive approach than NCLB's annual testing would be to integrate instruction and assessment. This is far from a new idea. When testing is an integral part of pedagogy, one is actually teaching to the test—no, rather, teaching with the test. As teachers, we are aware that testing, in the sense of raising questions to get students thinking, is an essential component of pedagogy. By embedding testing into the teaching process, we can try to ensure that students are thinking about the subject. An optimum marriage of questioning and explaining can enhance the learning process. This approach has a familiar name: classroom assessment.[4]

We believe that keypads combined with Internet technology can be used to achieve embedded assessment, day by day, even hour by hour, without imposing the deadly burden of high-stakes tests.

Educational research has defined two distinct types of assessment: summative and formative.[5] Formative assessment enhances instruction by deftly using questioning and quizzing to establish a feedback loop between students and teacher. An example of formative assessment, used in both lecture and laboratory, is "interactive engagement," in which a teacher leads students in activities that in some way yield timely feedback.[6] In contrast with formative assessment, summative assessment is similar in form and use—e.g., a final examination administered at the end of the semester or school year—to the high-stakes tests we have been criticizing.

Teachers can apply modest forms of technology to improve the use of formative assessment. In 1993, we at the Illinois Institute of Technology initiated the use of "keypads" during classroom lectures. Keypads are wireless electronic devices that enable students to respond immediately to multiple-choice questions that are projected onto a large screen throughout the course of a lecture. After about 30 seconds or at the instructor's discretion, the responses of all the students are compiled by a computer and presented in a histogram. Each individual student's response has also been recorded in the computer. We accidentally stumbled on this wireless electronic system—originally designed for interactive sales pitches—and modified its use for high school and college instruction based on actual classroom experience. We began making presentations on keypad-based instruction at meetings of the American Association of Physics Teachers in 1995 and have continued ever since.[7]

A decade ago, wireless keypad systems were available from only one source and cost $300 apiece. Now there are about five suppliers, selling hundreds of thousands of keypads per year (both radio frequency and infrared) to schools and universities at a fraction of the earlier price. The systems are often called electronic student response systems (ESRS), and their use represents an enhanced type of formative assessment.[8]

We propose using this technology to satisfy, in part, the new accountability requirements that have been imposed on schools in an attempt to address district, state, and federal concerns about the quality of education. We believe that keypads combined with Internet technology can be used to achieve embedded assessment, day by day, even hour by hour, without imposing the deadly burden of high-stakes tests. If this interactive student response system does, say, 70% of the job of assessing students' progress in grasping concepts and reaching understanding, a summative test could then be added in order to satisfy the accountability authorities with about one-third of the trauma we see in our current system.

We have, of course, nurtured and studied this technique in physics instruction only, but others have used wireless keypads for classes in English literature, biology, engineering, etc. The wide utility of ESRS should not be surprising since the technique is applicable to all subjects that can be assessed in part by multiple choice questions.

How Does Keypad-Based Instruction Work?

During a typical 40- to 75-minute high school or first-year college class, a teacher can interrupt six to 12 times to ask questions that are designed primarily to test students' grasp of the subject matter but also to generate discussion among students. Each question offers a choice of three to 10 possible answers. After a minute or so, the class results are presented as a histogram. If the histogram shows that most of the class missed the concept, the teacher has instant feedback and can take immediate steps to address the students' lack of understanding. One possible response to such feedback would be to encourage peer instruction, in which students discuss the question with their neighbors for several minutes.[9] Bedlam! Perhaps, but remember, the students are arguing over subject matter. The teacher then asks the same keypad-quiz question again to check whether the concept has been clarified. Moreover, this technique creates the possibility that discussion and argumentation among students will become a habit—one that is practiced outside the classroom as well.

The tabulation of one semester's keypad-quiz grades may result in as many as 300 to 600 scores for each student. This is enough to give the teacher a very good evaluation of each student's status and progress. The keypad quizzes may, of course, be supplemented by one or two full-period tests.

Keypad-based questions currently follow the traditional multiple-choice format. Multiple-choice questions are not essays, but they can be given essay-type features. Since the keypad quizzes are computer graded, an item can have more than one correct answer or offer the option of correct and "almost correct" answers. For example, a teacher can ask students to select from several sentences the one that offers the best explanation of a concept. When a student chooses a next-best sentence along with the best, that second choice can be added to the student's grade for the question. This scheme is far from being perfected, but, as we gain more experience with the technology, we can develop more incisive questions that will both test and sharpen student understanding. In this way, we can hope to extend the range of questions to higher-level cognitive domains[10] than would otherwise be available with the multiple-choice format, thereby making keypad-based formative assessment an even more effective testing procedure.

Keypad-Based Assessment and Accountability

High-stakes testing, even at its best, puts a strain on good pedagogy, places a huge burden on students and teachers, and creates winners and losers in an education system that needs to have all winners. Our federal and state education policy makers have not inspired confidence that their procedures can fix the current system. And we have not even mentioned the lack of sufficient funding for so massive a federal intervention as NCLB. As an alternative, classroom-embedded assessment can provide continuous, detailed information on the progress of students, and keypads and Internet technology can allow state and federal officials to augment their one-test approach.

With reasonable coordination between teachers, schools, and, say, accountability headquarters at the state and federal levels, an accountability system that combined keypad-based formative assessment with summative assessment could be created. State or federal education experts could develop standardized multiple choice accountability tests and require students to take them on a semester or annual basis. Teachers could download the tests via the Internet and administer them at the correct phase of the class. Such a system would no longer rely on single high-stakes tests since the keypad data collected by the teacher would contribute significantly to the overall assessment of student achievement and in a different way from the summative test.

As educational technology becomes an increasingly dominant factor in pre-K–12 education, we need to be creative in looking at how it can modify curricula, assist the student, ease the administrative burden, and support the teacher in providing exemplary and joyful instruction.

References

1. W. James Popham, "Standardized Achievement Tests: Misnamed and Misleading," *Education Week*, 19 September 2001, p. 46.
2. See, for example, W. James Popham, "The Trouble with Testing: Why Standards Based Assessment Doesn't Measure Up," *American School Board Journal*, February 2003, pp. 14–17.
3. The American Psychological Association's testing guidelines are available at **www.apa.org/pubinfo/testing.html.**
4. Thomas A. Angelo and K. Patricia Cross, *Classroom Assessment Techniques: A Handbook for College Teachers* (San Francisco: Jossey-Bass, 1993).
5. Paul Black and Dylan Wiliam, "Inside the Black Box: Raising Standards Through Classroom Assessment," *Phi Delta Kappan*, October 1998, pp. 139–49.
6. Richard R. Hake, "Interactive Engagement vs. Traditional Methods: A Six-Thousand-Student Survey of Mechanics Test Data for Introductory Physics Courses," *American Journal of Physics*, January 1998, pp. 64–74.
7. Ray A. Burnstein and Leon M. Lederman, "Interactive Lectures: Keeping Students Involved in a Lecture Course," AAPT Announcer, July 1995, p. 80; and idem, "Report on Progress in Using a Wireless Keypad Response System," in Edward F. Redish and John S. Rigden, eds., *The Changing Role of Physics Departments in Modern Universities: Proceedings of the International Conference on Undergraduate Physics Education* (College Park, Md.: American Institute of Physics, Conference Proceedings No. 399, October 1997), pp. 531–37.
8. For more information on the pedagogical value of ESRS, see Ray A. Burnstein and Leon M. Lederman, "Using Wireless Keypads in Lecture Classes," *Physics Teacher*, January 2001, pp. 8–11; and H. Arthur Woods and Charles Chiu, "Wireless Response Technology in College Classrooms," The Technology Source, September/October 2003, available at **http://ts.mivu.org/default.asp?show=article&id=1034**.
9. Eric Mazur, *Peer Instruction: A User's Manual* (Upper Saddle River, N.J.: Prentice-Hall, 1996).
10. Benjamin S. Bloom, *Taxonomy of Educational Objectives* (New York: Longmans, Green, 1956).

LEON M. LEDERMAN, Nobel Laureate, is resident scholar at the Illinois Mathematics and Science Academy, Aurora, and Pritzker Professor of Science at the Illinois Institute of Technology, Chicago. **RAY A. BURNSTEIN** is research and emeritus professor of physics at the Illinois Institute of Technology. © 2006, Leon M. Lederman.

What Colleges Forget to Teach

Higher education could heal itself by teaching civics—not race, class, and gender.

ROBERT P. GEORGE

The university is worth fighting for. No other institution can carry the burden of educating our young people. That's why we must redouble our efforts to restore integrity, civility, and rigorous standards in American higher education—particularly in the area of civic education.

I'll be the first to admit that the situation is dire. I sympathize when critics throw up their hands in despair. I sometimes feel that way myself. Darkness often prevails in places where the light of learning should shine. I often trade horror stories with my friend Hadley Arkes, a distinguished scholar of jurisprudence and political theory at Amherst. On one occasion, I explained that the Woodrow Wilson School of Public and International Affairs at Princeton was sponsoring a viciously anti-Catholic art exhibit—one that it would never even permit were some favored faith or cause, such as Islam or gay rights, its target. Every year, some outrage along these lines seems to prove that anti-Catholicism really is the anti-Semitism of the intellectuals, though anyone familiar with academic life today knows that anti-Semitism itself is making a run at being the anti-Semitism of the intellectuals.

Professor Arkes listened sympathetically and said, "Things have gotten pretty bad here at Amherst, too: we've granted tenure in political science to a guy promoting a theory explaining the foreign policy of George H. W. Bush by reference to his alleged homoerotic attraction to Ronald Reagan." "Well," I replied, "Princeton has topped that. We've given a distinguished chair in bioethics to a fellow who insists that eating animals is morally wrong, but that killing newborn human infants can be a perfectly moral choice." (This professor has since gone on to say that there would be nothing wrong with a society in which large numbers of children were conceived, born, and then killed in infancy to obtain transplantable organs.)

And so we go back and forth with each other, in a macabre game of one-upmanship.

Still, teaching at Princeton is in many ways a joy. I have the privilege of instructing students who actually know when the Civil War took place. Even before arriving at Princeton, they know that Lee surrendered to Grant, not to Eisenhower, at Appomattox Court House. Most know that Philadelphia, not Washington, D.C., played host to the constitutional convention. Few would list Alexander Hamilton among the most important presidents, because they know that he was never president. Some can identify the cabinet office that he held and even give a decent account of his differences with Thomas Jefferson. Speaking of whom, all my students know that Jefferson owned slaves—but then, everybody seems to know that, even those who know nothing else about him. My students, though, also know that it was Franklin D. Roosevelt, not his cousin Teddy, or Harry Truman, or JFK, who promised Americans a New Deal. Some can even tell you that the Supreme Court invalidated some early New Deal legislation and that FDR responded with a plan to pack the Court. Yes, my students and students at elite universities around the country come to campus knowing American history pretty well—and wanting to know it a lot better.

Many of these young men and women value historical knowledge not merely for its own sake but because they want to be good citizens. More, they seek to be of genuine service to fellow citizens. Many hope to be legislators, judges, even president. They know that knowledge of American history is vital to effective citizenship and service.

But they also need an understanding of American civics—particularly the principles of the Constitution. For all their academic achievement, students at Princeton and Yale and Stanford and Harvard and other schools that attract America's most talented young people rarely come to campus with a sound grasp of the philosophy of America's constitutional government. How did the Founding Fathers seek, via the institutions that the Constitution created, to build and maintain a regime of ordered liberty? Even some of our best-informed students think something along these lines: the Framers set down a list of basic freedoms in a Bill of Rights, which an independent judiciary, protected from the vicissitudes of politics, would then enforce.

It's the rare student indeed who enters the classroom already aware that the Framers believed that the true bulwark of liberty was limited government. Few students comprehend the crucial distinction between (on the one hand) the national government as one of delegated and enumerated powers, and (on the other) the states as governments of general jurisdiction, exercising police powers to protect public health, safety, and morals, and to advance the general welfare. If anything, they imagine that it's the other way around. Thus they have no comprehension as to why leading supporters of the Constitution objected to a Bill of Rights, worried that it could compromise the delegated-powers doctrine and thus undermine the true liberty-securing principle of limited government.

Good students these days have heard of federalism, yet they have little appreciation of how it works or why the Founders thought it so vital. They've heard of the separation of powers and often can sketch how the system of checks and balances should work. But if one asks, for example, "Who checks the courts?" they cannot give a satisfactory answer.

The students' lack of awareness flows partly from the conception of the American civic order that they have drunk in, which treats courts as if they aren't really part of the government. Judges, on this view, are "non-political" actors whose job is to keep politicians in line with what elite circles regard as enlightened opinions. Judicial supremacy, of the kind that Jefferson and Lincoln stingingly condemned, thus winds up uncritically assumed to be sound constitutional law. The idea that the courts themselves could violate the Constitution by, for example, usurping authority that the Constitution vests in other branches of government, is off the radar screen.

Lacking basic knowledge of the American Founders' political philosophy and of the principles that they enshrined in the Constitution, students often fall prey to the notion that ours is a "Living Constitution," whose actual words matter little. On the Living Constitution theory, judges—especially Supreme Court justices—serve as members of a kind of standing constitutional convention whose role is to invalidate legislation that progressive circles regard as antiquated or retrograde, all in the name of adapting the Constitution to keep up with the times.

It doesn't take much to expose the absurdity of this theory. The purpose of enshrining principles in a constitution is to ensure that the nation's fundamental values remain honored even if they fall out of fashion. As for adapting the nation's laws to keep up with the times, legislators can—and should—take care of that task. The proper role of courts when they exercise the power of judicial review is essentially a conserving (you could even say "conservative") one. It is not to change anything but rather to place limits on what one can change.

Does this mean that our Constitution is "dead"? No: the Constitution's principles are "living" in the sense that they can apply validly even to matters that the Founders themselves could not have anticipated. The original understanding of Fourth Amendment principles governing searches and seizures, for example, can reliably extend to cover today's controversies about computer files, cyber-storage, and electronic surveillance. So to reject, as we should, the Living Constitution and its anticonstitutional doctrine of virtually unlimited judicial power is by no means to treat our Constitution as a dead letter. Rather, it is to treat the Constitution as law—supreme law—binding on, and limiting the power of, every branch of government and agency of the state, including the courts.

What is the source of this educational breakdown? The trouble isn't the students—they're bright and eager to learn. It's that too few teachers are presenting students with the Founders' philosophy, much less introducing them to the great issues, some still with us today, that divided the Founders. And if teachers aren't teaching the Founding's principles, where will students learn them? They're not likely to get any sense of the distinction between the delegated powers of the national government and the general jurisdiction of the states from any newspapers, national magazines, or television news networks, that's for sure. Have the editors of the *New York Times* and the folks at CBS News even heard of that distinction yet? News travels slowly, true; but it shouldn't take 218 years.

The solution to this educational breakdown is straightforward: we need to make a commitment at every level of schooling and within the public media to promote a deep awareness of the principles of the American Founding. Why educate students into archaism? some will doubtless object. Surely governing principles set forth in the eighteenth century have little relevance to us in the twenty-first. But American ideals, as embodied preeminently in the Declaration of Independence, are universal and timeless. They have force wherever there are human beings, fallible (indeed, as the Founders recognized, fallen) creatures, yet images of God in their possession of reason and freedom—beings, as the Declaration says, "endowed by their Creator with certain unalienable rights."

The constitutional scheme that the Founders devised for the lawful governance of human beings and for the preservation of their sacred rights is the world's greatest triumph of practical political science. Of course, we shouldn't treat our institutions as if they're perfect—the Founders provided, after all, for their possible revision by constitutional amendment. True civic education isn't indoctrination. The Founders themselves weren't of one mind as to the proper interpretation of their handiwork in every respect. And reasonable people of goodwill, of course, disagree about key matters of constitutional interpretation. We do our students a wonderful service when we invite them into the great historical and contemporary debates about the meaning of our fundamental law in controversial cases. To do that, though, we must equip them with the historical knowledge and the philosophical understanding necessary if they're to evaluate intelligently the competing arguments.

We needn't teach that our institutions are uniquely just—that any polity that seeks to respect people's rights and preserve liberties must copy them precisely. But anyone who sincerely seeks the truth will see that ours are indeed worthy institutions that have served Americans well whenever our people and leaders have shown the wisdom and mustered the fortitude to honor and live by them. The fact is, freedom-loving people throughout the world—even in an age darkened by widespread anti-Americanism—draw inspiration from American ideals and look to American institutions as the gold standard of republican government. Even critics of American policy feel that they must pay lip service to our ideals of democracy, limited government, equality before the law, civil liberty, private property, the free economy, and the rule of law.

Madison did not doubt that it would be so: "The free system of government we have established," he wrote, "is so congenial with reason, with common sense, and with a universal feeling that it must produce approbation and a desire of imitation, as avenues may be found for truth to the knowledge of nations." In Eastern Europe, much of Latin America, and parts of South Asia, Africa, and the Middle East, "avenues have been found for truth to the knowledge of nations." Yet, at the same time, in the U.S. itself, public comprehension of "the free system of government" that Madison and his "founding brothers" bequeathed to us has eroded. We must reverse that trend. Otherwise, the quality of citizenship and statesmanship will inevitably suffer.

Madison famously observed that "only a well-educated people can be permanently a free people." Yet some today seem to think otherwise. They don't necessarily doubt that the impoverishment of civic understanding erodes citizenship and statesmanship, but they wonder why we can't get along perfectly well anyway. We are, after all, the richest, most powerful nation in world history. We're on top, and despite emerging economic challenges from China, maybe India, we're likely to stay there. Isn't that enough?

To this, a double reply. First, history shows us that basic freedoms are hard-won and easily lost. The institutions that preserve freedom can be crumbling even as they appear strong. Severe economic strains and other fundamental challenges can tempt people to compromise or sacrifice even basic freedoms. As Madison knew, it is *conviction* born of knowledge—civic understanding—that is our bulwark, our only true security, in the face of such temptations.

Second, as Plato (though no admirer of democracy) observes, the goal of the polis—the political order—isn't merely to establish security but also to provide the conditions for citizens to live good and decent lives, worthy of human beings as rational and moral creatures. Our founders saw this crucial philosophical point. The purpose of the Declaration of Independence and its principles of civic life, Jefferson wrote shortly before he died, were "not to find out new principles or new arguments never before thought of, nor merely to say things which had never been said before, but to place before mankind the common sense of the subject.... All its authority rests on the harmonizing sentiments of the day, whether expressed in conversation, in letters, printed essays, or in the elementary books of public right, as Aristotle, Cicero, Locke, Sydney, etc."

These "elementary books" inform us that statesmanship and, especially, citizenship, though key means to other ends, possess a value greater than merely instrumental. When we carry out our civic responsibilities in an informed way, we find ourselves ennobled as individuals and as a community. Even if a nation could remain on top in the global competition for military and economic superiority, and even if its basic political structure could last more or less indefinitely, the people of that nation, if they remain ignorant of the moral foundations of that structure, would be impoverished.

Whatever one thinks of the decision to invade Iraq, one cannot fail to find deeply moving the desire of the vast majority of Iraqis to be democratic citizens—a desire that cannot be accounted for merely by noting the tendency of democracies over time to be prosperous and stable. Rather, Iraqis proudly displaying ink-stained fingers are saying something that we Americans, at some level, still appreciate: that democratic citizenship fulfills an important aspect of our humanity. It is so inherently desirable that Iraqi men and women have risked their lives to exercise the franchise, just as it caused those eighteenth-century Americans who pledged their "lives, fortunes, and sacred honor" to risk the king's hangman's noose.

Our posture cannot be—must not be—complacent. We must firmly resolve to make reform and renewal—whatever the obstacles, whatever the costs—our constant endeavor. We must not let the resistance of entrenched interests or recalcitrant ideological forces in the academic establishment, the funding bureaucracies, or anywhere else intimidate us. Let us seize every opportunity, marshaling our resources and deploying our wits to advance the cause of reform wherever we detect an opening, however much the weeds may obscure it. The reform and renewal of civic education in our nation is a noble cause. We must make it an urgent priority.

Boys at Risk:
The Gender Achievement Gap

GLENN COOK
Managing Editor

Kelley King knows the drill. As principal of Douglass Elementary School in Boulder, Colo., she works annually on plans to improve student achievement. But little did she know that an initiative begun in 2004 would land her students on the cover of *Newsweek* this past January.

"Our school district was saying that we needed to specifically look for achievement gaps, and we had to have a stand-alone equity goal," King said.

"While we don't have a lot of English language learners or free and reduced lunch children to disaggregate, we still have subgroups of kids. Every school does. And our largest subgroup was boys."

Yes, you heard that right. Boys are now a subgroup, and their failure to achieve is causing ripples through the education community. But lest you think reporters are just hopping on the latest fad, researchers who study gender differences say it's been a problem for two decades. And they have the data to prove it.

"The industrial schooling system where you sit down, listen, read, and write in a strand-driven, project-driven type of learning is just not fit for a classroom of 30 kids when half of them are boys," said author and family therapist Michael Gurian, whose institute has trained almost 20,000 teachers on how to create boy-friendly classrooms. "That is not the way that boys learn best, and their grades show it."

And as schools like King's face pressure to increase student achievement, Gurian and other researchers say districts must pay attention to those learning styles to be successful.

"There are more boys who drop out and fewer boys who go on to college and graduate from college," said Julie Coates, co-author of *Smart Boys, Bad Grades,* a report released in March by the Learning Resources Network. "That's not a fad. Those are facts that are somewhat alarming. And schools have to do something about it now."

Boys have "consistently and increasingly underperformed" in school compared to girls since the 1980s, said Coates, who wrote the study with William Draves. Both blame boys' lack of performance on homework, which schools increasingly rely on as a measuring stick for good grades.

"Overnight, school boards—without any cost involved—could help put more than a million boys into college, simply by not penalizing them for late homework," Draves said. "As long as you continue to punish boys for late homework, they're not going to get into college. They may learn. They may increase their knowledge. But they won't have the grades."

The notion that boys and girls have different learning styles is nothing new, Coates and Draves said. Over the past two decades, scientists have said that brain chemistry and male sex hormones play a role in boys' physical and mental abilities. Girls develop language skills more quickly and typically are more patient, while boys tend to have better hand-eye coordination and less developed fine-motor skills.

"Up until fifth grade, a boy needs four to five recesses a day," said William Pollack, a Harvard psychologist and author of the 1998 book *Real Boys.* "What do we do if he squirms in his seat? We take away recess. If the child is a discipline problem, then we look for ways to have him diagnosed and put on medication. And people wonder why boys feel misunderstood and stupid."

Pollack is working on a K-6 "beta curriculum" that is being used in 27 schools—public and private—in the San Francisco Bay Area. The curriculum, which includes educational video games and computers as learning tools, is designed to "create classrooms that are more comfortable to boys."

"We're trying to find reading materials that are more interesting to boys and to get teachers to recognize that their biases and expectations don't meet boys' needs," Pollack said. "What we're finding is that by modifying the way we teach, it fits their style and speed. It makes the class run more smoothly and boys do better.

"It's very simple in concept, but so is knowing that boys and girls have learning styles that are different," he said. "The key is translating that concept into reality."

For King, that meant sharing Gurian's book, *The Minds of Boys,* with her faculty and asking them to come up with ways to structure their classrooms differently. As a result, lectures were replaced with lessons that move quickly, use small groups, and give boys an opportunity to perform.

Two years ago, boys at Douglass scored 10 points lower in reading and 14 points lower in writing than girls. By 2004–05, the gap had been cut in half, and *Newsweek* came calling.

"What I've been telling our staff is that we can be an excellent school and still have a long way to go," King said. "How boys have exceeded girls in terms of gains shows that it's doable, and we didn't leave girls behind. But even when our scores are excellent, we can't be satisfied. We're not truly excellent until every child—boy and girl—has gone as far as we can take them."

Standardized Students: The Problems with Writing for Tests Instead of People

BRONWYN T. WILLIAMS

I'm not usually a huge fan of bumper stickers, even the ones I agree with, because of the way they shout out simplistic positions on complex issues. I still remember, though, when I saw the one that read "Standardized Testing Produces Standardized Students." I smiled and nodded my head a bit in agreement. Simplistic as that phrase may be, over the years it comes back to me when I am involved in conversations about testing that seem bound in reductive and simplistic arguments about standards, rigor, and accountability. I don't use the phrase because I don't think using a bumper-sticker argument I agree with makes it superior to my opponents' bumper-sticker arguments. But I do try my best to nudge arguments about testing toward a more complex consideration of the myriad implications of the concept of standardization.

Some levels of standardization I rely on. I take great comfort that there are identifiable standards for inspecting elevators, for example. I also appreciate that most medical doctors go through some kind of standard training in human anatomy. And I believe that we teachers have a responsibility to assess whether students are learning the concepts, ideas, and ways of thinking that we believe are important and also to hold ourselves and our pedagogies accountable if we are failing to reach most of our students.

Like many of my colleagues, however, I am not convinced that literacy assessment is best achieved through standardized tests given to huge groups of students in high-stakes situations. More and more, it seems as if the point of literacy education—of all education—is becoming standardized assessment and rankings rather than learning. Standardized assessment differs from assessment that attempts to determine whether students are learning what we are trying to teach. No one I know is against the latter. What recent trends in standardized assessment emphasize, however, is not learning but the comparison and ranking of failure. Incessant testing regimes, such as the infamous No Child Left Behind (2002) law in the United States (known ruefully among many teachers as No Teacher Left

Standing), focus on broad comparisons of students, with little regard to their differences, and severe punishments for schools and teachers who fail to meet the "standards." As long as students meet the standards, what they may actually be learning seems to be beside the point.

The fervor for this kind of standardized testing reinforces the kind of ranking games that are a particular enthusiasm of Americans and are certainly not unknown in other countries. We're willing and eager to rank anything—from the 100 greatest movies to the 250 best cities in which to raise children. Never mind that the criteria for such rankings are hazy at best; if we can't put a number on it and rank it, then what good is it? Numbers seem scientific and technological. So we test and test and test, oblivious or resistant to the possibility that standardized literacy testing often produces numbers with about as much utility or connection to reality as ranking songs on the old American Bandstand television program. "It sounds good, has a good beat, and I can dance to it. I give it an 87."

Testing as Punishment

My concerns about the increasingly pervasive reliance on standardized testing in literacy education are about more than questionable methods of assessment and measurement, however. I am also deeply troubled about the implications for issues of literacy and identity. What effect does the unrelenting emphasis on standardized literacy testing have on students' perception of the purposes and possibilities of literacy? By extension, what effect does such testing have on their perception of the possibilities for themselves as readers and writers?

Many concerns about identity and standardized testing have been framed in terms of race and social class and have been well documented and well argued by others (McNeil, 2000; Murphy, 1997; Ohanian, 1999; Orfield & Kornhaber, 2001). These teachers and researchers have argued that standardized testing works not from a set of objective standards somehow as constant as the North Star but from a set of cultural conceptions about literacy that are neither objective nor static. Students whose race or social class is not part of the dominant culture often face more complex challenges in meeting the standards of that dominant culture. Much of the impulse behind standardized tests and their illusion of objectivity seems to be a drive to punish, ridicule, and marginalize those who already feel punished, ridiculed, and marginalized by the institutions of education. At the same time the standardized tests from the dominant culture reassure its members about the quality of their educational institutions as well as their children. Using literacy tests to reinforce dominant privileges and exclude others is nothing new; all we have to do is remember the literacy tests used to reject immigrants to the United States or to keep African Americans off U.S. voting rolls in the last century. The standardized testing movement today is just better able to cloak such motives within the rationale of "not leaving children behind."

I do have another concern about these methods of literacy assessment in terms of student identity. Most teachers have stories of bright students who "don't test well." I've seen such students at every level, from middle school to university, and all of them could do innovative, creative, fascinating work on a project or a paper. But for reasons stretching from learning disabilities to personality traits and cognitive ways of processing and communicating information, they could not score well on timed, standardized tests. Nevertheless, there are students who blossom in such test-taking situations—students who understand the rhetorical demands and structures of standardized exams, and whose minds organize and recall certain kinds of information quickly and efficiently.

I see one of each kind of student when I look at my twin adolescent sons, who were born just 15 minutes apart and raised in the same circumstances. One son excels at taking standardized tests of all kinds by understanding the rhetorical structure of the questions and the institutional demands of the exam. The other, though in some ways a more powerful writer and just as strong a student in school, has always found standardized tests rigid and bewildering. If all I knew about them were the results of their annual standardized tests, I would no doubt rejoice in how the school system was succeeding to educate one while worrying over its failure to reach the other. Their wildly divergent test scores tell me nothing about their abilities and nothing about the quality of teaching they receive.

Yet U.S. culture clings to standardized literacy tests as a means of providing meaningful information about students, teachers, and schools because such tests offer the illusion of scientific rigor (as well as those all-important quantifiable numbers) to an endeavor that ultimately can't be measured in a lab and for which numbers are meaningless. This infuriating numbers game allows politicians and media pundits to make facile judgments, and cynical proclamations, about education that they turn into a relentless cycle of testing, criticism, and punishment. From the administrators to the teachers and students, testing drives the curriculum, and the curriculum shapes student identities in terms of literacy practices.

Writing as a Human Endeavor

Standardized testing, to be standardized, must create questions and answers that leave no room for interpretation. Such rigid questions and answers remove the importance of context from literacy practices and allow for no independent meaning making from students. Yet it is in that moment when an individual makes meaning in writing and reading in a specific cultural context that identity and literacy come together. When literacy education becomes more about standardized assessment, it becomes less about writing and reading by individuals who make meaning and have something to say. In the drive to assess and quantify, what is forgotten is why we want students to read and write in the first place. Reading and writing is about communicating with other human beings—about being part of a society and its ongoing conversations. I think most literacy teachers dream that students, once their days of school are over, will be inspired and educated to read and write about what matters to them. That is the kind of literate identity we want for our students.

However, the increasing pressure of standardized testing disconnects literacy education from human concerns. Students face writing prompts and reading tests that have no connection to their lives, communities, or interests. The tests are created and then read by disconnected, uninvested, anonymous readers—and now perhaps even computers. Literacy practices become less about communicating with people and more about communicating with a faceless system or a machine. What students, like administrators and teachers, learn from this system is that only the numbers matter, not the meaning or the communication.

Students and teachers have also learned that, like any system, standardized tests can be "gamed." When work is written only to be assessed rather than to communicate ideas, the activity becomes more about ensuring that certain qualities are present (e.g., the use of examples, the complexity of sentences, transition devices, vocabulary) regardless of the overall effect of the piece of writing. In the United States, one example of such an activity is the brief writing section recently added to the Scholastic Aptitude Test (SAT)—the test taken by thousands of university bound students that is supposed to indicate their abilities to succeed in higher education. Using a 25-minute writing sample to determine a student's ability to write the kind of extended critical prose required in university is like using a person's ability to back a car down a driveway to determine whether the driver can make it through rush-hour traffic. The writing samples on the SAT are apparently scored on such generalizable characteristics of writing as smooth transitions and varied sentences rather than on content or overall effect (Klein, 2005).

So let's say specific examples are highly prized, particularly those that are not about personal experiences. Now, it doesn't matter if the specific examples are made up, as long as they are specific, and so pretty soon we'll find students sprinkling their essays with impressively "specific" examples. What the students will know, and what we as teachers will have to admit, is that writing as a means of communicating ideas does not matter in this situation; it's racking up the right number of smooth transitions and specific examples that does. It is difficult to imagine such a situation creating the conditions to inspire students to think of themselves as writers and readers and to engage in writing with any sense of ownership or passion.

Gaming the Testing Machines

Even more troubling is the recent trend toward evaluating student writing through computer software. No longer is the student writing for any person, even an anonymous person; instead it is writing done to be judged by a series of algorithms that look for quantifiable characteristics such as transitional phrases and complex syntax. But any of these programs can be easily "fooled." Give one an essay that is gibberish but includes the proper characteristics of syntax and vocabulary, and you receive high marks.

In fact, computer assessment software can be gamed by other computer software. Hesse (2005) pointed this out in a recent presentation. First he used the online Essay Generator (www.EssayGenerator.com) to create an essay. If you've never used this website, it is great fun. You enter any word or phrase and are immediately rewarded with an essay on that topic with complete sentences; sections on social, economic, and political factors; and even important-looking citations and a graph. But reading the essay more closely reveals its delightful ridiculousness. For example, I just entered the phrase "standardized testing" and received an essay with the following opening sentences:

The issues involving standardized testing has been a popular topic amongst scholars for many years. In depth analysis of standardized testing can be an enriching experience. Though standardized testing is a favourite topic of discussion amongst monarchs, presidents and dictators, there are just not enough blues songs written about standardized testing.

The essay continues with complex and syntactically correct sentences that make little or no sense at all. Hesse (2005) took his randomly generated essay, full of similar nonsense, and then submitted it to "intelligent" essay assessing software and received a report that praised the high quality of the writing, including the mature command of language and the effective use of examples and transitional devices. I replicated Hesse's experiment with similar results (and it's worth trying yourself if you want to be simultaneously amused and horrified). Perhaps this is the wave of the future: We can have computers write essays to be read and evaluated by other computers and leave students out of the process altogether.

Even so, the important concern in the use of computer assessment, as well as standardized testing, is not whether such systems can be fooled. Those advocating the development of such software maintain that someday computer software may be able to read student essays for content as well as for syntactic characteristics. They may be right. But the sophistication of the software is not the point. The more disturbing question is about what writing becomes when it is produced to be read and evaluated by a computer. What is the point of writing for a computer? Will there be writers who will care as deeply about what a computer thinks about their writing in the way that they care about pleasing a human audience?

Will anyone take writing for a computer seriously? Students may care whether they pass a test, but what will they learn about literacy and identity when there is no human connection to what they write?

I'm a die-hard humanist on this issue. Writing and reading are about touching the mind of another person, whether in a proposal, a poem, or a polemic. When advocates of computer software or standardized testing argue that their systems will be more objective, it is an argument that again strikes me as beside the point. Writing for other human beings—even when they are teachers—is by nature subjective. Everything about writing depends on context, culture, and the occasional unpredictability of human response. Such is the challenge and joy of writing, along with its intermittent frustration. Even as I write this column, thinking I have some sense of my audience and the context of this journal, I know that I cannot predict all the possible responses. I can't think of a writer who doesn't know in her or his bones that writing will always be responded to and judged subjectively. Yet standardized literacy testing and evaluation would have us pretend to students and their parents that such subjective responses can be overcome with scientific methods and better technology, and that such methods can generate a set of numbers that are meaningful about the quality of that writing. And we forget that even standardized test readers and computer software programmers are people with their own biases and preferences. We do these same students a significant disservice by acquiescing to this pretense of objectivity and by not talking to them about how real humans in real contexts read and how best we can try to identify and respond to such real people and situations.

In conversations with students about how real audiences in real situations respond to writing is where meaningful assessment can happen. If I want to know if students are learning to write, I first want to see those students write about subjects that matter to them for an interested audience and reflect on the reasons for their writing choices. Once students get a real response from an audience, I want them to reflect again on that response and what it might teach them about what they wrote and why. I always talk with students about assessment and how their work could be assessed. Then I discuss my choices during assessment and how I evaluate both their writing and their reflections on it. I'm not against assessing writing. I tell students that every piece of writing read by another person is assessed in some way, even if only in the reader's choice to read all the way to the end. I'm just against thinking that we can assess writing through some pseudoscientific, technology-driven, one-size-fits-all, a-contextual test.

Making a Difference with Human Response

Sommers and Saltz (2004), in their longitudinal study of more than 400 university student writers, found that the students who made the most progress in terms of writing shared two characteristics. First, these students, even if they began their university careers as relatively weak writers, were the ones who brought ideas and issues that mattered to them to their choice of courses and their responses to assignments. Equally important for these students was the ability to see writing assignments as something more than just fulfilling a requirement for a grade:

> When students begin to see writing as a transaction, an exchange in which they can "get and give," they begin to see a larger purpose for their writing. They have their first glimmerings of audience; they begin to understand that they are writing for flesh-and-blood human beings, readers who want them to bring their interests into a course, not simply teachers who are poised with red pens ready to evaluate what they don't know. (p. 139)

In addition, Sommers (2005) found that the responses from teachers that resulted in the most substantial improvement in student writers took the work and the ideas of the writers seriously and, along with constructive criticism, provided comments and questions that pointed the students toward what they might improve in future pieces of writing. Writing for a real audience about ideas that engage individual interests and intellects and having that audience provide thoughtful individualized responses not only helps students become better writers, it also helps them create their identities as writers. Such an approach to writing is the antithesis of standardized testing.

Of course, the sad fact is that there are people in and out of education who are not concerned about whether writing with passion for real readers will inspire students and help them develop identities as confident writers. This camp wants to ensure that students attain a functional literacy that makes them productive in the workplace—in clerical and service industry jobs. As I've argued before in this column, the way literacy instruction is conceived and enacted is often connected to issues of social class, and it's the same with standardized tests as well. One benefit of standardized testing as assessment is that it is much cheaper than the kind of individualized assessment I advocated earlier. Affluent students will be taught to "game" the standardized testing system. But these same students will also have abundant opportunities in small classes in elite schools to write for real readers and to read for meaning, pleasure, and enrichment. By contrast, it is working class and poor students, for whom pleasure and the construction of literate identities is deemed unimportant, who will encounter a curriculum driven by the fear of standardized testing. The administrators and teachers of those students, facing large classes, few resources, and the threat of punishments over low scores, will be forced to create a curriculum in which students will be taught to write only for the anonymous readers and machines that evaluate such tests. Certainly that will be cheaper than providing the resources and trust in poorer schools that would allow teachers to face the same class sizes and use the same approaches for teaching writing that affluent schools enjoy. But students from poorer schools will encounter fewer and fewer opportunities to think of themselves as writers communicating their interests and passions for real readers.

What Is to Be Done?

Many teachers, even when facing the pressure of standardized testing, continue to design assignments that fulfill the needs of assessment while providing students with places to do writing and reading that matters. And systems of assessment that are not bound up in concerns about time and technology, such as writing portfolios, can provide responsible assessment that is valuable for students, teachers, and institutions. However, writing portfolios can become as rigid and impersonal as any approach to assessment if the focus of the writing becomes the assessment itself rather than the communication of ideas.

The pressure toward standardized testing is such that more must be done than just designing good pedagogy around the margins of a test-driven curriculum. It is time for individual teachers at every level to take back the debate about assessment from the people who say the only valid evaluation of writing is timed, standardized, and faceless. It is time to take back the debate that maintains that only assessment that results in quantifiable numbers is valid. Engaging in this debate does not happen on a grand stage, it happens as a persistent, continuing conversation with the people in our communities. It is the responsibility of teachers to keep explaining to students, parents, administrators, neighbors, and newspaper editors that writing and reading that matters for real audiences is what creates literate citizens. It is the responsibility of teachers to explain how such writing can be assessed, that such instruction can be responsible and accountable, but that assessment and instruction happen differently in literacy education than in other fields. Finally, it is the responsibility of teachers not only to keep talking about what the best practices and outcomes for student literacy education should be but also to publicize our successes.

Reading and writing matter, and we teachers care deeply about them. If we want students to think of themselves as readers and writers, then those activities have to matter to students beyond learning how to game the test to avoid being punished. It is time we reclaimed the idea that having standards does not necessarily mean accepting or aspiring to standardization.

References

Hesse, D. (2005, March). *Who owns writing?* Keynote address at the Conference on College Composition and Communication, San Francisco, CA.

Klein, K. (2005, April 3). How I gamed the SAT. *The Los Angeles Times*, p. A20.

McNeil, L. (2000). *Contradictions of reform: Educational costs of standardized testing.* London: Routledge.

Murphy, S. (1997). Literacy assessment and the politics of identities. *Reading and Writing Quarterly*, 13, 261–278.

No Child Left Behind Act of 2001, Pub. L. No. 107–110, 115 Stat. 1425 (2002).

Ohanian, S. (1999). *One size fits few: The folly of educational standards.* Portsmouth, NH: Heinemann.

Orfield, G., & Kornhaber, M.L. (2001). *Raising standards or raising barriers? Inequality and high-stakes testing in public education.* New York: Century Foundation Press.

Sommers, N. (2005, March). *Across the drafts: Responding to writing, a longitudinal perspective*. Paper presented at the Conference on College Composition and Communication, San Francisco, CA.

Sommers, N., & Saltz, L. (2004). The novice as expert: Writing the freshman year. *College Composition and Communication*, 56, 124–149.

The department editor welcomes reader comments on this column. E-mail bronwyn.williams@Louisville.edu. Mail Bronwyn T. Williams, University of Louisville, Department of English, Humanities Building, Louisville, KY 40292, USA.

Observer: A Little Ethics Left Behind

It's easy to boost school test scores—if you don't care how you do it.

ALAN GREENBLATT

Whatever else the No Child Left Behind Act may accomplish, it is providing states with practice in civil disobedience. State policy makers have been busy all year passing regulations or preparing lawsuits to protest the strictures of the federal education testing law. Now, in many areas, they are questioning the results themselves.

Because promotions and other professional goodies are based on test outcomes, some principals and teachers are doing their utmost to guide students toward the right answers. "It's human nature that the more the pressure is increased, the more incentive there is to cheat," says Robert Embry, former president of the Maryland State Board of Education.

Teachers, in scattered but well-documented cases, have been found leading their students through practice exercises drawn from the supposedly secret tests. Others, rather than silently proctoring, coach frustrated students toward a correct answer. Some districts clean up answer sheets, erasing stray marks that can be read by machines as incorrect responses—and are sometimes a little too vigorous in their cleaning and correcting.

Several states are taking steps to address these problems, among them Texas, which has seen all of them, including some serious violations in the very district that provided the model for the federal law. Some states have increased training and bolstered security, sometimes sending independent monitors to schools on testing day. Others are creating separate assessment departments that can follow up on complaints about organized cheating.

Ironically, the stated purpose of No Child Left Behind—boosting test scores—has become a red flag. The more precipitous a district's gains, the more suspicious it may look. States are investing in software that will alert investigators when scores suddenly shoot up. There's no point, after all, in celebrating improvements that turn out to be frauds.

So far, it's all been rather ad hoc, and no one has come up with the perfect solution. John Fremer, a consultant who runs testing audits for states, predicts that security will become a central part of test design, which it hasn't been up until now. But the mere fact that states are taking the problem seriously is a preventive measure in and of itself. "The fact that people know they could be audited," says Gregory Cizek, an education professor at the University of North Carolina, "dissuades a lot of them."

Lost Art

The fine print in NCLB is worth reading.

Cheating may be the most worrisome issue that's come up under No Child Left Behind, but others keep appearing. States and school districts report that the rush to boost test scores in reading and math is crowding out other subjects. Perhaps the one that's been hurt the most is arts education. The NCLB law itself describes art as part of the "core curriculum," but that isn't how it's turning out.

One governor, Mike Huckabee of Arkansas, wants the language on arts education treated seriously. His campaign to make that happen has been a pleasant surprise to some who don't normally think of the Razorback State as an aesthetic oasis. "Huckabee planting the flag on arts education is hugely important," says Frederick Hess, education doyen at the American Enterprise Institute.

Beginning this September, Arkansas will require all public schools to provide instruction in art and music to every student. Huckabee fought off legislative attempts to water down the requirement, notably the minimum amount of time to be spent on arts each week and the mandate that every school hire at least one certified arts instructor.

A Baptist minister who has played the guitar since he was 11, Huckabee offers familiar arguments about how art and music help kids develop cognitive skills and boost scores in the basic subjects that are the main focus of school testing. But he makes other points as well. Active participation in the arts, he says, teaches the "great life lesson that successful people spend hours and hours preparing for the brief moments when they're in the spotlight."

Huckabee's state isn't entirely alone in its campaign for arts education. South Carolina and Virginia require it, and Denver voters approved a property tax increase last fall to pay for it. Right now, however, they are more the exception than the rule. The arts have long been a poor cousin when it comes to public funding, and amid the pressures of NCLB, school systems aren't tripping over each other in the race to change that. "It's a tough time for anybody to champion the arts," says Larry Peeno of the National Art Education Association.

Keeping Score

Why Standards and Accountability—Done Right— Are Good for Schools, Teachers, and Kids

JOHN COLE

Back in the 1980's, when Texas education reform got underway, I was often asked: "Why is the teachers union supporting the new school reform law?" The 1984 law required a lot of new accountability for teachers and students, including district report cards that contained information on student test scores and a high school exit exam. I'd be asked, "Isn't it a lot easier for you all when people aren't breathing down your neck about test scores?"

A lot of teachers were also dubious of the law. They worried that it would force them into a teaching straitjacket and that it might mean that a lot of decent kids would fail classes and might not even get a high school diploma. But I have always argued that standards and accountability, combined with the support that teachers and kids would need to reach the standards, are good for public schools, teachers, and kids—especially poor kids.

Why do I think this? Let me start with two anecdotes. First: I am an avid Dallas Cowboys fan. Back in 1993, my favorite running back, Emmitt Smith, was requesting something like $13 million for a four-year contract with the Cowboys. I immediately wrote to the Cowboys and offered to serve as their running back for much less—perhaps one-tenth of that amount, even a hundredth of that amount. Amazingly, the Cowboys never responded to my generous offer. I asked myself, "Why—why do they want to pay this guy $13 million when they could get me for just $100,000?" The answer, I think, has to do with keeping score. If you don't keep score, the quality of your players really doesn't matter. In Texas football, we keep score. The Cowboys keep score. And they care about scoring well. That's obviously why they're willing to pay Emmitt Smith all that money even though they could have me practically for free.

Here's the second anecdote: To pay for college, I sold insurance for a while. In my office there were about four guys and a manager. Three of us were young kids like myself and one was this older gent who had been selling insurance forever. This guy *never* came to the office. He missed *every* staff meeting. His accounts often didn't balance, which would have been bad news for the rest of us, but not for him. If his account was $10 over, he took $10 out. If it was $10 short, he pitched $10 in. The manager treated him like he was some sort of deity. The rest of us were treated more or less in accordance with our just desserts. Why was this? Because in the insurance business there's a way of keeping score. That manager's salary was determined by the amount of insurance sold out of our office. That older gent sold more than the rest of us put together—probably twice as much. So, the manager didn't care about whether he came to staff meetings or even behaved rudely (which he often did). What the manager knew was that this was the guy who produced good paychecks. Whatever would keep that guy selling was important to the manager, the rest was trivial.

I am a product of several decades of Texas education. I actually went through the schools here and then began teaching. And I can tell you, during all that time, no one was keeping score—or, to be more precise, no one was keeping score about matters like student achievement. And, when a school system doesn't keep score on student learning, there's not a lot of pressure for learning to improve. That means there's not a lot of pressure to pay the kinds of salaries that would attract qualified teachers. It means there's not a lot of pressure to make sure poor schools have books that aren't torn and old as dirt. It means martinet principals can focus on trivial matters like locker records instead of results.

Let's start with my initial years as a teacher in Corpus Christi. Schools in Corpus Christi weren't desegregated until 1976. So when I started teaching in the late 1960s, we had three sets of schools—one for whites, one for blacks, and one for Hispanics. I taught in the Hispanic junior high school. We were blessed, I suppose, in that we got the textbooks right after the white junior high school was finished with them—when we finished with them, we sent them over to the black junior high school.

The school had a lot of dedicated teachers, but as an institution, the public school system didn't really care too much about what went on in the school that I taught in—or in the other schools that Hispanic and African-American kids attended. For example, there were no standards for coursework. We had valedictorians from some of these schools who couldn't get into college because they hadn't taken the right courses. There were many places where kids took the same remedial math course four years in a row under a different name. They never got to algebra, never got beyond arithmetic. When I started teaching, I was told that four percent of the kids at my junior high went on to graduate from the Hispanic high school in Corpus Christi; the other 96 percent dropped out along the way. As far as I could tell, not one person cared if I ever taught a lick.

Here's how my school worked: One of the teachers was absolutely beloved by the principal. He was a coach who was assigned to teach English. He got every 16mm film that he could order and he showed one every day until the last couple of weeks of school when the film library was closed. Then, to wrap up the school year, he bought a bunch of coloring books. The grades in his class were based primarily upon attendance and comportment.

But this teacher never got into trouble for his behavior. (In fact, later on he became an administrator!) Again, I asked myself why? But the answer was easy. What, after all, was important to this principal? Certainly not learning. Above all else, what was important to him was that nobody showed up at his office door. He didn't want to see angry parents or kids complaining.

In this principal's mind, I was a terrible teacher. I complained that we had no program for the kids who didn't speak English. I complained that we were short of textbooks and that the ones I had were missing pages. I complained that we needed to get some eyeglasses for the kids whose parents were too poor to buy them. I was a source of problems and disruption; I caused grief for that principal.

The coach-turned-teacher, on the other hand, was a model that everyone was supposed to look to and admire. Why was that? Well, nobody kept score of the students' learning. The school system did keep score of some other things, though. If a teacher's textbook records showed up in disarray, that was a problem. If a teacher's locker records were in disarray, that was big trouble. But during the entire time that I taught, I never once had anybody ask me about the students' learning.

I n the late 1980s, several years after I became president of the Texas Federation of Teachers, I served for two years on an official state committee charged with recommending what indicators of performance should be included on school report cards. Our hope was that they would include information on test scores, dropout rates, and other factors. Part of my job was to hold public hearings in different parts of the state. The only people who came were school board members and superintendents, by and large. And at each hearing it was the same. I could have written the script. I would go through my presentation and have my charts. And they'd have one question: "Are we going to publish this information?" Well, yes. I'd tell them that the idea was to make this report card available to parents and the public. After a moment of general consternation, there would be an observation: "Wait a minute, if we do this, nobody is going to want his kid to go to this school over here." And then somebody else would say, "Oh, and what about that school over there? Everybody will want to be in that school."

"Wait a minute," I'd say. "Are you telling me there's a school in your district right now that doesn't teach kids, you know of it, and you're not telling anybody—you're just letting it sit there?" These school board members and superintendents knew good and well where education was happening and where it wasn't, but clearly they didn't want the public to know. Pressure would build to improve those schools. They'd actually have to find resources for those schools, offer salaries that would attract qualified teachers, and get them textbooks that weren't ripped up and old. They'd have to make sure kids were learning something before they were promoted or given a high school diploma. It was a lot easier for them to just pretend there was no problem. It was a conspiracy of silence. And, there was no way to blow the whistle on it because there was no objective way to compare student achievement across schools and districts.

> **These school board members and superintendents knew good and well where education was happening and where it wasn't, but clearly they didn't want the public to know. Pressure would build to improve those schools.**

Standards and Accountability Blow the Whistle

In Texas, we started keeping score when the school reform law passed in 1984—long before George Bush was governor, I should point out. And, because we started keeping score, that marked the beginning of the end of the conspiracy of silence. Yearly testing in reading, writing, and math in grades 1, 3, 5, 7, 9 and 11 began right away; and the 11th-grade test became a requirement for graduation in 1987. Not surprisingly, many districts resisted the idea of a state exam; they each wanted to decide on their own test, their own passing score. Districts had long played a game in which they would give their own test, and if scores were good, they'd use them to say how great their schools were; they ignored the scores if they were low. We ended that game once there was a single state test.[1]

Keeping score has made a world of difference—it has ended that conspiracy of silence, or at least made it a much harder game to play. There is absolutely no question that we've ratcheted up the quality of education in Texas dramatically. The test we gave 6th-graders this year was harder than the one we gave 11th-graders back in 1987. And despite dire predictions to the contrary, while we've raised the difficulty of our standards and curriculum pretty steadily since then, the drop-out rate has remained pretty constant (pretty constantly awful, I should say). But we have roughly the same percentage of kids in school, and they're passing tougher tests at higher rates. We haven't shut down the achievement gap between white and other children, but it's diminished.

Now, is that all we did—put tests and accountability into place? Absolutely not. Tests don't teach and tests don't produce miracles. We put the test in place, we put the standards in place, but we also put tons of new money in place. The standards and accountability have to be there, otherwise the districts get money, and who knows where it goes? It often winds up paying for wonderful lessons on self-esteem (or worse), but not the things that effect academic achievement.

Now, is that all we did—put tests and accountability into place? Absolutely not. Tests don't teach and tests don't produce miracles. We put the test in place, we put the standards in place, but we also put tons of new money in place.

But you can't expect to raise standards and get better teaching unless you commit the resources to pay for the good salaries that will lure qualified teachers into the classroom; to pay for the professional development that teachers need to teach better; to get extra help to the kids who really need it and the schools that really need it. When we passed the 1984 reform, we added 13 percent to our state aid per pupil. And that wasn't the end of it. We kept pumping in new money so that between 1984 and 2000, state aid per pupil increased by 24 percent (in constant dollars). And we didn't just add new money—we redirected the state's resources so that low-wealth school districts and school districts with high concentrations of disadvantaged children received the bulk of it. It was a revolution. We also created a minimum standard for teachers; it was suddenly much harder for administrators to hire unqualified people and call them teachers. Starting in 1986, all teachers had to take a basic reading and writing test; if they couldn't pass it, they lost their teaching certificate. But we also increased salaries, spectacularly so in the poorest districts, so that when new teachers were hired, we were able to attract teachers who met the higher standard.

In 1999 Texas enacted legislation, which the Texas Federation of Teachers initiated, that made passing the third-grade reading test a requirement for promotion to fourth grade. The requirement kicked in as of 2003 because that's when the 1999-2000 crop of kindergartners reached third grade. But that legislation didn't just create a barrier to promotion for those kids, it provided resources to pull together the key ingredients for success, including professional development for their teachers, diagnostic assessments, and immediate interventions. Beginning in 1999 with kindergarten teachers, and adding a grade each year, Texas provided paid professional development opportunities to virtually all the state's K-3 teachers. By 2001, nearly 60,000 teachers had already received the training. The student failure rate on this third-grade reading test prior to 2003 (the year it became a requirement for promotion) was about 20 percent. With professional development, early assessment, interventions, and accountability, we cut that failure down to about four percent in 2003.[2]

T ests don't teach; accountability on its own doesn't make teachers teach better. Shutting down schools when you have no better strategy for making them work the second time around does no one any good. But accountability makes people keep score. It helps stop the conspiracy of silence. And that helps get the resources flowing to schools—and it helps to make sure the resources are used well. It helps people see that giving out high school diplomas doesn't mean you've educated the kids. And, as with running backs, it helps people see that just calling someone a teacher doesn't make it so.

Clearly there's still much to do to increase achievement in Texas. From the 1980s to today, one of the main questions has been how to increase the level of difficulty on the student tests and provide the support that teachers need to make sure that students can pass. We still do not have the grade level or graduation tests where we want them to be. Salaries are higher, but still not where they should be. And, after years of support, this year the Texas legislature seems bent on grossly underfunding education. But we've come a long way in the last 21 years, and it would not have occurred without standards, professional development, additional resources, and the accountability that comes from the test.

Notes

1. Based on my experiences in Texas, I believe that No Child Left Behind (the federal legislation mandating school improvement) gave away the farm by allowing all states to have their own standards and tests. Without a common standard and a common test, there's a strong incentive for individual states to lower their passing bars thus making it look like their students are highly proficient.

2. This year we ratcheted up the standards again, so the passing rate on the first administration was 89 percent. I expect the final passing rate will be higher, but not as high as it has been for the past two years. In the past, whenever we ratcheted up standards, more money flowed to school districts to help them meet those standards. But this year the governor and legislature have cut money from education. So far, they have eliminated our master reading and math teachers, as well as our remedial programs.

JOHN COLE is president of the Texas Federation of Teachers and a vice president of the AFT. Previously, he was a teacher in Corpus Christi, Texas, and the founding member and president of the Corpus Christi Federation of Teachers.

UNIT 4
Values, Society, and Education

Unit Selections

Key Points to Consider

- What is character education? Why do so many people wish to see a form of character education in schools?

- Are there certain values about which most of us can agree? Should they be taught in schools? Why, or why not?

- What can teachers do to help students become caring, morally responsible persons?

- Do you agree with Aristotle that virtue can and should be taught in schools? Explain.

Student Website
www.mhcls.com/online

Internet References
Further information regarding these websites may be found in this book's preface or online.

Association for Moral Education
http://www.amenetwork.org/

Child Welfare League of America
http://www.cwla.org

Ethics Updates/Lawrence Hinman
http://ethics.acusd.edu

The National Academy for Child Development
http://www.nacd.org

All of us are situated as persons in social, political, and economic "locations" from which we develop our values. Our values usually derive from principles of conduct that we learn in each of our histories of interacting with ourselves (as they form) in interaction with others. This is to say that societal values develop in a cultural context. All of our values derive from the social process through which we become whatever we become. In democratic societies, such as the United States, alternative sets of values and morals co-exist. We are focusing in this unit on character education, citizenship education, the concept of patriotism, and the idea of "altruism" (selfless or self-sacrificial behavior), and the idea of "perseverance" in society. This editor recommends that the articles on patriotism be discussed together so that students can see any similarities or differences in the points of view taken by the authors of these essays.

Moral issues are ones where a person must decide the question: What should or ought I do? This is especially true when one's answer to this question will affect the well-being of one's self or others.

Morality has always been a concern of educators. There has possibly not been a more appropriate time to focus attention on ethics, on standards of principled conduct, in our schools. The many changes in American family structures in past years make this an important public concern, especially in the United States. We are told that all nations share concern for their cherished values. In addition to discerning how best to deal with moral and ethical educational issues, there are also substantive values controversies regarding curriculum content, such as the dialogue over how to infuse multicultural values into school curricula. On the one hand, educators need to help students learn how to reason and how to determine what principles should guide them in making decisions in situations where their own well-being and/or the well-being of another is at stake. On the other hand, educators need to develop reasoned and fair standards for resolving the substantive values issues to be faced in dealing with questions about what should or should not be taught.

Students need to develop a sense of genuine caring both for themselves and others. They need to learn alternatives to violence and human exploitation. Teachers need to be examples of responsible and caring persons who use reason and compassion in solving problems in school.

Some teachers voice their concerns that students need to develop a stronger sense of character that is rooted in a more defensible system of values. Other teachers express concerns that they cannot do everything and are hesitant to instruct on morality and values. Most believe that they must do something to help students become reasoning and ethical decision makers.

What teachers perceive to be worthwhile and defensible behavior informs our reflections on what we as educators should teach. We are conscious immediately of some of the values that affect our behavior, but we may not be as aware of what informs our preferences. Values that we hold without being conscious of

them are referred to as tacit values—values derived indirectly after reasoned reflection on our thoughts about teaching and learning. Much of our knowledge about teaching is tacit knowledge, which we need to bring into conscious cognition by analyzing the concepts that drive our practice. We need to acknowledge how all our values inform, and influence, our thoughts about teaching.

Teachers need to help students develop within themselves a sense of critical social consciousness and a genuine concern for social justice. Insight into the nature of moral decision making should be taught in the context of real current and past social problems and should lead students to develop their own skills in social analysis relating to the ethical dilemmas of human beings.

There is a need for teachers to develop principles of professional practice that will enable them to respond reasonably to the many ethical dilemmas that they now face. Knowledge of how teachers derive their sense of professional ethics is developing; further study of how teachers' values shape their professional practice is very important. Schooling should not only transmit national and cultural heritages, including our intellectual heritage; it should also be a fundamentally moral enterprise in which students learn how to develop tenable moral standards in the contexts of their own world visions.

One of the most compelling responsibilities of schools is that of preparing young people for their moral duties as free citizens of free nations. Governments have always wanted schools to teach the principles of civic morality based on their respective constitutional traditions. Indeed when the public school movement began in the 1830s and 1840s, the concept of universal public schooling as a mechanism for instilling a sense of national identity and civic morality was supported. In every nation, school curricula have certain value preferences embedded in them.

For whom do the schools exist? Is a teacher's primary responsibility to his or her client, the student, or to the student's parents? Do secondary school students have the right to study and to inquire into subjects not in officially sanctioned curricula? What are the moral issues surrounding censorship of student reading material? What ethical questions are raised by arbitrarily withholding information regarding alternative viewpoints on controversial topics?

Teachers cannot hide all of their moral preferences. They can, however, learn to conduct just and open discussions of moral topics without succumbing to the temptation to indoctrinate students with their own views.

Teaching students to respect all people, to revere the sanctity of life, to uphold the right of every citizen to dissent, to believe in the equality of all people before the law, to cherish freedom to learn, and to respect the right of all people to their own convictions—these are principles of democracy and ideals worthy of being cherished. An understanding of the processes of ethical decision making is needed by the citizens of any free nation; thus, this process should be taught in a free nation's schools.

Character and Academics: What Good Schools Do

Though there has been increasing interest in character education among policy makers and education professionals, many schools hesitate to do anything that might detract from their focus on increasing academic performance. The authors present evidence indicating that this may be misguided.

Jacques S. Benninga, Marvin W. Berkowitz, Phyllis Kuehn, and Karen Smith

The growth of character education programs in the United States has coincided with the rise in high-stakes testing of student achievement. The No Child Left Behind Act asks schools to contribute not only to students' academic performance but also to their character. Both the federal government and the National Education Association (NEA) agree that schools have this dual responsibility. In a statement introducing a new U.S. Department of Education character education website, then Secretary of Education Rod Paige outlined the need for such programs:

> Sadly, we live in a culture without role models, where millions of students are taught the wrong values—or no values at all. This culture of callousness has led to a staggering achievement gap, poor health status, overweight students, crime, violence, teenage pregnancy, and tobacco and alcohol abuse.... Good character is the product of good judgments made every day.[1]

And Bob Chase, the former president of the NEA, issued his own forceful call to action:

> We must make an explicit commitment to formal character education. We must integrate character education into the fabric of the curriculum and into extracurricular activities. We must train teachers in character education—both preservice and inservice. And we must consciously set about creating a moral climate within our schools.[2]

Despite the clear national interest in character education, many schools are leery of engaging in supplementary initiatives that, although worthy, might detract from what they see as their primary focus: increasing academic achievement. Moreover, many schools lack the resources to create new curricular initiatives. Yet the enhancement of student character is a bipartisan mandate that derives from the very core of public education.

The purpose of public schooling requires that schools seek to improve both academic and character education.

If it could be demonstrated that implementing character education programs is compatible with efforts to improve school achievement, then perhaps more schools would accept the challenge of doing both. But until now there has been little solid evidence of such successful coexistence.

Definitions and Research

Character education is the responsibility of adults. While the term *character education* has historically referred to the duty of the older generation to form the character of the young through experiences affecting their attitudes, knowledge, and behaviors, more recent definitions include such developmental outcomes as a positive perception of school, emotional literacy, and social justice activism.[3]

There are sweeping definitions of character education (e.g., Character Counts' six pillars, Community of Caring's five values, or the Character Education Partnership's 11 principles) and more narrow ones. Character education can be defined in terms of relationship virtues (e.g., respect, fairness, civility, tolerance), self-oriented virtues (e.g., fortitude, self-discipline, effort, perseverance) or a combination of the two. The state of California has incorporated character education criteria into the application process for its statewide distinguished school recognition program and, in the process, has created its own definition of character education. Each definition directs the practice of character education somewhat differently, so that programs calling themselves "character education" vary in purpose and scope.

There is some research evidence that character education programs enhance academic achievement. For example, an evaluation of the Peaceful Schools Project and research on the Responsive Classroom found that students in schools that implemented these programs had greater gains on standardized test scores than did students in comparison schools.[4] The Child Development Project (CDP) conducted follow-up studies of middle school students (through eighth grade) who had attended CDP elementary schools and found that they had higher course grades and higher achievement test scores than comparison middle school students.[5] Longitudinal studies have reported similar effects for middle school and high school students who had participated as elementary school students in the Seattle Social Development Project.[6]

A growing body of research supports the notion that high-quality character education can promote academic achievement. For example, Marvin Berkowitz and Melinda Bier have identified character education programs for elementary, middle, and high school students that enhance academic achievement.[7] These findings, however, are based on prepackaged curricular programs, and most schools do not rely on such programs. Instead, they create their own customized character education initiatives. It remains to be seen whether such initiatives also lead to academic gains.

Toward an Operational Definition of Character Education

We decided to see if we could determine a relationship between character education and academic achievement across a range of elementary schools. For our sample we used the elementary schools that applied in 2000 to the California Department of Education for recognition as distinguished elementary schools, California's highest level of school attainment. Eligibility to submit an application for the California School Recognition Program (CSRP) in 2000 was based on the previous year's academic performance index (API) results.

However, 1999 was the first year for California's Public School Accountability Act (PSAA), which created the API. Thus, while the state department stated that growth on the API was the central focus of the PSAA, schools applying for the CSRP in 1999-2000 did not receive their 1999 API scores until January 2000, after they had already written and submitted their award applications. Approximately 12.7% of California elementary schools (681 of 5,368 schools) submitted a full application for the award in 2000. The average API of these schools was higher than the average for the schools that did not apply, but both were below the state expectancy score of 800. The mean API for applicant schools was 751; for non-applicant schools, 612. The API range for applicant schools was 365–957; for non-applicant schools, 302–958. Hence the sample for this study is not representative of all California elementary schools. It is a sample of more academically successful schools, but it does represent a broad range of achievement from quite low to very high.

Specific wording related to character education was included for the first time in the CSRP application in 2000. Schools were asked to describe what they were doing to meet a set of nine standards. Of these, the one that most clearly pertained to character education was Standard 1 (Vision and Standards). For this standard, schools were required to include "specific examples and other evidence" of "expectations that promote positive character traits in students."[8] Other standards could also be seen as related to character education. For these, schools were asked to document activities and programs that ensured opportunities for students to contribute to the school, to others, and to the community.

We chose for our study a stratified random sample of 120 elementary schools that submitted applications. These 120 schools were not significantly different from the other 561 applicant schools on a variety of academic and demographic indicators. For the schools in our sample, we correlated the extent of their character education implementation with their API and SAT-9 scores—the academic scale and test used by California at that time.[9]

The first problem we needed to grapple with was how to define a character education program. We spent considerable time discussing an operational definition to use for this project. After conferring with experts, we chose our final set of character education criteria, drawn from both the standards used by the California Department of Education and the *Character Education Quality Standards* developed by the Character Education Partnership.[10] Six criteria emerged from this process:

- This school promotes core ethical values as the basis of good character.
- In this school, parents and other community members are active participants in the character education initiative.
- In this school, character education entails intentional promotion of core values in all phases of school life.
- Staff members share responsibility for and attempt to model character education.
- This school fosters an overall caring community.
- This school provides opportunities for most students to practice moral action.

Each of the six criteria addresses one important component of character education. We created a rubric encompassing these six criteria and listing indicators for each, along with a scoring scale.

Character Education and Academic Achievement

Our study of these high-performing California schools added further evidence of a relationship between academic achievement and the implementation of specific character education programs. In our sample, elementary schools with solid character education programs showed positive relationships between the extent of character education implementation and academic achievement not only in a single year but also across the next two academic years. Over a multi-year period from 1999 to 2002, higher rankings on the API and higher scores on the SAT-9 were significantly and positively correlated with four of our character education indicators: a school's ability to ensure a clean and safe physical environment; evidence that a school's parents and teachers modeled and promoted good character; high-quality opportunities at the school for students to contribute in meaningful ways to he school and its community; and promoting a caring community and positive social relationships.

These are promising results, particularly because the *total character education score* for the year of the school's application was significantly correlated with every language and mathematics achievement score on the SAT-9 for a period of three years. In two of those years, the same was true for reading achievement scores. In other words, good-quality character education was positively associated with academic achievement, both across academic domains and over time.

What Good Schools Do

From our research we derived principles—the four indicators mentioned above—that are common across schools with both thoughtful character education programs and high levels of academic achievement.

- *Good schools ensure a clean and secure physical environment.* Although all schools in our sample fit this description, the higher-scoring character education schools expressed great pride in keeping their buildings and grounds in good shape. This is consistent with what is reported about the virtues of clean and safe learning environments. For example, the Center for Prevention of School Violence notes that "the physical appearance of a school and its campus communicates a lot about the school and its people. Paying attention to appearance so that the facilities are inviting can create a sense of security."[11]

- One school in our sample reported that its buildings "are maintained well above district standards.... The custodial crew prides themselves in achieving a monthly cleaning score that has exceeded standards in 9 out of 12 months." And another noted, "A daily grounds check is performed to ensure continual safety and cleanliness." Each of the higher-scoring schools in our sample explicitly noted its success in keeping its campus in top shape and mentioned that parents were satisfied that their children were attending school in a physically and psychologically safe environment.

- All schools in California are required to have on file a written Safe School Plan, but the emphases in these plans vary. While some schools limited their safety plans to regulations controlling access to the building and defined procedures for violations and intrusions, the schools with better character education programs defined "safety" more broadly and deeply. For example, one school scoring high on our character education rubric explained that the mission of its Safe School Plan was "to provide all students with educational and personal opportunities in a positive and nurturing environment which will enable them to achieve current and future goals, and for all students to be accepted at their own social, emotional, and academic level of development." Another high-scoring school addressed three concerns in its Safe School Plan: identification of visitors on campus, cultural/ethnic harmony, and safe ingress and egress from school. To support these areas of focus, this school's teachers were all trained to conduct classroom meetings, to implement the Community of Caring core values, and to handle issues related to cultural diversity and communication.

- *Good schools promote and model fairness, equity, caring, and respect.* In schools with good character education programs and high academic achievement, adults model and promote the values and attitudes they wish the students to embrace, and they infuse character education throughout the school and across the curriculum. Rick Weissbourd drove home this point in a recent essay: "The moral development of students does not depend primarily on explicit character education efforts but on the maturity and ethical capacities of the adults with whom they interact.... Educators influence students' moral development not simply by being good role models— important as that is—but also by what they bring to their relationships with students day to day."[12] The staff of excellent character education schools in our sample tended to see themselves as involved, concerned professional educators, and others see them that way as well.

- Thus one school described its teachers as "pivotal in the [curriculum] development process; there is a high level of [teacher] ownership in the curriculum.... Fifty percent of our staff currently serves on district curriculum committees." Another school stated that it "fosters the belief that it takes an entire community pulling together to provide the best education for every child; that is best accomplished through communication, trust, and collaboration on ideas that reflect the needs of our school and the community.... Teachers are continually empowered and given opportunities to voice their convictions and shape the outcome of what the school represents." A third school described its teachers as "continually encouraged" to grow professionally and to use best practices based on research. In the best character education schools, teachers are recognized by their peers, by district personnel, and by professional organizations for their instructional prowess and their professionalism. They model the academic and prosocial characteristics that show their deep concern for the well-being of children.

- *In good schools students contribute in meaningful ways.* We found that academically excellent character education schools provided opportunities for students to contribute to their school and their community. These schools encouraged students to participate in volunteer activities, such as cross-age tutoring, recycling, fundraising for charities, community clean-up programs, food drives, visitations to local senior centers, and so on.

- One elementary school required 20 hours of community service, a program coordinated entirely by parent volunteers. Students in that school volunteered in community gardens and at convalescent hospitals, and they took part in community clean-up days. Such activities, while not directly connected to students' academic programs, were viewed as mechanisms to promote the development of healthy moral character.

According to William Damon, a crucial component of moral education is engaging children in positive activities—community service, sports, music, theater, or anything else that inspires them and gives them a sense of purpose.[13]

- *Good schools promote a caring community and positive social relationships.* One school in our sample that exemplified this principle was a school of choice in its community. The district had opened enrollment to students outside district boundaries, and this school not only provided an excellent academic program for its multilingual student population but also worked hard to include parents and community members in significant ways. Its Family Math Night attracted 250 family members, and its Family Literacy Night educated parents about read-aloud methods. Parents, grandparents, and friends were recruited to become classroom volunteers and donated thousands of hours.

- This particular school also rented its classrooms to an after-school Chinese educational program. The two sets of teachers have become professional colleagues, and insights from such cultural interaction have led both groups to a better understanding of the Chinese and American systems of education. One result has been that more English-speaking students are enrolling in the Chinese after-school program. And teachers in both programs now engage in dialogue about the specific needs of children. One parent wrote a letter to the principal that said in part, "It seems you are anxious to build up our young generation more healthy and successful.... I am so proud you are not only our children's principal, but also parents' principal."

- Other schools with strong social relationship programs provide meaningful opportunities for parent involvement and establish significant partnerships with local businesses. They encourage parents and teachers to work alongside students in service projects, to incorporate diverse communities into the school curriculum, and to partner with high school students who serve as physical education and academic mentors. As one such school put it, all stakeholders "must play an important and active role in the education of the child to ensure the future success of that child."

Conclusion

It is clear that well-conceived programs of character education can and should exist side by side with strong academic programs. It is no surprise that students need physically secure and psychologically safe schools, staffed by teachers who model professionalism and caring behaviors and who ask students to demonstrate caring for others. That students who attend such schools achieve academically makes intuitive sense as well. It is in schools with this dual emphasis that adults understand their role in preparing students for future citizenship in a democratic and diverse society. The behaviors and attitudes they model communicate important messages to the young people in their charge. Future research on the relationship between character education and academic achievement should include a greater representation of schools in the average and below-average achievement categories. In particular, a study of the extent of the implementation of character education in schools that may have test scores at the low end of the spectrum—but are nevertheless performing higher than their socioeconomic characteristics would predict—would be an important contribution to our understanding of the relationship between character education and academic achievement.

While this was our initial attempt to explore the relationship between these two important school purposes, we learned a good deal about what makes up a good character education curriculum in academically strong schools. We know that such a curriculum in such schools is positively related to academic outcomes over time and across content areas. We also know that, to be effective, character education requires adults to act like adults in an environment where children are respected and feel physically and psychologically safe to engage in the academic and social activities that prepare them best for later adult decision making.

At a time when resources are scarce, we see schools cutting programs and narrowing curricula to concentrate on skills measured by standardized tests. Our research suggests that school goals and activities that are associated with good character education programs are also associated with academic achievement. Thus our results argue for maintaining a rich curriculum with support for all aspects of student development and growth.

Notes

1. U.S. Department of Education, "ED Launches Character Education Web Site," **www.thechallenge.org/15-v12no4/v12n4-communitiesandschools.htm**.

2. Bob Chase, quoted in "Is Character Education the Answer?," *Education World*, 1999, **www.education-world.com/a_admin/admin097.shtml**.

3. Marvin W. Berkowitz, "The Science of Character Education," in William Damon, ed., *Bringing in a New Era in Character Education* (Stanford, Calif.: Hoover Institution Press, 2002), pp. 43–63.

4. Stuart W. Twemlow et al., "Creating a Peaceful School Learning Environment: A Controlled Study of an Elementary School Intervention to Reduce Violence," *American Journal of Psychiatry*, vol. 158, 2001, pp. 808–10; and Stephen N. Elliott, "Does a Classroom Promoting Social Skills Development Enable Higher Academic Functioning Among Its Students Over Time?," Northeast Foundation for Children, Greenfield, Mass., 1998.

5. Victor Battistich and Sehee Hong, "Enduring Effects of the Child Development Project: Second-Order Latent Linear Growth Modeling of Students' 'Connectedness' to School, Academic Performance, and Social Adjustment During Middle School," unpublished manuscript, Developmental Studies Center, Oakland, Calif., 2003.

6. J. David Hawkins et al., "Long-Term Effects of the Seattle Social Development Intervention on School Bonding Trajectories," *Applied Developmental Science*, vol. 5, 2001, pp. 225–36.

7. Marvin W. Berkowitz and Melinda C. Bier, *What Works in Character Education?* (Washington, D.C.: Character Education Partnership, 2005).

8. "California School Recognition Program, 2000 Elementary Schools Program, Elementary School Rubric," California Department of Education, 2001. (Data are available from Jacques Benninga.)

9. For more detail on the design of the study, see Jacques S. Benninga, Marvin W. Berkowitz, Phyllis Kuehn, and Karen Smith, "The Relationship of Character Education Implementation and Academic Achievement in Elementary Schools," *Journal of Research in Character Education*, vol. 1, 2003, pp. 17–30.

10. *Character Education Quality Standards: A Self-Assessment Tool for Schools and Districts* (Washington, D.C.: Character Education Partnership, 2001).

11. "What Is Character Education?," Center for the Fourth and Fifth Rs, 2003, **www.cortland.edu/c4n5rs/ce_iv.asp**.

12. Rick Weissbourd, "Moral Teachers, Moral Students," *Educational Leadership*, March 2003, pp. 6–7.

13. Damon is quoted in Susan Gilbert, "Scientists Explore the Molding of Children's Morals," *New York Times*, 18 March 2003.

JACQUES S. BENNINGA is a professor of education and director of the Bonner Center for Character Education, California State University, Fresno. **MARVIN W. BERKOWITZ** is Sanford N. McDonnell Professor of Character Education, University of Missouri, St. Louis. **PHYLLIS KUEHN** is a professor of educational research, California State University, Fresno. **KAREN SMITH** is principal of Mark Twain Elementary School, Brentwood, Mo. The research described in this article was funded by a grant from the John Templeton Foundation, but the opinions expressed are those of the authors.

Patriotism and Education: An Introduction

That patriotism is a complicated concept became clear in the immediate aftermath of 9/11. Mr. Westheimer, the guest editor of this *Kappan* special section, poses the question of how schools should approach the tension between loyalty to one's country and the importance of dissent.

JOEL WESTHEIMER

A cartoon published in the *New Yorker* in October 2001 shows a couple in a New York apartment entertaining friends. As the hosts clutch each other's hands, the woman confesses to their guests, "We're still getting used to feeling patriotic." Another *New Yorker* cartoon shows a policeman walking away from a car. Inside, reading the newly issued ticket, the driver asks his passenger incredulously, "Flagless in a patriotic zone?" In a third cartoon, an elegantly dressed woman hands a pile of expensive dresses, a fur coat, and her credit card to a sales clerk and says, "This isn't for me—it's for the economy."

New Yorker cartoons are hardly a barometer of national sentiment about patriotism following 9/11, but the magazine has a distribution of over 800,000—a large percentage of which are subscriptions in the city where the Twin Towers fell—and its authors, cartoonists, and even advertisers reflected a mélange of conflicted feelings about loyalty, solidarity, and the right to dissent in a democracy. Editor David Remnick was initially criticized for censoring authors and capitulating to pressure from the Bush Administration to lend support to military operations in Afghanistan and elsewhere, but the magazine also was where Susan Sontag furiously observed that "the unanimity of the sanctimonious, reality-concealing rhetoric spouted by American officials and media commentators in recent days seems, well, unworthy of a mature democracy." Perhaps the contributor who most plainly captured the confusion of the months to come was cartoonist Victoria Roberts, who drew a middle-aged husband and wife sitting down to dinner. Both look slightly perplexed as the husband says simply, "Who ever thought patriotism could be so complicated?"

The complexity of patriotism is further reflected in the great many ways it has been represented by politicians, the media, authors, critics, and religious leaders. Each has shaped various ideas about patriotism and its importance to national unity and sought to advance particular notions of patriotism over others. Nowhere are the debates around these various visions of patriotic attachment more pointed, more protracted, and more consequential than in our nation's schools. As several authors in this special section make clear, patriotism is highly contested territory.

The articles here explore the relationship between patriotism and education. Pedro Noguera and Robby Cohen ask readers to think about what educators' responsibilities are in wartime. Digging deep into the nation's past, they present provocative historical examples that do not lend themselves to facile analysis or pat good-guy/bad-guy stories. They ask whether, in an era of educational accountability, we are not ignoring our responsibility to students to present clear and accurate information on varying viewpoints about the "war on terrorism." "Given that our nation is at war in at least two countries," they ask, "shouldn't educators be accountable for ensuring that all students have some understanding of why we are fighting, of whom we are at war with, and of what is at stake?"

Diane Ravitch challenges us to think about what schools actually do to encourage students' appreciation of U.S. culture. She points out that educators stand strong in their belief that children's self-esteem is linked to knowledge and appreciation of their ancestral culture but not to that of the United States, where they live and will one day vote and raise children. "How strange," Ravitch muses, "to teach a student born in this country to be proud of his parents' or grandparents' land of birth but not of his or her own. Or to teach a student whose family fled to this country from a tyrannical regime or from dire poverty to identify with that nation rather than with the one that gave the family refuge." Critical of jingoistic conceptions of patriotism, Ravitch nonetheless calls for attention to traditional respect for and celebration of the nation's heritage and democratic principles and ideals.

Michael Bader offers a provocative contribution to our section on patriotism in education. A clinical psychologist, Bader asks readers to consider the psychological needs served by various expressions of patriotic fervor. He examines from a psychologist's perspective the collective responses both to 9/11 and to the devastation wrought by Hurricane Katrina. In a compelling analysis of the links between our need for security and protection and our early life experiences at home, Bader suggests that patriotism can be a force for good or evil, but that the key to understanding our own motivations is to understand their emotional and psychological roots in the universal need for attachment and affiliation. He draws on 25 years of clinical experience to show that patriotism often offers a symbolic resolution to longings we all experience for both safety and relatedness. Bader shows how both the political Left and the political Right "seek to link their partisan agendas to the evocation and satisfaction of these frustrated longings."

Gloria Ladson-Billings shares a deeply personal exploration of what it means to be a patriotic African American woman in the United States. "I am a patriot," she flatly declares, adding, "To most people who know me that statement probably comes as a surprise." Ladson-Billings, who is currently president of the American Educational Research Association, takes readers through her experiences growing up as an African American in the 1950s and 1960s and deftly examines the effects of those experiences on her thinking about the United States and about her patriotic attachments. How are we to understand patriotism, she asks, in a country where African Americans could be excluded from attending schools that white children attended or where "a 14-year-old boy from Chicago could be killed (beaten, lynched, castrated, and drowned) for whistling at a white woman"? Many members of Ladson-Billings' family served proudly in the military—in segregated units. Criticizing the "vacuous speeches" and "empty rhetoric" that politicians employ when they talk about what it means to be patriotic, Ladson-Billings reclaims the noble call to patriotic action on behalf of all U.S. citizens and those who are powerless around the globe.

In "Patriotism, Eh?" Sharon Cook adds a Canadian perspective on patriotism and education. As anthropologists know well, one's understanding of one's own culture is greatly improved by the study of another. My current country of residence, Canada offers a starkly different perspective on U.S. notions of patriotism. Canadians, Cook argues, have pride in peacefulness, in welcoming new immigrants (at a higher per-capita rate than virtually any Western nation), and in caring for the nation's citizens and other residents. By analyzing key historical events, Cook plumbs the significance of Canada's relationships to England and the U.S. She explains that national patriotism in Canada (though it too has had its excesses) is generally of a mild-mannered kind, perhaps because a more jingoistic form "seems unnecessary if one already finds inclusion in the family of a respected imperial power."

Patriotism and war have been intertwined in complex ways since the dawn of the nation-state. Many readers may know that the No Child Left Behind Act includes a provision that requires high schools to turn over personal information on students to military recruiters. In addition, the Pentagon now maintains a database of some 30 million 16- to 25-year-olds, including their names, ethnicities, addresses, cell phone numbers, family information, extracurricular activities, and areas of study (for more information, watch the 11-minute video at **www.LeaveMy-ChildAlone.org**). In "Hearts and Minds: Military Recruitment and the High School Battlefield," William Ayers tracks the recent explosion in the military presence in schools and classrooms throughout the U.S., paying special attention to Chicago. Ayers notes that Chicago has the largest JROTC program in the country and, according to some, the "most militarized" school system in America. His powerful stories of recruits, veterans, and Purple Heart recipients are as emotionally wrenching as they are deeply hopeful. What's more, his topic has important historical antecedents. For example, in 1911, Katherine Devereux Blake, a New York City elementary school principal, predicted an upcoming struggle in public education between those who advocate a greater military presence in the schools and those who want students to learn peace. "They are organized for war," Blake proclaimed. "We must be organized for peace."[1] In this article, Ayers details the heavy incursions those "organized for war" have made.

Joseph Kahne and Ellen Middaugh provide a systematic and sobering examination of high school students' attitudes toward patriotism. They surveyed over 2,000 seniors in 12 California high schools and conducted 50 focus groups to learn about students' patriotic commitments. Regardless of your beliefs about the importance of teaching patriotism in schools, it's reasonable to ask what should be taught about patriotism and what students already think and know. Kahne and Middaugh's findings are likely to challenge your assumptions. For example, although a majority of high school seniors believe that "if you love America, you should notice its problems and work to correct them," only 16% of high school seniors express consistent support for what the authors see as a democratic vision of patriotism. Moreover, most students do not necessarily see any connection between patriotism and civic participation.

Finally, my article, "Politics and Patriotism in Education," explores the ideological battles that are being waged in the name of patriotism in the nation's classrooms. Like Kahne and Middaugh, I suggest that patriotism and democratic ideals are not inherently at odds with one another but that a democratic form of patriotism is far from inevitable. To the contrary, there is much cause for concern over a far more dangerous brand of patriotic sentiment that is better described as "authoritarian" and that is widely on the rise.

This special section also features a series of Point of View opinion pieces. Nine prominent educators and public figures from a wide range of backgrounds and perspectives have provided short responses to the question "What should children learn in school about patriotism?" The answers are as diverse and fascinating as the contributing authors. After reading responses from Studs Terkel, Cindy Sheehan, Maxine Greene, Bill Bigelow, Walter Parker, Joan Kent Kvitka, Chester Finn, Denise Walsh, and Dean Wiles, you are unlikely to think about patriotism and education in precisely the same way as you did before.

Before I turn readers over to the contributing authors, let me return to the realm of comics, since they capture so well the mix of public sentiment around deeply complex political issues. A high school social studies teacher I know developed a curriculum for her students that would engage the full complexity of issues that arose following the U.S.-led war in Iraq. Frustrated with the lack of curricular resource materials available, she found, through the *Rethinking Schools* website, a suggestion to use political cartoons to examine the contentious issues arising from the war. Enthusiastically, she put together several lessons that would allow her students to examine critically all sides of the debates about the war by culling cartoons from across the political spectrum. But when two of the cartoons she used raised the ire of a parent of one of her students, her principal requested that she discontinue the lessons she had planned.

The two offending cartoons both came from the controversial comic strip "Boondocks," the brainchild of 28-year-old cartoonist Aaron McGruder. The strip stars Huey Freeman, a little African American kid living in suburbia who has attracted more than his share of controversy. The first cartoon the teacher used was originally published on Thanksgiving Day 2001, when polls suggested that President Bush's approval ratings were higher than 90% and when popular support for the war on terror was widespread. Huey is leading the Thanksgiving prayer: "Ahem," he begins. "In this time of war against Osama bin Laden and the oppressive Taliban regime, we are thankful that our leader isn't the spoiled son of a powerful politician from a wealthy oil family who is supported by religious fundamentalists, operates through clandestine organizations, has no respect for the democratic electoral process, bombs innocents, and uses war to deny people their civil liberties. Amen." The second shows Huey calling the FBI's antiterrorist hotline to report that he has the names of Americans who helped train and finance Osama bin Laden. "Okay, give me some names," the FBI agent says. And Huey responds: "All right, let's see, the first one is Reagan. That's R-E-A-G...."

Students responded to these and the other cartoons used with an enthusiasm for debate that the teacher reported she had rarely witnessed in her classroom. She was careful to ensure that students received exposure to the broad spectrum of political perspectives, and, she noted, a vast majority of her students sported a plethora of patriotic symbols on their clothes and schoolbags during the weeks following 9/11.

Schools, of course, did not invent the brand of patriotism that involves stifling democratic debate. The same fear of dissenting viewpoints sometimes witnessed in schools can also be seen outside. It was not only the 16- and 17-year-old students of this teacher who were prohibited from debating McGruder's critique of the war. Some of the 250 newspapers that run the strip pulled it either selectively or in its entirety after September 11. Many

noted that it was "too political." In what could arguably be a successful alignment, the school curriculum may actually prepare students well for the adult world they are soon to enter—one in which, as McGruder observes, the media have "become so conglomerated that there are really very few avenues left for people to express dissent."

Indeed, there is some evidence that many are learning the lessons of my-country-right-or-wrong patriotism very well. In response to a "Doonesbury" strip critical of Bush Administration policies, some readers posted notes on the "Doonesbury" website. From Maurepas, Louisiana: "Your ... biased state of mind has no place for a patriotic thinking America. Grow up.... We are at War!" From Melbourne, Florida: "Your disloyalty to our society and our country shine through quite clearly." In apparent confusion between former Canadian Prime Minister Pierre Trudeau and "Doonesbury" creator Garry Trudeau, one reader from Arkansas echoed the xenophobic sentiments so often part and parcel of jingoistic patriotic campaigns: "Why don't you go back to Canada, or even better France?" But perhaps Virginia Beach resident Stuart Schwartz best captured the attitude toward dissent shared by those who favor what I describe in my article as authoritarian patriotism: "Please do the public a service and die."

A Pew Research Center poll in 2003 found that 92% of respondents agreed either completely or mostly with the statement "I am very patriotic."[2] However, as will become clear when reading the articles that follow, what it means to be patriotic is a matter of considerable debate. And it always has been. As far back as the 1890s, policy makers realized that public schools could serve as a "mighty engine for the inculcation of patriotism."[3] But 116 years later, patriotism and its role in school curriculum remain disputed territory.

This special section of the *Kappan* sets out to capture the controversies surrounding patriotism and education. Like the teacher who wanted to show a range of controversial opinions, the articles that follow express a healthy variety of viewpoints and approaches to the topic. In *Spheres of Justice*, Michael Walzer argues that the democratic citizen must be "ready and able, when the time comes," to engage in dialogue and "to deliberate with fellow [citizens], listen and be listened to."[4] The contributors to this section of the *Kappan* write in that spirit.

Notes

1. Katherine D. Blake, "Peace in the Schools," *National Education Association Proceedings* (Chicago: University of Chicago Press, 1911), pp. 140–46, cited in Susan Zeiger, "The Schoolhouse vs. the Armory: U.S. Teachers and the Campaign Against Militarism in the Schools, 1914–1918," *Journal of Women's History*, Summer 2003, p. 150.
2. Pew Research Center, "The 2004 Political Landscape: Evenly Divided and Increasingly Polarized," November 2003.
3. George Balch, "Methods of Teaching Patriotism in Public Schools" (1890), cited in Cecilia O'Leary, *To Die For: The Paradox of American Patriotism* (Princeton, N.J.: Princeton University Press, 1999), p. 175.
4. Michael Walzer, *Spheres of Justice: A Defense of Pluralism and Equality* (New York: Basic Books, 1984), p. 310.

JOEL WESTHEIMER is University Research Chair in Democracy and Education, a professor of the social foundations of education, and co-director of Democratic Dialogue: Inquiry into Democracy, Education, and Society at the University of Ottawa, Ont. (joelw@uottawa.ca). He wishes to thank the Social Sciences and Humanities

Research Council of Canada, the Center for Information and Research on Civic Learning and Engagement, and Democratic Dialogue at the University of Ottawa (democraticdialogue.com) for their support in the preparation of this special section. Karen Suurtamm, Democratic Dialogue's project director, provided research and editing assistance.

Patriotism and Accountability: The Role of Educators in the War on Terrorism

Citizenship education, according to Mr. Noguera and Mr. Cohen, means providing students with the knowledge and skills to think critically about their country's actions.

PEDRO NOGUERA AND ROBBY COHEN

W hat are the responsibilities of educators while our nation is at war? This is not a question that comes up at most conferences or workshops on education, even though anyone familiar with our work as educators knows that it is nearly impossible to avoid taking a stance on the issue.

Should educators be expected to promote patriotism and support for the military effort in Iraq or Afghanistan? If our students seek our advice and counsel, should we encourage them to enlist? Or should we tell them that the decision is theirs to make? What about the Patriot Act? Should we urge our students to accept curtailments of our civil liberties as a necessary sacrifice in the "war on terrorism," a war against a stateless enemy that is not confined to a particular territory? Or should we warn them of the potential dangers that may arise when any government is allowed to invade the privacy of its citizens?

Ignoring these questions does not allow one to escape taking a stand. Even if you are uncomfortable speaking out for or against the war, it is important to understand that in times such as these we cannot pretend that education is apolitical work. Particularly now, when accountability has become a national mantra, we believe that educators must hold themselves accountable for ensuring that students acquire an intellectual grounding in history, civics, and culture that will enable them to develop informed opinions about the war, about U.S. foreign policy toward the Middle East, and about the implications of the war for civil liberties in American society.

Silence and inaction are nothing more than a form of complicity with the status quo. The war is raging now, and those who do not express opposition are in effect demonstrating complicity if not support. People—Iraqis, Afghanis, and Americans—are dying, and decisions are being made in Washington that will affect our future. Our schools are being used as recruiting grounds for the military because No Child Left Behind (NCLB) requires

schools to provide military recruiters with access to schools and student records.[1] Our schools are not required to provide antiwar groups with equal access, so it seems clear that our education system is tilted toward war rather than peace.

During the 1960s, universities and colleges were the sites of demonstrations and sit-ins when campus administrators provided the federal government with access to student records for the military draft during the Vietnam War. Today, the use of student records for military recruitment provokes relatively little protest. Fear of terrorist attack, fear of being perceived as sympathizing with terrorists or enemies of the U.S., and the undocumented but enduring belief that the war in Iraq will prevent terrorists from attacking us here—all combine to make it increasingly difficult for individuals to take public positions against the war. Sensitivities are also heightened whenever American men and women (actually one-third of those serving in our armed forces in Iraq and Afghanistan are not U.S. citizens) are deployed to fight in a foreign land, and this too contributes to the chilling effect on domestic dissent. However, as educators, we have a special responsibility to encourage critical thinking among our students. Indeed, citizens who think critically are essential for the functioning of our democracy. We ought not to allow our nation's schools to remain cogs in a war machine, nor should we allow ourselves to become unwitting supporters.

Linking Accountability and Patriotism

Over the past decade there has been a new emphasis on accountability in our nation's schools. NCLB has required schools to produce evidence that students are learning (as measured by performance on standardized tests) and that when they graduate from school they possess basic competencies in math and literacy. While many educators (including both of us) applaud certain aspects of NCLB, federal education policy under President Bush has been increasingly linked to other Administration initiatives, including the war. Thus educators are being held accountable in new ways. As a result of this linkage, the stakes are increasingly high for teachers, administrators, and students.

Educators who support the war, the President, and the policies of the Administration may experience little difficulty doing what they can to embrace the military effort and NCLB with patriotic enthusiasm. They may do so either because they trust the President and his policies or because they believe that obedience and loyalty are essential when the nation is at war. They may have no qualms about promoting a similar brand of patriotism among their students and encouraging them to enlist in the military, even if they do not encourage their own children to do the same.

Others may secretly oppose the war and the policies of the Administration but fear making their opposition known. Perhaps they fear being accused of disloyalty or being seen as a troublemaker. Or perhaps they are concerned that if they speak out they will be censured, fired, or worse.

It is not surprising that many who oppose the war (and polls show that a majority of Americans no longer support it[2]), who question the rationale and logic used to justify the military occupation of Iraq and Afghanistan, and who regard NCLB as a threat to the integrity of public education may be reluctant to express their views openly. In some parts of the country, critics of the war, including prominent politicians, journalists, and celebrities, have been castigated for being "soft" on terrorism, and their patriotism has been questioned. Just before launching the war in Afghanistan, the President declared, "You are either with us or with the terrorists." When the lines of debate are drawn so starkly, even passive neutrality may give rise to suspicion.

Yet educators who prefer to avoid controversy and who would rather remain silent on these polarizing issues may find a stance of neutrality difficult to maintain during these tense times. When the National Education Association is called a terrorist organization by one secretary of education and when the state superintendent of Connecticut is described as "un-American" by another, simply because both have been critical of NCLB and other aspects of federal education policy, it is clear that a link between war and education has been forged. It may seem odd—and even unfair—for one's attitudes and positions toward the war to be linked to one's position on NCLB and federal education policy, but these are not ordinary times.

While no one wants to risk being questioned by the FBI, blacklisted, or detained (or even deported if one is not a U.S. citizen) for taking public positions that are regarded as unpatriotic, it is important for us to remember that the right to dissent is an essential part of our democracy. It is also important to remember that, as educators, we have been given the great responsibility of imparting knowledge that will prepare our students to become citizens in this democracy. This is not a responsibility that can be taken lightly.

Accountability and Democratic Citizenship

As accountability has become the leading policy fixation in education, it might be helpful for educators to think of patriotism and citizenship in terms of accountability as well. Given that our nation is at war in at least two countries, shouldn't educators be accountable for ensuring that all students have some understanding of why we are fighting, of whom we are at war with, and of what is at stake?

Citizenship education is important in every society, but there is no place where it is more vital than in the U.S., the world's preeminent military power. Our government spends far more on the military than does any other nation. We have military bases and troops deployed in more than 100 foreign countries and hundreds of nuclear warheads ready to be launched on the order of the President. A nation with so strong a military and so vast a military presence must have an education system that is equally strong in teaching its future citizens to think critically and independently about the uses of American power and about the role of the American military in the world.

Unlike most military superpowers of the past, the U.S. is a democracy, and the results of our elections can influence the global policies we pursue. Since the rest of the world cannot vote in our elections, even though their fate may be determined by the outcomes, it is up to us, as citizens and as educators, to ensure that our teaching fosters the kind of informed debate and discussion that is necessary for the functioning of a healthy democracy.

Such an approach to teaching must include a willingness to discuss controversial issues, such as the nature and implications of American imperialism, our role as a global power, and our ongoing desire to intervene in the affairs of other nations. Every student in our nation's secondary schools should be exposed to both sides of the debate about how the U.S. uses its power in the world. All students should be able to understand the rationale given for American troop deployments and military actions abroad, and before graduating, they should be able to write a coherent essay exploring the merits of various courses of action and putting forward their own perspective on the ethics of U.S. foreign policy.

To acquire this form of political literacy, our students must have an understanding of American and world history that goes far beyond regurgitating facts and dates or passing state history exams. They must also understand the complexity of politics in ways that exceed the typical offerings of the mainstream media. In short, they must learn, as Paulo Freire once admonished, to "read the world" so that they might have a clearer understanding of the forces shaping their lives.

Let us use the concept of imperialism to illustrate how these educational goals might be pursued. The American Heritage Dictionary defines imperialism as "the policy of extending a nation's authority by territorial acquisition or by the establishment of economic and political hegemony over other nations." To determine whether it is appropriate to apply this term to the actions of the U.S., students would need to be exposed to a thematic approach to the history of America's territorial expansion, its ascendance to global power after the Spanish-Cuban-American War, and its emergence as the world's foremost superpower in the aftermath of World War II.

Such an approach to history would compel students to grapple with the meaning and significance of economic and political changes rather than merely to recall a chronology of isolated facts. It would also enable students to comprehend the significance of blatant contradictions in U.S. foreign policy. For example, many Americans do not realize that the United States once supported many of the groups that now are part of al Qaeda (including Osama bin Laden himself) when these individuals and groups were carrying out acts of terrorism in Afghanistan in opposition to the Soviet occupation of that country. They also may not know that Saddam Hussein was once a U.S. ally and that we supported him in his war against Iran, even when we knew he was using chemical weapons against the Kurds.[3]

We should teach history in ways that make it possible for students to make sense of contradictions such as these. Indeed, we must do so if our students are to appreciate the complex social processes that led to America's rise as an imperial power. This does not mean that we should engage in an unfair bashing of the United States. One way to avoid this is to provide readings that offer a variety of points of view on the same subject. However, even as we strive for balance and fairness, we should provide our students with the analytical skills to critique and evaluate the information they are exposed to so that they can develop a logical and historically grounded framework for comprehending present conflicts and foreign engagements.

To have a context for understanding the present war in Iraq, every student should know that war and violence were central to the founding and early development of the United States. What began as 13 states on the East Coast of North America eventually expanded from sea to sea through a process of conquest and conflict. Students should understand that, while some historians view this expansion in positive terms, as the growth of a liberty-loving republic, others see it as having been achieved by the near genocide of Native Americans and by the seizure of immense western territories from Mexico.[4]

Similarly, to appreciate the significance of President Bush's assertion that Saddam Hussein had weapons of mass destruction as a pretext for taking the nation to war, it would help students to know that similar tactics have been used in the past. The 1846 clash of U.S. and Mexican troops on lands that historically had belonged to Mexico; the sinking of the battleship Maine off the coast of Cuba in 1898, which Americans, without evidence, blamed on Spain; and the alleged but never confirmed second North Vietnamese attack on U.S. vessels in the Gulf of Tonkin in 1964 are examples of controversial rationales that were used to take the nation to war. Understanding the nature of these historical controversies—namely, who wanted the war, who opposed it, and why—would help students to appreciate the significance of the ongoing debate over how and why the U.S. entered the war with Iraq.

Accountability in teaching should also include ensuring that students have the ability to process the news and information they are exposed to each day so that they can understand how the war is being conducted and develop informed opinions about it. To be intelligent citizens today, students should be able to use the daily reporting from Iraq—from mainstream and alternative sources—to question and critique the claims of the Administration, such as Vice President Cheney's recent assertion that the insurgency in Iraq is in its "last throes." The parallels between such claims and the equally misleading claims made by the Johnson Administration during the Vietnam War are worth exploring, as they offer historical precedent as well as evidence that the Republicans have no monopoly on this kind of spin. As the saying goes, "In war, truth is the first casualty."

Students should understand both the risks involved if the U.S. leaves Iraq before peace and democracy are established and those involved in staying longer. Again, the parallels to Vietnam are haunting. Making sense of such issues and arriving at an intelligent, well-thought-out point of view requires an ability to critique arguments and opinions that are presented as facts and to recognize misleading statements.

In a recent essay titled "War and the American Constitutional Order," Mark Brandon asserts that, as of 2004, Americans had been involved in wars or military actions in 182 of the 228 years since the colonies declared independence in 1776.[5] He also points out that U.S. military actions became much more frequent in the 20th century. Remarkably, from 1900 to 2000 there were only six years in which the U.S. was not engaged in some form of military action. Today, we are pursuing an open-ended commitment to a global war on terrorism that knows no national or temporal boundaries.

Critics such as Andrew Bacevich write of a "new American militarism" whereby the nation's political elite, infatuated with the capabilities of high-tech weaponry and emboldened by the collapse of the Soviet Union and the lack of a countervailing superpower, has embraced military action as a first rather than a last resort to advance U.S. interests.[6] Our students need not accept Bacevich's arguments, but they do need to know enough about American history to be able to critique and debate them. Why has the U.S. been so reliant on military force for so much of its history? Do other nations have similar histories? What rationales have Americans used in the past to justify going to war? How do we reconcile this long history of U.S. warfare with the fact that U.S. territory has so rarely come under attack from foreign powers? Our students need to engage questions such as these with an understanding of history and with a critical frame of mind.

It is also well past time for U.S. schools to confront what is new about this latest U.S. war. This is the nation's first preemptive war. By conventional standards, the U.S. could well be seen as the aggressor in this war, since it invaded a far weaker state not in response to any immediate threat or attack on Americans but in response to a presumed threat (Iraq's alleged possession of weapons of mass destruction) that later proved to be nonexistent. Students need to grapple with the whole idea of preemptive war and its international implications. If the U.S. is entitled to wage such a war, attacking weaker nations whenever it construes a potential threat from them, then do we accord this same right to other major powers? Can China, for example, be given a green light to invade Taiwan if China's leaders believe that this smaller nation poses a threat to its security?

Our efforts to ensure that our students understand the war we are fighting should also include discussion of how our troops conduct themselves during the war. We must help our students to understand how it was possible for prisoners of war to be abused and tortured by American forces in Iraq and why it is that Amnesty International has referred to the prison at the Guantánamo military base in Cuba as the "Gulag of our times." Here the linkages between past and present can be made by simply asking why it is that the U.S. owns this naval base in Cuba.

We should encourage our students to debate who should be held accountable when atrocities such as these come to light. Those who torture, those who supervise and command them, both? They should know why the Geneva Conventions for the treatment of prisoners during war were adopted and why America's designation of certain prisoners as "unlawful combatants" represents a threat to Americans who may be captured. Likewise, similar kinds of questions must be asked of the Iraqi insurgents and of the terrorist groups whose suicide bombings and attacks on civilians have created the worst horrors of the war.

The extent to which our civil liberties should be curtailed as a result of the war on terrorism is yet another topic that should be fully explored. Is the Patriot Act fundamentally different from Sen. McCarthy's search for Communists during the Cold War years? Was President Roosevelt's decision to intern Japanese Americans during World War II similar to or different from the mass detentions of Muslims who are still being held without trial or legal representation throughout America today? With police searching bags at airports and security agencies possessing new powers to order wiretaps on Americans, students need to assess whether the national security rationales for these acts can stand up under critical scrutiny.

The Middle Eastern focus of much of the war on terrorism poses a serious challenge to our schools, because most students—indeed, most of our citizens—lack the kind of understanding of the history and culture of the region that would be needed to understand the complex issues. Not many public schools teach Arabic or have teachers with expertise in the history of Islam. With such educational deficiencies the norm in the U.S., it is little wonder that the American electorate was unable to sort out the secular tyranny of Saddam Hussein and the violent religious fanaticism of Osama bin Laden. Educators need to do better than politicians have in grappling with the complexities of the Middle East, and they need to make distinctions among those we regard as our enemies.

Perhaps the most provocative area of inquiry our students can explore as they reflect on their nation's international impact and posture is at the macrohistorical level. What is it that motivates the U.S. to act as it does internationally? Is American foreign policy and war-making driven by democratic altruism? Or do economics and the search for markets, cheap labor, and raw materials shape the American agenda? Should the U.S. work with and support the United Nations, the international body we helped to create, or should we denounce the UN as an anti-American institution and reject the idea of allowing outsiders to debate questions pertinent to our defense and security?

While many of the topics we have highlighted are most easily dealt with in social studies and English classes, teachers in other subject areas should not shy away from participating in the process of citizenship education. American students need to understand how the rest of the world perceives us and why so many people who sympathized with the U.S. after September 11th no longer do. Teachers of all kinds should raise these issues with their students, not to dictate what they should think, but simply to encourage them to think. Too much is at stake for citizenship education to be treated as an isolated unit to be covered solely in a social studies class.

My Country Right or Wrong?

If we are honest in our approach to teaching history and getting our students to think critically about the war, we will point out that there is a tension between flag-waving nationalism and a willingness to confront the ugly side of American history. For example, American nationalism impels us to think of 9/11 not merely as a day of U.S. suffering or as an act of brutal violence, but as a rallying cry for a global war on terror. If we can put aside our nationalist lenses for a moment, we might seek to understand why many developing countries regard us as an international bully, a nation motivated more by power and greed than by altruism and a sincere commitment to human rights and democracy.

Chilean writer Ariel Dorfman reminds us that there is "more than one America and more than one September 11th."[7] Dorfman and millions of others remember another September 11, this one in 1973, as a day of mourning. That was the day that a U.S.-backed coup overthrew the democratically elected socialist president of Chile, Salvador Allende, and replaced his government with a military junta led by Gen. Augusto Pinochet. Dorfman asks Americans to recognize that their suffering is neither unique nor exclusive. He challenges us as educators to see that, when we push beyond the boundaries of a narrow patriotism, we see a world in which the U.S. plays a complex and contradictory role—sometimes as victim, sometimes as perpetrator, of antidemocratic violence.

Criticizing Islamic fundamentalists and rabid nationalists in other countries is easy. It is far more difficult to challenge the patriotic assumptions and biases of one's own country, especially during wartime.

The pioneers of the idea of public education—Thomas Jefferson, Horace Mann, and John Dewey—argued that schools were essential to the health and well-being of our republic. They understood that an uneducated citizenry would doom the republic because ignorant citizens would be incapable of electing good leaders or voting out of office those who abused their power. As educators, it is our democratic responsibility to foster critical thinking among our students.

Those who deem taking up such challenges as unpatriotic would do well to heed the warning of English writer G. K. Chesterton: "My country right or wrong is a thing that no patriot would think of saying except in a desperate case. It is like saying, 'My mother, drunk or sober.'"[8]

With NCLB seeing to it that our schools become sites of military recruitment, educators have an even stronger obligation to ensure that their students are able to make informed decisions about their future. They must be exposed to all sides of the debates over America's role as a superpower. They must be able to draw lessons from the past so that they will be more informed about the present. In short, they must be made to understand what they may be putting their young lives on the line for. To do anything less is irresponsible and a willful neglect of our professional duties as educators.

Notes

1. John Gehring, "Recruiting in Schools, a Priority for Military, Is Targeted by Critics," *Education Week*, 22 June 2005, p. 6.
2. See David Jackson, "Bush Continues to Stump for War Support," *USA Today*, 13 January 2006.
3. See Mahmood Mamdani, *Good Muslim, Bad Muslim: America, the Cold War, and the Roots of Terror* (New York: Doubleday, 2004).
4. James W. Loewen, *Lies My Teacher Told Me: Everything Your American History Textbook Got Wrong* (New York: New Press, 1995), pp. 67–129; and Walker LaFeber, *The American Age: U.S. Foreign Policy at Home and Abroad, 1750 to the Present* (New York: Norton, 1994), pp. 1–125.
5. Mark E. Brandon, "War and the American Constitutional Order," in Mark Tushnet, ed., *The Constitution in Wartime: Beyond Alarmism and Complacency* (Durham, N.C.: Duke University Press, 2005), p. 11.
6. Andrew J. Bacevich, *The New American Militarism: How Americans Are Seduced by War* (New York: Oxford University Press, 2005), passim.
7. Ariel Dorfman, *Other Septembers, Many Americas: Selected Provocations, 1980–2004* (New York: Seven Stories Press, 2004), p. 41.
8. Quoted in William B. Whitman, *The Quotable Politician* (Guilford, Conn.: Lyons Press, 2003), p. 242.

PEDRO NOGUERA and **ROBBY COHEN** are professors in the Department of Teaching and Learning at New York University, New York City. © 2006, Pedro Noguera.

Should We Teach Patriotism?

America has long relied on its public schools to teach young citizens about the workings of a self-governing democracy. But does this entail teaching "patriotism"? Ms. Ravitch believes that it should—as long as students learn to appreciate their country without ignoring its faults.

DIANE RAVITCH

Not long ago, I was among a group of visitors to a public elementary school in New York City. The school had achieved a certain renown for its programs in the arts, and we came to learn more about what the staff was doing. The principal met us at the door and soon began to speak glowingly about the school's accomplishments. He mentioned that the school was attended by children from nearly 40 different nations and cultures and that it went to great lengths to encourage the students to have pride in their cultural heritage. There were children in the school from Asia, Latin America, Africa, Europe, and India. All of them were learning to appreciate the foods, dances, customs, and literature of their native countries. Quietly, I asked him whether the school did anything to encourage students to appreciate American culture, and he admitted with embarrassment that it did not.

This seems to me a great paradox in American public education today. Educators believe that children's self-esteem is firmly linked to a positive relationship to their ancestral culture but not to the culture of the country in which they live and are citizens of and in which they will one day raise a family, earn a living, and participate in elections. How strange to teach a student born in this country to be proud of his parents' or grandparents' land of birth but not of his or her own. Or to teach a student whose family fled to this country from a tyrannical regime or from dire poverty to identify with that nation rather than with the one that gave the family refuge.

The extent to which we abhor or admire patriotism in the schools depends on how it is taught. If we teach it narrowly as jingoistic, uncritical self-praise of our nation, then such instruction is wrong. It would be indoctrination rather than education. If, however, we teach civic education and define patriotism as a respectful understanding and appreciation of the principles and practices of democratic self-government, then patriotism should be woven through the daily life and teachings of the public schools.

Until the last generation, American public schools took the teaching of patriotism very seriously. The school day began with the Pledge of Allegiance, every classroom displayed an American flag, the flag was raised each day over the school, and students learned the songs of the American civil religion—the national anthem, "God Bless America," "Columbia, the Gem of the Ocean," "America the Beautiful," "My Country, 'Tis of Thee," etc. Since the earliest days of public education, the schools were expected to teach students about the history, culture, and symbols of America and to encourage them to feel part of the nation. If anything, the public schools in the United States were generally viewed by the public as an institutional expression of national pride, because they were considered the quintessential governmental instrument for building a strong and vibrant national community. It was understood that students and families came from a wide variety of national and ethnic origins, and the public schools were expected to teach everyone about the duties and privileges of citizenship in the United States. The public schools were to instruct students about voting and jury duty, about how the government works, and about national ideals and aspirations.

In many ways, American schools were very much like the state schools of every other nation, which invariably teach students to respect the larger community that supplies and funds their education. No state system teaches its children to despise their own government. But American schools probably went further in their patriotic spirit than the schools of other nations, for two reasons. First, other nations are based on ties of blood or religion, but the United States is a social creation, evolving not from common inherited features but from a shared adherence to the democratic ideology embedded in the Declaration of Independence and the Constitution. The public schools were expected to help forge the American people anew in each generation by teaching children about the nature and workings of democratic self-government. Second, the public school is itself an expression of the nation's democratic ideology, a vehicle created to realize the nation's belief in individualism, self-improvement, and progress. It was in the public schools that students not only would learn what it meant to be an American but would gain the education necessary to make their way in an open society, one in which rank and privilege were less important than talent and merit. If the public schools were ever to abandon their role as an instrument of democratic ideology, they would risk losing their place in the American imagination as well as their claim on the public purse.

Obviously, if teaching patriotism degenerates into vulgar national boasting and a mandate for conformity, then it has failed in teaching the Constitution. For an essential part of the promise of the democratic ideology involves teaching children about the rights of a free people, including the rights of free speech, free expression, and dissent. It is impossible to teach American history without recognizing the important roles played by outsiders, dissenters, and critics, who often turned out to be visionary and prescient in their rejection of the status quo.

The teaching of patriotism in American schools should not be a separate subject. There should not be time set aside for instruction in patriotism. Students who have a solid civic education will study the ideas and institutions of the Founders and learn how democratic institutions work, where they falter, and how they can be strengthened. Students who study American history will learn about the sacrifices of previous generations who sought to safeguard our liberties and improve our society, and they will learn about the men and women of all races and backgrounds who struggled to create a land of freedom, justice, and opportunity. Students must learn too about the failings of our democracy, about the denials of freedom and justice that blight our history.

But to deprive students of an education that allows them to see themselves as part of this land and its history and culture would be a crying shame. Just as students must learn to value themselves as individuals, to value their families, and to value their community, so too should they learn to value the nation of which they are citizens. To love one's country does not require

one to ignore its faults. To love one's country does not require one to dismiss the virtues of other countries. Indeed, those who are patriotic about their own country tend to respect those who live elsewhere and also love their respective countries. Love of country may mean love of place, love of the landscape and the people, love of what is familiar. Surely people who have been persecuted may be excused for not having an attachment to their homeland. But for most of us, whatever place we call home and whatever our nationality, Sir Walter Scott's words ring true:

Breathes there the man with soul so dead
Who never to himself hath said,
"This is my own, my native land!"
Whose heart hath ne'er within him burned,
As home his footsteps he hath turned
From wandering on a foreign strand?
If such there breathe, go, mark him well;
For him no minstrel raptures swell;
High though his titles, proud his name,
Boundless his wealth as wish can claim
Despite those titles, power, and pelf,
The wretch, concentred all in self,
Living, shall forfeit fair renown,
And, doubly dying, shall go down
To the vile dust from whence he sprung,
Unwept, unhonored, and unsung.

DIANE RAVITCH is a research professor at New York University; a senior fellow at the Hoover Institution, Stanford, Calif.; a nonresident senior fellow at the Brookings Institution, Washington, D.C.; and a graduate of the Houston public schools. She is the author of *The Language Police: How Pressure Groups Restrict What Students Learn* (Knopf, 2003) and co-editor, with Michael Ravitch, of *The English Reader* (Oxford University Press, 2006).

From *Phi Delta Kappan*, April 2006, pp. 579-581. Copyright © 2006 by Phi Delta Kappan. Reprinted by permission of the publisher and author.

Promoting Altruism in the Classroom

Altruism is the purest form of caring—selfless and non-contingent upon reward—and thus the predecessor of pro-social cognitions and behaviors.

E.H. MIKE ROBINSON III AND JENNIFER R. CURRY

Pro-social behavior is described as "behavior intended to benefit another" (Eisenberg et al., 1999, p. 1360). Such behaviors may include comforting, sharing, working or playing cooperatively, and displaying empathy for others (Simmons & Sands-Dudelczyk, 1983), all of which have an element of altruism. Altruism is defined by Eisenberg et al. (1999) as "behavior motivated by concern for others or by internalized values, goals, and self-rewards rather than by the expectation of concrete or social rewards, or the desire to avoid punishment or sanctions" (p. 1360). Therefore, it is our contention that altruism is the purest form of caring—selfless and non-contingent upon reward—and thus the predecessor of pro-social cognitions and behaviors (Smith, 1976). While many character education programs focus on promoting pro-social behavior, the literature holds very few suggestions for specifically promoting altruism. This article will outline some hypotheses about the need to develop altruism as a base for pro-social behavior, describe how altruism develops, and propose strategies educators can use to foster altruism in the classroom.

Many hypotheses have been proposed regarding the origination and nature of altruism; it is also debated whether an altruistic personality type exists and, if so, whether such a characteristic is stable over time and across situations (Eisenberg et al., 1999). Historically, research has centered on the reasons why a person is either a bystander or a helper in situations involving a stranger in need. Interest in altruism heightened after the fatal stabbing of Kitty Genovese, when 38 people either saw or heard her being attacked yet did not intervene (Dovidio, 1991). This phenomenon of not intervening became known as the bystander effect, wherein the diffusion of responsibility, brought on by being in a group, negates individual action to respond to a person in crisis.

Since the 1960s, the research conducted on altruism and acts of selfless giving has helped researchers develop multiple theories about why people choose to perform altruistic acts. One theory is that altruistic tendencies are biological, in that self-sacrificing behavior may be performed with the unconscious idea that this behavior will be reciprocated in the future. Evidence supporting this hypothesis comes from monozygotic and dizygotic twin studies (Eisenberg et al., 1999), and through observations of infants' responses that reflect signs of distress exhibited by their caregivers (Zahn-Waxler, Radke-Yarrow, Wagner, & Chapman, 1992). However, the biology hypothesis does not explain why a person would help a stranger who may never have the occasion to reciprocate.

Another hypothesis comes from social learning theory, which posits that children learn to be altruistic through multiple social interactions, including adult role modeling of ideal behaviors, dialectic conversations that stimulate cognitive formation and development of altruistic ideas, and role playing and instruction that increase children's perceptions of their own competencies for helping others (Konecni & Ebbesen, 1975). In addition, Eisenberg and Fabes (1998) found that parenting style and social context may affect the development of pro-social behaviors that have an altruistic base.

Researchers have found that the type of help children offer is directly related to the repertoire of behaviors they have gleaned from their school environment. Specifically, children who attended a transactional analysis school were most likely to offer spontaneous help, children from a Montessori school were most likely to wait for a specific request for help before giving assistance, and students from a traditional school were most likely to try finding an adult to help another child rather than directly assisting the child themselves. The researchers believe that differences in helping behavior are correlated with the socialization of children in their respective education environments (Simmons & Sands-Dudelczyk, 1983).

Further evidence supporting the social learning theory of altruism comes from research by Konecni and Ebbesen (1975), who found that children have a greater response to adults who behave altruistically (through role modeling) versus adults who merely make statements in favor of altruism. Similarly, Bryan and Walbek (1970) found that children learn more and respond more positively to role modeling than to didactic instruction on altruism. They also concluded that parents and adult role models can help train children to recognize situational cues for assistance (e.g., signs of distress in another person) and also may prescribe norms for helping others (Konecni & Ebbesen, 1975). This socialization into the helping process may be the key for understanding how children discern who needs help, based on such factors as age, race, gender, and ethnicity.

One last connection of social learning theory and altruism comes from research on gender and altruistic behavior. It appears that males and females differ in the type of assistance they are likely to give, and that this qualitative difference may be based on beliefs and social norms about appropriate helping behaviors for each gender. For example, females may be more likely to attend to others empathically and verbally—giving support, empathy, and encouragement. Conversely, males are more likely to offer physically oriented altruism, with few verbally altruistic behaviors (Monk-Turner et al., 2002; Zeldin, Savin-Williams, & Small, 1984). Bihm, Gaudet, and Sale (1979) found that the amount of help offered did not differ between males and females. Furthermore, the greatest determinant of helping behavior appears to be the same in both genders: an empathic orientation toward others, characterized by cognitive and affective perspective taking and the ability to empathize accurately (Fry, 1976; Oswald, 1996).

Another hypothesis about altruism addresses cognition and internalized beliefs about helping others from a cognitive development theory basis. Cognitive schemas for altruism appear to change as children mature. Children who are high in empathic orientation or social sensitivity may internalize the helping concept and integrate these behaviors into self-concepts by incorporating the helping orientation into their belief systems (Fry, 1976). In addition, McGuire (2003) found that persons high in empathic orientation cognitively downplayed the self-cost for helping others and increased their perception of benefit to the recipient of help. This cognitive bias, which McGuire labeled a "modesty bias," serves to perpetuate and reinforce helping behavior in persons displaying altruistic tendencies.

Support exists in the literature for the cognitive schema hypothesis of altruism. Specifically, a general consensus indicates that with age, and the development of cognitive ability to take others' perspectives, comes a concomitant increase in altruistic behaviors (Eisenberg, Miller, Shell, McNalley, & Shea, 1991). However, this relationship is not linear. The relationship between age and altruistic behaviors actually appears to be curvilinear—there is an increase from birth to about 6 years of age, and then a decrease in altruistic behavior around age 7, followed by a subsequent sustained increase throughout late childhood and adolescence (Grunberg, Maycock, & Anthony, 1985).

Whether altruism has a biological basis, is socially learned, or is a cognitive schema that produces internalized beliefs that foster altruistic behaviors is a fascinating topic for consideration. According to Cushman (1990), society expanded and changed drastically with the post-modern era of industrialization and automation. These changes, in effect, produced massive social changes; however, the infrastructure did not exist to create the bonds of caring, kinship, and connectivity that were lost due to urbanization and isolation in the modern-day systems. Therefore, in order to fill the gap in the absence of these connections, our culture has become one of self-focus and consumerism—driven by the need to pursue tangibles to replace social cohesion and support networks (Cushman, 1990).

If caring is a natural, biological process, then how do we develop the innate propensity to care for others in a culture that largely promotes self-preservation and the enhancement of individuality? Children's truly innate altruistic tendencies may be discouraged through the climate of self-promotion and self-care that cultures often promote. Noddings (1992) suggests that educators must create opportunities for natural caring in the classroom if children are to develop their own instinctive caring, while simultaneously promoting ethical, intentional caring to develop those tendencies under the influence of cognition and social learning (Noddings, 1992).

While ethical caring may develop a sense of connection and community—along with notions of service and civic mindedness—natural caring also should be fostered in order to develop the individual's unique competencies and constructive ways of knowing about caring. The benefit would be a caring classroom community. In classrooms where caring is promoted, children may be more likely to offer assistance to other children and to connect with other students and teachers. These connections may, in turn, increase the child's school success (Noddings, 1995a). But should educators be teaching values? According to Noddings (1991), values already are implicit in schools through the rules established by teachers and administrators and through messages conveyed by the behavior of adults in the school building. Values are inherently present in schools and communities; we can be intentional and choose the values that we pass on to the children in our care (Noddings, 1995b).

So, how can educators increase students' altruistic behaviors? There are multiple means for achieving this goal. Teachers can be great role models for caring and altruistic behavior; they can demonstrate caring, empathy, and compassion toward others in their day-to-day interactions with students. Teachers are also in a position to structure the classroom so that opportunities exist for the expression of altruism, and to recognize and acknowledge children's altruistic acts of kindness to others. An additional way that teachers can promote altruism is by infusing altruism into the curriculum in the classroom. Kohn (1993) writes that teachers may increase caring opportunities by modeling caring, using caring to problem solve, utilizing art that illustrates caring, and by teaching it directly. Here are some suggestions of ways to increase altruistic behavior, accompanied by explanations of how to execute the suggestions in the classroom.

Increasing Student Awareness of Altruism and Greed

In order to foster altruistic behaviors, we have to make children aware of what constitutes altruism and the opposite of altruism—greed. We will examine ways to increase student awareness of altruism and greed-related acts through different subjects.

Young children may be exposed to the concepts of greed and altruism through literature (children's stories are rich with these ideas), commercials on television, and children's movies. After watching movies or reading stories, discuss the actions of characters that showed kindness and caring versus those that did not.

Discuss with children how acts of caring and acts of greed affected the outcomes of the story for different characters. History and social studies also provide great avenues for discussion about greed and altruism. The concept of greed may be expanded to non-material things, such as social status (greed may be about more than money—it might concern power and control). Let students be artistic, and have them create collages from magazines that represent acts of greed and/or altruism. Tap into kids' love of music by encouraging them to discuss themes of greed and altruism in songs. Teachers may want to create writing assignments about these concepts; for example, students could write about the kindest thing anyone ever did for them.

Teachers can be great role models for caring and altruistic behavior; they can demonstrate caring, empathy, and compassion toward others in their day-to-day interactions with students.

Older students can do research on altruistic activities. For example, what is involved in being a blood donor? What is volunteerism? Another activity may be to put students in groups and have each group research a different charitable organization (such as the YMCA, The Leukemia/Lymphoma Society, March of Dimes, Muscular Dystrophy Association, The American Cancer Society, The Humane Society, United Way, etc.). Have each group complete a research project outlining the mission of their assigned organization; how the organization is funded (such as private and corporate sponsorship, government grants, etc.); what services the organization provides and who benefits from those services; volunteer opportunities with the organization; etc. If you don't want to assign, you could let students choose from a list—we recommend that you ensure that every group has a different organization so as to increase student exposure to different organizations. After they have completed their research, teams can present their information to the entire class. You can make this creative by letting them develop commercials for their organization, as well as brochures, fliers, newspaper articles, posters, and much more!

Increasing Empathic Orientation

Making students aware of their feelings and other people's feelings increases their empathic orientation. This, in turn, allows them to recognize signs of distress in other people and to empathize with others. Consequently, this type of affective response can increase their propensity for aiding and comforting others.

Literature provides a platform from which to explore a myriad of emotions. It is important to move young children beyond identifying emotions as "mad" and "sad." Have discussions about the differences between mad, frustrated, angry, furious, disappointed, etc. After reading stories, allow for a discussion of how the characters emotionally reacted to events. Encourage

children to examine how a character's body language or voice let the child know what the character was feeling. Here is an example:

> *"Big Bear shouted, 'I want some honey right now!' He slammed his paw on the table and growled."*

If you were discussing this example with students, you would want to have them tell you how Big Bear is feeling. What things did Big Bear do that let the students know how he felt?

Have students discuss a time they experienced similar emotions to that of characters in literature. Have them discuss how they know when others are: sad, angry, confused, excited, happy, tired, etc. In order to have students understand the physical cues of emotions, you can have them act out different emotions with a partner or in groups. Tell students they are not allowed to talk; they can only show emotions through body language. Read them a statement and have them act out an emotion to go with the statement. (You may have to model this process for younger students.) For example, you state:

> *"Greta realized she was all alone in the forest. She did not know her way home. How do you think she was feeling?"*

Students then would act out the body language for being scared. Discuss with students what fearful or scared looks like (nail biting, turning pale, increased heart rate, widened eyes, etc.).

Another way to utilize literature is to have students recognize altruistic acts in books they are reading; conversely, you also can have children identify greedy acts. This dichotomy often exists in children's literature. Students may recount multiple altruistic acts or acts of greed performed by various characters, and then analyze and document the impact these behaviors had on other characters. Table 1 provides a sample list of authors and books that may be used for this purpose.

Developing Personal Values About Helping

Developing the classroom as a community is essential in promoting children's internalization of values about helping and altruism. Creating community classrooms can be done in a variety of ways. Teachers can establish tasks that each individual performs for the good of the classroom community.

Table 1 Sample Books Containing Altruistic Acts

Author	Title	Appropriate Age Group
Shel Silverstein	*The Giving Tree*	5–8 years old
E.B. White	*Charlotte's Web*	7–10 years old
Harper Lee	*To Kill a Mockingbird*	12–14 years old

Instead of making children responsible for cleaning up their own desk areas, make them responsible for one task that affects the whole classroom. For instance, make one student the chair monitor each day, and that student can be responsible for ensuring that chairs are pushed in and that no coats or backpacks are left on chairs. That same child may be in charge of erasing the boards in the classroom on the next day, and be assigned on a following day to ensuring that all of the textbooks are shelved correctly. It is important that every child be given a task each day (this could be done on a rotating basis and assignments could be given at the beginning of the day), and that the tasks are manageable and easy enough to be done quickly. One other way to facilitate the feeling of community in the classroom is by designating the classroom supplies as community property. Instead of each child needing a pencil box, one box of pencils can be shared by the entire class.

Teachers train students for life success by encouraging students to be lifelong learners and contributing members of society. They can utilize the classroom as a source of socialization.

Another way to develop personal values and beliefs about helping others is to use group discussion about moral dilemmas. Many books and stories focus on characters with a moral dilemma. Students can brainstorm ways that characters in the stories could have responded and what different outcomes would have resulted. Also, allowing students to explore their own personal values regarding helping others can contribute to the internalization of helping as a belief system. Children can write stories in which they perform an act of kindness for another person. Because children enjoy being creative, you also can have them write and perform skits or puppet shows about kindness, caring, and helping.

During the holiday season, you could discuss as a class why it is important to help others in the community. Perhaps instead of throwing a traditional school holiday party, students could benefit others in the community by hosting a holiday party for residents from a local nursing home. Students also could throw a party in honor of the school volunteers, such as parents and community members. Students may want to create expressive works, such as poems, short stories, pictures, paintings, etc., of ways that they have benefited from volunteers' contributions and present these expressions at the party. This allows students to connect their own appreciation with the acts of others, thereby creating a mental schema for helping others and the benefits of helping behaviors.

Increasing Self-Perceived Competencies for Helping

Teachers can give students opportunities to increase their knowledge of the skills they possess that they can use to help others. In- *creasing children's self-perceived competencies for helping will aid them in recognizing skills they already have that allow them to be helpful to others.*

Peer helper programs are a great way to encourage students to help others. An example of a peer helping program is Peer Tutoring, which trains students to help other students with math or reading assignments. Another type of peer helping, one that is especially useful with transient populations, such as urban or military schools, is Peer Buddies for new students. A Peer Buddy shows the new child around the classroom and acclimates him or her to the daily schedule; explains the routine of lunch and bathroom breaks; helps the student locate the library, lunchroom, lockers, and other key areas around the building; and introduces the new student to other students and teachers.

Another way to promote self-perceived competencies is to give students increased opportunities for creative problem solving. Ask the students, for example, how the class can show their appreciation and respect to the janitors. Students may come up with ideas that the teacher never would have conceived of. Allowing students to be creative and problem solve also increases their commitment to the resolution of an action plan. In the above example, the students might be more likely to follow through with the work of setting up a day to honor the workers if they are allowed to help plan the event and can create a vision for how the day will proceed.

Teachers also can help students become aware of helping opportunities by incorporating altruism into everyday activities. For example, if you are studying plant life in science, you could plan a small garden for the school yard that your class can maintain throughout the year. This does not have to require large amounts of time or money. Depending on the children's age, projects could include developing and implementing a school-wide recycling plan, organizing a canned food drive, or petitioning the school to adopt a nonprofit organization. These types of projects require research, planning, marketing, and a proposal for action. All of these requirements help students develop public speaking skills, writing skills, and organization, which exercises their creativity. Mathematics is infused in the agenda if you require students to calculate project costs, count donations, and track expenditures over time.

Conclusion

Altruism is evidenced in society through volunteerism, philanthropic support, and random acts of kindness performed every day. If our students are going to behave in altruistic ways, we first must help them recognize what altruism is, increase their awareness of others' feelings, develop their own personal values and style for helping, and increase their knowledge of their own helping competencies. Teachers are invaluable in this process. Altruism will continue to play a part in increasing the cohesion and connectivity of individuals and groups, both locally and globally. Teachers train students for life success by encouraging students to be lifelong learners and contributing members of society. They can utilize the classroom as a source of socialization to influence the moral development of children, creating opportunities for interpersonal success and engaging students to participate responsibly in the communities in which they reside.

References

Bihm, E., Gaudet, I., & Sale, O. (1979). Altruistic responses under conditions of anonymity. *The Journal of Social Psychology, 109*, 25–30.

Bryan, J. H., & Walbek, N. H. (1970). The impact of words and deeds concerning altruism upon children. *Child Development, 41*, 747–757.

Cushman, P. (1990). Why the self is empty. *American Psychologist, 45*(5), 599–611.

Dovidio, J. (1991). The empathy-altruism hypothesis: Paradigm and promise. *Psychological Inquiry, 2*(2), 126–128.

Eisenberg, N., & Fabes, R. A. (1998). Shyness and children's emotionality, regulation, and coping: Contemporaneous, longitudinal, and across context relations. *Child Development, 69*(3), 767–790.

Eisenberg, N., Guthrie, I. K., Murphy, B. C., Shepard, S. A., Cumberland, A., & Carlo, G. (1999). Consistency and development of prosocial dispositions: A longitudinal study. *Child Development, 70*(6), 1360–1372.

Eisenberg, N., Miller, P. A., Shell, R., McNalley, S., & Shea, C. (1991). Prosocial development in adolescence: A longitudinal study. *Developmental Psychology, 27*(5), 849–858.

Fry, P. S. (1976). Children's social sensitivity, altruism, and self-gratification. The *Journal of Social Psychology, 98*, 77–88.

Grunberg, N. E., Maycock, V. A., & Anthony, B. J. (1985). Material altruism in children. *Basic and Applied Social Psychology, 6*(1), 1–11.

Kohn, A. (1993). Punished by rewards. Boston: Houghton Mifflin.

Konecni, V. J., & Ebbesen, E. B. (1975). Effects of the presence of children on adults' helping behavior and compliance: Two field studies. *The Journal of Social Psychology, 97*, 181–193.

McGuire, A. M. (2003). "It was nothing"—Extending evolutionary models of altruism by two social cognitive biases in judgments of the costs and benefits of helping. *Social Cognition, 21*(5), 363–394.

Monk-Turner, E., Blake, V., Chniel, F., Forbes, S., Lensey, L., & Madzuma, J. (2002). Helping hands: A study of altruistic behavior. *Gender Issues, 20*(4), 70–76.

Noddings, N. (1991). Values by deliberation of default. *Clearing House, 64*(5), 320–323.

Noddings, N. (1992). *The challenge to care in schools: An alternative approach to education.* New York: Teachers College Press.

Noddings, N. (1995a). Teaching themes of care. *Phi Delta Kappan, 76*(9), 24–29.

Noddings, N. (1995b). A morally defensible mission for schools in the 21st century. *Phi Delta Kappan, 76*(5), 365–369.

Oswald, P. A. (1996). The effects of cognitive and affective perspective taking on empathic concern and altruistic helping. *Journal of Social Psychology, 136*(5), 613–623.

Simmons, C. H., & Sands-Dudelczyk, K. (1983). Children helping peers: Altruism and preschool environment. *The Journal of Psychology, 115*, 203–207.

Smith, A. (1976). *The theory of moral sentiments* (D. D. Raphael & A. L. Macfie, Eds.). Indianapolis, IN: Liberty Fund.

Zahn-Waxler, C., Radke-Yarrow, M., Wagner, E., & Chapman, M. (1992). Development of concern for others. *Developmental Psychology, 28*(1), 126–137.

Zeldin, R. S., Savin-Williams, R. C., & Small, S. A. (1984). Dimensions of prosocial behavior in adolescent males. *The Journal of Social Psychology, 123*, 159–168.

E.H. MIKE ROBINSON III is the Robert N. Heintzelman Eminent Scholar Chair for the study of greed and promotion of altruism and **JENNIFER R. CURRY** is a doctoral research assistant, University of Central Florida, Orlando.

"In the End You Are Sure to Succeed": Lincoln on Perseverance

Harold Holzer

I f there was one quality Abraham Lincoln believed essential both to individual success and to social advancement, it was industriousness. A child of the impoverished frontier who went on to take proud advantage of what historian Gabor Boritt has called "the right to rise" in America, Lincoln expected others to share his ambition for advancement. As he put it: "I am always for the man who wishes to work."

Politically, this meant opposing slavery and advocating full opportunity: the hope, as he put it once, that "the weights should be lifted from the shoulders of all men, and that *all* should have an equal chance." Personally, it meant urging friends and relatives to pursue the unfettered path toward upward mobility. "Free labor," he insisted, "has the inspiration of hope."

Lincoln occasionally provided such inspiration himself. When a school teacher from Pleasant Plains, Illinois, wrote in 1860 to inquire how best to transform himself into a lawyer, Lincoln's advice was simple and straightforward: "Work, work, work is the main thing." Later, as President, supervising the vast federal bureaucracy, Lincoln discovered that not everyone in government shared his enthusiasm for tireless labor. When asked by a needy mother in October 1861 to supply army jobs for her eager boys, the new President was barely able to contain a newfound cynicism when he obliged with a letter of referral. "Set them at it," he instructed an army major. "Wanting to work is so rare a merit, that it should be encouraged." His own step-brother, John D. Johnston, was guilty of one sin that Lincoln could not pardon: laziness. "You are destitute because you have *idled* away all your time.… Go to *work* is the only cure for your case."

Such was his advice for George Clayton Latham of Springfield, Illinois, a young man whose aching disappointments and unique relationship with the Lincoln family inspired one of the most rousing personal letters in the entire Lincoln canon. Young Latham was the son of Ohio native Catherine Rue Taber Latham and Kentucky-born Philip C. Latham, one of Springfield's early settlers. The elder Latham joined the county clerks office in 1827, and within eleven years had built a new home in town. Son George was born on May 16, 1842.

But then tragedy struck. On May 25, 1844, the elder Latham was hit and killed by lightning near the village of Shawneetown. George and his four brothers and sisters were left fatherless. But not friendless. The Latham house stood only a few blocks from the Lincoln's Jackson Street dwelling, and George grew close to the Lincoln's eldest son, Robert. Together, they attended the local Estabrook Academy, then, beginning in 1854, the preparatory school of the new Illinois State University, which held classes in a onetime Presbyterian Church called the Mechanics' Union.

Robert Lincoln, who was a year younger than George, took the Harvard University entrance exams in 1859—and failed miserably. To prepare him to take the tests anew his parents sent him off that September to Phillips Exeter Academy in New Hampshire (annual tuition: $24). George Latham joined Robert at Exeter as a fellow student, and the two were soon rooming together at the home of Mr. and Mrs. Samuel B. Clarke (at an additional cost of $2.25 per week).

Stopping at Exeter on a publicity-generating trip in the northeast, Lincoln was re-united on February 29 not only with Robert, but with George Latham. The two teenagers then accompanied Lincoln to Concord and Manchester and were doubtless on the scene as well on March 3 when Lincoln returned to Exeter and spoke at the local Young Men's Working Club. The boys may not have realized it, but they were bearing witness to a political and historical transformation. Within months, Lincoln would win the Republican nomination for President. Meanwhile, Robert would enjoy a triumph of his own: on his second attempt, he passed the rigorous entrance tests and entered Harvard.

Unfortunately, George Latham did not fare as well. He failed the Harvard entrance exams. The younger Lincoln reported the bad news to his father, prompting Lincoln on July 22 to compose the magnificent letter of encouragement that is reproduced here. The mere fact that the busy and preoccupied candidate took time to do so in the midst of his campaign gives the effort particular poignancy.

He began by confiding that he had "scarcely felt greater pain" than on learning of George's disappointment, but hastened to insist that the young man "allow no feeling of <u>discouragement</u> to seize, and prey upon you." Surely George would have another opportunity, and when he did, Lincoln declared, "you <u>can</u> not fail, if you resolutely determine that you <u>will</u> not." Above all, the nominee advised, "having made the attempt, you <u>must</u> succeed in it. '<u>Must</u>' is the word." Echoing throughout the letter was that

Transcript of GLC 3876: A letter from Abraham Lincoln to George Clayton Latham, July 22, 1860.

Springfield, Ills. July 22,1860.

My dear George

I have scarcely felt greater pain in my life than on learning yesterday from Bob's letter, that you had failed to enter Harvard University—And yet there is very little in it, if you will allow no feeling of <u>discouragement</u> to seize, and prey upon you—It is a <u>certain</u> truth, that you <u>can</u> enter, and graduate in, Harvard University; and having made the attempt, you <u>must</u> succeed in it. "<u>Must</u>" is the word—

I know not how to aid you, save in the assurance of one of mature age, and much severe experience, that you <u>can</u> not fail, if you resolutely determine, that you <u>will</u> not.

The President of the institution, can scarcely be other than a kind man; and doubtless he would grant you an interview, and point out the readiest way to remove, or overcome, the obstacles which have thwarted you—

In your temporary failure there is no evidence that you may not yet be a better scholar, and a more successful man in the great struggle of life, than many others, who have entered college more easily—

Again I say let no feeling of discouragement prey upon you, and in the end you are sure to succeed—

With more than a common interest I subscribe myself

Very truly your friend.
A. Lincoln.

Lincolnian ethic: "Work, work, work is the main thing." For George, it likely made all the difference.

Eventually, Latham returned to live in Springfield, where he was reunited with Robert in May 1865 for a heartbreaking event: the martyred President's funeral and burial. Two years later, Latham married Olive Priest, and entered his father-in-law's shoe business. The Lathams went on to raise three children of their own. George Latham died in his old home town on February 1, 1921, at the age of 78, and was buried in the same cemetery where Abraham Lincoln had been interred more than fifty years earlier. Saddened by the loss of his old companion, Robert Lincoln confessed: "With the death of ... Mr. George Latham, there is not now in Springfield, I feel quite sure, a single one of my old men friends or even acquaintances who might write to me."

But Robert's father had written—famously and inspiringly—to George Latham, motivating him beyond a potentially crushing early failure. One of Lincoln's most accomplished personal letters, this gem of optimistic correspondence testifies as eloquently to Lincoln's own perseverance, discipline, and uncompromising work ethic as it does to his extraordinary ability to inspire others.

One thing is certain: Lincoln's words had not been lost on George Latham. The young man took Lincoln's advice to heart, studied hard, and went on to pass his college entrance exams and enter one of the great American universities.

But not Harvard. George Clayton Latham went to Yale.

HAROLD HOLZER has authored, co-authored, and edited twenty-four books on Abraham Lincoln and the Civil War. His book *Lincoln at Cooper Union: The Speech That Made Abraham Lincoln President*, was the second place Lincoln Prize winner in 2005. He is the senior vice president of the Metropolitan Museum of Art and co-chairman of the U.S. Lincoln Bicentennial Commission.

This document with an expanded version of the essay by Harold Holzer was previously published in booklet form by the Gilder Lehrman Institute as the keepsake for the Lincoln Prize dinner in 2001.

UNIT 5
Managing Life in Classrooms

Unit Selections

Key Points to Consider

- Describe some of the myths associated with bullying behavior. How do you see the reality of bullying? What do you think school policy and teachers in particular can do to control bullying?

- Prepare your own road map of how you would create positive and productive approaches to the classroom instruction of middle-school-age children. Summarize your ideas about what features would lead to effective classroom management in a given school system.

Student Website
www.mhcls.com/online

Internet References
Further information regarding these websites may be found in this book's preface or online.

Classroom Connect
http://www.classroom.com
Global SchoolNet Foundation
http://www.gsn.org
Teacher Talk Forum
http://education.indiana.edu/cas/tt/tthmpg.html

All teachers have concerns regarding the "quality of life" in classroom settings. All teachers and students want to feel safe and accepted when they are in school. There exists today a reliable, effective knowledge base on classroom management and the prevention of disorder in schools. This knowledge base has been developed from hundreds of studies of teacher/student interaction and student/student interaction that have been conducted in schools in North America and Europe. We speak of managing life in classrooms because we now know that there are many factors that go into building effective teacher/student and student/student relationships. The traditional term *discipline* is too narrow and refers primarily to teachers' reactions to undesired student behavior. We can better understand methods of managing student behavior when we look at the totality of what goes on in classrooms, with teachers' responses to student behavior as a part of that totality. Teachers have tremendous responsibility for the emotional climate that is set in a classroom. Whether students feel secure and safe and whether they want to learn depends to an enormous extent on the psychological frame of mind of the teacher. Teachers must be able to manage their own selves first in order to effectively manage the development of a humane and caring classroom environment.

Teachers bear moral and ethical responsibilities for being witnesses to and examples of responsible social behavior in the classroom. There are many models of observing life in classrooms. Arranging the total physical environment of the room is a very important part of the teacher's planning for learning activities. Teachers need to expect from students the best work and behavior that they are capable of achieving. Respect and caring are attitudes that a teacher must communicate to receive them in return. Open lines of communication between teachers and students enhance the possibility for congenial, fair dialogical resolution of problems as they occur.

Developing a high level of task orientation among students and encouraging cooperative learning and shared task achievement will foster camaraderie and self-confidence among students. Shared decision making will build an *esprit de corps*, a sense of pride and confidence, which will feed on itself and blossom into high-quality performance. Good class morale, well managed, never hurts academic achievement. The importance of emphasizing quality, helping students to achieve levels of performance that they can feel proud of having attained, and encouraging positive dialogue among them leads them to take ownership in their individual educative efforts. When that happens, they literally empower themselves to do their best.

When teachers (and prospective teachers) discuss what concerns them about their roles (and prospective roles) in the classroom, the issue of discipline—how to manage student behavior—will usually rank near or at the top of their lists. A teacher needs a clear understanding of what kinds of learning environments are most appropriate for the subject matter and ages of the students. Any person who wants to teach must also want his or her students to learn well, to acquire basic values of respect for others, and to become more effective citizens.

There is considerable debate among educators regarding certain approaches used in schools to achieve a form of order in classrooms that also develop respect for self and others. The dialogue about this point is spirited and informative. The bottom line for any effective and humane approach to discipline in the classroom, the necessary starting point, is the teacher's emotional balance and capacity for self-control. This precondition creates a further one—that the teacher wants to be in the classroom with his or her students in the first place. Unmotivated teachers cannot motivate students.

Helping young people learn the skills of self-control and motivation to become productive, contributing, and knowledgeable adult participants in society is one of the most important tasks that good teachers undertake. These are teachable and learnable skills; they do not relate to heredity or social conditions. They can be learned by any human being who wants to learn them and who is cognitively able to learn them. There is a large knowledge base on how teachers can help students learn self-control. All that is required is the willingness of teachers to learn these skills themselves and to teach them to their students. There are many sound techniques that new teachers can use to achieve success in managing students' classroom behavior, and they should not be afraid to ask colleagues questions and to develop peer support groups with whom they can work with confidence and trust.

Teachers' core ethical principles come into play when deciding what constitutes defensible and desirable standards of student conduct. Teachers need to realize that before they can control behavior, they must identify what student behaviors are desired in their classrooms. They need to reflect, as well, on the emotional tone and ethical principles implied by their own behaviors. To optimize their chances of achieving the classroom atmosphere that they wish, teachers must strive for emotional balance within themselves; they must learn to be accurate observers; and they must develop just, fair strategies of intervention to aid students in learning self-control and good behavior. A teacher should be a good model of courtesy, respect, tact, and discretion. Children learn by observing how other persons behave and not just by being told how they are to behave. There is no substitute for positive, assertive teacher interaction with students in class.

This unit addresses many of the topics covered in basic foundations courses. The selections shed light on classroom management issues, teacher leadership skills, and the rights and responsibilities of teachers and students. In addition, the articles can be discussed in foundations courses involving curricula and instruction. This unit falls between the units on moral education and equal opportunity because it can be directly related to either or both of them.

Welcome to the House System

A junior high school finds that its new system of social houses hasn't only improved school climate—it's raised student achievement.

Daniel G. Green

J.K. Rowling's *Harry Potter* series provides a fictitious yet surprisingly instructive approach to school community building. The adolescent wizards who attend Hogwarts all belong to one of four social houses, which cross gender, racial, ethnic, social-class, age, and academic boundaries. This structure and the system in which students' behavior and accomplishments gain points for their houses provide Rowling's characters with a strong sense of community spirit and identity.

Three years ago, Goleta Valley Junior High, located in Goleta, California, was looking for some "wizardry" to improve its school climate. The school serves 900 7th and 8th graders; approximately 50 percent of our students are white and 40 percent Hispanic, with 26 percent eligible for free or reduced-price lunch. The school suffered from problems that plague early adolescents in junior high schools across the United States. In addition to their natural hormonal changes and identity struggles, our tweens were experiencing an increase in bullying, fighting, and racial segregation, and suspension rates were on the rise. Teachers observed a striking correlation between student unrest and declining academic performance.

As a staff, we searched for ways to help connect students to one another and to the school community as a whole. We considered dividing the school into small learning communities. As research has shown, small school environments can bolster "student affiliation with the school community" while increasing safety and order (Cotton, 2001, p. 50). Students are more likely to participate in extracurricular activities and less likely to engage in risky behaviors, such as truancy or dropping out of school. The end results are more positive student attitudes and higher achievement for all.

Despite this encouraging research, the prospect of entirely reorganizing the school into multiple academies or academic houses seemed daunting. We had a new principal and a 20 percent staff turnover rate since the previous year. Statistics indicated that we would have a difficult time meeting No Child Left Behind objectives for all populations, which meant that we would need to dedicate significant time and resources to avoiding future sanctions. The time was not right for a major structural change. However, we still wanted to harness the benefits of small learning communities. Our principal, Paul Turnbull, who had observed social houses while growing up and teaching in Ontario and British Columbia, suggested we give the system a try.

Used in schools across Canada and Europe, social houses divide students into multiple social units rather than into separate academic entities. Each unit has its own identity and theme. At Goleta Valley, all students mix during the day in regular classrooms but divide into their four houses during social and academic competitions, community service activities, and school-wide leadership meetings. The houses reflect the school's diversity, encompassing students of various races, ethnicities, ages, and academic abilities. Teachers and staff members are assigned to the houses to encourage stronger relationships between adults and students. Each house has approximately 230 students and 17 staff members. Once the houses are formed, they compete against one another for points and build a greater sense of community in the process.

Many faculty members endorsed the social house program, pointing out that it would fit the developmental needs of our junior high population. Social houses have the potential to lessen the anxiety caused by the transition from all-inclusive elementary classrooms to secondary school. A smaller environment can also reduce insecurities caused by rapid physical and psychological changes. At the same time, engaging house activities can harness and enhance some of the more positive attributes of early adolescence, such as students' burgeoning idealism and interest in the world.

Ready, Set, Go!

We actively solicited student involvement in designing the program. For example, students participated in the initial step of naming the four houses. After submitting names and voting on the possibilities, students chose "Blue Pirates," "Red Sea Monkeys," "White Buccaneers," and "Golden Vikings." A local artist created a logo for each house to place on posters, T-shirts, flags, and ID cards. Students selected the winning artwork.

Students, teachers, cafeteria employees, office staff, custodians, and even the security guard were assigned to one of the four houses. To help students and staff identify fellow members of their new social teams, we distributed T-shirts and campus IDs with house logos and displayed group pictures of the houses throughout the campus.

Our primary goal was to use social houses as a means of building school community. We hoped that a smaller-feeling school would promote new friendships among students and help them develop citizenship skills, stronger relationships with staff, and a greater sense of identity. A wide body of research suggested that improved school climate would also translate into better academic results in the classroom (Hoy & Hannum, 1997).

We communicated these goals to students at an opening assembly and described the programs point system. The house that earned the most points between September and June would earn a trophy called the Mariner Cup. Houses could accumulate points through acts of citizenship or achievement by individual students, participation in group competitions, and housewide contributions to the local community. With much anticipation and excitement, in November 2003 we officially commenced the first year of the social house program.

House Activities

Opportunities for Individuals to Earn Points

Organizing students into social houses provides staff with an effective and easy way to reinforce positive behaviors on campus. Teachers can give points to students who assist others, participate in class, demonstrate effort, or attend the homework center. For instance, an English teacher might award points to a shy student who overcomes his fear of public speaking by reading in front of the class. The teacher might also reward a fidgety student who, for the first time in two weeks, has managed to stay in her seat for the whole period. Outside the classroom, cafeteria employees might award points to students for picking up and throwing away someone else's trash. The librarian can offer points to students who are silent during quiet hours.

Students love the feeling of being "caught doing something good" by a staff member and feel excited about contributing points to their small communities. Staff members jot down the names of the point-earning students and the houses they represent in a standardized house point form that they send to the office secretary at the end of the week. The secretary tallies the points for each house and posts the results on campus the following week.

Our administration has capitalized on student enthusiasm for this system by creating additional academic incentives. Vice principals randomly enter classrooms to offer points to those students who have written down homework assignments in their agendas or brought writing instruments to class. In this way, our school leaders reinforce routines needed for academic success while interacting with the students in a fun, nonbureaucratic manner.

Although the main focus of the program is social and school climate improvement, we have implemented a few academics-related contests. For instance, we calculate the combined grade point averages of all students in each house at the end of the school year, awarding points to the group with the highest GPA. Also, some teachers choose to award individual points to students on the basis of academic criteria—for making particularly insightful comments in class, for example, or reaching their academic potential on an exam.

Group Competitions

Students can also gain points for their houses by participating in a myriad of interactive group activities on campus. House competitions, such as trivia matches, relay races, dodgeball games, or dance contests, take place every Tuesday at lunch. Students enthusiastically represent their houses and participate in activities that they might otherwise ignore. In the process, they build connections and friendships with people outside their normal peer groups. As one student told me,

> I used to hate lunch until the house activities started. Now I can participate in fun events, get points for my house, and make new friends instead of being bored.

Some teachers replicate the success of these lunchtime activities within their own classrooms. Because every class contains students from all four houses, teachers can easily divide the students into teams by house to participate in academic contests. The kids love joining their fellow housemates in games of history Jeopardy, science scavenger hunts, or grammar bingo. This sense of competition among house groups exponentially increases student engagement in the classroom. As one teacher remarked,

> I can take a regular activity and transform it into a house competition, making it one of the most thrilling lessons of the week. For example, I'll split the kids into their four house groups as part of a test review Jeopardy game. Students who are normally unenthusiastic in class practically jump out of their seats as they try to earn points for their houses.

Community Involvement

The house system also serves as a perfect forum for introducing the importance of community service. Many students enter junior high never having experienced the value of giving to others in need. We conduct annual clothing drives, book collections for our feeder elementary schools, and fund-raisers for the homeless. All houses receive points for their participation, but the real reward for students is experiencing the thrill of connecting with their local communities. Exposure to such opportunities can encourage lifelong commitments to community involvement.

Student Leadership

Faculty members nominate 8th graders as house representatives at the beginning of each school year, with 7th graders joining the mix in the spring. The representatives develop leadership capabilities through joint seminars and eventually divide into their four individual house committees to plan specific activities. Under the supervision of a teacher from their respective houses, the committees plan one lunchtime activity each month, a schoolwide dance, special theme days, and a community service fund-raiser—for example, the annual book drive, which garnered more than 1,700 books to be donated to Goleta Valley's feeder elementary schools.

Concerns About the House Program

Some teachers have asked whether competition among social houses might actually hurt school climate rather than making it more robust. If students were to take the house point system too seriously, fragmentation within the student body and lower self-esteem among the losing houses might result.

To address these concerns, during the last two years we have calibrated the point system to award participation, effort, and growth just as much as achievement. For instance, all house participants in a game of trivia are awarded points for effort, with the winning house getting only a few more points than the other teams. Students also receive benchmark rewards that recognize growth throughout the year. For example, the Golden Vikings could win a barbeque served by the principal if house members recycled more bottles in April than in March. Finally, all of our competitions are cooperative so that students never feel singled out for failure in front of their peers.

Another area of concern involves 8th graders, who seem to lose interest in the house program toward the end of their 8th grade year. To keep these students engaged, we are developing new opportunities for student leadership. For instance, 8th graders will gain life skills by mentoring 7th grade future house leaders. We are also creating 8th grade-only house competitions, such as a talent show and kickball matches, in which students compete against staff members. We also hope that our schoolwide international festival this spring, which will include multicultural poetry, sports, drama, trivia, and board game competitions, will reinvigorate 8th grade interest in the house program.

> **Social houses divide students into multiple social units rather than into separate academic entities.**

Another challenge of the program is getting teacher buy-in. Teachers who were not part of the original planning process might not understand how the program works or see the benefits of social houses. We are remedying this problem by putting on presentations about the program's benefits at the beginning of each school year and involving new faculty members in planning future house activities.

The Results

We have noticed numerous benefits of our social house program. Interviews with members of the school community indicate stronger and more relaxed bonds between students and staff. Students seem to enjoy working side by side with teachers as part of on-campus house activities and community service fund-raisers. One student explained,

> I feel closer to teachers who roll up their sleeves and join us in the house events. They're not just giving us grades—they're more on our level.

Paul Campbell, a 7th grade teacher, concurs:

> Students don't see us as the bad guys so much. They think it's great when we award them points or work with them to win a tug-of-war. There's more of a "we're in this together" feeling that spills into the classroom.

We have also observed significant decreases in school suspension and bullying rates. During the last two years, suspensions fell by almost 50 percent. Moreover, a two-year study conducted by the University of California–Santa Barbara found that reports of teasing, harmful rumors, and physical violence have decreased significantly since the inception of the house program (Greif & Furlong, 2005). We believe that houses have played an integral role in improving school climate to a point where students can focus on what matters most: achieving social and academic success. In fact, in the last year, Goleta Valley's Academic Performance Indicator (API) test score rose 35 points. This was four times greater than the previous year's API increase.

Word of the program has reached the six elementary schools that feed into Goleta Valley Junior High. As we conduct site visits to 6th grade classes within the district, students inundate us with questions like "Can I be a Pirate?" or "When will I find out what house I'm in?" Rather than feeling anxious about possible 8th grade bullies or getting lost on a large campus, these 6th graders are focusing on a positive aspect of junior high. And because they will enter the school in the fall with a positive attitude, they are more likely to be successful from the start.

One of the best ways to measure the impact of social houses is to observe our campus during lunchtime. A visitor will notice happy, smiling students of diverse backgrounds and ethnicities participating together in house activities. The overall atmosphere of our campus today is more upbeat, safe, and energetic. Social houses may have been just the stroke of magic that our school community needed.

References

Cotton, K. (2001). New small learning communities: Findings from recent literature. *School Improvement Research Series*. Portland, OR: Northwest Regional Educational Laboratory.

Greif, J. L., & Furlong, M. J. (2005). *Survey of bullying: Goleta Valley Junior High*. Unpublished report. University of California-Santa Barbara, Center for School-Based Youth Development.

Hoy, W. K., & Hannum, J. W. (1997). Middle school climate: An empirical assessment of organizational health and student achievement. *Educational Administration Quarterly, 33*, 290–311.

DANIEL G. GREEN is House Program Coordinator and a social studies teacher at Goleta Valley Junior High School in Goleta, California; **dgreen@sbsdk12.org**.

Discipline: Responding to Socioeconomic and Racial Differences

The use of prejudicial classroom management techniques with minority students, particularly African American and Hispanics, is well-documented.

DORIS WALKER-DALHOUSE

Changing school demographics, coupled with a teaching force that is predominantly white and female, has created a growing discrepancy between teachers and the students they teach. Many children of color and children in poverty do not display the behaviors or experience the type or degree of success in school as white or middle-class students do. Consequently, they create challenges for the teacher. They may pose disciplinary problems, and so teachers may underteach these students as they focus on addressing the behavior.

In what follows, I will share my experiences teaching in a 4th-grade class of predominantly African American children for a year. After residing in the midwestern United States for 12 years, I decided to return to the state where I received my teacher preparation to pursue a teaching opportunity in the public school system during a year-long sabbatical from a university faculty position. The sabbatical provided me with the opportunity to work with predominantly African American, lower socioeconomic students in a magnet school program—a school within a school program founded on the philosophy of educator Marva Collins.

Review of Research

Children from minority and low-income backgrounds are less likely, when compared to middle-class and majority students, to have positive relationships with their middle-class teachers. A number of explanations have been offered for this situation (Pianta & Nimetz, 1991; Townsend, Thomas, Witty, & Lee, 1996; Vondra, Shaw, Swearingen, Cohen, & Owens, 1999). One explanation is that these differences reflect teachers' biases, classroom management styles, and disparities in the severity of practices used for discipline. The use of prejudicial classroom management techniques with minority students, particularly African American and Hispanics, is well-documented (Banks & Banks, 1993; Sheets & Gay, 1998; Skiba, Michael, Nardo, & Peterson, 2002). Teachers perceive that the behavior of African American males is more aggressive and severe than that of their white counterparts.

African American males who misbehave in the same way as their white counterparts are more likely to be punished (Ferguson, 2000; Obidah & Teel, 2001; Sheets & Gay, 1998), resulting in suspensions and expulsions (Costenbader & Markson, 1994; Pauken & Daniel, 1999; Townsend, 2000). The severity of these disciplinary practices against minority students impedes their achievement in the classroom, excludes them from courses, alienates them, increases misbehavior, and leads to higher drop-out rates, lowered expectations, and more frequent grade retention (Garibaldi, 1992; Irvine, 1990; Meisels & Liaw, 1993; Oakes, 1994; Rodney, Grafter, Rodney, & Mupier, 1999).

Rodney et al. (1999) pointed out that suspensions of African American males, 13–17 years old, are associated with poor academic performance. Yet poor academic performance by African American males is not likely to improve unless the school environment improves for African American males. According to Gottfredson, Fink, and Graham (1994), grade retention is a generally preferable alternative to suspension and expulsion for African American males. Retention could reduce rebellious behavior in school, reduce feelings of alienation, and increase 6th- and 7th-grade African American males' feelings of attachment to school. However, there is evidence that retention does not reduce in-school rebelliousness or feelings of alienation in these students (Gottfredson et al., 1994). Indeed, accumulated research shows that most students who are retained perform less well and misbehave more than those who are socially promoted.

Classroom disciplinary practices also are influenced by students' socioeconomic level. Teachers frequently view low-income students as having the highest potential for behavior problems (Malone, Bonitz, & Rickett, 1998). Consequently, students from low-income homes, regardless of ethnicity, are disciplined more often by teachers than middle-class white students. Additionally, teachers of low socioeconomic children most often use or support the use of corporal punishment, verbal punishment, or suspension, compared to teachers of middle-class students (Lezotte, 1998–99). Lezotte argued that some of the behaviors by culturally diverse lower socioeconomic level students that teachers may find annoying and/or problematic are behaviors that serve a function in the students' world outside of school.

There is a scarcity of literature and discussion about culturally responsive teachers and issues associated with classroom management (Weinstein, Tomlinson-Clarke, & Curran, 2004) and limited scholarship that addresses disciplinary practices (Monroe & Obidah, 2004). Especially lacking is systematic research with African American children that addresses behavioral problems and ways to promote successful classroom experiences. In one of the few published studies on the subject, Tucker, Herman, Pedersen, and Vogel (1998) conducted interviews with 13 African American teachers as part of a pilot study on the behavior of African American students (five elementary and eight high school teachers). The five elementary teachers reported that the most common classroom behavioral problem of African American males that they encountered was inattentive behavior and failure to follow directions. Next in order of frequency were inappropriate talking and horseplay, followed by talking back to teachers in a disrespectful manner. The high school teachers reported that the most common behavior problems they encountered with African American males were talking back to teachers in a disrespectful and argumentative manner and inappropriate talking and horseplay in the classroom.

Ecological behavioral theorists explain that children's behavior is influenced directly by aspects of their immediate environment (e.g., interactions with their peers and family), as well as indirectly by aspects of the environment in which they themselves are not participants (e.g., the stress their parents face at work) (Tucker, 1999). Educators of students from diverse backgrounds must teach them to separate school behavior from nonschool behavior. Most important, the behaviors presented must be grounded in structure and choice. The element of choice is important because it moves these students from being dependent upon others for controlling their behaviors to self-control of behaviors they choose to perform.

The school, home, and students must work together to clearly identify appropriate school behaviors, and the consequences for not choosing those behaviors must be clearly stated (Delpit, 1995; Lezotte, 1998–1999). For students who perceive that there is no good reason to control their behavior, appeals can be made to their ethnic pride, or to their community or family values and expectations. In other words, teachers must acquire cross-cultural literacy, or the ability to use students' cultural backgrounds, to help them develop more adaptive classroom behaviors (Cartledge, Tillman, & Johnson, 2001). Ladson-Billings's (1994) research involving successful African American teachers of African American children reinforces the need to employ culturally relevant teaching practices.

Three principles of culturally relevant teaching that are especially important for discipline include judicious use of authority in the classroom, viewing students as extended family members, and changing one's perceptions about student achievement. Among things that majority and minority teachers must do to employ culturally relevant classroom management practices are the following: 1) recognize their own ethnocentrism and biases; 2) increase their knowledge of their students' cultural backgrounds; 3) understand the effect of broader social,

economic, and political contexts in interpreting and responding to the students' behavior; 4) use culturally appropriate classroom strategies to help students assume responsibility for behaving appropriately; and 5) display a commitment to creating caring classroom communities (Weinstein, Tomlinson-Clarke, & Curran, 2004). Strategies that help establish culturally responsive classroom management include: 1) establishing behavioral expectations for students, 2) developing a caring classroom environment, 3) working with families, and 4) using appropriate interventions to assist students with behavioral problems (Weinstein, Curran, & Tomlinson-Clarke, 2003).

Marva Collins's Methods

Marva Collins, a noted African American educator, employs humanistic principles to manage urban classrooms in Chicago. At the center of her approach is the belief that teachers who display high expectations and recognize that teaching itself is discipline will be successful (Collins, 1999). Collins tells her students that she expects them to behave in ways that contribute to the learning process and benefit other children. Teachers are encouraged to establish a positive relationship with their students before discipline problems develop. When it is necessary to discipline a student, Collins believes that it must be done in a caring manner (Collins, 1992; Collins & Tamarkin, 1982). Collins encourages teachers not only to praise, or, if need be, express concern for, student behavior, but also to demonstrate tough love. That is, teachers should show empathy and understanding for students' out-of-class problems/stressors that may contribute to problem behaviors, while continuing to hold high expectations for their achievement and behavior. Collins expects teachers to be direct with students about the negative consequences of inappropriate behavior, and work diligently to teach them that self-discipline and self-determination are necessary for success (Collins & Tamarkin, 1982).

Collins's philosophy of teaching includes informing students of their freedom to make choices about learning or not learning, and making them aware of the consequences for choosing not to learn. Teachers are responsible for encouraging students to demonstrate leadership, display confidence in their convictions, engage in reflective thinking, and assume control over their futures. If teachers want to eliminate discipline problems, they must create an organized classroom environment and adopt a consistent strategy of presenting information to students. The presentation strategy that Collins uses informs students about what they will be learning, outlines the methods and techniques to be used in presenting content, and makes connections between the content to be learned and the students' short-term and long-term goals (Hollins, 1982). The opportunity for success is greater if the process is started with children in the early grades. If students do not possess the skills of self-control or positive socialization, they may need assistance from a counselor in addition to the support provided by the regular classroom teacher.

Collins (1999) argues that teachers who hold low expectations for low-income African American children are not helping them to be successful in controlling their behavior or in achieving academically. Teachers should let their students know that they are confident of their abilities to exhibit self-control and to analyze and reflect about their behaviors. Self-control and reflection can be taught directly through systematic and situational-based instruction, and indirectly through discussion and teacher modeling. Collins (1999) reports that she successfully used writing as an integral part of a reflective process in which students are asked to record the reasons why they are too intelligent to engage in disruptive behavior. Collins also reports that she taught students proverbs and had them write and recite the proverbs as a means of teaching the students how to change disruptive behaviors (Collins & Tamarkin, 1982). Proverbs, poems, humor, and multicultural literature are powerful forms of language that have historically been used in African American culture to teach life lessons and can be used to convey expectations for success. Such poems as Maya Angelou's "On the Pulse of Morning" and Langston Hughes's "I, Too" can be used to motivate students and provide them with culturally relevant messages about establishing self-control by being optimistic about their future, setting goals, and maintaining high expectations.

At the center of her approach is the belief that teachers who display high expectations and recognize that teaching itself is discipline will be successful.

The Marva Collins plan requires students to establish individual expectations for behaviors. Students are challenged to change their inappropriate behavior because of teacher expectations, or because of situations in which they are placed. Teachers are encouraged to promote student self-reflection, as opposed to recording students' infractions with a penalty system (Collins, 1999).

The state where I taught established the magnet school concept in an effort to provide alternate instructional models to meet students' varying talents and needs. The enrollment in the magnet program was approximately 50 percent white and 40 percent African American. Approximately 63.4 percent of the students received free or reduced lunch. My class of 14 students was 79 percent African American and 21 percent white. Seventy-one percent (10) were female and 29 percent (4) were male. Sixty-seven percent of the students were designated as limited income. Student performance on the Gates-MacGinitie Reading Test indicated that only four of the fourteen 4th-grade students (30 percent) were reading at the 4th-grade level. None of the students scored higher than 50 percent on the Inventory and Cumulative tests associated with the Addison-Wesley mathematics series.

I learned the basics of teaching in a teacher education program at a historically African American university in the southeastern region of the United States and applied those principles and practices during my initial teaching experiences in a predominantly white, middle-class school setting. My teacher education program did not include a specific course in classroom management.

Prior to student teaching, we were told that it was important that we maintain control over our respective classrooms if the students were to learn and we were to be effective teachers. We were taught indirectly that we needed to maintain order through appropriate punishment (firmly warning against misconduct, sending students to time-out, using assigned seating, and removing students from the classroom and sending them to the principal's office). Disciplinary challenges were expected to be few in number; to be successful, we should only need to make examples of a few students and the rest of the class would know that certain behaviors would not be tolerated. Before embarking on my sabbatical, I thought about what I knew and realized that more would be required if I intended to be successful in working with students facing great challenges at home.

Drawing upon my personal knowledge of African American culture and classroom experiences teaching African American children in integrated classroom settings, I re-entered the classroom feeling prepared for the challenges ahead. I knew that my year would not be without problems but I was prepared to facilitate and support my students' decision making, academic success, and self-concept, and to expect nothing less than their very best behavior and work.

Implementation of the Marva Collins Methods

At the beginning of the school year, my attempts to impose discipline were most frequently met with shrugs, eye rolling, and talking back. Students engaged in verbal disputes and ridiculed each other, often disrupting the daily class functioning. It was clear that these behavior problems had to be resolved if students were going to achieve the individual goals reflected in their mission statements, as well as reach the district-level academic goals for 4th grade. While I was concerned about fostering a classroom environment where all students could learn, I was particularly interested in helping those students at high risk for failure and alienation from school. The students who were the most disruptive and presented the greatest disciplinary challenges were two low-income, low-achieving males.

The teachers in our magnet program believed that parents were a key to preparing students to learn. The parents were expected to sign a contract that identified the goals of the academy, the expected learner outcomes, and the expected teacher, parent, and student commitments to achieving the goals and outcomes. Parents, teachers, and students signed contracts during a special ceremony at the beginning of the year. A parent advisory board, consisting of parents with children in kindergarten through 4th grade, was formed to assist teachers with grade level and program level issues, including discipline.

Marva Collins suggests that teachers begin the school year by having students write a mission statement that puts into words what they hope to be or to accomplish in life. She recommends that these statements be taped to students' desks so that they can be reread each time students misbehave. I modified this process slightly by having students write their mission statement and goals in a journal at the beginning of the school year.

Each day, I read selections from the *Children's Book of Virtues* (Bennett, 1995) to provide them with stories and sayings that related to various aspects of self-control and motivation. I also wrote proverbs on the board and asked students to write their reactions to the proverbs in their individual journals. For example, students copied down a statement by Martin Luther King, Jr.—"We must all live together as brothers or perish as fools"—in their journals and then wrote what it meant to them. This exercise was followed by class sharing and discussion.

Some of the children brought unresolved conflicts with classmates from the previous school year, thereby creating early disciplinary challenges. Other conflicts in the classroom resulted from agitated feelings about race, economics, and social interactions. Another issue that challenged the class was the perceived differences in physical or personal attributes between both boys and girls. I used excerpts from the Marva Collins Creed to assist students in self-reflection when they engaged in verbal put-downs. The Creed, 22 verses long, emphasizes that achievement is an individual choice and that positive thinking and taking personal responsibility are important. Students were asked to select lines from the creed and to recite the line needed to redirect their behavior and/or thinking (e.g., "I was born to win, if I do not spend too much time trying to fail"). I also incorporated writing into the disciplinary plan by having students make journal entries in which they described how they had lost sight of their mission. They were expected to use appropriate lines from the Marva Collins Creed, the *Book of Virtues*, or from African proverbs or poetry, such as the poem "Perseverance" (author unknown), in an effort to help them learn from their mistakes and refocus their efforts in a positive direction. I found that students who were asked to write apology poems as a result of specific behaviors found new outlets to express their creativity and humor. I discovered that my students usually ended up learning by trying to outdo their fellow students in their written apologies. Creating and sharing songs or stories about conflicts or classroom situations also can be used to generate laughter and move students to view a situation from a different and more positive perspective. Again, students are presented with the opportunity to take responsibility for their behavior and recognize that they have choices.

I implemented the Marva Collins approach and the above techniques with my 4th-grade class at the beginning of my sabbatical year. By the end of the year, this group of students, which had a history of behavior problems and whose reading performance averaged two levels below grade, became a class with minimal behavior problems and an average improvement of two grade levels in reading performance.

What I Learned About Discipline

Teachers need to take time to examine their disciplinary and instructional practices and to change their attitudes and beliefs about African American children and their families (Townsend, 2000). There are no easy answers to finding the right combinations of actions that will help children to behave in ways that will allow them to be successful in the school environment. As more and more economically, ethnically, linguistically, and culturally diverse students enter schools, teachers must continually seek ways to engage these students mentally and to channel their energies so that they have some control over their future, if not their present circumstances. New teachers must be informed about family/community norms and recognize and respond to the learning characteristics of diverse students. They must get to know the children as people who are not responsible for the quality of their lives and accept their parents as people who often have the desire but not necessarily the resources or skills to provide a better life for their children.

The most important lesson I learned is that it is critical for the teacher to establish a caring and supportive relationship with African American children. This relationship can manifest itself in individual and group conversations in which teachers share their interests, cultures, and beliefs with students. The teachers also might learn about the communities, the issues affecting students in their community, and the resources that those communities provide. Reading community newsletters or special African American newspapers, attending community events, or listening to radio stations or programs will provide teachers with background information. The information learned can be used to engage and motivate students by creating authentic learning experiences that address students' home environments. Relevance in learning through cultural connections is an essential component of classroom management. Enforcing classroom rules, by itself, will not necessarily create a classroom environment that is conducive to learning for African American children. It is more critical to make connections with students or nurture teacher-student relationships so as to convey to students that they are important—first, because of who they are and, second, because of who they have the potential to become.

I found it essential to establish communication links with parents before problems arose in the classroom. Home visits, if acceptable both to teachers and parents, can be used to make initial contact. Alternate sites for such meetings might be public library meeting rooms, churches, or other public places. Teachers should periodically follow up by calling parents to share children's school successes. I recall making one such call to a parent who thanked me for my interest in her child and said that it was the first time that she had been called to be told something good about her son. I found it important to dispel the fear that many African American parents have—that any communication from the teacher means the start of trouble for the child and spells conflict between teacher and parent.

I inquired from parents, via telephone and/or conferences, about family expectations for their children's behavior. The shared home and school expectations were recorded and used selectively to remind students of appropriate classroom and school behaviors. Middle-class or white teachers often need help in interpreting family expectations in light of cultural norms or values. I would recommend creating a parent advisory board. African American fathers, single mothers, and two-parent families should be asked to engage in dialogue about problem classroom behaviors and ways to empower African American students. The parent advisory board for our magnet program and the room parents worked in conjunction with our teachers in this area.

I learned that it is important to convey, both orally and in writing, the classroom expectations to students and parents. It is important to teach students what is expected of them and model appropriate responses to situations. It is essential that teachers demonstrate, through their language and actions, their belief that students are capable of working cooperatively to achieve class goals. Student-created mission statements and contracts can be effective tools in creating a classroom environment where students can be challenged to learn. I used individual conferences with students to develop contracts that were signed by parents as an expression of support for their children's efforts; these were used to establish benchmarks for behavioral and academic goals. Both documents were used as assessment tools for student reflection and teacher planning. By sharing their goals with parents, teachers can make essential cultural connections with the child's family and community by informing them of the goals and implicitly asking for help in supporting the child's efforts.

I learned that in the classroom, teachers must behave as compassionate but firm authority figures who will support their students in their efforts to reach their goals; they must not be afraid to hold them accountable for inappropriate behaviors. Middle-class white teachers must especially earn students' trust and respect by being assertive and strong in conveying their expectations for learning and behaving. They should treat their students as they would their own children (Obidah & Teel, 2001).

Summary

Monroe and Obidah (2004) believe that it is crucial to build cultural bridges between teachers and students in order to reverse the effects of students' misbehavior. Culturally based classroom management must be used in all classrooms—suburban, urban, and rural—where ethnically and culturally diverse students are found. It is incumbent on the teachers in these schools to analyze their perceptions of and interactions with African American students, especially boys. These teachers must establish a classroom environment that affirms and celebrates their students' cultures, promotes student control in setting and achieving academic and behavioral goals, communicates clear expectations for success, and promotes connections and communication between the school and each child's home and community (Cooper, 2003; Sheldon, 2002; Vondra, 1999). As teacher educators and researchers, we also must challenge ourselves to make cultural diversity an integral part of our discussions about classroom management as we strive to prepare preservice teachers to become multiculturally competent (Weinstein, Tomlinson-Clarke, & Curran, 2004).

References

Banks, J., & Banks, C. A. M. (Eds.). (1993). *Multicultural education: Issues and perspectives* (2nd ed.). Boston: Allyn & Bacon.

Bennett, W. (Ed.). (1995). *The children's book of virtues*. New York: Simon & Schuster.

Cartledge, G., Tillman, L., & Johnson, C. (2001). Professional ethics within the context of student discipline and diversity. *Teacher Education and Special Education, 24*(1), 25–37.

Collins, M., & Tamarkin, C. (1982). *Marva Collins' way*. Los Angeles: J. P. Tarcher.

Collins, M. (1992). *Ordinary children, extraordinary teachers*. Norfolk, VA: Hampton Roads Publishers.

Collins, M. (1999). *Marva Collins's teacher power seminar 2000 workbook*. Chicago: Marva Collins Publisher.

Cooper, P. M. (2003). Effective white teachers of black children: Teaching within a community. *Journal of Teacher Education, 54*(5), 413–427.

Costenbader, V., & Markson, S. (1994, October). School suspension: A survey of current policies and practices. *NASSP Bulletin*, 103–107.

Delpit, L. (1995). *Other people's children*. New York: The New Press.

Ferguson, A. A. (2000). *Bad boys: Public schools in the making of Black masculinity*. Ann Arbor, MI: University of Michigan Press.

Garibaldi, A. M. (1992). Educating and motivating African American males to succeed. *Journal of Negro Education, 61*(1), 12–18.

Gottfredson, D. C., Fink, C., & Graham, N. (1994). Grade retention and problem behavior. *American Educational Research Journal, 31*(4), 761–784.

Hollins, E. R. (1982). The Marva Collins story revisited: Implications for regular classroom instruction. *Journal of Teacher Education, 33*(1), 37–40.

Irvine, J. (1990). *Black students and school failure: Policies, practices, and prescriptions*. New York: Greenwood Press.

Ladson-Billings, G. (1994). *The dreamkeepers: Successful teachers of black children*. San Francisco: Jossey-Bass.

Lezotte, L. (1998-99). Home-school relations. *Effective Schools: Research Abstracts, 13*(7), 1–2.

Malone, B., Bonitz, D., & Rickett, M. (1998). Teacher perceptions of disruptive behavior. *Educational Horizons, 76*(4), 189–194.

Meisels, S. J., & Liaw, F. (1993). Failure in grade: Do retained students catch up? *Journal of Educational Research, 87*(2), 69–77.

Monroe, C., & Obidah, J. (2004). The influence of cultural synchronization on a teacher's perceptions of disruption: A case study of an African American middle-school classroom. *Journal of Teacher Education, 55*(3), 256–268.

Oakes, J. (1994). Tracking, inequality and the rhetoric of reform: Why schools don't change. In J. Kretovics & E. J. Nussel (Eds.), *Transforming urban education* (pp. 146–164). Needham Heights, MA: Allyn & Bacon.

Obidah, J., & Teel, K. M. (2001). *Because of the kids: Facing racial and cultural differences in schools*. New York: Teachers College Press.

Pauken, P. D., & Daniel, P. T. K. (1999). Race and disability discrimination in school discipline: A legal and statistical analysis. *Education Law Reporter*, Dec. 1999.

Pianta, R. C., & Nimetz, S. L. (1991). Relationships between children and teachers: Associations with classroom and home behavior. *Journal of Applied Developmental Psychology, 12*, 379–393.

Rodney, L., Crafter, G., Rodney, H. E., & Mupier, R. (1999). Variables contributing to grade retention among African American adolescents. *Journal of Educational Research, 92*(3), 185–190.

Sheets, R., & Gay, G. (1998). Student perceptions of disciplinary conflict in ethnically diverse classrooms. *NASSP Bulletin, 80*(5), 84–94.

Sheldon, S. (2002). Improving student behavior and school discipline with family and community involvement. *Education and Urban Society, 35*(1), 4–26.

Skiba, R., Michael, R. S., Nardo, A., & Peterson, R. (2002). The color of discipline: Sources of racial and gender disproportionality in school punishment. *The Urban Review, 34*(4), 317–342.

Townsend, B. (2000). The disproportionate discipline of African-American learners: Reducing school suspensions and expulsions. *Exceptional Children, 66*(3), 381–391.

Townsend, B., Thomas, D., Witty, J., & Lee, R. (1996). Diversity and school restructuring: Creating partnerships in a world of difference. *Teacher Education and Special Education, 19*(2), 102–188.

Tucker, C. (1999). *African American children: A self-empowerment approach to modifying behavior problems and preventing academic failure.* Boston: Allyn & Bacon.

Tucker, C. M., Herman, K., Pedersen, T., & Vogel, D. (1998). *The research-based model partnership education program: A 4-year outcome study.* Unpublished manuscript.

Vondra, J. I. (1999). Commentary for "Schooling and high-risk populations: The Chicago Longitudinal Study." *Journal of School Psychology, 37*(4), 471–479.

Vondra, J. I., Shaw, D. S., Swearingen, L., Cohen, M., & Owens, E. B. (1999). Early education and early relationship from home to school: A longitudinal study. *Early Education and Development, 10*, 163–190.

Weinstein, C. S., Curran, M., & Tomlinson-Clarke, S. (2003). Culturally responsive classroom management: Awareness into action. *Theory Into Practice, 42*(4), 269–276.

Weinstein, C. S., Tomlinson-Clarke, S., & Curran, M. (2004). Toward a conception of culturally responsive classroom management. *Journal of Teacher Education, 55*(1), 25–38.

DORIS WALKER-DALHOUSE is Professor of Reading, Department of Elementary & Early Childhood Education, Minnesota State University Moorhead.

Reach Them to Teach Them

Four high school teachers show that teaching adolescents is about relevance and challenge, affection and respect.

CAROL ANN TOMLINSON AND KRISTINA DOUBET

Two observations from teachers of adolescents are so prevalent these days that they sound like theme music. The more recurrent refrain says that there's no time for covering anything in high school classes other than curriculum or standards: There's no time for discussion, for student interests, for products beyond mandatory quizzes and tests, or for activities. Teachers are under relentless pressure to prepare students for high-stakes tests and for advanced placement or International Baccalaureate exams. The amount of material to cover simply exceeds the time available for covering it.

The second refrain has to do with the impracticality—if not impossibility—of really knowing one's students in a high school setting. There are too many of them, and they are indifferent—or ill-behaved. Combined with the avalanche of pressure for high test scores, these factors make it unfeasible for teachers to know their students more than superficially.

Snapshots of four high school classrooms challenge these two pervasive beliefs. We profile four teachers who connect with their students and who persevere in making learning a process that engages the minds and imaginations of the adolescents they teach. These teachers' professional work centers on knowing their students well enough to make learning interesting and on knowing their content well enough to shape it to their students' needs. These snapshots serve as an antidote to the very real pressures that can make us forget what lies at the core of transformational high school classrooms.

Katie Carson's Classroom:

A Labor of Love

Katie Carson, a fifth-year teacher at Fauquier High School in Warrenton, Virginia, teaches English to 9th and 11th graders. She is a young teacher who spends some of her free time acting in and directing a comedy improvisation troupe in Washington, D.C. But teaching is her labor of love.

With the exception of a few overachievers in each class, says Carson, kids in high school "have zero desire to learn more about grammar, literature, and punctuation." The magic of early experiences with reading and writing is gone. So unless I create a class in which they discover one another's gifts and challenge one another, or unless they have a relationship with me," she adds, "students have no desire to learn those things."

Getting to Know One Another

Carson creates an environment in which students learn about one another and get to know their peers' strengths. She places students in groups in which they'll work for a quarter of the year. Once a week, on a randomly selected day, she gives the groups five-minute challenges, such as building the tallest tower in the class out of bits of paper and paper clips. You can hear students saying among themselves, "We need Steven for this job. He's the man!" This kind of focus is particularly important for students who are not initially seen as academic contributors.

The room is set up to welcome students who can sit in armchairs, on a couch, or at tables. Carson also studies learning preferences and gives students opportunities to learn in ways that meet their various needs. "It's part of showing respect," she says.

Attendance-taking begins with an "attendance question" as soon as the bell rings. As Carson calls their names, students respond to the day's question, providing a brief justification for their responses.

"OK, people, this is a big one today. Definitive answer. Coke or Pepsi?" On another day, she begins, "OK, folks, you've just been given a sampler box of Russell Stover candy, but the map is missing. You bite into a piece and much to your dismay, find you've chosen a_____." Students answer by filling in the blank. Before long, students bring her slips of paper, whispering, "Here's an attendance question. It's really good!"

Sharing Stories

Carson encourages students to tell their own stories. "I'll even delay a test for a few minutes for a good story," she says, "but it has to be a good one." On the first day of class, she puts on the board a story arc, which contains seven numbered lines:

1. Once upon a time …
2. And every day …
3. Until one day …

4. And then …

5. And then …

6. Until finally …

7. And ever since …

This is her way of teaching students about exposition, rising action, conflict, climax, and denouement. Teacher and students use the academic words in their conversations about stories, but the story arc serves as a barometer for assessing the stories that they share with one another. "You all have experiences that make good stories," she reminds the students. "But it's all in how you tell them."

Mastering the Content

Carson embeds the required content standards in her instruction, but the students feel that she's teaching them, not just "covering material." In a recent Utopia project, nearly all her juniors said that they would do away with state standards if they could. "What's the point?" they asked, and they lamented the number of times their teachers say, "Now you'll need to remember this because it's on the standards test."

Carson reminded those juniors that this was, in fact, a standards test year and that in three weeks, they would be taking the standards test in her class. "Yeah, but you don't bring it up all the time," they responded. "You prepare us without teaching to the test."

This is evident in a unit on 19th century American poetry. As the students compare various poems with artwork and photographs, Carson presents a quotation from a British author indicating that Americans have no literature. The students argue heatedly against the author's sentiment, using works that they have read as evidence to the contrary, and they ask whether they'll be able to "critique more artwork" after lunch.

Making Writing Relevant

When her class discusses a golden age of literature, Carson asks students to describe golden ages in their own lives and uses their descriptors as a segue into a serious discussion of literature. She notes,

> My job is to make sure the kids know that I care, that I appreciate their sharing the truth about their lives, and that I value their opinions. When we have that personal trust, it's not so horrifying for them to write and turn that writing in to me.

Too often, she says, writing in high school is an exercise of turning in a paper to get it back covered with red marks. We forget, she suggests, how important it is for students to know that they have stories to tell and that those stories are full of discoveries about human nature.

Ned, for example, was a low-achieving student who did not—would not—write. Then he made the junior varsity football team. Carson told him that she was impressed because she'd never understood football. "Gosh," he said, "you must be dumb." For the rest of the year, he wrote about football in his journal, and she wrote back about football. In passing, she would mention in class that she had watched part of a game on TV or at school. "I under-

stood why the flag was thrown. Thanks so much, Ned!" His stories had helped someone—and he was proud.

George Murphy's Classroom:

It's All About Inquiry

As Students enter George Murphy's 10th grade biology class, he chats with them individually about their reading and experiments. Murphy is science department chair at Fauquier High School in Warrenton, Virginia, and has taught for 24 years. When class begins, he proclaims, "Welcome to your favorite class of the day!" Students grin as he launches into the daily agenda posted on the board. There's a sense of urgency and excitement about the class: Important work is waiting, and there's no time to waste.

Demonstrating Understanding

The current science unit centers on energy and respiration. Murphy has embedded the key understandings in an exploration of diet and energy. He begins the unit with an Interactive demonstration that introduces the key concepts of energy, action, and reaction. Students observe a new piece of equipment—an empty fermentation apparatus—and they hypothesize about its possible use. Their ideas initiate a demonstration of a basic working fermentation setup. Once students are clear about what is required for fermentation, they launch into an inquiry process to determine what caused the reaction they witnessed in the demonstration. Murphy carefully guides the process to be sure that students "get it" before they design their own experiments, in which they will pose and test a hypothesis about the nature of energy. Murphy's students demonstrate their understandings about energy both by completing a lab report and by creating a product that they choose from a list of teacher-provided and student-designed options.

Students select one of three tasks to continue learning about energy: Some students finish their experiments; some work with a study guide on the topic; and others work on laptops to complete a diet planner, an exercise that helps them analyze energy consumed and energy expended in their own lives.

There is no class textbook. Instead, Murphy guides students in finding authentic and reputable information sources, in print or on the Web.

Very real pressures can make us forget what lies at the core of transformational high school classrooms.

Making It Relevant

Inquiry is at the root of Murphy's instruction. "I think everything in biology should be relevant to what students experience in their own lives," he says. "It's the study of life, so a student should be able to connect biology with everything we do."

He tells his students that if they can't see how a given topic connects to their lives, they probably shouldn't be studying it—either because it's not biology or because he hasn't clearly communicated the essence of the topic. He realizes that he must sometimes reteach material in new ways to help students find that connection. "We can talk about the ATP cycle, photosynthesis, and respiration, but that doesn't grab kids," Murphy says. What *does* rouse their curiosity is analyzing the foods they're eating and burning and figuring out the caloric content.

Murphy teaches his students on a half-year block schedule. That constricts the time he has to get to know them, so he makes his curriculum and instruction compelling from the start.

He explains,

It's not the standards that will make school relevant and vital for students. I want to get them interested in what they're doing. I'm not up front to dance for them. I want to present the students with a challenge, see them rise to the challenge, see them *want* to learn. I want to dare them to have a good time with science.

Probing Student Thinking

Murphy moves among the students as they work with absorption on their tasks. Two girls who are using computers and the Body Mass Index (BMI) instrument to work on their diet profiles commiserate with him about their results, declaring that switching from whole to low-fat milk is doable but that giving up cookies in exchange for fruit is asking too much. A sturdy football player tells Murphy, "That's two pieces of bad news today. I have to lower my carbs—and I love carbs. I also have to lower my fat, and that stinks." Another boy is searching on the Internet for a formula that he believes could call into question the figure generated by the BMI device. Two girls discuss the feasibility of "fooling" the instrument by combining their weights.

Two boys in the design phase of their experiment explain their hypothesis and how they arrived at it and then return to a discussion about what amount of glucose and water will work best in their experiment. A boy working with the study guide talks with Murphy about his topic, his research, and the Internet itself.

That Murphy engages both the interest and trust of his students is evident in the purposefulness of the classroom, in the respectful exchanges between Murphy and his students, and in the spirit of cooperation among the students themselves. As the students learn about biology, they discover its capacity to reveal life and to help them develop as thinkers. His instruction has nothing to do with coverage—it's about inquiry and community.

Chad Prather's Classroom:

Making Connections

Chad Prather is a second-year teacher who teaches 9th graders world geography and world history at Charlottesville High School in Charlottesville, Virginia. Most of his world geog-

raphy students read well below grade level, and they have little motivation to learn. Says Prather,

These students haven't been celebrated throughout their education. They've gotten used to tracking and very used to worksheets. When teachers give them something challenging, the students rebel because they're so used to worksheets that [the new assignment] just seems too hard.

Prather finds this situation tragic and is determined to show the students their untapped potential.

He's discovered that success lies in making two kinds of connections: connecting students with important ideas and establishing his own connection with students as individuals.

Connecting with Ideas

Prather organizes curriculum around key concepts rather than memorization of facts. Too much of what goes on in school, he believes, is focused on knowledge rather than on understanding. Knowledge, he says, may get students to answer "who" and "what" questions on a state test, but it falls short of helping them answer the more meaningful "how" and "why" questions. He adds,

Teachers have given these kids worksheets over the years in the hope that the worksheets would pound knowledge into their heads, that repetition would create memory. It doesn't. No one expects these students to understand. I tell them that I won't give them what they're used to. They need to step up to the challenge of understanding. Then the knowledge will take care of itself.

Prather's students work with units that raise important ideas in geography. The unit on space and interaction, for example, probes how humans adapt to and alter the environments in which they live. He explains,

When I prepare a lesson, I try to imagine myself as one of my students, and I ask myself—as though I were that student—Is this an engaging use of my time? Then I ask myself—as the teacher now—Is this an effective way of demonstrating meaning?

Connecting with Students

Prather says that connecting with his students is even more important than his sustained work to connect his students with the curriculum. "I had the idea early on." he says, that if I were assertive and hard-core with the rules, then the students would work hard for me." That's not proven to be the case. What *does* work is connecting with students. Not only does it more successfully get them to work, but it also encourages them to accept living within the classroom rules. "The curriculum that I write has to come from a place that the kids are comfortable with," says Prather. "And that obviously starts with the teacher-student relationship."

The world geography class begins with a review that prepares students for a brief Jeopardy-like game. "I don't hear all of you reviewing," prompts Prather, "and that gives me great displeasure. My heart is breaking as though it were the Earth's crust during plate tectonics." Students grin and begin reviewing individually, in pairs, or in small groups. In the 10-minute Jeopardy game that follows, excitement builds to a pinnacle when an unlikely student selects and correctly answers a 1,000-point question. The class erupts in whoops of joy and praise.

Prather quickly transitions to a slide presentation designed to give his students images of the Earth's power. He understands that the process of a hurricane forming over an ocean means little to his students because most have never seen the ocean. He gives them cues about what matters most for them to understand, and he emphasizes the relationships, causes, and effects among the ideas depicted in the images.

Students move next to their "Thug Nasty Big Eartha" projects. For the unit's final product, students are asked to assume the role of lead producer of a new CD and select a project from a number of options that demonstrate that the Earth is a "thug nasty" place. Some students choose in write the lyrics for the hit single. "Big Eartha's House"; others may choose to design the CD cover. All product options focus on the Earth's

power. "It's hard-core," says Prather, "It doesn't back down." Students look at ways in which the Earth exerts its supremacy, especially in terms of extreme weather and climatic forces. Students use teacher-provided grids to take notes on "molten hot performers," such as Twisted Sister (tornado), Dry Bones (drought), and Grand Rapid (flood). Each product choice has a checklist for success, and all choices focus on the important information and ideas from the unit. Product options address varied student interests and learning modes.

In class, students work on their products as their teacher walks among them, coaching them. Because many of Prather's students have difficulty completing schoolwork at home, he said some colleagues provide a place in school in the afternoons for the many students who need time, space, and support for their work.

Prather knows he has much to learn about his students and about how best to connect them with ideas that they thought were out of their reach, but his students send him signals that he's working in the right direction: They talk with him about issues related to race and school, write him thank-you notes, and come by his classroom to share their successes.

From *Educational Leadership,* April 2005, pp. 8-13. Reprinted by permission of the Association for Supervision and Curriculum Development. Copyright © 2005 by ASCD. All rights reserved. The Association for Supervision and Curriculum Development is a worldwide community of educators advocating sound policies and sharing best practices to achieve the success of each learner. To learn more, visit ASCD at **www.ascd.org**

Dealing with Rumors, Secrets, and Lies: Tools of Aggression for Middle School Girls

BETSY LANE

Getting Started

My own middle school years remain vivid in my memory. I was excluded, and I manipulated the exclusion of others. I could be mean, yet, in turn, I was deeply hurt by others. If my friends and I did speak to an adult about these problems, we heard such clichés as: "There are plenty of other girls who would love to be your friends" or "Can't you just try to be nice to each other" or my all time favorite, "Sticks and stones may break my bones, but words can never hurt me." Words break your heart and scar you for life instead.

The difference now, in addition to e-mail and instant messenger, is that young girls are more apt to seek an adult to help them problem solve, and I must confess before going any further that, as an assistant principal of a middle school, I hate to see them coming!

In complete frustration as a fledgling administrator, I assigned a group of sixth grade girls an office detention when I could not determine who was mad at whom, or why, or how it started, or why they could not just end it, and neither could they. My decision to assign detention, made in desperation, unsettled these girls, and certainly stopped them from coming to see me. Moreover, I have no doubt that the unrest and mean comments flourished insidiously.

A particular difficulty with girls' stories is that they can be long and involved, impossible to decipher, and excruciatingly boring. Minute details are provided with sincere emotion and expression while my mind swirls and screams, "Enough already!" However, it is important to remain focused on the primary goal: to get the girls talking and to develop a level of trust. In all likelihood, they only want someone to listen. Listening and reflecting provides an opportunity to help them figure out strategies for their problem (Wiseman, 2002).

Learning More

I decided it was my professional responsibility to learn more about the development of girls and constructive ways in which to help them work through these seemingly endless and painful struggles. My search for understanding or, more truthfully, for strategies to cope with the turbulence of young adolescent relationships, was the catalyst for this article. I weave together the following four themes: why and how girls bully, the applications and results of alternative aggressions, the phenomenon of popularity and cliques, and how adults might offer guidance and support.

Bullying in school, a form of social aggression, has recently become a hot topic nationally and has been referred to by some as an epidemic. The real surprise is not that bullying occurs in our schools, but that our bullies are not only boys. As early as fifth grade, girls can be extremely cruel, mean spirited and aggressive as they begin to form social hierarchies. According to Wiseman (2002), 99.99% of girls gossip and they will almost always blame their behavior on something or someone else. When a girl is accused of spreading a rumor, her initial response is to ask indignantly who told on her, as if that person is actually to blame.

The consensus that girls are less aggressive than boys began to change after Kaj Bjorkqvist, a Finnish professor, shared information from interviews with young adolescent girls. Bjorkqvist exposed the fact that girls are just as aggressive as boys, though the aggression manifests itself differently. Talbot (2002, February 24):

> They are not as likely to engage in physical fights, for example, but their superior social intelligence enabled them to wage complicated battles with other girls aimed at damaging relationships or reputations … leaving nasty messages by cell phone or spreading scurrilous rumors by e-mail, making friends with one girl as revenge against another, gossiping about someone just loudly enough to be overheard. Turning the notion of women's greater empathy on its head, Bjorkqvist focused on the destructive uses to which such emotional attunement could be put. "Girls can better understand how other girls feel," as he puts it; "so they better know how to harm them." (p. 4–5)

The anecdotes and information from each author are equally compelling. Simmons (2002) postulated that the roots of girls' bullying, which is not new, can be traced to society's expectations of females. Girls internalize a powerful and damaging message, reinforced while growing up, that they must be *good* above all else. It is difficult at best, not to mention tiresome, to be constantly *good*.

> Girls strive to be perfect, thinking that this is what adults want. The only way to preserve this image is to constantly judge others thus creating anxiety that divides and separates girls. The intensity with which girls gossip is connected to their own shame of not measuring up to a false, but pervasive, ideal of the perfect girl. (Nagel, 2002; p. 3–4)

Giannetti and Sagarese (2001) observed that young adolescent girls pour their hearts and souls into their relationships. Unfortunately, relationships erupt weekly, daily, even hourly in middle school and the psychological ramifications can be extremely harsh. Day to day, recess to recess, class period to class period, teachers hear the cruel comments and note the fearful expressions, as social status waxes and wanes. Simmons' (2002) research supports this:

> In friendship, girls share secrets to grow closer. Relational competitions corrupt this process, transforming secrets into social currency and, later, ammunition. These girls spread gossip: they tell other people's secrets. They spread rumors: they invent other people's secrets. They gain access to each other using intimate information. (p. 172)

It does not take long for girls to find power and satisfaction in such tactics as backstabbing, gossiping, belittling, and rumor spreading. The modern media of e-mail and instant messaging adds to the excitement and the fury of it all. The position of these girls as they reign over their cliques is temporarily tightened and secured by these tactics.

Middle level students' primary concerns are focused on their peers and what others think of them. It is a time of tremendous insecurity for both boys and girls, and most of them experience some kind of rejection or exclusion exactly when being included is of utmost importance. In particular, the deterioration of female relationships begins in middle school and tends to escalate as the girls mature. Friendship and belonging are key elements of adolescence, yet as Simmons (2002) reported, instead of being nurtured, they are abused and rejected:

> Girls' fierce attachment to their friends illustrates the powerful influence relationships exert over their lives. As they grow more socially sophisticated, the love between girls takes them into a new, enchanting territory. But for girls on the popularity treadmill, friendship is rarely just friendship: it's a ticket, a tool, an opportunity—or a deadweight. You can own anything Abercrombie ever made, but if you don't have the right friends, you're nobody. (p. 158–159)

Girls are passionate about their friends and share secrets as a means of bonding and securing the relationship. However, the relentless quest to be popular can destroy even the closest friendship. The powerful need to be included can outweigh any sense of loyalty or confidentiality.

Cliques are the unfortunate result of judgments made by the very few. Who is pretty enough, smart enough, athletic enough, or nice enough to belong to a particular group? As young adolescents divide themselves into groups, cliques are formed. Giannetti and Sagarese (2001) wrote:

> The term "clique" is used loosely to define a particular group of friends, but more often to define a group that revolves around more than camaraderie. Cliques deal in social power. Formed around a leader or two, the pack lets it be known that *not* everyone is welcome. Certain children are dubbed "worthy" while others are judged *not good enough*. "Excluding becomes a primary activity. The mentality is like a junior country club. The guest list to this invitation-only party is always changing."

Cliques are divisive and destructive to relationships as girls quickly abandon loyalty to close friends to be included in a group, if only briefly. The authority and power given temporarily to these *popular* girls gives them tremendous clout to include and exclude.

Unexpected exclusion or expulsion from a clique can happen to even the most popular girls. To be suddenly shut out is devastating and excruciatingly cruel. This abrupt and unexplainable change most likely happens because girls are unable to appropriately express feelings of anger. Remember, that they are taught to be nice above all else and have not learned how to deal with feelings of anger and jealousy. It is very difficult and confusing to be angry and nice simultaneously. Therefore, girls have learned to appear nice to bystanders, such as teachers, administrators, and parents, while cutting each other to shreds with vicious rumors, broken confidences, and harsh criticisms.

Researchers have contributed to understanding this phenomenon. They found that when threatened or presented with immediate danger, boys tend to choose "fight or flight" and girls are more apt to choose "tend and befriend," seeking group support which is more nurturing and less aggressive.

Relational aggression, one form of alternative aggression used frequently by girls, uses relationships as the swift sword to destroy friendships or exclude members of cliques or groups. Because girls crave close relationships and inclusion, relational aggression causes great emotional suffering for many girls. At one time or another, we have all witnessed this aggression that Simmons (2002) so clearly explains:

> Relationally aggressive behavior is ignoring someone to punish them or get one's way, excluding someone socially for revenge, using negative body language or facial expressions, sabotaging someone's relationships, or threatening to end a relationship unless the friend agrees to a request. In these acts, the bully uses her relationship with the victim as a weapon.

Stepping Forward

Honoring my relatively new determination to learn more and become involved and helpful with middle level girls and their social distress in grades five through eight, I welcomed into my office a small group of upset fifth graders. An instant message had circulated rapidly in cyberspace the night before in which one girl said that Amy was *stuck up*. One girl took it upon herself to print the message at home and bring it to the one accused of being *stuck up* because she did not have instant messenger at home. She did not really know why she delivered the message other than she thought that Amy should know. I took a deep breath, rallied my patience and compassion, and attempted to help them resolve the tangle of feelings and misunderstandings amid the tears and accusations. I asked them to keep a journal of their feelings and observations during the week following our discussion. My intent with this strategy was to return them to class (these sessions have the potential to absorb huge amounts of time and interfere with learning), yet honor the seriousness of the conflict by providing time and a place for them to vent and sort out their feelings. Following are a few interesting entries in their journals:

From Cathy:
I am very upset right after my counseling session with Mrs. Lane. Lisa started to get mad at me and I have no idea what to do. Everyone is telling me to give her the silent treatment until she forgives me, but I think to myself that I would hate it if someone did that to me so I stick to my instincts and don't do that. I asked Lisa why she was mad at me and she said that I already know and she already told me. Lisa is now forming a group of people to be mad at me. These people I have been in fights with before so they don't have a great impression of me and I don't have one of them. I went to see Mrs. Lane about Lisa and she called Lisa and me down to her office. Lisa and I worked everything out and Lisa said she was mad at me because I said I could not trust her because she told a secret that I told her not to tell.

From Lisa:
I want to punch Cathy in the face. She's been lying and crying every single second. I think that I could start hanging around Nancy (the author of the message that inflamed the initial argument) a little more at recess. She understands a little more of what she's been doing over the years. It's a lot funner to be friends again.

From Kate:
People are still crying and I don't think there is anything to cry about. Some people are talking in groups of 2s and 3s. Amy and Ellen are friends again and that made me feel good. I hate this fight and people are still mad and I hate it.

From Beth:
Tension at lunch. Cathy is still crying. I found out that Nancy is out of school today because she is troubled not because she is sick. Amy told me that she has no friends and she either wants to move to California or go to NYA. This is harsh! Everyone is trying to cheer Cathy up with songs, but it's not working. Amy says that everyone is ignoring her and she starts crying. Lisa said that she is mad at Cathy because she lied even if she did correct it.

And on and on the dialogue goes, written or spoken, swirling round and round losing its beginning as the drama and emotion ebb and flow. It is no wonder teachers and administrators often only shake their heads and wonder where to begin. These four sample journal entries are typical of girls' feelings as they twist and tangle through changes. Perhaps Lisa is the most honest of all in saying that she would just like to punch Cathy (direct aggression) and get on with things. Throughout the journals, there is strong evidence that girls criticize and judge while assuming nurturing and caring roles. This portrays the façade of kindness and caring while fully enjoying their involvement in the fight. Simmons (2002) affirmed my assumptions in her statement explaining the strong need girls have to belong:

> Girls have multiple incentives to become embroiled in others' conflicts. First alliance building offers a chance for girls to belong, even briefly, to an ad hoc clique. Jumping on another girl's bandwagon to show support in her time of conflict affords a rare moment of inclusion and comfort. One girl stated, "People don't know what we're fighting about, but they want to be in it. They want to be part of the gossip." (pp. 81–82)

I have learned through experience that the outcome to girls' fights can be unsettling because actually being *in* the fight, even if only briefly included, seems to be much more important than the fight itself. Asking girls to apologize with "sorry" does nothing more than get them to "act nice" to one another, while driving the hostility further underground. The spark that ignited the fight in the first place is left to smolder and will undoubtedly reignite. Apologizing temporarily reduces the heat and makes the involved adult feel somewhat helpful and, perhaps, a bit smug because the problem is *solved*, but it does nothing to discover the source of the flames and extinguish them.

Listening Carefully

As my interest in this social epidemic grew, I had the opportunity to interview a student who was once traumatized by alternative aggression. Kate vividly and painfully remembers sixth grade—a year in which her life as a middle school girl was "pure hell." As a college sophomore, the memories still prevent her from returning to the school and she avoids this small coastal town as much as possible. She continues to have trust issues with friends and does not like the middle school age group. Relocating in the middle of her sixth grade year, Kate found her new classmates to be reserved and tightly networked. A few of the girls in her class made Kate's life unbearable. In addition to snide comments, there were notes left in her locker ordering her to go back to New Jersey or threatening to burn her house down. Kate remains adamant that the students in this school system are not accepting of new students no matter at what age they join the system. "You're always seen as the new kid," she remembered.

At home in the safety of her family, Kate would cry and beg her family to return to New Jersey. Her parents went to the school and spoke with teachers, administrators, and the guidance counselor, yet the problem persisted. The teachers were oblivious because it was all underground. Suggestions such as "just ignore them" and "try to be nice" and discussions with the guidance counselor proved useless.

"The cafeteria for a new kid is a war zone, a place of complete humiliation. It's a place of hell because there is no one to turn to," Kate painfully explained. When she would sit at a table, the girls would rise and move to the end of the table. If she joined a friendlier group, the girls gave those students a hard time. Kate described the middle school cafeteria as *intense*, a place where *who likes who* is determined. They continually haunted her, never relenting regardless of what was said or done. Kate's parents considered putting their house back on the market in sheer frustration and concern for their daughter, who was once a happy, confident student.

The girls involved in Kate's torment were not the so-called cool girls. Kate explained, "They were the *bottom dwellers* and that's why it didn't spread up through the popular chain." The popular chain had definite lines and seemed to be defined around a hierarchy of athletics. Kate's athletic ability proved to be a tremendous asset in helping her overcome the ridicule and humiliation from the few classmates.

Kate made new friends through soccer, basketball, and softball. She was accepted by her teammates and things began to improve with her new status. "Once I got the power of popular, they didn't mess with me because you don't cross the line."

Kate offered a few suggestions for me as an administrator to help students who find themselves in the same hostile situation. She fondly remembers two young teachers who really helped and "didn't try to intervene, they were my friends." In Kate's opinion, students who are being ostracized and isolated need a friend and not a psychiatrist. "They are lonely and need someone besides their mothers to talk with about school issues."

Kate's story is all too familiar. As stated by Giannetti and Sagarese (2001):

> Nearly every young adolescent gets victimized by a peer or group of peers at some time or other during the middle school years. That is a fact of life for our children. The push and pull of social gathering during early adolescence creates outcasts and crises by the dozen. (p. 90)

As the assistant principal of the school that Kate abhors, I am deeply concerned, yet fascinated with the social dynamics that develop between these young adolescent girls. They are fickle and unsure of themselves, willing to turn their backs on a good friend to gain acceptance by someone deemed more popular. Many friendships are tenuous and require frenetic energy to keep up with the unstable dynamics. The use of e-mail and instant messaging feeds and exacerbates rumors that are often at the heart of hurt feelings, exclusion, broken trusts, and friendships.

Reaching Out

My interest in this social phenomenon inspired me to design a survey for students in grades six through eight, which was administered to students in health science classes. The students were asked to list five words that describe popular and five words that describe unpopular. The 54 sixth graders who participated in the survey most often described popular as cool, athletic, good looking, nice, and included/well known. They described unpopular as unattractive, mean, not many friends, not athletic, and stupid/dumb.

The 40 seventh graders who took the survey described popular as: athletic, nice, cool, lots of friends, and funny. To them, unpopular is described as mean, not athletic, ugly/overweight, different/weird, and shy/quiet. The 57 eighth graders described popular as athletic, good looking, funny, nice, and cool. Unpopular was described as ugly/fat, weird/not cool, not athletic, nice, and quiet. Just as Kate claimed, the survey results support the idea that athletics play a highly prominent role in determining one's social status in today's middle schools. The literature supported this as well. Based on the work of Colorado sociologists Patricia and Peter Adler, Giannetti and Sagarese (2001) offered a summary of four basic social groups:

> **Popular Clique** This is the cool group. The beautiful, the athletic, the charming, the affluent; these young adolescents combine to make up about 35% of the population.
>
> **The Fringe** About 10% of children hover around the popular set. The fringers accept their part-time superiority because running with the "in crowd" some of the time is worth being left behind the rest of the time.
>
> **Middle Friendship Circle** The majority of boys and girls, nearly half at 45%, form small groups of several friends apiece. They carry on with their daily lives with assorted measures of confidence and satisfaction.
>
> **The Loners** These are the boys and girls who have no friends. Usually 10% of a class falls into this category. (p. 20 and 21)

I recently had lunch with two seventh grade girls who are most likely classified by themselves and others as unpopular. They talked about the cafeteria and how it is understood where certain students sit. The unpopular girls tend to sit near the stage and the more popular girls fill the tables on the opposite side. They proceeded to tell me that anywhere from 20 to 30 students join their group each day, which to me sounded like a very popular group. The difference in popular, to them, means hanging out with only certain people and making other students feel invisible. "They have a way of looking right through you, they even turn their backs as if we don't exist," explained Susan.

Observing students in the cafeteria is both enlightening and heart wrenching. I know how the cafeteria *works*. The delineation and pattern is very clear and predictable, I know where to look for certain students at each grade level.

Making a Difference

Based on what is known about girls and their social development, it is no longer acceptable for me or other educators to shrug off alternative aggression between girls. "Girls need active guidance in how to stay clear and centered in their anger and disagreement, and they need to be encouraged to bring their strong feelings into public life in constructive ways," reported Nagle (2002, p. 4).

Simmons (2002) suggested that teachers, guidance counselors, and administrators, with very little training, offer the best chance of making significant change with this phenomenon. We have the ability to create cultures in our schools that do not tolerate alternative aggressive behaviors. Students must be held accountable and must come to understand the source of their anger or jealousy and the seriousness and painful results of their words and actions. School personnel must no longer look the other way and say, "That's just the way it is."

This will not be enough on its own. Adults need to model assertive, respectful relationships for all students. Girls, in particular, need to be taught how to manage their anger and resolve their conflicts constructively. It is imperative that we talk about alternative aggression with our students and teach them that it is indeed harmful and unacceptable.

In our genuine attempts to reduce the overall amount of aggression in our schools, we must accept the fact that exclusion does happen. It always has and always will in both childhood and adult relationships. It is as much a natural part of life as is the desire to be popular. Caring adults must try to be objective and distinguish between what is the natural social ordering of children and what is deliberately mean and hurtful. I offer several suggestions and interventions taken from the literature for your consideration:

- Make it a point to acknowledge students personally to let them know you care. Young adolescents crave our attention. Give students your full attention when they are talking to you and avoid' interjecting your own feelings.
- Encourage girls to write in journals. If students want to talk and are "stuck," ask them to write down words and phrases or draw pictures that describe how they feel.
- Emphasize a student's strengths and accomplishments to refocus identifiers away from social behaviors. Point out that he or she is an outstanding artist instead of shy or charming.
- When a student reports being humiliated by gossip, do not dismiss it with casual comments such as "I'm sure that no one even noticed." It is a very big deal, and students need to know that you understand and care.
- Insist that students apologize sincerely. Apologies are a public acknowledgement of the consequences of hurtful behavior and are, therefore, powerful.
- Avoid punishing or restricting privileges (as I did!). They may be appropriate and deserved, however, the most important thing is to get girls to accept responsibility for their harmful actions.

- "Don't say 'behavior' when you're talking about accountability, say 'actions' 'Behavior,' like, 'watch your tone of voice,' makes girls crazy."(Wiseman, 2002, p. 117)
- Assure students that you will not be offended or shocked by bad language if it is, a part of their story. Encourage them to talk freely and openly.
- Offer academic curricula or hold discussions that address the issues of social aggression and how to recognize and manage it.
- Get to know the girls who appear to be alone, and intervene with strategies and social skills to involve them more with others.
- Structure activities that allow girls opportunities to belong and gain confidence and a sense of competence. Girls may become bored and thus, turn to gossiping to spice up the approximate 2.5 hours a day they spend talking with friends.
- "The power of peers' immediately resisting negative evaluations of others suggests that intervention programs could teach girls strategies for quickly challenging malicious gossip, and perhaps also social exclusion. Because girls are prone to being agreeable, it would likely be important to teach them very specific statements and to practice these in role plays.... Although challenges, could be effective from high and low status youth (Eder and Enke, 1991) it might be especially effective to teach these skills to high status girls who' are already prone to assuming the defender role and likely to have the greatest impact on their peers." (Underwood, 2003, p. 227)
- "Helping [students] understand and deal with anger is perhaps one of the greatest lessons you can teach them. Anger is caused by hurt feelings and a loss of control. No age group feels less in control than young adolescents. They may get angry when ordered around by parents and teachers. And, they get angry when they cannot control their friendships. You cannot control their friendships either, but you can help them deal with anger that these liaisons may produce." (Giannetti & Sagarese, 2001, p. 55–56)
- "The best way to eliminate cliques and bullies is to encourage the silent majority to speak up. The kids, who stand on the sidelines, watching other children be humiliated, hold the key to reform in their hands. Standing by silently reaffirms the clique's power. Speaking up nullifies it."(Giannetti & Sagarese, 2001, p. 192)

Closing Thoughts

As I continue to work with middle school girls, I pledge to enforce antibullying strategies that alert girls to the dangers of their behavior. Earlier, I hated to see distraught and squabbling girls coming because I was unprepared and doubtful as to what to do. I clearly did not understand the dynamics behind girl fights and their perpetual scramble to be noticed and accepted. Now, I am better informed about alternative aggression and its negative impact on young adolescent girls. I look forward to working with them and helping middle level teachers and parents to have more understanding and compassion for the phenomenon. It seems that this is the least I can do since, mercifully, returning to my own middle school days and making better choices for my own behavior is not an option. I choose to be proactive and involved in an effort to make a difference for girls like Kate.

A special thank you to students:
Anne, Brenna, Caitlyn, Chaya, Emily, Kristin, Lizzie, Margaret, Maryann, and Suvanna

References

Brown, L., & Gilligan, C. (1992). *Meeting at the Crossroads: Women's psychology and girls' development*. New York: Ballantine Books.

Giannetti, C., & Sagarese, M. (2001). *Cliques: 8 steps to help your child survive the jungle*. New York: Broadway Books.

Nagle, M. (2002, Sept./Oct.). Fighting to be somebody: Research on girls' aggression shows the need for activism. *UMaine Today*, 2–4.

Simmons, R. (2002). *Odd girl out: The hidden culture of aggression in girls*. New York: Harcourt.

Talbot, M. (2002, February 24). *Girls just want to be mean*. The New York Times. Retrieved February 26, 2002, from **http://www.nytimes.com/2002/02/24/magazine/24GIRLS.html**

Underwood, M., (2003). *Social aggression among girls*. New York: The Guilford Press.

Wiseman, R., (2002). *Queen bees and wannabees*. New York: Three Rivers Press.

BETSY LANE is an assistant principal at Frank H. Harrison Middle School in Yarmouth, Maine. E-mail: **Betsy_Lane@yarmouth.k12.me.us**

UNIT 6

Cultural Diversity and Schooling

Unit Selections

Key Points to Consider

- What is multicultural education? To what does the national debate over multiculturalism in the schools relate? What are the issues regarding it?

- How would you define the equity issues in the field of education? How would you rank them?

- What are the ways that a teacher can employ to help students understand the concept of culture?

- Critique the slogan, "Every child can learn." Do you find it true or false? Explain.

Student Website

www.mhcls.com/online

Internet References

Further information regarding these websites may be found in this book's preface or online.

American Scientist
http://www.amsci.org/amsci/amsci.html

American Studies Web
http://www.georgetown.edu/crossroads/asw/

National Institute on the Education of At-Risk Students
http://www.ed.gov/offices/OERI/At-Risk/

Prospects: The Congressionally Mandated Study of Educational Growth and Opportunity
http://www.ed.gov/pubs/Prospects/index.html

The concept of "culture" encompasses all of the life ways, customs, traditions, and institutions that people develop as they create and experience their history and identity as people. In the United States of America, many very different cultures coexist within the civic framework of a shared constitutional tradition that guarantees equality before the law for all. So, as we all have been taught, out of many peoples we are also one nation united by our constitutional heritage.

The civil rights movement in the United States in the 1950s and 1960s was about the struggle of cultural minorities to achieve equity: social justice before the law under our federal Constitution. The articles in this unit attempt to address some of these equity issues.

There is an immense amount of unfinished business before us in the area of intercultural relations in the schools and in educating all Americans regarding how multicultural our national population demographics really are. We are becoming more and more multicultural with every passing decade. This further requires us to take steps to ensure that all of our educational opportunity structures remain open to all persons regardless of their cultural backgrounds or gender. There is much unfinished business as well with regard to improving educational opportunities for girls and young women; the remaining gender issues in

American education are very real and directly related to the issue of equality of educational opportunity.

Issues of racial prejudice and bigotry still plague us in American education, despite massive efforts in many school systems to improve racial and intercultural relations in the schools. Many American adolescents are in crisis as their basic health and social needs are not adequately met and their educational development is affected by crises in their personal lives. The articles in this unit reflect all of the above concerns plus others related to efforts to provide equality of educational opportunity to all American youth and attempts to clarify what multicultural education is and what it is not.

The "equity agenda," or social justice agenda, in the field of education is a complex matrix of gender- and culture-related issues aggravated by incredibly wide gaps in the social and economic opportunity structures available to citizens. We are each situated by cultural, gender-based, and socioeconomic factors in society; this is true of all persons everywhere. We have witnessed a great and glorious struggle for human rights in our time and in our nation. The struggle continues to deal more effectively with educational opportunity issues related to cultural diversity and gender.

The "Western canon" is being challenged by advocates' multicultural perspectives in school curriculum development. Multicultural educational programming, which will reflect the rapidly changing cultural demographics of North American schooling, is being advocated by some and strongly opposed by others. This controversy centers around several different issues regarding what it means to provide equality of opportunities for culturally diverse students. The traditional Western cultural content of general and social studies and language arts curricula is being challenged as Eurocentric.

Helping teachers to broaden their cultural perspectives and to take a more global view of curriculum content is something that the advocates of culturally pluralistic approaches to curriculum development would like to see integrated into the entire elementary and secondary school curriculum structure. North America is as multicultural a region of the world as exists anywhere. Our enormous cultural diversity encompasses populations from many indigenous "First Americans" as well as people from every European culture, plus many people of Asian, African, and Latin American nations and the Central and South Pacific Island groups. There is spirited controversy over how to help all Americans to better understand our collective multicultural heritage. There are spirited defenders and opponents of the traditional Eurocentric curriculum.

The problem of inequality of educational opportunity is of great concern to American educators. One in four American children does not have all of basic needs met and lives under poverty conditions. Almost one in three lives in a single-parent home, which in itself is no disadvantage, but under conditions of poverty, it often is. More and more concern is expressed over how to help children of poverty. The equity agenda of our time has to do with many issues related to gender, race, and ethnicity. All forms of social deprivation and discrimination are aggravated by great disparities in income and accumulated wealth. How can students be helped to have an equal opportunity to succeed in school?

Some of us are still proud to say that we are a nation of immigrants. In addition to the traditional minority/majority group relationships that evolved in the United States, new waves of immigrants today are again enhancing the importance of concerns for achieving equality of opportunity in education. In light of these vast sociological and demographic changes, we must ensure that we will remain a multicultural democracy.

The social psychology of prejudice is something that psychiatrists, social psychologists, anthropologists, and sociologists have studied in great depth since the 1930s. Tolerance, acceptance, and a valuing of the unique worth of every person are teachable and learnable attitudes. A just society must be constantly challenged to find meaningful ways to raise human aspirations, to heal human hurt, and to help in the task of optimizing every citizen's potential. Education is a vital component to that end. Teachers can incorporate into their lessons an emphasis on acceptance of difference, toleration of and respect for the beliefs of others, and the skills of reasoned debate and dialogue.

The struggle for optimal representation of minority perspectives in the schools will be a matter of serious concern to educators for the foreseeable future. From the many court decisions upholding the rights of women and cultural minorities in the schools over the past years has emerged a national consensus that we must strive for the greatest degree of equality in education as may be possible. The triumph of constitutional law over prejudice and bigotry must continue.

The Heightened Significance of *Brown* v. *Board of Education* in Our Time

Most people associate *Brown* v. *Board of Education* solely with the issue of school desegregation. But the landmark decision also illuminated several other fundamental ideals of education in a democracy. Mr. Wraga fears that today's prevailing trends in education policy are a threat to those ideals.

WILLIAM G. WRAGA

Two years ago, numerous commemorative essays and analyses retold the familiar and now-famous story. On 17 May 1954, the U.S. Supreme Court issued its landmark decision in the case of *Brown* v. *Board of Education of Topeka*,[1] which struck down the "separate but equal" doctrine of the 1896 *Plessy* v. *Ferguson* decision. The Court claimed, "To separate them [African American children] from others of similar age and qualifications solely because of their race generates a feeling of inferiority as to their status in the community that may affect their hearts and minds in a way unlikely ever to be undone." The Court concluded that "in the field of public education the doctrine of 'separate but equal' has no place. Separate educational facilities are inherently unequal."[2]

The implications of this decision for the rights of African Americans and indeed for all of American society were profound and engendered decades of efforts to desegregate public schools. Although desegregation has yet to be satisfactorily achieved and gains toward that end stalled during the 1990s—halted by federal court decisions—the impact of the Supreme Court's 1954 *Brown* decision remains significant. The significance, however, extends beyond the ongoing and crucial project of achieving racial integration and equality in our schools. In the process of rendering "separate but equal" schooling illegal, the Court also articulated fundamental ideals of American education, which, in the current education reform environment, merit renewed consideration. Let us revisit three of these ideals.

Unifying Function of Public Schools

By insisting that all students attend school under the same roof, the High Court affirmed both the importance of the concept of equal educational opportunity and, implicitly, the unifying function of public education in a democracy. The potential unifying effect of schooling had long been advocated as a central purpose of American education. Lawrence Cremin observed, for example, that, during the mid-19th century, such reformers as Horace Mann conceived of the common school as "a school not common in the traditional European sense of 'for the common people,' but common in a new sense of common to all of the people."[3] Cremin continued, "Only in a school where children of all economic classes, religious creeds, and political persuasions could meet on a free and equal basis did these leaders see the amelioration of divisive influences which threatened the social cohesion so necessary to the new Republic."[4]

During the early 20th century, educators extended the idea of the common school from the elementary to the secondary level. At this time, a debate raged over whether the United States should adopt a dual, European-style system in which 20% of the student population would attend academic high schools conducted by educators, while the remaining 80% of adolescents would attend trade schools controlled by business interests.[5] Dewey spoke for many educators when he wrote, "Most of us have probably settled back in a conviction that the unity of the public school system is the best guarantee we possess of a unifying agency to deal successfully with the diversified heterogeneity of our population."[6] This debate was decided in favor of the comprehensive high school model, which houses academic and vocational programs and students under one roof, thus expressly embracing a unifying function through which future citizens will "obtain those common ideas, ideals, and common modes of thought, feeling, and action that make for cooperation, social cohesion, and social solidarity."[7]

Prevailing social norms, of course, always determined the extent of social unification that was acceptable and therefore feasible in educational settings. Over time, however, visions of unification through public schooling became increasingly inclusive. Although by the mid-20th century educational leaders had extended the unifying function of education by calling for the public schools to mitigate the inequalities instigated by racism, it was not until the *Brown* decision that this ideal could begin to become a reality.[8] One year after the *Brown* decision, the Court issued an implementation directive that left the logistical details to the states. Given the vagueness of the Court's directive, states and localities enjoyed wide latitude, which they exploited and which led, more often than not, to flagrant noncompliance.

School Choice and Segregation

Significantly for education reform in the early 21st century, one of the tactics employed during the 1950s and 1960s to dodge the High Court's desegregation order involved instituting "free choice" schemes, under which "any student assigned to a school where she was a member of the racial majority could transfer to a school where she would be in the minority."[9] Even if such transfers did not occur, districts could claim to have ended de jure segregation. Diane Ravitch described the situation this way:

> Deep South districts overwhelmingly submitted free-choice plans, permitting students to choose their schools, presumably to maintain segregation-by-choice or to establish token desegregation; the U.S. Civil Rights Commission identified 102 free-choice districts where not a single black student was in school with whites. Southern districts thought that the adoption of a free-choice plan fully satisfied the requirements of the Civil Rights Act, but the Office of Education considered free-choice only a means to the end of complete integration.[10]

Ravitch reported that such schemes resulted in the "resegregation" of schools. In addition, "voucher-like programs" were devised "to provide public support to private segregationist academies."[11]

Yet, since the 1980s, when proposals for vouchers and other forms of school choice began to be increasingly advocated as a veritable educational panacea, proponents of school choice have omitted these earliest cases of such strategies from their historical sketches. Instead, they have traced choice to the alternative schools movement of the 1960s and 1970s or presented it as a new idea justified by free-market ideology. Although school systems that implement choice plans endeavor to maintain racially balanced schools, the historical origins of free-choice schools as mechanisms of segregation should give policy makers and educators pause. In fact, at least in terms of access, racial bias tends to persist in school-choice arrangements, as well as in charter schools, a form of school choice.[12] Furthermore, research points to the conclusion that "large-scale unregulated-choice programs are likely to lead to some increase in stratification."[13]

Moreover, segregation occurs not only along racial and socioeconomic lines. Proposals for school choice, charter schools, and magnet schools often promote segregation in a variety of ways, targeting students on the basis of academic or vocational ability, aptitude, or aspiration; gender; and even race. The orga-

nization of the curricula of magnet, charter, and choice schools around narrow themes or specializations—such as the humanities, science and engineering, the performing arts, or even an Afrocentric focus—can result in curricular fragmentation and balkanization and in academic and educational segregation of students. Such schools, like gated educational communities, fly in the face of the historical commitment to the unifying function of public schooling in the United States. Integration and multicultural understanding emerge from actual association.[14] At a time when the nation's population continues to diversify and when socioeconomic divisions have been aggravated by two decades of economic policies that have increased disparities in income and wealth, the unifying function of a common school experience that the Supreme Court affirmed in *Brown* v. *Board of Education* becomes increasingly vital to the social fabric of the United States.[15]

Returning to the *Brown* decision, the High Court situated the case and its ruling squarely in the context of the history and purpose of public education in a democracy. The Court stated in *Brown*:

> Today, education is perhaps the most important function of state and local governments. Compulsory school attendance laws and the great expenditures for education both demonstrate our recognition of the importance of education to our democratic society. It is required in the performance of our most basic public responsibilities, even in the armed services. It is the very foundation of good citizenship. Today it is a principal instrument in awakening the child to cultural values, in preparing him for later professional training, and in helping him adjust normally to his environment. In these days, it is doubtful that any child may reasonably be expected to succeed in life if he is denied the opportunity of an education. Such an opportunity, where the state has undertaken to provide it, is a right which must be made available to all on equal terms.[16]

This passage contains at least two additional fundamentally American educational ideals that we too often take for granted and that are currently threatened by education reform policies.

Educating Enlightened Citizens

One of these ideals holds that an important function of public education should be to educate enlightened citizens. Thomas Jefferson's reflections on this subject have been a touchstone for citizenship education in a democracy: "Every government degenerates when trusted to the rulers of the people alone. The people themselves are its only safe depositors. And to render them safe, their minds must be improved to a certain degree."[17] For Jefferson, an enlightened citizenry not only would make informed decisions about common problems but also would serve as a check against the power of the government.

Recent reform efforts, however, have exalted academic achievement and the training of productive workers at the expense of the preparation of future citizens. The No Child Left Behind (NCLB) Act, for example, omits any mention of education for citizenship as part of its express purpose. Although Subpart 3 of NCLB, titled the "Education for Democracy Act," authorizes the secretary of education to award grants to organizations that promote civics education, even the purposes articulated in this passage make no reference to the kind of citizenship that Jefferson called for.[18] In the current reform climate, the Supreme Court's affirmation in *Brown* of the role of public education in educating enlightened citizens for democracy warrants renewed attention.

Publicly Supported Education

A third ideal the Court affirmed in *Brown* v. *Board of Education* has become so ingrained in American thinking about education that it is surprising that thoughtful reformers can so brazenly dismiss it. Philosophers from Aristotle to Adam Smith long ago identified education as a primary function of the state.[19] According to Cremin, for 19th-century education reformers in the United States, "Not only was this common school to serve the public, it was also to be supported and controlled by the public. In this way," he continued, "no child could ever be banned for poverty, and no partisan political, economic, or religious group could ever control the school for its own private purposes."[20] Recognizing this imperative, during the 20th century, industrial democracies adopted state-supported systems of education.

Yet recently in the United States—the first nation in history to provide universal access to publicly supported education—efforts to commercialize and even privatize public education have proliferated.[21] For example, NCLB authorizes the secretary of education to provide grants to for-profit organizations that engage in teacher recruitment and permits charter schools to use public money "to access private-sector capital" to invest in property or subsidize capital improvements.[22] Vouchers and school choice were only the first such efforts. In recent years, numerous aspects of the school program—from food and custodial services to curriculum and even wholesale management of schools—have been privatized or contracted to private concerns. In the process, the public voice—and possibly the public interest—is in danger of becoming of secondary importance to private profit.

Moreover, the statistically unattainable expectations for "adequate yearly progress" mandated in NCLB can be understood, as Gerald Bracey put it, as part of "a campaign of shock and awe" intended to discredit the public schools, to erode public confidence in the institution, and ultimately to pave the way for privatization of our public education system.[23] In an era in which powerful interests are poised to commercialize and even privatize a range of public services, including the public schools, the ideal of a publicly financed and governed system of education that the Supreme Court affirmed in *Brown* v. *Board of Education* deserves renewed commitment.

In deciding to render "separate but equal" educational facilities unconstitutional, the Supreme Court affirmed fundamental educational ideals: implicitly, the unifying function of common schooling and explicitly, the imperatives for citizenship education and for a publicly supported system of education. The jus-

tices took these fundamental ideals, which formed the basis of the *Brown* decision, as givens. No longer can these ideals be taken for granted. Taking our cue from the High Court, it is time that we reaffirm our commitment to the unifying function of common schooling, to the necessity for citizenship education, and to the imperative for a publicly supported system of education. At a time when such fundamental ideals have become increasingly vulnerable, the sage judgment of the Court in *Brown* assumes heightened significance.

References

1. *Brown* v. *Board of Education*, 347 U.S. 483 (1954).
2. Ibid., pp. 495–96.
3. Lawrence A. Cremin, "The Curriculum Maker and His Critics: A Persistent American Problem," *Teachers College Record*, February 1953, p. 235.
4. Ibid.
5. Committee on Industrial Education, *Report of the Committee on Industrial Education* (New York: National Association of Manufacturers, 1915).
6. John Dewey, "Splitting Up the School System," in Jo Ann Boydston, ed., *John Dewey: The Middle Works*, vol. 8 (Carbondale: Southern Illinois University Press, 1985), p. 123.
7. Commission on the Reorganization of Secondary Education, *Cardinal Principles of Secondary Education,* Department of the Interior, Bureau of Education, Bulletin 1918, No. 35, p. 21.
8. For calls that preceded *Brown,* see, for example, Educational Policies Commission, *Education for ALL American Youth* (Washington, D.C.: National Education Association, 1944), pp. 16, 79, 233; and Hollis L. Caswell, ed., *The American High School: Its Responsibility and Opportunity* (New York: Harper & Row, 1946), p. 137.
9. Brian Gill et al., *Rhetoric vs. Reality: What We Know and What We Need to Know About Vouchers and Charter Schools* (Santa Monica, Calif.: RAND Corporation, 2001), p. 159.
10. Diane Ravitch, *The Troubled Crusade: American Education, 1945–1980* (New York: Basic Books, 1983), p. 164. In 1968, the Supreme Court ruled that "free choice" schemes were inadequate responses to segregation.
11. Gill et al., p. 159.
12. Gill et al., op. cit.; and Jeffrey R. Henig, "School Choice Outcomes," in Stephen D. Sugarman and Frank R. Kemerer, eds., *School Choice and Social Controversy: Politics, Policy, and Law* (Washington, D.C.: Brookings Institution Press, 1999), pp. 68–110.
13. Gill et al., p. 204.
14. Robert E. Slavin, "Integrating the Desegregated Classroom: Action Speaks Louder Than Words," *Educational Leadership,* February 1979, pp. 322–24; and idem, "Effects of Biracial Learning Teams on Cross-Racial Friendships," *Journal of Educational Psychology,* vol. 71, 1979, pp. 381–87.
15. Harold Hodgkinson, "Educational Demographics: What Teachers Should Know," *Educational Leadership*, December 2000/January 2001, pp. 6–11; and Kevin Phillips, *Wealth and Democracy* (New York: Broadway Books, 2002).
16. *Brown* v. *Board of Education*, p. 493.
17. Thomas Jefferson, "Notes on the State of Virginia" (1781/1785), in Gordon C. Lee, ed., *Crusade Against Ignorance: Thomas Jefferson on Education* (New York: Teachers College Press, 1961), p. 97.

18. No Child Left Behind Act of 2001 (P.L. 107–110, 8 January 2002), United States Statutes at Large, pp. 1662–66. For the purpose of the act, see p. 1439.

19. *The Politics of Aristotle*, trans. Benjamin Jowett (Oxford: Clarendon Press, 1885), Book VIII, p. 244; and Adam Smith, *An Inquiry into the Nature and Causes of the Wealth of Nations* (New York: Modern Library, 1937), pp. 734–37, 768.

20. Cremin, pp. 235–36.

21. For the wider trend, see Paul Krugman, *The Great Unraveling: Losing Our Way in the New Century* (New York: Norton, 2003), esp. pp. 6, 216. For discussions of efforts to commercialize and privatize public schools, see Alex Molnar, *Giving Kids the Business: The Commercialization of America's Schools* (Boulder, Co-lo.: Westview Press, 1996); and Gerald W. Bracey, *The War Against America's Public Schools: Privatizing Schools, Commercializing Education* (Boston: Allyn and Bacon, 2002).

22. No Child Left Behind, pp. 1656, 1801.

23. Gerald W. Bracey, "The 13th Bracey Report on the Condition of Public Education," *Phi Delta Kappan*, October 2003, p. 149.

WILLIAM G. WRAGA is a professor in the Department of Lifelong Education, Administration, and Policy, College of Education, University of Georgia, Athens. He wishes to thank Elizabeth DeBray for constructive suggestions on an earlier version of this article.

The Role of Social Foundations in Preparing Teachers for Culturally Relevant Practice

ANN MARIE RYAN

The 2003 National Assessment of Educational Progress fourth grade reading results indicate that while 75% of white children across the nation read at or above a basic level—partial mastery of knowledge and skills required for grade level work—only 40% of African American and 44% of Latino fourth graders do (National Center for Education Statistics, 2003a). Results were similarly discouraging for children from low-income families of whom 45% scored at or above a basic level, while 76% of those not eligible for free/reduced-price school lunches scored at or above a basic level (National Center for Education Statistics, 2003b).

The entrenched social inequities responsible for this crisis of access and equity in education are historically rooted in broad social and institutional issues that influence the pedagogical practices of schools and teachers. They play a significant role in shaping teacher beliefs, teacher attitudes, and teacher expectations of students of color and those in poverty and how they should be taught.

To leave these socialized beliefs unexamined can produce devastating consequences, as evidenced by the over-representation of African American children placed in special education. In 1998, while representing only 17% of the total school enrollment, African American children accounted for 33% of those labeled mentally retarded (Losen & Orfield, 2002, p. xvi). In a qualitative study of the special education referral process in a particular district, Harry, Klingner, Sturges, and Moore (2002) found that teachers referred children seen as behavior problems and oftentimes blamed that behavior on what they perceived to be dysfunctional families (p. 78).

In this process, teachers often made "implicit or explicit references to ethnicity, culture, and/or socioeconomic status of the families" in explaining the reasons for students' behavior (Harry, Klingner, Sturges & Moore, 2002, p. 79). Many preservice teachers hold similar beliefs about students of color and those in poverty. Bondy and Ross (1998) found that these misguided beliefs contribute to a notion that many African American children require special education.

These myths held by teacher candidates include believing that poor African American students fail because their parents do not care about their education; that they are unmotivated and uncooperative; and that they have grown up with few literacy experiences (Bondy & Ross, 1998, pp. 243–246). These notions, derived from social stereotypes of African Americans and low-income families, perpetuate low teacher expectations and intensify an already disturbing picture of over-representation in special education and low student achievement in general education settings.

Addressing the issue of teachers' low expectations of students of color and those in poverty poses significant challenges to teacher education. The growing body of research focused on this issue documents ways teachers can make a real difference in the educational lives of children. Ladson-Billings' (1992; 1994; 1995) and others demonstrate that teachers can work with students to challenge socio-economic inequities, succeed academically, and retain pride in their cultural backgrounds.

Based on a review of literature about preparing culturally competent teachers, this article argues that social foundations courses, especially courses in the history and sociology of education, are critical for teacher candidates to understand the power of racial, ethnic, and socio-economic inequities and the relationship of these factors to the pedagogical practices of schools and teachers in order for teachers to engage in culturally relevant practice.

Culturally Relevant Pedagogy

Much of the literature addressing the challenges of preparing teachers for teaching students of color and those in poverty is increasingly focused on culturally relevant pedagogy.[1] Ladson-Billings (1992) defines culturally relevant pedagogy as that which empowers students intellectually, socially, emotionally, and politically by using cultural referents to impart knowledge, skills, and attitudes (p. 382). She argues that it urges collective action grounded in cultural understandings, experiences, and ways of knowing the world. Culturally relevant teachers treat students as competent and provide instructional scaffolding so that students can use what they know to access what they need to know (Ladson-Billings, 1994, pp. 123–124).]

Shujaa (1995) asserts that the intent of culturally relevant pedagogy is to increase student achievement, to help students develop the skills to achieve economic self-sufficiency, and to develop citizenship skills based on a realistic and thorough understanding of the political system (p. 200). Mehan, Lintz, Okamoto, and Wills (1995) argue that when culturally sensitive teaching is not accompanied by an academically rigorous curriculum, minority students will most likely not benefit from it (p. 141).

Therefore, culturally relevant pedagogy works to assist students from marginalized communities by focusing on academic achievement toward political and economic access. This requires teachers who possess in-depth knowledge of students, subject matter, pedagogy and the social implications of education.

Implications for Teacher Preparation

The complex and substantive demands of culturally relevant pedagogy pose urgent challenges to teacher preparation programs, especially since the demographic reality is one of an increasingly diverse student population and a considerably homogeneous teaching population. In 1999, 63% of all elementary and high school students were white; however, in that same year one out of every five elementary and high school students had one foreign-born parent (Jamieson, Curry, & Martinez, 2001).

The demographic background of teachers in the same year was 84% white and 16% minority (Hoffman, 2003). This trend shows little sign of changing since the majority of students enrolled in teacher education programs continues to be white. In the fall of 2001, white students represented 78% of all those enrolled in teacher education programs (American Association of Colleges for Teacher Education, 2002). As a result, teachers are more frequently being asked to teach students who have different backgrounds and life experiences from their own. This demographic reality makes it necessary for teacher preparation programs to better prepare their teacher candidates for the diversity of students they will teach.

Exploring the connections between racial and ethnic identities and pedagogy is essential for all teachers, since teachers and students belong to a host of microcultures (Gollnick, 1992). Zeichner (1996) argues that even if efforts to recruit and retain students of color in teacher preparation programs are successful and there is an increase in their number, the need to bridge cultural knowledge and pedagogy is still of great importance (p. 133). This also holds true for teachers who share a significant part of their cultural background with students.

It cannot be assumed that teachers can easily translate cultural knowledge into culturally relevant pedagogy (Montecinos, 1994, p. 41). Although a teacher may share many cultural aspects with his or her students, including racial or ethnic background, other differences, such as socioeconomic status, can create challenges for teachers. Hence all teachers need to be-

come aware of the many cultures they are a part of and how it might affect their teaching and their students' learning.

Making Race and Class Matter

Teachers holding high expectations, scaffolding from home to school, and involving parents and community members in schools are essential to increasing teachers' effectiveness with students of color and those in poverty (Villegas, 1991; Zeichner, 1996). However, an increased emphasis on the importance of teachers having a clear sense of their own cultural identities and their relationship to teachers' understanding of socio-economic inequities is evident in recent literature (Villegas & Lucas, 2002, pp. 27–35).

Thus, successful teaching of students of diverse backgrounds calls for teachers who understand relationships between racial and ethnic identity and pedagogy and are aware of how schools can perpetuate socio-economic inequities. These elements are critical in preparing teacher candidates to effectively teach students of color and those in poverty.

Addressing relationships of race, ethnicity, and pedagogy and issues of socio-economic inequity and schooling connect the more personal and social dimensions of teaching. An examination of these important dimensions in social foundations courses complicates and sophisticates teachers' understandings, resulting in less paternalistic and more authentic engagements with students. It allows teachers to see that they are socially constructed beings and that schools and classrooms are microcosms of larger societies. This elevates critical elements of culturally relevant pedagogy—high expectations, scaffolding, and parent involvement—to more than educational buzzwords with predictable and measured outcomes.

Teacher candidates become aware that their expectations of students are affected by the ways they have been socialized as individuals *and* as teachers. This then allows them to appreciate that their ability to scaffold students' learning is dependent on a deep understanding of their students, beyond what they have come to know through socialized and filtered means.

Effective teachers of students of color and students in poverty have an awareness of the social construction of their identities and those of their students and what those identities represent in broader social contexts.[2] These teachers are aware that identity is shaped by cultural experiences and that both the individual and the cultures they represent have an impact on teaching and learning. This becomes especially poignant in the case of white middle and upper class teachers, where there is a need for them to recognize what they symbolize. Their whiteness, along with the power and privilege it embodies, will be a defining characteristic in a classroom.

These teachers will need to understand issues of representation and how their whiteness shapes the way they see students of color and those in poverty. Consequently, not only do teachers need to be competent in their subject matter and teaching methodologies, but they also need to address the personal and social realties of race and class and their pedagogical implications. This will require middle and upper class white teachers to acknowledge that social systems and specifically schools are inequitable and that in many cases they have personally benefited from this inequity.

There is powerful evidence demonstrating how social class shapes schooling and how teachers play a role in this process. In a review of literature on social class and schooling, Knapp and Woolverton (1995) assert that teachers' social-class identification is critical to understanding how they see themselves as teachers and how they understand their students. This conclusion is supported by Shujaa's (1995) study of several initiatives in U.S. school districts to integrate African and/or African American content into the curriculum to make instruction more culturally relevant for African American students.

Shujaa (1995) contends that in order to support culturally relevant teaching, professional development must be directed toward enabling teachers to focus on their conceptions of themselves and others, their cultural knowledge, and their classrooms' social structure. Shujaa (1995) further argues that culturally relevant pedagogy is more than an infusion of content; it requires teachers to recognize who they are racially, culturally, and economically as individuals and how they have learned to view others who are racially, culturally, and economically different from themselves in order to effectively implement culturally relevant pedagogy.

Culturally Relevant Teachers

Recent research on effective teachers of students of color and those in poverty illustrates that teachers can make a difference and assist in increasing their students' academic achievement. Ladson-Billings (1992) found that those teachers most successful with African American students, encouraging children to choose academic excellence and maintain their cultural identity, are aware of the position of African Americans in society and how it affects expectations of students (p. 389).

These teachers are concerned about the inequities in society and schooling. They see their role as helping students become aware of these inequities and use pedagogy that is liberating, rather than maintaining the status quo, by explicitly teaching students how to gain social and political access (Ladson-Billings 1992, p. 388). From additional research on successful teachers of African American students, Ladson-Billings (1994) found that these teachers encourage individual achievement and help students develop a broader socio-political consciousness allowing them to critique cultural norms, values, and institutions that produce and maintain socio-economic inequities (p. 118).

Villegas (1991) found that although successful teachers of culturally diverse students are aware of the institutional obstacles that many of their students face, they do not adopt a pessimistic outlook toward their students' ability to achieve (p.18). On the contrary many of these teachers explicitly work with students to understand these obstacles and acquire strategies to deal with them.

According to Haberman (1995), successful teachers of students in poverty see how education, schools, and teachers contribute to the failure of students and work against perpetuating these practices and policies (pp. 52–53). Effective teachers of students in poverty believe that regardless of the life conditions their

students face, they as teachers bear the primary responsibility for sparking their students' desire to learn (Haberman, 1995, p. 53).

A strong sense of efficacy on the part of a teacher is vital to the academic achievement of students. The belief that one has or can acquire the skills and resources to teach a child regardless of race or class is an essential quality that includes relying on personal and professional experiences, as well as students, parents, and communities as resources for teaching. Teachers need to demonstrate that they believe all students are capable of learning and that they believe they are capable of making a difference in the educational lives of children.[3]

Building a Foundation for Culturally Relevant Pedagogy

Prospective teachers' beliefs have a great impact on their attitudes and behaviors towards culturally different students; therefore teacher educators need to make beliefs an important feature of preparation programs and legitimate sources of inquiry (Sia & Mosher, 1994, p. 2). Courses in social foundations provide opportunities for such examinations and can scaffold teacher candidates from their own experiences and beliefs to complex understandings of educational access and equity.

Teacher candidates need to be familiar with the critical discourses of social foundations, examining the historical and sociological aspects of education, to heighten their awareness of their socialization and foster an understanding of how instructional methods are shaped by these forces. Teacher education can sometimes be a series of isolated courses rather than a program reflecting the integrated nature of teaching, lacking explicit connections between the social contexts of schooling, the actual content taught, and the methods used to teach that content. Social foundations courses can provide an integrated experience where content is wedded to the practice of teaching in such a way that students can see how individual and social issues have real implications for everyday pedagogical practice.

History of American education courses, a common requirement in teacher education programs, often focus on understanding how education has been shaped by broader historical, political, economic, regional, and social forces. In the case of the over-representation of African Americans in special education described earlier, teacher candidates would examine historically how such beliefs came to be and what forces were at work in shaping those beliefs. Examining the expanded access to formal schooling for African Americans as a result of the Civil War and Reconstruction Era and the limitations to that access in the late nineteenth century as a result of Jim Crow laws and the "separate but equal" Supreme Court decision in the 1892 case of *Plessy v. Ferguson* are critical in this process.

Alongside that, the study of movements in the early-twentieth century that led to the introduction of IQ testing further complicates students' understanding of how racial stereotypes combined with institutional barriers resulted in grave misconceptions of African Americans and in particular the intellectual potential of African American children. The rigorous examination of such equity issues over time has the potential to challenge the validity of current beliefs and perhaps dispel dangerous myths.

Through historical and sociological inquiries into education, teacher candidates have the opportunity to raise their awareness of past and current social inequities and the role of schools and teachers in perpetuating and resisting them. While teacher candidates may assume access to universal public schooling is a given, courses in the social foundations allow them to examine the gradual and oftentimes reluctant move toward this reality by focusing on the evolution of public schooling and the educational experiences of diverse groups at various points in the history of the United States. Teacher candidates begin to distinguish between historical and contemporary perspectives on access to schooling and come to understand the efforts that led to wider educational access and the challenges that remain in providing educational equity for all.

These types of understandings are critical in preparing teacher candidates to practice culturally relevant pedagogy and begin to address the long-standing crisis of achievement for students of color and those in poverty. Addressing this crisis requires a considerable amount of flexibility and sophistication on the part of teachers. It calls for a strong sense of self, an awareness of how broader social and historical issues affect teaching and learning, a thorough understanding of subject matter and pedagogy, and a commitment to learning from students and their communities. Such a complex outcome can only be met with a concerted and coordinated effort by social foundations and teacher preparation faculty.

Notes

1. For examples on how to prepare culturally responsive teachers and how to integrate culturally responsive pedagogy into teacher preparation programs see Gay, 2000; Villegas and Lucas, 2002.
2. The importance of teacher self-efficacy is examined in Banks and McGee Banks, 1995; Bondy and Ross, 1998; Canella and Reiff, 1994; Haberman, 1995; Ladson-Billings, 1992, 1995; Kailin, 1994; Lawrence and Tatum, 1997; Mazzei, 1997; Montecinos, 1994.
3. This is especially important given that studies have shown how powerful social class is in determining the types of education children are provided. Metz (1998) studied the affects of social class on five high schools from different classes in 1985 and again in 1995 and found that "… even where classes were task-oriented, the level of discourse and the kind of discourse was noticeably more advanced the higher one went in SES among these schools" (p. 28). Anyon (1981) found, "… that even in an elementary school context, where there is a fairly 'standardized' curriculum, social stratification of knowledge is possible" (pp. 3–4).

References

American Association of Colleges for Teacher Education. (2002). *Professional education data system (PEDS) report*. Washington, DC: AACTE. Retrieved April 25, 2005, from **http://www.aacte.org/programs/multicultural/enrollment_ethnicity_yr89-91–95.htm**.

Anyon, J. (1981). Social class and school knowledge. *Curriculum Inquiry, 11(1)*, 3–42.

Banks, C. McGee, & Banks J. (1995). Equity pedagogy: An essential component of multicultural education. *Theory Into Practice, 34(3)*, 152–158.

Bondy, E., & Ross, D. (1998). Confronting myths about teaching black children: A challenge for teacher educators. *Teacher Education and Special Education, 21(4)*, 241–254.

Cannella, G., & Reiff, J. (1994). Teacher preparation for diversity. *Equity and Excellence in Education, 27(3)*, 28–33.

Gay, G. (2000). *Culturally responsive teaching: Theory, research, & practice*. New York: Teachers College Press.

Gollnick, D. (1992). Understanding the dynamics of race, class, and gender. In M. Dilworth (Ed.), *Diversity in teacher education: New expectations* (pp. 63–72). San Francisco: Jossey-Bass.

Haberman, M. (1995). *Star teachers of children in poverty*. West Lafayette, IN: Kappa Delta Pi.

Harry, B., Klingner, J. K., Sturges, K. M., & Moore, R. F. (2002). Of rocks and soft places: Using qualitative methods to investigate disproportionality. In D. J. Losen & G. Orfield (Eds.), *Racial inequity in special education* (pp. 71–92). Cambridge, MA: Civil Rights Project at Harvard University, Harvard Education Press.

Hoffman, C. M. (2003). *Mini-digest of education statistics, 2002* (NCES 2003-061). Washington, DC: U.S. Department of Education, National Center for Education Statistics.

Jamieson, A., Curry, A., & Martinez, G. (2001). *School enrollment in the United States—social and economic characteristics of students, October 1999* (P20-533). Washington, DC: U.S. Department of Commerce, Economics and Statistics Administration, U.S. Census Bureau.

Kailin, J. (1994). Antiracist staff development for teachers: Considerations of race, class, and gender. *Teaching and Teacher Education, 10(2)*, 169–184.

Kleinfeld, J. (1998). The use of case studies in preparing teachers for cultural diversity. *Theory Into Practice, 37(2)*, 140–147.

Knapp, M. S. & Woolverton, S. (1995) "Social class and schooling," In J. A. Banks & C. A. McGee Banks (eds.), *Handbook of research on multicultural education* (pp. 548–569). New York: Macmillan Publishing.

Ladson-Billings, G. (1992). Liberatory consequences of literacy: A case of culturally relevant instruction for African American students. *Journal of Negro Education, 61(3)*, 378–391.

Ladson-Billings, G. (1994). *The Dreamkeepers: Successful teachers of African American children*. San Francisco: Jossey-Bass.

Ladson-Billings, G. (1995). But that's just good teaching: The case for culturally relevant pedagogy. *Theory Into Practice, 34(3)*, 159–165.

Lawrence, S., & Tatum, B. D. (1997). Teachers in transition: the impact of antiracist professional development on classroom practice. *Teachers College Record, 99(1)*, 162–178.

Losen, D. J., & Orfield, G. (2002). *Racial inequity in special education*. Cambridge, MA: Civil Rights Project at Harvard University, Harvard Education Press.

Mazzei, L. (1997, March). Making our white selves intelligible to ourselves: Implications for teacher education. Paper presented at the Annual Meeting of the American Educational Research Association, Chicago, IL. (ERIC Document Reproduction Service No. ED410215).

Mehan, H., Lintz, A., Okamoto, D., & Wills, J. S. (1995). Ethnographic studies of multicultural education in classrooms and schools. In J. A. Banks & C. A. McGee Banks (Eds.), *Handbook of research on multicultural education* (pp. 129–144). New York: Macmillan Publishing.

Metz, M. H. (1998, April). Veiled inequalities: The hidden effects of community social class on high school teachers' perspectives and practices. Paper presented at the Annual Meeting of the American Educational Researchers Association (AERA), San Diego, CA. (ERIC Document Reproduction Service No. ED420629)

Montecinos, C. (1994). Teachers of color and multiculturalism. *Equity and Excellence in Education, 27(3),* 34–42.

National Center for Education Statistics. (2003a). *National assessment of educational progress 2003.* Washington, DC: U.S. Department of Education. Retrieved April 25, 2005, from **http://nces.ed.gov/ nationsreportcard/ reading/results2003/natachieve-re-g4.asp**.

National Center for Education Statistics. (2003b). *National assessment of educational progress 2003.* Washington, DC: U.S. Department of Education. Retrieved April 25, 2005, from **http:// www.nces.ed.gov/nationsreportcard/ reading/results2003/ natachieve-lunch-gr4. asp**.

Shujaa, M. (1995). Cultural self meets cultural other in the African American experience: Teachers' responses to a curriculum content reform. *Theory Into Practice, 34(5),* 194–201.

Sia, A. & Mosher, D. (1994, February). Perception of multicultural concepts by pre-service teachers in two institutions. Paper presented at the 74th Annual Meeting of the Association of Teacher Educators, Atlanta, GA. (ERIC Document Reproduction Service No. ED367603)

Villegas, A. M. (1991). *Culturally responsive pedagogy for the 1990's and beyond.* (Trends and Issues Paper No. 6). Washington, DC: ERIC Clearinghouse on Teacher Education. (ERIC Document Reproduction Service No. ED339698)

Villegas, A. M. & Lucas, T. (2002). *Educating culturally responsive teachers: A coherent approach.* Albany, NY: State University of New York Press.

Zeichner, K. (1996). Educating teachers for cultural diversity. In K. Zeichner, S. Melnick, & M. L. Gomez, (Eds.), *Currents of reform in pre-service teacher education* (pp. 133–175). New York: Teachers College Press.

ANN MARIE RYAN is an assistant professor with the School of Education at Loyola University Chicago, Chicago, Illinois.

Tolerance in Teacher Education

Restructuring the Curriculum in a Diverse But Segregated University Classroom

SANDY WHITE WATSON AND LINDA JOHNSTON

Introduction

Many of us teach undergraduate and graduate teacher education courses that include a cultural hodgepodge of future teachers who differ not only in ethnicity, but in age, sexual preference, religion, language, and a host of other microcultural areas. Occasionally it is clear within the first couple of class sessions that these groups are reluctant to interact with one another in any format. In these instances, those few cliques that could possibly develop do so early on and class discussions may be almost nonexistent at the outset of the courses. In later discussions we have witnessed angry encampments of student groups lashing out at one another.

What follows is our attempt at bringing diverse and segregated class groups together in some sense of understanding and respect for one another through a restructured, reconceptualized, multicultural curriculum. After all, these very groups of non-cooperative students will very soon be serving as teachers in schools across the United States and will need to develop the skills necessary to foster multicultural tolerance among their own students.

The Call for Multicultural Education in Higher Education

Gollnick and Chinn (2002) provide a list of fundamental characteristics of multicultural higher education:

1. Cultural differences have strength and value.
2. Schools and institutions of higher learning should be models for the community in reflecting respect for cultural differences and expression of human rights.
3. Social justice and equality for all people should be of paramount importance in the design and delivery of curricula.
4. Attitudes and values necessary for the continuation of a democratic society can be promoted in schools and institutions of higher learning.
5. Schooling can provide the knowledge, skills, and dispositions, for redistribution of power and income among diverse groups of people.
6. Educators at institutes of higher learning work with local communities to create an environment that is supportive of respect for diversity and multiculturalism.

Because institutions of higher education are models for academic excellence and democratic human values, it is paramount that university faculty and administrators embrace the above characteristics. We are the exemplary models for public schools and the community (Ameny-Dixon, 2004).

Preparing Pre-Service Teachers to Be Culturally Responsive

As a culturally responsive teacher one must celebrate each student as part of the learning community. To be culturally responsive and find the commonalities within a classroom, a teacher must recognize that he/she must work toward social justice for his/her students (Kroeger & Bauer, 2004). In order for teachers to learn and practice this concept, institutions of higher education must make this happen. Teacher candidates must be prepared to be culturally responsive teachers.

Colleges of education must adhere to the National Council for Accreditation of Teacher Education (NCATE, 2002) Standard # 4, *Diversity*. Standard 4 states:

> The unit designs, implements and evaluates curriculum and experiences for candidates to acquire and apply the knowledge, skills and dispositions necessary to help all students learn. These experiences include working with diverse higher education and school faculty, diverse candidates and diverse students in P-12 schools.

In addition, the Interstate New Teacher Assessment and Support Consortium (1992) (INTASC) Principle # 3 provides colleges and universities with a venue for teacher candidates to adhere to cultural sensitivity. INTASC (1992) Principle # 3 states:

> The teacher understands how students differ in their approaches to learning and creates instructional opportunities that are adapted to diverse learners.

Teachers must be prepared in such a way as to become role models in effectuating change. The faces of America's school children have changed at a rapid pace. The number of school age children who are disabled, have limited English proficiencies, and who are from various ethnic groups of color has increased during the last ten years. Therefore, teacher candidates must understand exactly what it means to be culturally responsive.

According to Gay (2000) a culturally responsive teacher:

Acknowledges the legitimacy of cultural heritages as legacies that affect students' dispositions, attitudes, and approaches to learning and as worthy content to be taught in the formal curriculum.

Builds on meaningfulness between home and school experiences as well as between academic abstractions and lived sociocultural realities.

Uses a variety of instructional strategies that are connected to different learning styles.

Teaches students to know and praise their own and each others' cultural heritages.

Incorporates multicultural information, resources and materials in all subjects and skills taught in school. (as cited in Kroeger & Bauer, 2004, p. 25)

To enhance a teacher candidate's perceptions of multicultural education as well as to begin the process of bringing various groups together, it is imperative that faculty within colleges of education provide various activities to stimulate this endeavor.

Microcultures

Within the larger macroculture in the United States are countless smaller subsocieties or subcultures known as microcultures. According to Gollnick and Chinn (2002), microcultres share cultural patterns of the macroculture but also have their own distinct sets of cultural patterns and "People who belong to the same microculture share traits and values that bind them together as a group" (p. 18).

Microcultural examples could include place of residence (farm, urban, etc.), abilities (marathon runner, gardener, etc.), age, career (physician, teacher, construction worker, etc.), socioeconomic status, group member, gender, etc. Individuals belonging to one microculture may not all belong to another.

All of us are members of numerous microcultural groups and if we could step back and view the interactions of those groups, we could see commonalities emerging that perhaps we did not know existed. And it is that interconnectedness that we wish to emphasize as a means of fostering commonalities in diverse groups.

Microcultural Mapping

A very effective initial classroom exercise involves the identification of one's microcultural self (this is an activity modified from *Awareness Activities*, part of the *Multicultural Pavilion*

Internet Project). After a discussion of culture and microculture, students are asked to define who they are via the identification of the microcultures to which they belong. They are provided outlines of human forms that represent themselves and they are then asked to draw lines from the forms outward to six or seven circles in which they write the names of microcultures to which they hold membership—what they feel demonstrates the most important dimensions of their personal identity.

Their papers are collected and from those papers a list is generated of all identified microcultures; no group is identified more than once. On a very large sheet of bulletin board paper all the identified microcultural groups are recorded randomly, all over the paper. Each student is then provided a cutout of a human with his or her name on it and is asked to glue his/her cutout somewhere on the large paper among the various microcultures.

During the next class session students are given yardsticks and are asked to draw lines from themselves to all of the microcultures to which they belong. The professor's personal cutout and connections are drawn to serve as an example and to also show students that he/she is willing to share his/her microcultural connections with the students. What results, is a very large microcultural "map" or "web." During the activity, some students may realize membership in groups they had not previously identified.

When the "mapping" is complete, students should see the commonalities they share with others in the class. Often, students find connections with individuals that they previously claimed to have nothing in common with.

Professional Development School Tolerance Activities

The Professional Development School (PDS) semester is designed for candidates to spend a semester in an actual urban public school setting. They work in the classroom under the supervision of a teacher for part of the day. University faculty teach the courses on site for the remainder of the day.

This semester occurs early in the students' college careers in order to provide them with exposure to the world of teaching. If candidates decide not to pursue a degree in the field of education, because the PDS experience occurs early in their college career it provides them with ample time to change majors.

The PDS semester is structured in such a way by both the school-based faculty and the university faculty to enhance students' awareness and provide them with a venue to begin thinking about the value of microculture connections. Microculture connections are a means for teacher education candidates to find commonalities among the diverse students they will teach. During the PDS semester they grow to appreciate heterogeneous classrooms and better understand how to be culturally sensitive in order to teach a very diverse student population. These activities can be held in reserve and then used by the candidates when they have their own classrooms.

The magazine *Teaching Tolerance* has a wealth of articles that are thought provoking. These articles are used to stimulate class discussions about topics many students have had little or no exposure to during their lifetime. During the 50th anniversary of the *Brown vs. Board of Education* decision, these articles were the basis of research projects, poems, reflective writings, dramatic presentations, and unit developments.

These activities were also utilized by school-based faculty who provided seminars to candidates. Individuals from around the community, who were part of that era and were educated in segregated environments, were brought in to facilitate small group discussions with candidates. Comments such as "I never thought about how the other side felt, until now," or "What vision and strength those individuals had," are part of a reflective process that brings sensitivity awareness to various events and cultures that the students had never thought about.

Community Mapping

Another awareness activity to stimulate sensitivity about the community where students actually live is community mapping. Candidates are divided into small groups and given instructions to go out into the community and spend one half day. They are to stop at restaurants, churches, community buildings, grocery stores, quick stop markets, etc., and talk with people in each of these settings to gain a deeper understanding about where students in the area's K-12 schools reside.

They are asked to inform individuals who they are and what they are doing in this process. After returning to class they compile a list of things they learned from their time in the community. As a result, they have a deeper understanding of the role of the school within the community. Candidates always enjoy this activity and come back with a greater sensitivity to students attending the schools where they are teaching. This activity is conducted at the beginning of the PDS semester and provides teacher candidates with the opportunity to begin thinking about their role as teachers in relation to the students within the school.

100% Smart Activity

The 100% smart activity is one in which students determine the learning styles of the class members. Candidates are given a paper plate and then divided into groups of four or five. They are given a list of eleven different styles of learning: auditory, visual, kinesthetic, interpersonal, intrapersonal, spatial, tactile, musical, logical-mathematical, linguistic, and naturalistic. From this list they are to determine what percentage of students in the class represent each learning style based on their own perception of themselves.

They are then asked to divide the plate into pie shaped slices representing the percentage of each learning style. The total must equal 100%. The average is compiled for each group and then for the class as a whole in order for all to see the variation in the number of learning styles that are represented in the group.

The discussion that follows relates to the commonalities within the class as students are asked to consider what they think the class, as a whole, has in common and how the class members differ from one another. They are then asked to consider ways in which they could connect with one another considering their differences and then considering their commonalities.

This activity is designed to allow students to recognize awareness of diversity within the classroom and how teachers need to be sensitive to each student's learning style. It is emphasized that candidates must learn to connect with their classmates, no matter what their differences might be, and carry these strategies to their future classrooms as teachers.

Diverse Grouping

During the PDS semester candidates are divided into small groups to work on various projects throughout the semester. Candidates are divided into groups for the semester that are balanced with respect to learning styles, gender, race, and ethnicity. This is done by both site-based faculty and university faculty to promote an appreciation for all candidates and provide a means for candidates to begin learning how to collaborate with a wide range of individuals. This provides a learning experience in acceptance, professionalism, and tolerance.

English Language Learners

An activity that stimulates much discussion related to English Language Learners (ELL) is one that is astounding to some of the candidates. An ELL teacher is invited to conduct a seminar during the semester. The teacher is of Hispanic origin and begins the activity by speaking in Spanish. He/she continues to hand out papers and pencils and presents an activity on an overhead projector, all the time speaking in Spanish. Candidates find themselves both lost and frustrated.

What follows is a discussion related to the feelings they may have experienced during the activity, including isolation, frustration, anger, upsetness, and confusion. Candidates reflect on their feelings and in the process have a better understanding of what ELL students experience. This is an informative session and one that creates a huge awareness and better understanding related to sensitivity for students who may come to their classroom as non-English speakers.

Teacher candidates must develop a knowledge base and appreciation for teaching all students. They must also understand that students must feel an ownership in their own education. Shor (1992) suggests that women, minorities, and non-elite whites make up the bulk of students, and democratic education should be reflective of the cultures, conditions, needs, and history of those students. Participation should be a means for empowering education.

Cultural diversity is a strength, as well as a persistent, vitalizing force in personal and civic lives. It is a very useful resource for improving educational effectiveness for all students (Gay, 2000). Accepting diversity and celebrating that diversity within the classroom should be a day to day part of teaching.

Conclusion

American schools (K-12 and beyond) are currently housing the most culturally diverse group of students in the history of American education (Gollnick & Chinn, 2002). Certain ethnic populations have experienced phenomenal growth in the United States in the last decade. According to the Social Science Data Analysis Network (2001), the Hispanic population in the U.S. has increased by 45 percent, while the Asian community grew by 45 percent and the Black and Native American populations have each increased by 15 percent.

Increased ethnic diversity likewise means increased religious and linguistic differences. With this increase in diversity among U.S. student populations comes an increased responsibility to better prepare future educators to deal with the complex issues and needs of such diverse student groups. But before preservice teachers can master teaching for tolerance, they must first demonstrate respect and tolerance for one another as students.

References

Ameny-Dixon, G.M. (2004). Why multicultural education is more important in higher education now than ever: A global perspective. *International Journal of Scholarly Academic Intellectual Diversity*, (8)1.

Gay, G. (2000). *Culturally responsive teaching: Theory, research, and practice*. New York: Teachers College Press.

Gollnick, D.M. & Chinn, P.C. (2002). *Multicultural education in a pluralistic society (6th Ed.)*. Upper Saddle River, NJ, & Columbus, OH: Merrill/Prentice Hall.

Interstate New Teacher Assessment and Support Consortium [INTASC]. (1992). *Model standards For beginning teacher licensing, assessment, and development: A resource for state dialogue*. Washington, DC: Council of Chief State School Officers.

Kroeger, S.D., & Bauer, A. M. (2004). *Exploring diversity*. Boston: Pearson Education.

Multicultural Pavilion Internet Project (2002).(on-line): *Awareness activities*. Available: http://curry.edschool.virginia.edu/go/multicultural/pavboard/pavboard.html. Retrieved June 1, 2005.

National Council for Accreditation of Teacher Education [NCATE]. (2002). *Professional standards for the accreditation of schools, colleges, and departments of education* (on-line). Available: http://www.ncate.org. Retrieved June 1, 2005.

Shor, I., (1992). *Empowering education, critical teaching for social change*. Chicago: University of Chicago Press.

Social Science Data Analysis Network. (2000). *Census in the classroom* (on-line). Available: http://www.ssdan.net/ Retrieved May 30, 2005.

SANDY WHITE WATSON is an assistant professor and **LINDA JOHNSTON** is an associate professor, both with the Teacher Preparation Academy at the University of Tennessee at Chattanooga Chattanooga, Tennessee.

Dialogue Across Cultures: Teachers' Perceptions about Communication with Diverse Families

Arti Joshi, Jody Eberly, and Jean Konzal

Introduction

It is well accepted in the field of home-school relations and child development that parents and teachers must work together to build common expectations and to support student learning (Bronfenbrenner, 1986, 1979; Coleman & Hoffer, 1987; Epstein, 2001; Henderson & Berla, 1994). It follows, therefore, that the teacher must establish good relations and open communication with parents.[1] Building strong, trusting, and mutually respectful relationships between parents and teachers who share similar cultural backgrounds is difficult enough. Doing so between parents and teachers who come from different backgrounds is even more difficult.

New Jersey, like many other states, is experiencing a significant influx of new immigrants—from countries such as India, Pakistan, China, Russia, Poland, Nigeria, Liberia, Mexico, Dominican Republic, and Haiti. In addition, New Jersey remains one of the most segregated states in the country, educating the majority of its African-American families in the inner city and first-ring communities that surround the cities. Our teaching profession consists primarily of European-American women who are, in Lisa Delpit's words, teaching "other people's children" and who need help in doing so (1995).

Given this diversity in New Jersey classrooms, we conceptualized a multiphase research project with the ultimate goal of helping teachers understand family values, beliefs, and practices in order to create a learning environment at school that acknowledges and builds upon these. Simultaneously, the project aims to facilitate parents' understanding of the school's values, beliefs, and practices so they can create a congruent learning environment at home.

It is the first goal that this study seeks to address. We need to learn more about how teachers currently understand their students' family cultures, how they come to these understandings, and how this understanding influences how they reach out to parents. Little has been written about this "missing link" in our knowledge base related to parent involvement (Caspe, 2003, p. 128).

Towards this end, we designed a survey to assess New Jersey teachers' current knowledge and practices. Therefore the following questions are addressed in the article:

1. How do teachers define parent involvement; how do they define culture?
2. What practices do teachers use in working with families in general and, more specifically, with families from cultures different from their own?
3. What is the extent and nature of awareness of teachers with respect to the cultural beliefs and practices of the families in their classrooms?
4. What aspects of culture do teachers identify as important influences on children's education?
5. In what ways do teachers currently make use of what they know about their students' cultural backgrounds when planning instruction?

The Impact of Culture on Child Development and Learning

Bronfenbrenner's ecological theory of development (1979, 1986) and Super and Harkness's developmental niche theory (1997) argue that a child's development is influenced not only by their parents, but by other systems as well, including the family's culture, the caregivers' "ethnotheories" related to child development, and school and community values and beliefs.

Related to this, Gutierrez and Rogoff's (2003) definition of culture as a dynamic, situational, and historic construct stresses that a person's culture is not solely influenced by their ethnicity or race, but rather by a number of additional varibles as well: i.e., historical context, geographic location, gender, generation, age, religion, group memberships, and level of education. Gutierrez and Rogoff (2003) argue that the way one approaches learning is influenced by the practices inherent within the individual's cultural community characterized by all of the variables mentioned above—not solely a person's ethnicity.

Even Patricia Greenfield (1994), whose theory of cultural differences based on child-rearing goals towards either independence or interdependence, warns against jumping to conclusions that a person is automatically inclined towards either one or the other solely based on their ethnicity. Therefore, this study raises questions of how to translate understandings of a child's multi-faceted culture into classroom practices that open communication with parents and engage the child in a culturally responsive way.

The Importance of Parent/School Communication

Since it is acknowledged that both parents and teachers are responsible for educating our children, it would seem that it would be in the child's best interest for us all to be working towards the same goals. This common-sense notion is also supported by research. For example, studies into the impact of facilitating ongoing interactions with parents in order to help parents reinforce the school's goals and objectives at home (Berger, 1996; Epstein, 1990), the impact of parental interest in and encouragement of school activities on positive attitudes towards school and learning (Epstein, 2001), and finally the impact of communication and cooperation between home and school on children's learning (Epstein, 1990) all point to the critical importance of this relationship.

When dealing with parents from cultures different from their own, open lines of communication with parents are even more essential. If teachers are to create learning environments conducive to learning for children from different cultures, they need insight into the values, beliefs, and practices of those cultures (Bensman, 2000; Trumbull, Rothstein-Fisch, Greenfield, & Quiroz, 2001; Delpit, 1995; Lee, Spencer, & Harpalani, 2003).

Bensman (2000) argues that cultural interchange, the process by which teachers learn about cultures that their students bring to class and parents learn about the school/classroom culture, is the way to facilitate student success. Delpit (1995), Lee, et al. (2003), and Trumbull (2001) argue that this knowledge can then be translated into classroom activities that honor and incorporate culturally-based knowledge.

Unfortunately such open communication between parents and teachers is not common place. The dynamics of the parent-teacher relationship create communication problems that under the best of circumstances can be problematic. However, teachers and parents carry many preconceived notions about each other that make communication even more difficult.

Barriers to Good Parent/School Relations

Researchers have identified a variety of factors that inhibit open communication between parents and teachers regardless of cultural backgrounds (Epstein & Becker, 1982; Dodd & Konzal, 1999, 2001). These include different knowledge bases of teachers and parents, different perspectives in relation to "my" child versus "all children," use of jargon or "educator-speak"[2] when communicating with parents (Dodd & Konzal, 1999, 2001), lack of time for informal opportunities to get to know each other in non-stressful, non-bureaucratic encounters (Henry, 1996), and, finally, different understandings of the "proper" roles for teachers and parents (Greenwood & Hickman, 1991; Hughes & MacNaughton, 2000; Joshi, 2002).

Unfortunately, when parents and teachers come from different backgrounds, the barriers listed above are exacerbated and further barriers are introduced. Reviewing the literature, Bermudez and Marquez (1996) identified the following additional barriers that prevent parents and teachers from communicating openly and honestly, "... lack of English language skills, lack of understanding of the home-school partnership, lack of understanding of the school system, lack of confidence, work interference, negative past experiences with schools, and insensitivity or hostility on the part of the school personnel" (p. 3). These (and other) teacher attitudes towards parents many times lead to what parents perceive as insensitivity and even hostility (Bermudez & Marquez, 1996). Many times these negative and/or stereotypical teacher attitudes towards parents derive from cultural blinders.

Trumbull, et al. (2001) argue that the major barrier to parent-school communication is the lack of understanding of the very different beliefs that parents and educators may hold in relation to the purposes, goals, and outcomes of schooling. They argue "... it, is rare that schools (or those in charge of them) get below the surface to understand how those differences can lead not only to different goals but also completely different views of schooling and, hence, parent involvement" (p. 31).

This lack of understanding of the underlying beliefs about the parents' goals for child-rearing and education may lead to an unarticulated clash with educators' values and beliefs. In such cases, parents and educators are each pulling in different directions without necessarily being aware of what is happening. The child, of course, is in the middle, receiving one set of messages at home and another set at school. Surfacing these unarticulated different belief systems is in the best interests of the children—but it is not easy.

Translating Cross-Cultural Understandings into Practice

For communication between parents and teachers to be meaningful and responsive, it is necessary to understand the cultural frameworks within which parents' function, since parental attitudes are influenced by cultural and economic factors (Greenfield, 1994; Trumbull et al, 2001). Parents foster the development of children through developmental pathways which are couched within a given culture (Weisner, 1998). Aspects of culture like communication, education, dress, religion, and values for socialization and interactions influence an individual's behavior, values, and attitudes.

"The schools then become the agents who help children build bridges between the cultures of the family and other communities, by means of practices that respect and respond to the diversity of families" (Wright & Stegelin, 2003). In order to do this, is important for teachers to understand the cultural frameworks from which they function (Caspe, 2003).

Unfortunately, more often than not, teachers don't have deep understandings of either their own or their students' family cultural pathways and do not know how to build these bridges (e.g., see Gonzalez-Mena, 2000). There has been significant work in identifying the need for and developing strategies for culturally responsive teaching (Caspe, 2003; Delpit, 1995; Ladson-Billings, 1991; Marion, 1980; Trumbull, et al, 2001; Voltz, 1994). However, in the schools we visit we see little evidence that teachers are familiar with these practices.

Being able to build bridges for families and teachers so that they have insight into each other's worlds is essential for the well being of the children we hold in common. As a first step towards helping teachers understand how culture influences beliefs, values, and practices related to education and to connecting this understanding to their professional practice, we conducted a survey in order to find out (1) what teachers currently know and believe about the influence of culture on learning and (2) the practices they currently use to interact with parents and to design instructional activities for children from cultures different from their own.

Method

Participants were practicing teachers, specialists, and administrators in public and private central New Jersey schools serving children from preschool to 5th grade. One of the local elementary schools was approached and permission of the principal was obtained. The purpose of the survey was explained to the teachers and other faculty members in a faculty meeting. Subsequently, at a second faculty meeting, surveys were distributed and completed by all teachers, administrators, and other faculty members.

The total number of the respondents from this school was 25. The remaining respondents were working in preschools that were state funded and were enrolled in a graduate class at a local college. The purpose of the research was explained. All the students agreed to participate in the research. Informed consent was received from all of the participants. The final sample consisted of 40 respondents.

A majority of the respondents were females (92%) and PK-3 classroom teachers (82%). Of the respondents who reported their teaching experience, 42% (14) had 3 years or less teaching experience, while 30% (10) had more than 14 years of teaching experience. Ninety percent of the respondents identified their

ethnicity, out of which 83% (30) were European American 11% (4) were African American, 3% (1 each) were Hispanic/Latino and Middle Eastern. In terms of the demographic composition of the children, many of the classrooms had approximately half European American, while the remaining were African American, Hispanic, or Asian.

In order to design the questionnaire for this study an extensive review of literature on parent involvement and culture was undertaken. Based on the literature, common practices of parent involvement and components of culture were identified and a draft of the questions was developed (Bennett, 2003; Shade, Kelly, & Oberg, 1997; Wright & Stegelin, 2003). The questionnaire was refined from feedback from a focus group of practicing teachers and parents who had similar demographics as the final sample. To further refine the questionnaire, it was piloted with a group of central and southern New Jersey teachers enrolled in a graduate class at a local college.

The final questionnaire was comprised of three types of questions: open ended, ranking, and Likert type rating questions. The survey had two main sections: (1) parental involvement and (2) knowledge of culture and its impact upon a child's education. The first section of the survey consisted of questions where participants were asked to define parental involvement and to address means and challenges of involving parents.

In the second section, participants were first asked to define culture and then rank the most important components of understanding culture. The components of culture consisted of six different categories: communication patterns, social values, ways of learning, child rearing, outward displays, and religious practices (See Benett, 2003; Shade, Kelly, & Oberg, 1997; Wright & Stegelin, 2003).

Other questions asked participants to rate, on a 4-point scale, their awareness of cultural components and the components of culture that they felt most influenced a child's academic success. Open ended questions were used to seek the participants' definitions of parent involvement and culture along with their own practices regarding the same.

Likert type and ranking scales were used for all other questions. After the data were collected, the open ended questions were read by each of the researchers and emergent themes were identified. Consensus was reached amongst the researchers on the themes that emerged.

Findings About Parent Involvement

When asked to define parent involvement, the most common response was participation in school activities. Other common responses included communicating with school, demonstrating interest in school, and supporting children at home. Respondents were then asked to identify the important ways in which parents should be involved in their child(ren)'s education. The parent involvement practices most frequently rated as being important were communicating with teachers (38%), teaching children family values and beliefs (28%), and attending parent conferences/meetings (23%).

When asked to describe how parents are currently involved in their classrooms, the most common themes were participating in the classroom, attending special events and parties, chaperoning field trips, and attending parent-teacher conferences. Teachers also reported that written communication and conferences were the strategies that they most often employed in their efforts to involve parents and less frequently responded that home reading logs, telephone calls home, and class presentations were also effective strategies for including parents in their child's education.

The survey also sought to investigate the teachers' perceptions about the reasons for lack of parental involvement in their child(ren)'s education. About half of the teachers identified parents' other time commitments as being the number one reason for lack of involvement (53%). Parents' struggle to provide basic needs of the families emerged as the second reason by about one third of the respondents (35%). Other reasons for lack of parental involvement were difficulty in comprehending language (18%), educational constraints of the parents (18%), and parental difficulty in understanding the school culture (18%). An open-ended question about the challenges of involving parents revealed similar findings: parents' lack of time and language barriers. A third theme, though, also emerged: parents' lack of interest in their child's education.

Findings About Culture

The second section of the survey focused on identifying the respondents' beliefs and knowledge related to developing an understanding of cultures of families in their classrooms. Respondents were first asked to define culture. An overwhelming number of them defined culture as a set of beliefs and values. The next most frequently used definition of culture was customs and traditions, followed by religion and language.

In a second open-ended question, respondents were asked to explain whether or not they felt it was important to understand the different cultures of the families of the children in their classroom. Although all of the respondents answered in the affirmative, they gave varying reasons for doing so. The most common theme was to understand their students' backgrounds, followed by the effect it has on children's education and learning, and that it aids in communicating with parents.

With respect to how teachers acknowledge culture in their curriculum, the most common responses included reading multicultural books, celebrating holidays, implementing cultural heritage units, and inviting parents to participate in the classroom. In their interactions with families, teachers stated that they addressed culture through their own awareness of holidays and celebrations, through discussion of culture, and by translating communication into the families' preferred language.

For the purposes of this study, culture was conceptualized as having six main components: patterns of communication (body language, personal space, comfort with touching, talking and listening); social values (do's and don'ts of behavior, determi-nation of status, and definitions of achievement); preferred ways of learning and knowledge most valued in a given culture; ideas about raising children (child rearing patterns and goals, family structure, adult-child interactions, discipline, dependence-independence orientation); outward displays of culture (celebrations, artifacts, food, art, literature, and music); and religious values practiced in any given culture.

Table 1 reports on teacher responses to the following survey questions: To what degree are you aware of these cultural components of the families in your classroom? Which of these components of culture do you think most influence a child's academic learning/performance? On which of these areas have you sought information from parents?

David Bensman (2000) defines cultural interchange as "the process by which members of groups with different traditions, values, beliefs, and experiences gained a greater degree of mutual understanding" (p. iii). It is our contention that this "cultural interchange" is essential if teachers are to design culturally responsive instruction. In order for teachers to develop this knowledge-base and to translate it into practice, it is first important to surface their current and often unarticulated knowledge and beliefs about how cultural traditions, values, and beliefs influence learning and how teachers can take an active role in promoting open communication that leads to mutual understandings. Our findings suggest that the teachers we surveyed may have conflicting beliefs and practices in both of these areas.

Parent Involvement

The findings indicated that the common understanding of parent involvement was having the parents participate in the school. However, whether or not these practices actually lead to cultural interchange is not known.

Are teachers and parents getting to know each other during these activities in ways that lead to building trusting relationships? (Bensman, 2000; Dodd & Konzal, 2001). During these activities, are teachers communicating in ways that encourage parents to share their cultural beliefs and values? Are teachers able to observe how parents interact with their children and other children in order to gain cultural insights (Caspe, 2003 Trumbull, et al, 2001)? This will be investigated in future research subsequent to the current study.

When asked about their most effective strategies for involving parents, teachers responded that written communication and conferences were most effective. The teachers in our study recognized what the researchers tell us about the importance of communicating with parents, but it is unclear of the actual usage of these parent/teacher conferences. Researchers tell us that two-way communication is essential for building mutual trust and respect between parents and teachers; that two-way communication invites parents to tell teachers what they know about their children, their community, and their culture (Bensman, 2000; Dodd & Konzal, 2001; Edwards, 1999; Atkin & Bastiani, 1988).

Written communication is clearly one-way communication either from the parent or the teacher. It serves to maintain the so-

Table 1 Dissonance Between Teacher Beliefs and Practice

	Teacher Responses to Survey Questions Percentages			
	High Awareness	Little Awareness	High Influence on Learning	Seeks Information About
Patterns of Communication	66	34	95	63
Social Values	60	40	92	54
Ways of Learning	49	51	97	57
Child Rearing Practices	43	57	79	63
Outward Displays	50	50	41	66
Religious Values	15	85	44	37

cial distance of teachers from parents (Powell, 1978). Parent-teacher conferences, on the other hand, are a perfect opportunity for parents and teachers to have two-way communication. However, many times these conferences, rather than promoting cultural interchange, revert to another form of one-way communication—teachers telling parents (Lawrence-Light-foot, 2003, Trumbull, et al, 2001).

Therefore, concluding the findings about parent involvement, it is unclear whether or not the teachers use the parent/teacher conference as a means of promoting two-way communication and cultural interchange (Bensman, 2000) or use it more as a unidirectional way of passing information.

Cultural Knowledge

One of the most interesting findings is that at times there appears to be a disparity between what teachers report about their awareness of culture, what they say about how culture influences learning, their actual practice in the classroom, and the topics about which they seek information. While we did expect some disparity between teacher beliefs and practices (Lee et al, 2003; Trumbull, et al, 2001), we did find it surprising that the information that teachers seek about culture was also a part of this disparity. (See Table 1)

One possible reason for this disparity could be that teachers on a conceptual level understand the importance and influence of culture, however might be ill-equipped to translate it into actual practice. It might reflect the teachers' narrow view of culture (e.g., emphasis on overt aspects like food, celebrations, dress). They might also lack skills or training in integrating other more or less tangible aspects of culture into the curriculum and classroom practice.

Teachers overwhelmingly felt that patterns of communication, social values, preferred ways of learning and knowledge, and child raising patterns had a strong influence on students' learning. However, with respect to the outward displays of culture (dress, celebrations, food, art, literature, etc.) and religious values, less than half of the respondents felt that these had an influence on students' learning.

Yet, when asked how they acknowledge culture in their classrooms, the most common themes that emerged were books, holidays, and cultural heritage units, all of which fall under the category of outward displays of culture. Likewise, when asked how they affirm culture in their interactions with families, they reported that they demonstrate their own awareness of the culture's holidays.

Therefore, there seems to be a discrepancy between the fact that teachers feel that outward displays of culture do not have an important influence in learning and the fact that that is exactly what they choose to incorporate in their curriculum and interactions with families and what they mostly seek information about from parents.

Another interesting finding related to religious values. While 44% felt that religious values have some influence on learning, only a little over one-third of the respondents seek information on these values. It appears that teachers are uncomfortable with discussions related to religious values, especially in public school settings.

This is understandable given the confusion in schools about what is allowed and what is not allowed in relation to talking about and teaching about religion. We find it a problem since it is generally acknowledged that religious values significantly influence parents' beliefs about child rearing and education.

Limitations and Implications

This study is comprised of a small sample of preschool through third grade teachers in one state. These participants were volunteers and a sample of convenience. This leads to limitations of generalizability of the findings of the study. However, this study is a pilot for subsequent research that will be more extensive in its outreach as well as its depth. Additionally, this study was specifically implemented to provide data for the design and formulation of a in-service professional development program for schools.

This study reveals that the New Jersey teachers who responded to this survey have a rhetorical understanding of the important aspects of culture, but lack the ability to interpret that knowledge into practices. It leaves us wondering what they mean when they say that culture is the beliefs and values people hold. How do they operationalize this concept? The same is true for their understanding of parent involvement practices. They identify communication and parent/ teacher conferences as important, but we are left wondering about the specific strategies they use and if they use them for the purpose of cultural interchange. Future research will be designed to further probe these questions.

Notes

1. We use the term parents to include all family members who act as caregivers
2. Parent term for educational jargon from Konzal, 1996.

References

Atkin, J. & Bastiani, J. (1988). *Listening to parents: An approach to the improvement of home/school relations*. London, UK: Croom Helm.

Bensman, D. (2000). *Building school-family partnerships in a South Bronx classroom*. New York: NCREST.

Bennett, C. L. (2003). *Comprehensive multicultural education: Theory and practice*. Boston: Allyn & Bacon.

Berger, E. H. (1996). Working with families. Communication: Key to parent involvement. *Early Childhood Journal, 23*(3), 179–183.

Bermudez, A. B. & Marquez, J. A. (1996). An examination of a four-way collaborative to increase parental involvement in schools. *The Journal of Educational Issues of Language Minority Students, 16*(6), 1–16.

Bronfenbrenner, U. (1986). Ecology of the family as a context for human development: Research perspectives. *Developmental Psychology, 22*(6), 723–742.

Bronfenbrenner, U. (1979). *The ecology of human development: Experiments by nature and design*. Cambridge, MA: Harvard University Press.

Caspe, M. S. (2003). How teachers come to understand families. *The School Community Journal, 13*(1), 115–131.

Coleman, J. S. & Hoffer T. (1987). *Public and private high schools*. New York: Basic Books.

Delpit, L. (1995). *Other people's children: Cultural conflict in the classroom*. New York: New Press. ED 387274.

Dodd, A.W. & Konzal, J. L. (2002). *How communities build stronger schools: Stories, strategies and promising practices for educating every child*. New York: Palgrave Macmillan.

Dodd, A.W. & Konzal, J. L. (1999). *Making our high schools better: How parents and teachers can work together*. New York: St. Martin's Press.

Edwards, P. A. (1999). *A path to follow: learning to listen to parents*. Portsmouth, NH: Heinemann.

Epstein, J. L. (2001). *School, family, and community partnerships: Preparing educators and improving schools*. Colorado: Westview Press.

Epstein, J. L. (1990). School and family connections: Theory, research and implications for integrating sociologies of education and family. *Marriage and Family Review, 15*(1), 99–126.

Epstein, J. L. & Becker, H. J. (1982). Teachers' reported practices of parent involvement: problems and possibilities. *The Elementary School Journal, 83*(2), 103–113.

Gonzalez-Mena, J. (2000). High-maintenance parent or cultural differences? *Child Care Information Exchange, 134*, 40–42.

Greenfield, P. M. (1994). Independence and interdependence as developmental scripts: Implications for theory, research, and practice. In Greenfield, P. M. & Cocking, R. R. (Eds.), *Cross-cultural roots of minority child development*. Hillsdale, NJ: Lawrence Erlbaum Associates.

Greenwood, G. E. & Hickman, C. W. (1991). Research and practice in parent involvement: Implications for teacher education. *Elementary School Journal, 91*(3), 279–288.

Gutierrez, K. D. & Rogoff, B. (2003). Cultural ways of learning: Individual traits or repertoires of practice. *Educational Researcher, 32*(5), 19–25.

Henderson, A. T. & Berla, N. (1994). *A new generation of evidence: The family is critical to student achievement*. Washington, DC: National Committee for Citizens in Education, ERIC [On-line]. Available: Doc. No. 375968.

Henry, M. E. (1996). *Parent-school collaboration: Feminist organizational structure and school leadership*. New York: State University of New York Press.

Hughes, P., & MacNaughton, G. (2000). Building equitable staff parent communication in early childhood settings: An Australian case study. Paper presented at the Annual Conference and Exhibition of the Association for Childhood Education International, Baltimore, MD. ERIC [On-line]. Available: Doc. No. 444647.

Joshi, A. (2002). Effectiveness of early childhood teachers in the Indian context. Unpublished Doctoral Dissertation. Syracuse University.

Ladson-Billings, G. (1991). *The dreamkeepers: Successful teachers of African American children*. San Francisco: Jossey-Bass.

Lasky, S. (2000). *The cultural and emotional politics of teacher-parent interactions. Teaching and Teacher Education, 16*, 843–860.

Lawrence-Lightfoot, S.(2003). *The essential conversation: What parents and teachers can learn from each other*. New York: Random House.

Lee, C. K., Spencer, M. B. & Harpalani, V. (2003). "Every shut eye ain't sleep": Studying how people live culturally. *Educational Researcher, 32*(5), 6–13.

Marion, R. L. (1980). Communicating with parents of culturally diverse exceptional children. *Exceptional Children, 46*(8), 616–623.

Powell, D. R. (1978). Correlates of parent-teacher communication frequency and diversity, *The Journal of Educational Research., 71*, 333–341.

Shade, B. J., Kelly, C., & Oberg, M. (1997). *Creating culturally responsive classrooms*. Washington, D.C.: American Psychological Association.

Super, C. M., & Harkness, S. (1997). The cultural structuring of child development. In J. Berry, P. Dasen, & T. Saraswathi (Eds.), *Handbook of cross-cultural psychology: Basic processes & human development* (pp. 1–39). Needham, MA: Allyn & Bacon.

Trumbull, E, Rothstein-Fisch, C., Greenfield, P. M. & Quiroz, B. (2001). *Bridging cultures between home and school: A guide for teachers*. Mahwah, NJ: Lawrence Erlbaum Associates.

Voltz, D. L. (1994). Developing collaborative parent-teacher relationships with culturally diverse parents. *Intervention in School and Clinic, 29*(5), 288–291.

Weisner, T. S. (1998). Human development, child well-being, and the cultural project of development. *New Directions for Child Development, 81*, 69–147.

Wright, K., & Stegelin, D. A. (2003). *Building school and community partnerships through parent involvement*. Upper Saddle River, NJ: Merrill Prentice Hall.

ARTI JOSHI, JODY EBERLY, and **JEAN KONZAL** are professors in the Department of Elementary and Early Childhood Education at The College of New Jersey, Ewing, New Jersey.

African American Boys and the Discipline Gap: Balancing Educators' Uneven Hand

CARLA R. MONROE

I n a classic essay, "A Talk to Teachers," the writer and educator James Baldwin reflected: "It is your responsibility to change society if you think of yourself as an educated person" (1963/1988, 11). To apply his observation to the teaching profession, he articulated the ways in which he would better Black communities through the educational enterprise. Situating present realities in a historical context, strengthening individuals' resolve to overcome injustice, and encouraging young people's willingness to question the world around them were among the most fundamental of Baldwin's instructional aims. He concluded by urging individuals to exercise their agency toward transformative ends and to work with the country at large toward national advancement and cohesion. Despite publication more than forty years ago, "A Talk to Teachers" has remained persistently relevant for public school educators as professionals grapple with equity-based dilemmas involving Black populations. The schooling experiences of African American boys, by many accounts, require the greatest strides toward improvement (Noguera 2003).

Although educators are challenged to address a number of issues in Black male education, school discipline has surfaced as one of the most troubling aspects. According to data collected during the past thirty years, Black students are disciplined at rates that far exceed their statistical representation, particularly on measures of suspension and expulsion, in almost all major school systems (Children's Defense Fund 1975; Drakeford 2004; Skiba, Peterson, and Williams 1997; Williams 1989). For example, Skiba's study of a major Midwestern school district revealed that African American students represented 66.1 percent of all office referrals, 68.5 percent of out-of-school suspensions, and 80.9 percent of expulsions despite constituting only 52 percent of the district population (2001).

Both qualitative and quantitative examinations of the discipline gap, or overrepresentation of students of color in behavioral sanctions, suggest that the problem is most acute among Black boys (Ferguson 2000). Notably, racialized and gendered differences endure across both elementary and secondary grade

levels (Skiba et al. 2000;Taylor and Foster 1986). A small yet compelling body of literature further reveals that teachers are most likely to discipline Black boys even when students of other races participate in identical behaviors (Emihovich 1983; McCadden 1998). Although disproportionality based on race and gender is independently disturbing, there is abundant evidence that students' disciplinary trajectories influence additional problems such as dropout rates (DeRidder 1990), standardized test scores (Skiba and Rausch 2004), and teachers' decisions to leave the profession (Public Agenda 2004).

Social scientists have established a promising information base intended to push educators toward a sound comprehension of the problem's development and endurance. Research conducted within this strand has been particularly useful in identifying recurrent trends, isolating reasons that prompt behavioral sanctions, and drawing connections to sociocultural factors that invite unequal treatment (Monroe 2005; Skiba et al. 2000; Weinstein, Curran, and Tomlinson-Clarke 2004). Yet despite the increase in scholarship focused on underlying motivations for disproportionality, few researchers have set forth works designed to guide teachers' daily practice in redressing the matter.

This article seeks to broaden the present literature by connecting conceptual knowledge about African American and male culture to pedagogical and disciplinary techniques intended to support teachers' work. Heeding Baldwin's call for schools to become conduits of change, the article is written with an appreciation for the interplay of context and agency in closing the discipline gap. To this end, I first set forth theoretical reasons for African American males' location in national disciplinary trends. Special emphasis is placed on the role of culture as a key factor in why Black boys lead most measures of behavioral sanctions. I next analyze how research findings centered on African American and boys' cultural orientations may shape classroom life to promote positive results. More specifically, I sketch and discuss pedagogical strategies and teaching resources for K–12 educators. Finally, I conclude with a brief discussion of how future scholars may extend the ideas raised to remedy the discipline gap and further assist the academic pursuits of Black youth. Jacqueline Jordan Irvine's framework of cultural synchronization (1990) guides the article's interpretive stance.

Bad Boys: Disentangling a Cultural Construct

"Black boys in public schools either cannot or will not behave themselves": based on most statistical reports, the aforementioned statement would seem to be more an affirmation of reality than rhetorical conjecture. Nationally, African American boys are overrepresented on indexes of school discipline ranging from classroom penalties, such as verbal reprimands, to institutional punishments including suspensions and expulsions (Gordon, Piana, and Keleher 2000; Gouldner 1979). Given the remarkable consistency of disciplinary action exacted on African American boys, questions about their personal dispositions, family backgrounds, and socialization would appear reasonable, as articulated in works by McWhorter (2000) and Ogbu (1990). However, there is considerable evidence that deficit explanations for the discipline gap are grossly inaccurate. In fact, no compelling research studies support the claim that African American boys are more disruptive than their peers (Skiba and Peterson 1999; Skiba, Peterson, and Williams 1997; Wu et al. 1982). Moreover, the high value that African American students place on scholastic, personal, and professional aspirations is corroborated across studies in abundance (MSAN 2003; Thompson 2002). Cultural constructs, however, appear to be a weighty influence on racial disparities in school discipline (Townsend 2000; Weinstein, Curran, and Tomlinson-Clarke 2004).

In analyzing the relationship between culture and school failure, Irvine hypothesized that impediments to youths' success stem largely from a lack of cultural synchronization between students and their teachers (1990). African American pupils, she argued, tend to possess a distinct cultural orientation based on their African heritage. Tenets of cultural continuity are identifiable in students' attitudes, speech, behaviors, referents, and so forth. Commonly cited examples of African-influenced norms include overlapping speech, candor in dialogue, animation, rhythmic presentation styles, cadence variation, and interactions marked by physical expression (Hale-Benson 1982). White communities, in contrast, frequently uphold different communicative standards such as linear conversations, deference to mainstream points of authority, and impulse control (Irvine 1990). As a consequence, cross-cultural interactions in schools may lead to culturally based misunderstandings that end in disciplinary action (Weinstein, Tomlinson-Clarke, and Curran 2003). For example, Hanna's study of a Texas elementary school indicated that Black children engaged in play fighting and ritualized insults for amusement or self-defense, whereas teachers in the study perceived the children's actions as authentic aggression (1988). Practitioners' mistaken understanding of the intent behind the students' actions had the most deleterious effect on referrals for Black boys. Because the education profession is disproportionately composed of White professionals (NCES 1997), many of whom have a limited understanding of Black culture, there is a strong tendency to sanc-

tion African American children both recurrently and inappropriately. Per cultural forces that accompany school failure, Irvine has called for teachers to approach their craft with a keen sensibility for aligning professional practice with community and familial norms (2003). In the area of the discipline gap, teachers are subsequently encouraged to shift their thinking from "Why can't Black boys behave themselves?" to "How can my teaching and classroom ecology support Black male success?"

Engaging and Involving African American Boys: A Blueprint for Closing the Gap

When working with pre- and in-service teachers, I am often queried for suggestions on effective classroom-discipline techniques. I typically respond with my own series of questions about the quality of individuals' classroom instruction, background knowledge of enrolled students, and interpersonal bonds with students and their families. Although the desire for a quick checklist of ideas for promoting on-task time and eliciting student compliance typically prompts the initial question, my response is offered in the hope that listeners will better understand that student behavior, like any classroom phenomenon, cannot be divorced from its context. Beyond increasing cultural competency regarding African American children's communal orientations, teachers can substantially alter negative behavioral trends by creating strong learning communities and promoting a firm sense of attachment among students, families, and educators. When students are intellectually immersed in the academic tasks at hand and hold positive feelings about their schools, teachers, and roles as students, they are clearly more likely to become productive citizens. Although a wealth of information sheds insight into the theoretical and empirical components of culturally responsive education (Banks and Banks 1995), scant research provides guidelines specific to the needs of African American boys. To deliver powerful instruction and, in turn, affect behavioral outcomes, teachers must consciously shape their instruction to fit the needs of the young learners they serve. Despite the breadth and complexity of such a responsibility, a number of tools exist to support practitioners' efforts. The strategies presented below represent starting points for best practice with African American boys.

Completion of Student Inventories. At the start of the academic year, teachers should deliberately gather information about their students' personal, cultural, familial, and neighborhood backgrounds. In contrast to cursory or imposed knowledge about students' lives and interests, practitioners should elicit data-based answers regarding who students are, which topics interest them, how they learn best, and the like. These insights may be gathered through completing a student inventory list that is expanded and revised throughout the term. Categories should reflect areas such as family demographics, personal interests and skills, desired areas of knowledge, and so forth. Techniques for gathering information should range from informal strategies, such as listening to students' naturalistic conversations, to formal methods such as classroom activities and homework assignments. Teachers acquainted with the lived realities of their charges are positioned to create meaningful learning experiences.

Adopting a Proactive Stance toward Discipline. Along with a commitment to providing good teaching should come explicit standards for acceptable conduct. Effective teachers of African American students devote considerable time to explaining classroom policies, procedures, and the implications of those rules for students (Monroe and Obidah 2004). Moreover, they provide examples of the kind of classroom they hope to develop and continually revisit the vision set forth throughout the school year. Making expectations explicit is a critical step in avoiding misunderstandings and socializing students for classroom success.

Literacy as a Core Classroom Feature. There is growing evidence that teachers should focus their efforts on literacy initiatives to help African American boys thrive (Slaughter-Defoe and Richards 1995; Thompson 2002). For instance, in her work with African American students and their families, Thompson found that weak skills in reading comprehension, among other academic areas, were correlated with behavioral problems (2003). Additionally, many parents in her study articulated the belief that non-challenging course content contributed to student boredom and, subsequently, problematic behavior. Fortunately, teachers may consult a number of sources to locate materials of interest to Black males while attending to instructional mandates, varying ability levels, and different subject areas. Resources include the African American Booklist maintained by the National Education Association (NEA); winners of the Coretta Scott King Book Award offered through the American Library Association (ALA); and selections from the Carter G. Woodson Book Award sponsored by the National Council for Social Studies (NCSS). Other useful series directed toward K–12 readers include the Harry Potter and Lemony Snicket texts and the Dorling Kindersely readers,as well as the Time Warp Trio,Green Light/Red Light, and Rookie Reader books. Popular authors among African American youths also include Walter Dean Myers, Gary Paulsen, Christopher Curtis, Mildred Taylor, Louis Sachar, Carol Greene, and Patricia McKissack.*

Incorporating Physical Movement in the Classroom. Although not explicitly focused on African Americans,Gurian and Stevens's research on gender differences suggests that traditional classrooms should be modified to become "boy friendly" environments (2005). Among the authors' suggestions for teachers are weaving kinesthetic movement into well-designed lesson plans; increasing their tolerance for elevated noise levels; limiting "teacher talk"; incorporating multisensory experiences; and valuing self-directed learning. Specific pedagogical techniques to achieve those efforts are encouraging performance-based activities in which students draw on their dramatic talents; making use of manipulatives; establishing learning centers throughout the classroom; engaging students in play, music, and art as forums for learning; and selecting opportunities for outdoor and community-based discovery and application.

*I am grateful to Cheryl Fields-Smith, Patrice Grimes, Lowry Hemphill, Susan Harris-Sharples, and Renarta Tompkins for their suggestions regarding reading materials.

Summary and Reflections on Future Research Directions

Currents in school disciplinary action have been uneven for more than three decades. Most reports and inquiries provide substantial evidence that African American boys receive the majority of behavioral sanctions in K–12 public schools. Consequently, the national prevalence of disproportionality based on race and gender raises critical questions about the educational hazards that confront African American boys. Theoretical frameworks demanding close scrutiny of cultural constructs and naturalistic contexts have set forth compelling explanations for recurrent problems in contemporary African American education (Delpit 1995; Ladson-Billings 1994; Shade 1989). Clearly, alternative frames of reference for normative behavior, coupled with shallow or faulty interpretations of others' conduct, can unduly penalize students whose experiences deviate from teacher- or institution-defined norms. Whereas Irvine's framework of cultural synchronization provides a necessary and thorough basis from which to remedy such problems (1990), few researchers have explored the concept in relation to the discipline gap. There is a striking lack of research in which community voices are captured.

Social scientists are encouraged to forge new directions related to the scope and tools of their inquiries. Many critical questions meriting further consideration are located in the intersection of culture, gender, and behavior. For example, linking the discipline gap to cultural explanations narrowly focused on race is problematic, because gender distinctions between Black boys' and girls' experiences are unresolved. Whereas some works address the roles of societal, environmental, and peer forces in shaping outcomes specific to Black males (Anderson 1999;Monroe 2005; Noguera 2003), the information is largely conceptual or situated outside the physical boundaries of public educational organizations. Future inquiries should reflect a tighter focus on the school and classroom levels to reveal how and why disciplinary moments emerge within learning environments themselves. Texturing cultural arguments with an appreciation for gender dynamics would lend a more nuanced perspective to the discipline gap than currently exists.

Much may be gleaned, of course, from research approaches that convey the perspectives, actions, and latent understandings of relevant stakeholders. Research methodologists, in fact, argue that community-based interpretations and portrayals of educational phenomena are an essential road toward significant contributions to the field (Merriam 2001). Hence, studies reliant on qualitative data sources are needed to facilitate fruitful conversations among relevant stakeholders such as teachers, paraprofessionals and other instructional personnel, administrators, parents, and of course, students themselves. Information gathered from youths and school officials should highlight how and why individuals attach meaning to behavioral actions, especially among Black males. Researchers should make particular efforts to learn from examples of teachers who work successfully with African American students and their families. Finally, parents should receive prominent consideration both in identifying highly regarded teachers and informing educators how they can best meet the needs of school-age youths in their communities.

References

Anderson, E. 1999. *Code of the Street: Decency, Violence, and the Moral Life of the Inner-City.* New York: W. W. Norton.

Baldwin, J. 1963/1988. "A Talk to Teachers." In *Multi-cultural Literacy*, edited by R. Simonson and S. Walker. St. Paul, Minn.: Graywolf Press, 3–12.

Banks, J. A., and C. A. M. Banks, eds. 1995. *Handbook of Research on Multicultural Education.* New York: Macmillan.

Children's Defense Fund. 1975. *School Suspensions: Are They Helping Children?* Cambridge, Mass.: Washington Research Project.

Delpit, L. 1995. *Other People's Children: Cultural Conflict in the Classroom.* New York: New Press.

DeRidder, L. M. 1990. "How Suspension and Expulsion Contribute to Dropping Out." *Education Digest* 56: 44–47.

Drakeford, W. 2004. *Racial Disproportionality in School Disciplinary Practices.* Denver: National Center for Culturally Responsive Educational Systems.

Emihovich, C. A. 1983. "The Color of Misbehaving: Two Case Studies of Deviant Boys." *Journal of Black Studies* 13: 259–274.

Ferguson, A. A. 2000. *Bad Boys: Public Schools in the Making of Black Masculinity.* Ann Arbor: University of Michigan Press.

Gordon, R., L. D. Piana, and T. Keleher. 2000. *Facing the Consequences: An Examination of Racial Discrimination in U.S. Public Schools.* Oakland, Calif.: Applied Research Center.

Gouldner, H. 1979. *Teachers' Pets, Troublemakers, and Nobodies: Black Children in Elementary School.* Westport, Conn.: Greenwood Press.

Gurian, M., and K. Stevens. 2005. "What Is Happening with Boys in School?" *Teachers College Record.*

Hale-Benson, J. E. 1982. *Black Children: Their Roots, Culture, and Learning Styles.* Baltimore: Johns Hopkins University Press.

Hanna, J. L. 1988. *Disruptive School Behavior.* New York: Holmes and Meier.

Irvine, J. J. 1990. *Black Students and School Failure: Policies, Practices, and Prescriptions.* New York: Praeger.

———. 2003. *Educating Teachers for Diversity: Seeing with a Cultural Eye.* New York: Teachers College Press.

Ladson-Billings, G. 1994. *The Dreamkeepers: Successful Teachers of African American Children.* San Francisco: Jossey-Bass.

McCadden, B. M. 1998. "Why Is Michael Always Getting Timed Out? Race, Class, and the Disciplining of Other People's Children." In *Classroom Discipline in American Schools: Problems and Possibilities for Democratic Education*, edited by R. E. Butchart and B. McEwan. Albany: State University of New York Press, 109–134.

McWhorter, J. 2000. *Losing the Race: Self-Sabotage in Black America.* New York: HarperCollins.

Merriam, S. B. 2001. *Qualitative Research and Case Study Applications in Education.* San Francisco: Jossey-Bass.

Minority Student Achievement Network (MSAN). 2003. *New Study Challenges Notion about African-American and Hispanic Students' Achievement.* Evanston, Ill.: Author.

Monroe, C. R. 2005. "Why Are 'Bad Boys' Always Black? Causes of Disproportionality in School Discipline and Recommendations for Change." *The Clearing House* 79(1): 45–50.

Monroe, C. R., and J. E. Obidah. 2004. "The Impact of Cultural Synchronization on a Teacher's Perceptions of Disruption: A Case Study of an African American Middle-School Classroom." *Journal of Teacher Education* 55 (3): 256–268.

National Center for Education Statistics (NCES). 1997. *America's Teachers: Profile of a Profession, 1993–94.* Retrieved June 14, 2003, from <**http://nces.ed.gov/pubs97/97460.pdf**>.

Noguera, P. A. 2003. "The Trouble with Black Boys: The Role and Influence of Environmental and Cultural Factors on the Academic Performance of African American Males." *Urban Education* 38 (4): 431–459.

Ogbu, J. U. 1990. "Minority Education in Comparative Perspective." *Journal of Negro Education*: 45–56.

Public Agenda. 2004. "Teaching Interrupted: Do Discipline Policies in Today's Public Schools Foster the Common Good?" Available at <**http://www.publicagenda.org**>.

Shade, B. J. R. 1989. *Culture, Style and the Educative Process.* Springfield, Ill.: Charles C. Thomas.

Skiba, R. J. 2001. "When Is Disproportionality Discrimination? The Overrepresentation of Black Students in School Suspension." In *Zero Tolerance: Resisting the Drive for Punishment in Our Schools*, edited by W. Ayers, B. Dohrn, and R. Ayers. New York: New Press, 176–187.

Skiba, R. J., R. S. Michael, A. C. Nardo, and R. Peterson. 2000. *The Color of Discipline: Sources of Racial and Gender Disproportionality in School Punishment.* Bloomington, Ind.: Indiana Education Policy Center. Indiana Education Policy Center Policy Research Report #SRS1.

Skiba, R., and R. Peterson. 1999. "The Dark Side of Zero Tolerance: Can Punishment Lead to Safe Schools?" Retrieved November 4, 2001, from <**http://www.pdkintl.org/kappan/ski9901.htm**>.

Skiba, R. J., R. L. Peterson, and T. Williams. 1997. "Office Referrals and Suspension: Disciplinary Intervention in Middle Schools." *Education and Treatment of Children* 20: 295–315.

Skiba, R., and M. K. Rausch. 2004. "The Relationship between Achievement, Discipline, and Race: An Analysis of Factors Predicting ISTEP Scores." Center for Evaluation and Education Policy, 9 July.

Slaughter-Defoe, D. T., and H. Richards. 1995. "Literacy for Empowerment: The Case of Black Males." In *Literacy among African-American Youth: Issues in Learning, Teaching, and Schooling*, edited by V. L. Gadsden and D. A. Wagner. Cresskill, N.J.: Hampton Press, 125–147.

Taylor, M. C., and G. A. Foster. 1986. "Bad Boys and School Suspensions: Public Policy Implications for Black Males." *Sociological Inquiry* 56: 498–506.

Thompson, G. L. 2002. *African American Teens Discuss Their Schooling Experiences.* Westport, Conn.: Bergin and Garvey.

———. 2003. *What African American Parents Want Educators to Know.* Westport, Conn.: Praeger.

Townsend, B. L. 2000. "The Disproportionate Discipline of African American Learners: Reducing School Suspensions and Expulsions." *Exceptional Children* 66 (3): 381–391.

Weinstein, C., M. Curran, and S. Tomlinson-Clarke. 2004. "Toward a Conception of Culturally Responsive Classroom Management." *Journal of Teacher Education* 55: 25–38.

Weinstein, C., S. Tomlinson-Clarke, and M. Curran. 2003. "Culturally Responsive Classroom Management: Awareness into Action." *Theory into Practice* 42: 269–276.

Williams, J. 1989. "Reducing the Disproportionately High Frequency of Disciplinary Actions against Minority Students: An

Assessment-based Policy Approach." *Equity and Excellence in Education* 24: 31–37.

Wu, S.,W. Pink, R. Crain, and O. Moles. 1982. "Student Suspension: A Critical Reappraisal." *The Urban Review* 14: 245–303.

CARLA R. MONROE is an assistant professor in the Department of Foundations, Secondary, and Special Education, School of Education, College of Charleston, Charleston, South Carolina.

Grooming Great Urban Teachers

Master teachers working in real urban classrooms share exemplary teaching practices in an after-school pedagogical lab.

MICHÈLE FOSTER, JEFFREY LEWIS, AND LAURA ONAFOWORA

Teacher 1: "You know the lull you get when there's learning versus playing going on? It was like that. I want to hear more of it in my class."

Teacher 2: "What did it sound like?"

Teacher 1: "It's like people were doing what they were supposed to be doing. I've finally learned to identify it. I heard it, and it felt good."

Teacher 3: "You hear noise, but it's not sticking to you."

Teacher 4: "And it's not conflict. It's a hum."

This conversation about the hum of classrooms in which students are actively engaged in learning took place among a group of novice teachers who were meeting for the third time. These teachers participate in Learning through Teaching in an After-School Pedagogical Laboratory (L-TAPL), a program for elementary students that also serves as a practice-rich professional development site for teachers. The program aims to improve the achievement of urban students and the competence of their teachers.[1]

The L-TAPL enrichment program curriculum includes language arts, math, and science, as well as the arts. Elementary students in grades 1–4 who have volunteered for the lab meet after school for two hours, three days a week. The program, which runs for three to six months, has been launched in three urban school districts in California and New Jersey. At each site, master teachers work with 9 to 15 less experienced teachers who are grouped in cohorts of three, four, or five. Each cohort attends the after-school program once a week and meets for an additional hour of discussion.

Master teachers, who are paid extra for teaching in that capacity, are nominated by school and district personnel because of their demonstrated ability over time to effectively teach low-income urban students. They are wholly responsible for the program's curriculum and for the teaching strategies employed. The program recruits participating teachers from the schools that house L-TAPL as well as from neighboring elementary schools. Participating teachers receive a variety of incentives, such as college credit, additional pay, and up to $1,000 in mini-grants. With the program now in its fourth year, approximately 90 students and 40 teachers have participated in L-TAPL sites in California and New Jersey.

The enrichment program simultaneously addresses two issues: the underachievement of African American students and the preparation of teachers who can work successfully with these students. The goals of the program are

- To serve as a pedagogical laboratory and professional development site for inexperienced teachers.
- To link inexperienced teachers with effective, experienced teachers of poor urban students.
- To document and examine the processes of student learning.
- To document and analyze the processes by which inexperienced teachers learn to teach.

Through a collaborative process, participating teachers learn new strategies and identify the conditions required to make these strategies effective. Less experienced teachers can put their new knowledge and understanding into practice within the supportive context of the after-school program as well as within their regular classrooms.

Good Teachers Matter

Numerous studies, policies, and programs have addressed the persistent problem of underachievement among poor urban students and its array of possible causes. The No Child Left Behind Act (NCLB) links teacher quality to improved student achievement, especially among low-income urban children of color. Consequently, improving teacher quality has become one of the hallmarks of current reform efforts.

There is some disagreement, however, about the best approach to recruiting and developing competent teachers. One response is to stiffen certification requirements by requiring additional coursework. Another response aims to recruit new teachers with higher college grade point averages and higher standardized test scores or students who have graduated from elite universities. Other approaches stress selecting teacher candidates on the basis of certain underlying dispositions that will contribute to making them effective teachers of urban students of color (Haberman, 1995). Teacher induction programs are increasingly trying to teach culturally sensitive pedagogy as well (Glass & Wong, 2003).

According to Goldhaber (2002), teacher experience, degree attained, and other readily measurable and observable characteristics account for only 3 percent of the contribution teacher make to student achievement. The remaining 97 percent is associated with what researchers refer to as "elusive qualities."

Findings from the Research

A principal recommendation for improving teachers' practice is high-quality professional development. Programs enhance learning when they provide teachers with sustained opportunities to experiment with and receive feedback on innovative practices, to collaborate with peers in and out of school, and to interact with external researchers. Nevertheless, much of the professional development that occurs in schools is still not organized around these crucial features (CEO Forum on Education and Technology, 1999; Corcoran, 1995; Hawley & Valli, 1999).

Less experienced teachers can put their new knowledge and understanding into practice within the supportive context of the after-school program.

Although urban schools have served as research and implementation sites for more than 40 years, a huge gap remains between the world of university researchers and the realities of urban teachers (Fischer et al., 2004). Researchers and teachers in urban schools can work collaboratively, however, to bridge the university-school gap and provide a stronger link between theory and practice (Samuels, Rodenberg, Frey, & Fisher, 2001). Two recent models that engage university researchers and teachers in collaborative work are professional development schools—university-school partnerships designed to improve learning in K–12 schools—and deeply embedded professional development (Fischer et al., 2004). In both models, university researchers function as consultants and bring their expertise to bear on teacher and student needs.

A Look into the Lab

It's nearly an hour into the first day of the after-school lab. Students move from individual workstations into a semicircle around the master teacher. They're going to discuss the name the teacher has assigned the after-school program—the Mind, Body, and Spirit Club. The teacher asks the students to tell her the first word of the club's name. A boy responds jokingly; unbothered, she waves the joke off and directs her question to a second boy, who cannot remember the club's name. Although she has known the students for only an hour, she comfortably and inoffensively blends a mock challenge into her question. "You don't know?" Her tone is incredulous. "You sittin' in here

and don't know where you are?" Other students are raising their hands, making sounds of excitement, clearly anxious to show that *they* know.

A girl offers, "Spirit and Body Club." The teacher acknowledges that this is partly correct but is missing the first word. Finally, a second gift responds with the correct name, but mispronounces *mind* as *mine*. The teacher leans forward, directing her attention to the entire group, and says *mind*, stressing the final *D* sound. She then has the students repeat the word *mind* in unison, stressing the *D*. She provides a brief example of what *mine* means and then asks the students to tell her what *mind* means. The first two respondents continue to confuse *mine* with *mind*. A third student answers, "Like 'mind your business.'" The teacher affirms that this is correct, but she's looking for more. The next student again confuses *mine* with *mind* but catches her mistake. She pauses, apparently thinking about how to correct herself when other hands go up with impatient "oohs." At this point, the teacher stops the activity and says to the class,

> You know what? When someone's thinking, it's best
> to be nice and quiet because when you're on the hot
> seat and I'm waiting for you to say something, you
> want to be able to think.

The students settle down, and then one offers, "It's when you're thinking with your brain." With this, the teacher exclaims, "Yes! When you're thinking with your brain, you're using your *mind*!"

This vignette demonstrates some of the "elusive qualities" that characterize effective practice with urban African American students. In this brief five-minute segment, the teacher accomplishes several crucial things related to learning and community. First, she instructs, reinforcing proper pronunciation of a word that many speakers of vernacular African American English have difficulty pronouncing. She accomplishes this seamlessly, helping pupils define the word through group work that does not stigmatize any particular student. The teacher elicits from the students definitions of *mind* by drawing on and extending their knowledge and understanding while incorporating their contributions. She also nurtures mutual respect among students, pointing out that a person may need time to think before responding to a question.

Master teachers in L-TAPL engage in pedagogical practices that reflect a set of underlying principles. Each master teacher manages to create a respectful and vibrant classroom by discussing, teaching, and modeling specific values—such as self-discipline, self-regulation, inquisitiveness, purposefulness, camaraderie, and persistence in serious academic work. Despite attending punitive schools where authoritarian, inflexible classroom rules and unresponsive curriculum are the rule, students quickly respond to this different classroom environment. New, positive behaviors soon eclipse negative ones. When misbehavior does occur, teachers use the incident as an opportunity for the class as a whole to learn a lesson.

Students spend most of their time focused on activities that engage and stimulate both their minds and their emotions. This dual emphasis is apparent in the names that the master teachers independently assigned to the after-school labs: Mind, Body, and Spirit Club; Minds-On, Hands-On Learning; and Beautiful Minds, Beautiful Hearts.

Teachers as Learners

Less than a month after she began participating in the lab, a novice teacher from Trenton, New Jersey, commented, "I like the way the master teacher has the children learn the rules; the students are self-directed." Another teacher noticed that when interacting with the students, the master teacher was able to "stay calm, maintain an even tone, and treat the students with a great deal of respect."

After the first session, a teacher from Los Angeles remarked,

> The first thing I noticed was that the children seemed comfortable with their surroundings and with each other. They were intrigued, and they were trying to listen. And I saw Hassan. I don't even know him, but I *know* him: I have about three of them in my class. He tried this little distraction thing to get the others to go along. But they seemed more interested in paying attention to what was going on in class. He was just by himself, so he fell back in line.

At first, novice teachers are surprised by the absence of negative student behavior in the program. But as they become accustomed to seeing the students behave in positive ways—associating the students' behavior with that of the master teacher—the novice teachers begin altering their expectations for their own students and making small changes in their practice.

A teacher from Los Angeles noted that

> It's hard for me to let go of the reins. But today, I did. I let the kids get up and go to the trash can. I wanted to see what would happen if I wasn't constantly saying, "Why are you up? Sit down!" At first, the kids were looking at their friends, smiling as though to say, "What are you going to do?" But when they saw that I didn't say anything, they just got up on an as-needed basis. There wasn't any power in it anymore. So I saw how that could work. That's baby steps for me, but I'm going to get there.

The Learning Gains

Working in urban schools is challenging. Payne (1998) cites such impediments as teacher isolation, skepticism about students, weak sense of teacher agency, teacher factions, and student transience and mobility. Despite these obstacles, however, students, teachers, and schools can benefit from L-TAPL. The positive behavior demonstrated by students in the after-school lab trickles into and subtly influences their regular classrooms. Lewis and Kim found that

> Within the context of supportive teacher-student relationships [in LTAPL] where teachers explicitly cared about, trusted, and believed in their students, African American children developed positive individual and collective identities at school and responded with hard

work and enthusiasm to the challenge of rising expectations from their teachers. (2004, p. 11)

Benefits for Students

L-TAPL, now in its fourth year, clearly contributes to enhanced student learning. L-TAPL students at the New Jersey site demonstrated significant learning gains in reading, math, and writing on the basis of pre-tests and post-tests. L-TAPL students also outperformed a matched district sample of students in reading and math on the Terra Nova, a district-administered test. These gains were achieved in as little as 12 weeks (72 hours) of instructional time, which represents less than two and one-half weeks of instructional time in a regular classroom.

Benefits for Teachers

In L-TAPL, inexperienced teachers are able to observe how experienced teachers address and resolve problems and challenges that they encounter in their work with students who are similar to, or even the very same students as, those of the inexperienced teachers. Novice teachers explore why strategies work or don't work and connect their lab observations and group discussions to their own classrooms. This provides teachers with a window into the classrooms of their peers, easing the isolation they often experience and giving them the opportunity to support one another in responding creatively to challenges that they share in their practice.

One of L-TAPL's strengths is that it encourages participating teachers to develop professionally as a community as they discover and apply new knowledge and insights within the context of their shared everyday work. By observing a model of effective teaching of students like their own—and seeing these students respond in unexpected and productive ways—inexperienced teachers are challenged to become aware of how their own assumptions and biases affect their daffy practice, limiting their effectiveness. Moreover, through the process of reflection and discussion, teachers are able to share ideas and concrete examples of how they can "search for responsible ways to mitigate [the] impact" of such biases (Glass & Wong, 2003, p. 76), a process that affects them in profoundly personal ways and deepens their understanding of their practice.

Students quickly respond to this different classroom environment. New, positive behaviors soon eclipse negative ones.

During the course of the L-TAPL program, inexperienced teachers begin to shift their perceptions of their students and of their own practice. At the beginning of the lab, teachers tend to view their task through the lens of things they cannot control, such as the poverty and disorder of communities and schools and curriculum and testing mandates. By the end of the lab year, however, teachers are focusing on creating conditions for implementing more effective teaching strategies—something they can control. Teachers go from seeing students primarily in terms of deficits to seeing them as knowledgeable and capable—as possessing assets to build on.

Benefits for Schools

Although professional development is increasingly focusing on supporting teachers in urban schools, too few models effectively link the exemplary practices of experienced urban schoolteachers directly to the professional development of novices. L-TAPL does just that: It provides a powerful link between the after-school pedagogical laboratory and the teachers' regular classrooms.

L-TAPL is also efficient and cost-effective. The resources targeted to help underachieving students come from the school system itself rather than from some outside company. This builds on local expertise and increases capacity within the system. Many school districts have interpreted student support to mean individual tutoring, but insufficient funds can make it unfeasible to provide this kind of service to all the students who need it (Chan, 2004). L-TAPL teachers, however, work with groups, thereby providing a greater number of students with increased instructional hours.

Teachers in the L-TAPL program continually grapple with what it means to be an effective teacher. They see firsthand how to teach the curriculum, structure a classroom, organize and facilitate small-group work, and orchestrate large-group instruction. But perhaps more important, as they observe master teachers and begin to implement the effective strategies that they witness, they begin to grasp those "elusive qualities" that merge to create great teachers.

Note

1. This program was made possible through a National Science Foundation (NSF) Small Grant for Exploratory Research (REC-0004452) and a Field Initiated Studies grant award from the Office of Educational Research and Improvement (OERD. The opinions expressed in this paper do not necessarily reflect the views of either NSF or OERI. Michèle Foster is Principal Investigator; Jeffrey Lewis and Laura Onafowora are co-Principal Investigators.

References

CEO Forum on Education and Technology. (1999). *Professional development: A link to better learning.* Washington, DC: Author.

Chan, S. (2004, Aug. 4). Thousands of pupils qualify for help. *Washington Post*, p. B1.

Corcoran, T. (1995). *Helping teachers teach well: Transforming professional development.* Philadelphia: CPRE.

Fischer, J. M., Hamer, L., Zimmerman, J., Sidorkin, A., Samel, A., Long, L., et al. (2004). The unlikely faces of professional development in urban schools: Preparing at-risk students and colleges for each other. *Educational Horizons, 82*(3), 203–212.

Glass, R. D., & Wong, P. L. (2003). Engaged pedagogy: Meeting the demands for justice in urban professional development schools. *Teacher Education Quarterly, 30*(2), 69–87.

Goldhaber, D. (2002, Spring). The mystery of good teaching. *Education Next*, 50–55.

Haberman, M. (1995). *Star teachers of children in poverty.* West Lafayette, IN: Kappa Delta Pi.

Hawley, W. D., & Valli, L. (1999). The essentials of effective professional development. In L. Darling-Hammond & G. Sykes (Eds.), *Teaching as a learning profession: Handbook of policy and practice* (pp. 127–150). San Francisco: Jossey-Bass.

Lewis, J. L., & Kim, E. (2004). *A desire to learn: African American children's positive attitudes toward learning within a school culture of low expectations.* Unpublished manuscript.

Payne, C. (1998). *So much reform, so little change: Building-level obstacles to urban school reform.* Unpublished paper.

Samuels, P., Rodenberg, K., Frey, N., & Fisher, D. (2001). Growing a community of high quality teachers: An urban professional development middle school. *Education, 122*(2), 310–319.

MICHÈLE FOSTER is Professor in the School of Educational Studies at Claremont Graduate University in Claremont, California, and Distinguished Visiting Professor at Mills College in Oakland, California, in 2004–2005; michelefoster@sbcglobal.net.

JEFFREY LEWIS is Assistant Professor in the College of Human Ecology at the University of Wisconsin–Madison.

LAURA ONAFOWORA is Assistant Professor in the School of Education at North Carolina Central University in Durham, North Carolina.

UNIT 7

Serving Special Needs and Concerns

Unit Selections

Key Points to Consider

- What can schools do to encourage students to read during the summer months? What can teachers do to encourage reading for pleasure throughout the school year?

- Describe life in an American suburban high school. What concerns do you have about student experience in this setting? If possible, use your own experiences as a guide.

Student Website

www.mhcls.com/online

Internet References

Further information regarding these websites may be found in this book's preface or online.

Constructivism: From Philosophy to Practice
  http://www.stemnet.nf.ca/~elmurphy/emurphy/cle.html
National Association for Gifted Children
  http://www.nagc.org/home00.htm
National Information Center for Children and Youth with Disabilities (NICHCY)
  http://www.nichcy.org/index.html

People who educate serve many special needs and concerns of their students. This effort requires a special commitment to students on the part of their teachers. We celebrate this effort, and each year we seem to address special types of general concern.

People learn under many different sets of circumstances that involve a variety of educational concerns both within schools and in alternative learning contexts. Each year we include in this section articles on a variety of special topics that we believe our readers will find interesting and will grow with.

The general literature thematically varies from year to year. Issues on which several good articles may have been published in one year may not be covered well in other years in professional and trade publications. Likewise, some issues are covered in depth every year such as articles on social class, education, or school choice.

The articles in this unit cover a broad spectrum of issues not easily included in the other parts of the book. We hope that you will find these topics of interest. Each of them can spark spirited classroom discussion.

First, there is an essay on the role of United States military recruiters in American high schools attempting to recruit high school students to volunteer for military service after their graduation from high school. As part of his preparation to write this essay, the author also interviewed a group of wounded American veterans from the war in Iraq, each of whom had one thing in common: each has received the Purple Heart. The essay will spark spirited debate.

The next essay's author explores some of the political dimensions in the operations of large urban school systems. He is very critical of the claimed effectiveness of mayoral control of major city school systems. This has been a trend in urban school systems in recent years. The author argues that much publicity is addressed to parents and students supporting this idea, yet there is less hope for students because of the political power plays in urban school systems.

In the next article, the authors discuss how reading instruction in school systems has now been conducted on the Internet as well as with traditional hard-copy reading materials. The authors explain clearly some examples as to how this can be done.

The following article discusses how "looking white" can either socially help or harm high-achieving students of color, depending on which levels of their peer cultures they move in. "Acting White" can have possible adverse long-term effects on minority students. The author documents the reasons for this.

Next, there is a truly informative article on how boys learn in school. The authors distinguish the differences in the develop-

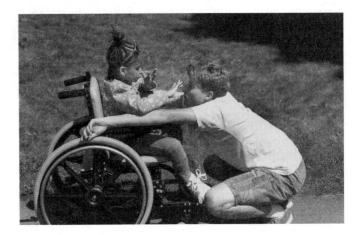

ment of boys' and girls' minds from infancy through childhood, and how these differences lead in school to major differences in how boys and girls respond to traditional school learning environments (and to testing). They raise important questions as to what teachers might do to help boys perform better in school. They argue that gender differences really occur in the brain. This is a "must read" essay. It will spark good class discussion.

The next article raises the question as to whether there is an over-abundance of the use of computers in the schools. The author raises questions as to whether or not we ought to seek a balance between the use of computers and traditional methods of learning.

Finally, there is an article on the role of physical education in schools and why students should have access to physical education. He offers a normative moral line of defense of physical education as a vital and necessary part of the education of a person. This is a very scholarly and well-researched article.

Since first issued in 1973, this ongoing anthology has sought to provide discussion of special social or curriculum issues affecting the teaching/learning conditions in schools. Fundamental forces at work in our culture during the past several years have greatly affected millions of students. These social, cultural, and economic pressures on families have produced several special problems of great concerns to teachers. Serving special needs and concerns requires greater degrees of individualization of instruction, and greater attention paid to the development and maintenance of healthier self-concepts by students.

Hearts and Minds: Military Recruitment And the High School Battlefield

In recent years, military recruitment has failed, with rare exceptions, to meet its quotas. The nation's high schools have thus become battlefields for the hearts and minds of young people, Mr. Ayers tells us, as recruiters dangle gifts and promises of future benefits before teenagers in an effort to fill the ranks of an all-volunteer military.

WILLIAM AYERS

I N HER BOOK *Purple Hearts*, the documentary photographer Nina Berman presents 40 photographs—two each of 20 U.S. veterans of the American war in Iraq—plus a couple of accompanying paragraphs of commentary from each vet in his or her own words.[1] Their comments cohere around their service, their sacrifice, their suffering. The Purple Heart binds them together—this award is their common experience, this distinction is what they embrace and what embraces them. This is what they live with.

Their views on war, on their time in arms, on where they hope they are headed with their lives, are various; their ways of making sense about the U.S. military mission, wildly divergent.

Josh Olson, 24 years old, begins: "We bent over backwards for these people, but they ended up screwing us over, stabbing us in the back. A lot of them, I mean, they're going to have to be killed…. As Americans we've taken it upon ourselves to almost cure the world's problems I guess, give everybody else a chance. I guess that's how we're good-hearted…." He's missing his right leg now and was presented with his Purple Heart at Walter Reed Military Hospital by President Bush himself. He feels it all—pride, anger, loss.

Jermaine Lewis, 23, describes growing up in a Chicago neighborhood where "death has always been around." He describes basic training as a place where "they break you down and then they try to build you up." To him, the "reasons for going to war were bogus, but we were right to go in there."

The vets are all young, and several recall deciding to enlist when they were much younger still, more innocent, more vulnerable, but feeling somehow invincible. Jermaine Lewis says: "I've been dealing with the military since I was a sophomore in high school. They came to the school like six times a year, all military branches. They had a recruiting station like a block from our high school. It was just right there."

Tyson Johnson III, 22, wanted to get away from the poverty and death he saw all around him. His life was going nowhere, he thought, and so he signed on: "And here I am, back here … I don't know where it's going to end up."

Joseph Mosner enrolled when he was 19. "There was nothing out there," he writes. "There was no good jobs so I figured this would have been a good thing."

Frederick Allen thought going to war would be "jumping out of planes." He joined up when recruiters came to his high school. "I thought it would be fun."

Adam Zaremba, 20, also enlisted while still in high school: "The recruiter called the house, he was actually looking for my brother and he happened to get me. I think it was because I didn't want to do homework for a while, and then I don't know, you get to wear a cool uniform. It just went on from there. I still don't even understand a lot about the Army." The Purple Heart seemed like a good thing from a distance, "but then when it happens you realize that you have to do something, or something has to happen to you in order to get it."

Recruiting High-Schoolers

Military recruiting in high schools has been a mainstay of the so-called all-volunteer armed forces from the start. High school kids are at an age when being a member of an identifiable group with a grand mission and a shared spirit—and never underestimate a distinctive uniform—is of exaggerated importance, something gang recruiters in big cities also note with interest and exploit with skill. Kathy Dobie, quoting a military historian, notes that "basic training has been essentially the same in every army in every age, because it works with the same raw material that's always been there in teenage boys: a fair amount of aggression, a strong tendency to hang around in groups, and an absolute desperate desire to fit in."[2] Being cool and going along with the crowd are big things. Add the need to prove oneself to be a macho, strong, tough, capable person, combined with an unrealistic calculus of vulnerability and a constricted sense of options specifically in poor and working-class communities—all of this creates the toxic mix in a young person's head that can be a military recruiter's dream.

One of the most effective recruitment tools is Junior Reserve Officers' Training Corps (JROTC), the high school version of ROTC that was established by an act of Congress in 1916 "to develop citizenship and responsibility in young people."[3] JROTC is now experiencing the most rapid expansion in its history. Some credit the upsurge to Colin Powell's visit to South Central Los Angeles after the 1992 riots, when he was head of the Joint Chiefs of Staff. Powell stated that the solution to the problems of city youths was the kind of discipline and structure offered by the U.S. military. In the ensuing decade the number of JROTC programs doubled, with over half a million students enrolled at over 3,000 schools coast-to-coast, and an annual Pentagon budget allocation in excess of $250 million. Today the evidence is clear: 40% of JROTC graduates eventually join the military, making the program a powerful recruiting device.

Chicago has the largest JROTC program in the country and the "most militarized school system in America,"[4] with more than 9,000 students enrolled in 45 JROTC programs, including one Navy and five Army JROTC academies that are run as "schools-within-a-school" and two full-time Army military academies, with another slated to open next year. That distinction is only the start: Chicago is also in the vanguard of the Middle School Cadet Corps (MSCC), with 26 programs in junior highs and middle schools involving 850 kids, some as young as 11.[5]

Defenders of the JROTC and MSCC claim that the goal is leadership and citizen development, dropout prevention, or simply the fun of dressing up and parading around. Skeptics point out that the Pentagon money for these programs provides needed resources for starving public schools and question why the military has become such an important route to adequate school funding. Chicago spends $2.8 million on JROTC and another $5 million on two military academies—"more than it spends on any other special or magnet program"[6]—and the Defense Department puts in an additional $600,000 for salaries and supplies.

There is no doubt that JROTC programs target poor, black, and Latino kids who don't have the widest range of options to begin with. Recruiters know where to go: Whitney Young High School, a large, selective magnet school in Chicago, had seven military recruiter visits last year, compared to 150 visits from university recruiters; Schurz High School, which is 80% Hispanic, had nine military and 10 university visits.[7] New York Times columnist Bob Herbert points out that all high schools are not equal in the eyes of the recruiters: "Schools with kids from wealthier families (and a high percentage of college-bound students) are not viewed as good prospects.... The kids in those schools are not the kids who fight America's wars."[8] Absent arts and sports programs or a generous array of clubs and activities, JROTC and its accompanying culture of war—militarism, aggression, violence, repression, the demonization of others,

and mindless obedience—becomes the default choice for poor kids attending low-income schools.

The military culture seeps in at all levels and has a more generally corrosive impact on education itself, narrowing curriculum choices and promoting a model of teaching as training and of learning as "just following orders." In reality, good teaching always involves thoughtful and complicated judgments, careful attention to relationships, complex choices about how to challenge and nurture each student. Good teachers are not drill instructors. Authentic learning, too, is multidimensional and requires the constant construction and reconstruction of knowledge built on expanding experiences.

The educational model that employs teachers to simply pour imperial gallons of facts into empty vessels—ridiculed by Charles Dickens 150 years ago and discredited as a path to learning by modern psychologists and educational researchers—is making a roaring comeback. The rise of the military in schools adds energy to that malignant effort.

A vibrant democratic culture requires free people with minds of their own capable of making independent judgments. Education in a democracy resists obedience and conformity in favor of free inquiry and the widest possible exploration. Obedience training may have a place in instructing dogs, but not in educating citizens.

'My Recruiter Lied To Me'

Today, two years into the invasion of Iraq, recruiters are consistently failing to meet monthly enlistment quotas, despite deep penetration into high schools, sponsorship of NASCAR and other sporting events, and a $3-billion Pentagon recruitment budget. Increasingly, recruiters are offering higher bonuses and shortened tours of duty, and violations of ethical guidelines and the military's own putative standards are becoming commonplace—in one highly publicized case, a recruiter was heard on tape coaching a high school kid about how to fake a mandatory drug test. "One of the most common lies told by recruiters," writes Kathy Dobie, "is that it's easy to get out of the military if you change your mind. But once they arrive at training, the recruits are told there's no exit, period."[9] Although recruiters are known to lie, the number of young people signing up is still plummeting.

The military manpower crisis includes escalating desertions: 4,739 Army deserters in 2001 compared to 1,509 in 1995. According to an Army study, deserters tend to be "younger when they enlist, less educated ... come from 'broken homes,' and [have] 'engaged in delinquent behavior.'"[10] In times of war, rates of desertion tend to spike upward, and so after 9/11 the Army "issued a new policy regarding deserters, hoping to staunch the flow." The new rules required deserters to be returned to their units in the hope that they could be "integrated back into the ranks." This has not been a happy circumstance for either soldiers or officers: "I can't afford to babysit problem children every day," says one commander.

At the end of March 2005, the Pentagon announced that the active-duty Army achieved only about two-thirds of its March goal and was 3,973 recruits short for the year; the Army Reserve was 1,382 short of its year-to-date goal.[11] According to military statistics, 2005 was the toughest recruiting year since 1973, the first year of the all-volunteer Army. Americans don't want to fight this war, and a huge investment in high school recruiting is the military's latest desperate hope.

The high school itself has become a battlefield for hearts and minds. On one side: the power of the federal government; claims (often unsubstantiated) of financial benefits; humvees on school grounds; goody bags filled with donuts, key chains, video games, and T-shirts. Most ominous of all is No Child Left Behind, the controversial omnibus education bill passed in 2001. Section 9528 reverses policies in place in many cities that keep organizations that discriminate on the basis of race, gender, or sexual orientation—including the military—out of schools. It mandates that military recruiters have the same access to students as colleges. The bill also requires schools to turn over students' addresses and home phone numbers to the military unless parents expressly opt out.

On the other side of the recruitment battle: a mounting death toll in Iraq, a growing sense among the citizenry that politicians lied and manipulated us at every turn in order to wage an aggressive war outside any broad popular interest, and organized groups of parents mobilizing to oppose high school recruitment.

A front-page story in the *New York Times* reported a "Growing Problem for Military Recruiters: Parents." The resistance to recruiters, according to the *Times* report, is spreading coast to coast, and "was provoked by the very law that was supposed to make it easier for recruiters to reach students more directly. 'No Child Left Behind' … is often the spark that ignites parental resistance."[12]

And parents, it turns out, can be a formidable obstacle to a volunteer Army. Unlike the universal draft, signing up requires an affirmative act, and parents can and often do exercise a strong negative drag on their kids' stepping forward. A Department of Defense survey from November 2004 found that "only 25 percent of parents would recommend military service to their children, down from 42 percent in August 2003."[13]

In a column called "Uncle Sam Really Wants You," Bob Herbert focuses attention on an Army publication called "School Recruiting Program Handbook." The goal of the program is straightforward: "school ownership that can only lead to a greater number of Army enlistments." This means promoting military participation in every feasible dimension, from making classroom presentations to involvement in Hispanic Heritage and Black History months. The handbook recommends that recruiters contact athletic coaches and volunteer to lead calisthenics, get involved with the homecoming committee and organize a presence in the parade, donate coffee and donuts to the faculty on a regular basis, eat in the cafeteria, and target "influential students" who, while they may not enlist, can refer others who might.[14]

The military injunction—hierarchy, obedience, conformity, and aggression—stands in stark opposition to the democratic imperative of respect, cooperation, and equality. The noted New Zealand educator Sylvia Ashton-Warner wrote that war and peace—acknowledged or hidden— "wait and vie" in every classroom. She argued that all human beings are like volcanoes

with two vents, one destructive and the other creative. If the creative vent is open, she maintained, then the destructive vent will atrophy and close; on the other hand, if the creative vent is shut down, the destructive will have free rein. "Creativity in this time of life," she wrote, "when character can be influenced forever, is the solution to the problem of war." She quoted Erich Fromm: "The amount of destructiveness in a child is proportionate to the amount to which the expansiveness of his life has been curtailed. Destructiveness is the outcome of the unlived life."[15]

Herbert, himself a Vietnam combat vet, is deeply troubled by the deceptive and manipulative tactics of recruiters: "Let the Army be honest and upfront in its recruitment," he writes. "War is not child's play, and warriors shouldn't be assembled through the use of seductive sales pitches to youngsters too immature to make an informed decision on matters that might well result in them having to kill others, or being killed themselves."[16]

The Reality of War

A little truth-telling, then. War is catastrophic for human beings, and, indeed, for the continuation of life on Earth. With over 120 military bases around the globe and the second largest military force ever assembled, the U.S. government is engaged in a constant state of war, and American society is necessarily distorted and disfigured around the aims of war. Chris Hedges provides an annotated catalogue—unadorned, uninflected—of the catastrophe:

- 108 million people were slaughtered in wars during the 20th century.
- During the last decade of that spectacular century, two million children were killed, 20 million displaced, six million disabled.
- From 1900 to 1990, 43 million soldiers died in wars and 62 million civilians were killed. In the wars of the 1990s the ratio was up: between 75% and 90% of all war deaths were civilian deaths.
- Today 21.3 million people are under arms—China has the largest military with 2.4 million people in service (from a population of 1.3 billion citizens), followed by the U.S. with 1.4 million (from a population of 300 million). About 1.3 million Americans are in Reserve and National Guard units.
- Vets suffer long-term health consequences including greater risk of depression, alcoholism, drug addiction, sleep disorders, and more. About one-third of Vietnam vets suffered full-blown post-traumatic stress disorder. Another 22% suffered partial post-traumatic stress disorder.[17] This is the nature of the beast. Anyone who's been there knows.

On and on, 119 densely packed pages, fact sheet upon fact sheet, 24 pages of evidentiary footnotes, 15 pages of bibliography, all of it adding up to an inescapable conclusion: war is the greatest organized misfortune human beings have ever constructed and visited on one another. And as Adromache, captive widow of Hector, says at the opening of Seneca's Trojan Women: "It is not finished yet. There is always more and worse to fear, beyond imagination."[18] In the course of the play, her young son will be thrown from a tower and murdered, and the daughter of Hecuba and Priam will also be sacrificed. Beyond imagination.

There are now more than 300,000 child soldiers worldwide. Why do children join? Here is Hedges' entire answer to that question: "They are often forced to. Some are given alcohol or drugs, or exposed to atrocities, to desensitize them to violence. Some join to help feed or protect their families. Some are offered up by their parents in exchange for protection. Children can be fearless because they lack a clear concept of death."[19]

The United States, which consistently refused to ratify the UN Convention on the Rights of the Child, agreed in 2002 to sign on to the "Optional Protocol" to the Convention, covering the involvement of children in armed conflicts. In its "Declarations and Reservations," the U.S. stipulated that signing the Protocol in no way carries any obligations under the Convention and that "nothing in the Protocol establishes a basis for jurisdiction by any international tribunal, including the International Criminal Court." It lists several other reservations, including an objection to Article 1 of the Protocol, which states, "Parties shall take all feasible measures to ensure that members of their armed forces who have not attained the age of 18 years do not take direct part in hostilities." The U.S. stipulates that the term "feasible measures" means what is "practical" when taking into account all circumstances, "including humanitarian and military considerations," and that the article does not apply to "indirect participation in hostilities, such as gathering and transmitting military information, transporting weapons, ammunition, or other supplies, or forward deployment."

Because recruiters do lie, because the U.S. steps back from international law and standards, and because the cost of an education for too many poor and working-class kids is constructed as a trip through a minefield and a pact with the devil, teachers should consider Bill Bigelow's advice to make a critical examination of the "Enlistment/Reenlistment Document—Armed Forces of the United States" that recruits sign when they join up. (Copies can be downloaded as a PDF at rethinking-schools. org.) There they will find a host of loopholes and disclaimers, like this one in section 9b: "Laws and regulations that govern military personnel may change without notice to me. Such changes may affect my status, pay, allowances, benefits, and responsibilities as a member of the armed forces regardless of the provisions of this enlistment/reenlistment document."

When Bigelow's students analyzed the entire contract, they concluded that it would be more honest to simply say something like, "Just sign up.... Now you belong to us." They offer sage advice to other students: "Read the contract thoroughly.... Don't sign unless you're 100% sure, 100% of the time." One of Bigelow's students, who had suffered through the war in Bosnia, recommended that students inclined to enlist might "shoot a bird, and then think about whether you can kill a human."[20]

Jermaine Lewis, the 23-year-old vet from Chicago who spoke about the war being "bogus" in the book *Purple Hearts*, always wanted to be a teacher but worried about the low pay. Now, with both legs gone, he calculates that a teacher's salary plus disability pay will earn him an adequate income: "So I want to go to college and study education—public school, primarily middle school, sixth to eighth grade." He went through the minefield to get what more privileged kids have access to without asking. It's something.

Notes

1. Nina Berman, *Purple Hearts: Back from Iraq* (New York: Trolley, 2004).

2. Kathy Dobie, "AWOL in America," *Harper's*, March 2005, p. 35.

3. David Goodman, "Recruiting the Class of 2005," *Mother Jones*, January/February 2002, pp. 1–8. All information in this paragraph comes from Goodman.

4. Ibid., p. 1.

5. Jennifer Wedekind, "The Children's Crusade," *In These Times*, 20 June 2005, pp. 6–7.

6. Goodman, p. 3.

7. Cheryl L. Reed, "Military Finally Gives Hispanic War Dead Proper Recognition," *Chicago Sun Times*, 3 July 2005, pp. A-18–A-19.

8. Bob Herbert, "Uncle Sam Really Wants You," *New York Times*, 16 June 2005, p. A–29.

9. Dobie, p. 40.

10. All quotes in this paragraph are from Dobie, pp. 34, 35.

11. Michael Kilian and Deborah Horan, "Enlistment Drought Spurs New Strategies," *Chicago Tribune*, 31 March 2005, p. 1.

12. Damien Cave, "Growing Problem for Military Recruiters: Parents," *New York Times*, 3 June 2005, p. B-6.

13. Ibid., p. A-1.

14. Herbert, op. cit.

15. Sylvia Ashton-Warner, *Teacher* (New York: Simon & Schuster, 1963), p. 100.

16. Herbert, op. cit.

17. Chris Hedges, *What Every Person Should Know About War* (New York: Free Press, 2003), pp. 1, 7, 3, 115.

18. David R. Slavitt, ed., *Seneca: The Tragedies, Volume I* (Baltimore: Johns Hopkins University Press, 1992), p. 17.

19. Hedges, p. 8.

20. Bill Bigelow, "The Recruitment Minefield," *Rethinking Schools*, Spring 2005, p. 46.

WILLIAM AYERS is a distinguished professor of education and senior university scholar at the University of Illinois at Chicago and author of *Teaching Toward Freedom: Moral Commitment and Ethical Action in the Classroom* (Beacon, 2004) and *Teaching the Personal and the Political* (Teachers College Press, 2004).

City's Pupils Get More Hype than Hope

Test scores show little payoff for mayoral control.

SOL STERN

"Judge me by the results," Mayor Michael Bloomberg announced in May 2002 as the state legislature gave him absolute control of New York City's schools. Everyone who cared about improving education in the city, it seemed, was smiling. After all, under the old Board of Education, with its seven voting members appointed by six different elected officials, it was impossible to hold anyone fully responsible for the city's dysfunctional school system and its dismal student outcomes. Our new billionaire mayor not only welcomed being accountable for the schools; he also made it clear that he intended to invest political capital in the risky business of education reform.

Unfortunately, it's now evident that what Mike Bloomberg really meant when he said that we should judge him by "the results" was nothing more than one vote, one time. If New Yorkers believed that the schools had made insufficient progress by the 2005 mayoral election (Bloomberg's last, because of term limits), they could vote to fire him and pick a new education CEO. That's a pretty constricted interpretation of education accountability under mayoral control: no one can plausibly argue that last year's desultory mayoral election was a fair referendum on Bloomberg's education record. With hapless Freddy Ferrer leading the opposition, New York didn't come close to having a serious debate on the schools. When asked how people who didn't like his education policies might express their concerns after Election Day, Mayor Bloomberg quipped: "They can boo me at parades."

If more New Yorkers knew how the schools were really doing, there'd be a lot of boos.

The mayor has made it harder for the public to know, however. A major rationale behind mayoral control of the schools was that a mayor's political future would be endangered if voters felt that he presided over continued education failure, thus motivating him (in theory) to press harder for school improvement. But in a classic case of unintended consequences, mayoral control has given this particular mayor the means to shape the education debate on his own terms—to deflect criticism, dominate the media, and use the schools as campaign props. Admittedly, some such distortion would have occurred anyway, thanks to Bloomberg's unique talent for co-opting potential opposition through his prodigious philanthropy and extensive social and business contacts. But the mayor's co-optation effort also got a giant boost from his taking control of a $16 billion education empire that doles out jobs and no-bid contracts and that spends millions on a well-oiled public-relations machine, while disdaining independent research and evaluation of its new classroom programs.

The administration has used its new powers to cut off the flow of essential information to the media, to education reform groups, and to scholars—the institutions and people that citizens normally count on to help them make informed judgments on school performance. Journalists routinely complain of having even less access to the schools than they did under the Board of Education. "It's easier to get information from private schools," said Joe Williams of the *Daily News* to a Columbia Journalism School publication. The *New York Times*'s Elissa Gootman grumbled: "I think the department officials are afraid of what you will see if you go into the schools." *Newsday* education reporter Ellen Yan went so far as to compare the Department of Ed's information control techniques with the KGB's. Still, the barriers to information that reporters cite cannot adequately explain Bloomberg's free ride on education. Neither the city's editorial boards nor its business organizations nor its universities have shown much interest lately in playing the crucial role of independent education watchdog, as the almost universally complacent response to the mayor's failure to win significant reforms in the teachers' contract shows.

Partly because of this abdication, the mayor could sell most New Yorkers on the falsehood that students were making significant academic progress, thus "proving" that his new education programs worked.

The most egregious case in point: the administration's hyping of fourth-grade reading scores just a few months before the mayoral election. In 2005, the percentage of city fourth-graders who achieved at Level Three or above on the statewide reading exam (defined as "meeting standards" or "demonstrating proficiency") rose ten points, to 59.5 percent. Bloomberg trumpeted this rise as "historic" and "record setting," and most of New York's media accepted his view more or less at face value. Banner headlines such as MINORITY KIDS SOAR IN READING dominated the city's tabloids; editorials congratulated the mayor, crediting him with the achievement. Hardly noted was a disturbing fact: almost 70 percent of the city's eighth-graders remained mired in near illiteracy. The percentage of that cohort of students meeting state reading standards actually *fell* 2.5 points, to a pitiful 32.8 percent.

There's no denying, of course, that it would be huge news if the higher fourth-grade test scores meant real gains in reading skills. Fourth-grade reading is probably the most important indicator of future academic progress. A leap forward would also vindicate several of the Bloomberg administration's key early decisions. Shortly after gaining control of the schools, Bloomberg handpicked Joel Klein, a former Clinton Justice Department official with no previous education experience, as schools chancellor. An even bigger gamble was Klein's subsequent decision to hire Diana Lam as deputy chancellor for instruction and then give her carte blanche to revolutionize the city's reading instruction. She promptly banished a phonics program, "Success for All," from dozens of predominantly minority schools where it seemed to be working, and installed a controversial "progressive" alternative called "Balanced Literacy" in almost all the city's elementary schools. This was quite a leap of faith for Klein, since the scientific research on reading in the early grades is abundant and clear: systematic phonics is the best teaching method, particularly for kids from disadvantaged homes. A nepotism scandal eventually forced Lam out, but Klein stubbornly continued to support her pedagogical choices. His pick to succeed her, Carmen Farina, is cut from the same progressive-ed cloth.

Having made these bold decisions, however, Bloomberg and Klein *had* to show significant progress in fourth-grade reading. Otherwise, the administration might come under fire for using schoolchildren as guinea pigs in a failed pedagogical experiment. Klein thus pulled out the stops to boost fourth-grade reading results. The city shelled out hundreds of millions of dollars to retrain teachers in Balanced Literacy. Schools had to devote 150 minutes of every school day (essentially half of available classroom time) to the reading program, and they spent countless hours on test-preparation drills. Klein even hired a "literacy coach" for every school.

Despite this massive effort, the 2004 fourth-grade reading scores actually dropped a few percentage points. Yet Klein and Bloomberg could reasonably argue that a single year wasn't enough time to judge the effect of a new program on a vast school system. Then came the ten-percentage-point upward bump on the 2005 state tests. The stars finally seemed in alignment for Klein. He seized the bully pulpit to proclaim that the fourth-grade gains proved that his new programs were "paying off" for the kids.

But the fourth-grade test scores proved no such thing. For starters, 2005 scores also rose significantly throughout the state. In large urban districts, such as Rochester, Syracuse, and Yon-

kers, they went up by even higher percentages than in New York City. Since none of these districts used the Balanced Literacy program (or other Klein-favored interventions), there's no logical reason to credit the Bloomberg administration for the Gotham gains. What's more, the fourth-grade scores of the city's Catholic schools also rose about seven percentage points, keeping the same ten-point lead that they've enjoyed over the public schools for years. If the city's new literacy initiatives really were "paying off," wouldn't that achievement gap have narrowed—especially since almost all the Catholic schools use the explicit phonics approach that Klein drove from the public schools?

There's another, unimpeachable source confirming that the Bloomberg administration's claims of spectacular progress on fourth-grade reading are bogus: the National Assessment of Education Progress, or NAEP. The NAEP has served as the federal education department's authoritative and "above politics" testing agency since 1990, with its fourth- and eighth-grade reading and math tests often described as the "nation's report card" and the "gold standard" for assessing student achievement. Every two years, the NAEP tests a representative sample of students in every state, with an enhanced sample set for about a dozen of the nation's largest urban districts.

In passing the No Child Left Behind act, Congress intended the NAEP to serve as an accountability check on state compliance with the new law's testing requirements. The NAEP tries to ensure that its tests are uniformly rigorous and don't change in difficulty from year to year. Thus, when NAEP tests show a notably lower percentage of students meeting minimum proficiency than do a particular state's tests, the discrepancy should raise suspicions that the state is dumbing down its tests to meet NCLB's performance goals and timetables. The NAEP's urban component provides an additional objective look at whether city students are making sufficient academic progress.

The NAEP administered its 2005 fourth-grade reading tests within weeks of the New York State tests, and the results clearly revealed that New York education officials—city and state—have indulged in unwarranted self-congratulation about student achievement. Where the state assessments showed 70 percent of students statewide as reading-proficient, the NAEP had only 33 percent attaining that level. And compared with the nearly 60 percent of city students reaching proficiency on the state test, only 22 percent of city kids reached the comparable NAEP level. Also, the NAEP showed no upward movement toward proficiency for New York City students since 2003, the last time it tested them. In other words, not only were the city's fourth-graders reading at a shamefully low level; the Bloomberg/Klein reforms had produced no significant academic improvement.

Confronted with the NAEP results, Klein changed the subject. In a press statement, he boasted that New York City fourth-graders did better in reading than kids in most other urban districts. That's true—but irrelevant. New York City's achievement levels have always been higher (though still lousy) than those of cities like Chicago, Detroit,

Los Angeles, and Washington, D.C. The reason: Gotham's schools have suffered less from white middle-class flight than most other old cities, while at the same time benefiting from an influx of striving and stable immigrant families.

Klein also heralded a three-percentage-point increase over two years in the number of kids moving from "Below Basic" (the functional equivalent of illiteracy) to "Basic" (somewhere short of grade level)—not exactly headline-grabbing news. He celebrated a much more impressive-sounding ten-percentage-point shrinking of the reading achievement gap between white and black fourth-graders. It became somewhat less impressive, however, after a closer look showed that half the "improvement" resulted from a still-unexplained five-percentage-point drop for white students (perhaps brought about by abandoning phonics). It said much that the "reform" chancellor who claimed a historic breakthrough in reading before the election was now grasping at straws.

Klein could put a slightly better spin on the poor reading results in part because of the Bush education department's diminished enthusiasm for maintaining the NAEP's watchdog function. Like other pols, the Bushies don't like bad news. Just as some state officials have tried to head off bad news on their inability to meet NCLB standards by dumbing down tests—as certainly seems to have happened in New York—Bush education officials have lately tried to show that NCLB is working by easing some of the NAEP's strict standards. Darvin Winnick, former education secretary Rod Paige's appointee to chair the NAEP governing board and a Texas friend of W.'s, has pushed the NAEP staff to argue publicly that getting children to meet the "Basic" standard—one level below the "Proficiency" benchmark—is a sign of reasonable progress. This move waters down official NAEP guidelines, which clearly state that "the overall achievement goal for students is performance at the Proficient level or higher" and that "the Basic level is not the desired goal."

The news out of Washington wasn't uniformly bad for New York City. NAEP did detect a five-percentage-point gain in the number of fourth-grade students who reached the "desired" Proficiency level in math. But without further statistical analysis, there's no way to attribute the gain to any particular factor. It might be due to new math programs that Klein introduced, but it could just as easily reflect a nationwide trend toward small but steady improvement in math achievement in lower grades. Indeed, several other cities showed greater math improvement than New York City.

With media attention focused on the Bloomberg administration's claims about fourth-grade scores, almost no one has paid attention to student performance data for the school system's upper levels. The administration doubtless prefers it that way.

Not only did Gotham's eighth-graders score abysmally in reading on the state test and the NAEP, but their math results were stagnant—and crummy—on both tests, too. And only 20 percent of city students met the not very high eighth-grade state proficiency standard in social studies (NAEP has no social studies test). That means that four out of five of our students entering high school are blank slates in civics, geography, and history.

Other astonishingly bad student results only came to light thanks to the dogged efforts of Eva Moskowitz, chair of the City Council's Education Committee. Among the revelations produced in a series of post-election hearings that she chaired: the percentage of city eighth-graders meeting state science standards has plummeted from 54 percent to 45 percent under Bloomberg. At one hearing, Moskowitz badgered the top science official in Klein's education department until the official conceded that the quality of science education in the city was "horrendous" and that the department didn't even know how many certified science teachers worked in the schools.

A later hearing uncovered that the percentage of students graduating with a Regents diploma—requiring one to pass exit exams in at least five subject areas—has shrunk from 35 percent to an even more dismal 33 percent during the Bloomberg term. Fewer than one in ten black and Hispanic students earned Regents degrees.

For those who want to look, the picture of student achievement during the first Bloomberg term is coming into clearer focus—and it's not pretty. Aside from fourth-grade math, stagnation or decline has marked every important benchmark test from the early grades to high school exit exams. If not for the expectations that mayoral control raised, one might merely note that the present administration's results are no worse than those obtained under Harold Levy, Klein's immediate predecessor, during the bad old Board of Ed days.

But the prospects for real education reform suffer terrible damage when a taxpayer-funded public-relations juggernaut gets away with spinning poor test outcomes as "historic" in order to improve a mayor's electoral prospects. It's not good for the city—and it's especially not good for the city's schoolchildren—if the public comes to believe that remedies for school failure are working, when they indisputably aren't. Eventually the public will wake up and realize that it's been getting Soviet-style statistics about a brighter future when the factories still can't produce shoes.

Dare we ask whether mayoral control—at least under *this* mayor—might actually have undermined democratic accountability in the schools and made things worse, not better?

From *City Journal*, Winter 2006, pp. 62-67. Copyright © 2006 by the Manhattan Institute, Inc Reprinted by permission of *City Journal*.

Approaching the Unavoidable: Literacy Instruction and the Internet

ABSTRACT: This column addresses the rapid pace of technological change and the implications for our classrooms. Jackie Malloy is currently working with the Internet Reading Research Group (Clemson University, South Carolina) and the New Literacies Research Team (University of Connecticut, Storrs) on a three-year U.S. Department of Education Institute of Education Sciences grant to explore the nature and promise of using the Internet to enhance reading comprehension and engagement with middle-grade students at risk to dropout. The work that they and other researchers produce will have an impact on how we prepare our elementary students for the literacies they will need in later grades and in life.(Linda B. Gambrell)

JACQUELYNN A. MALLOY AND LINDA B. GAMBRELL

All education springs from some image of the future.

(Toffler, 1974, p. 3)

"How do you spell *volcano,* Mom?" Connor asked, squinting at the computer screen. I looked over from the kitchen sink, my hands deep into the pots and pans I was scrubbing. "*V-o-l-c-a-n-o,* sweetie," I replied. "No silent *e* on that one." Connor, a third grader who struggles with reading and spelling, eagerly typed in the letters as I spoke them and waited for the search engine to do its job. It has always been difficult to get Connor interested in listening to books and even harder to interest him in reading them. Reading does not come as easily to him as it did with my first two children, but the quest for knowledge of things that are of great interest to him is unabated. The Internet is his salvation, and if he should have to read and spell in order to retrieve the information about volcanoes or tarantulas or Star Wars characters he craves, then he gladly does so.

Although Connor is a struggling reader, this story exemplifies a growing literacy that engages readers of all ages and abilities-the Internet. It is far from new; words like *Googling* and *IMing* (instant messaging) have become almost commonplace and highlight the effect that using the Internet is having on popular culture. It is important for teachers of elementary students to realize that leisure-time use of the Internet is no longer the sole realm of teenagers and adults; many elementary students are already adept at searching and surfing, using reading and spelling in ways not explicitly taught. Reading online is not only something that many students do in their leisure time but is also a skill they will need to develop as they learn to research and create in their middle school years and beyond. Searching and comprehending online text is an unavoidable literacy and an approachable one. These skills can help to prepare students as they strive to become fully literate adults in a technological age. It is our job as teachers to understand and appreciate the unavoidable and prepare for it.

To get a sense of the future of technology, you have only to look back about 10 years. The Internet was still new, and e-mail was only beginning to be used as a common form of communication. In today's classrooms, the use of e-mail and the Internet is widespread, and new technologies are emerging at breakneck speed. It is therefore not difficult to imagine that the next 5 to 10 years will bring even more changes. The "new literacies" will soon be replaced by even newer ones. As new technologies creep ever closer to the primary classroom, the wise teacher must find ways to use these tools to enhance instruction in ways that engage students and prepare them for what is yet to be.

How Does Reading Online Differ from Reading Print?

In looking at the differences between reading hypertext and print, consider first our purposes for reading. Although we can use either the Internet or printed text to discover things that interest, inform, and entertain us, the Internet has a greater number of pages and variety of text than hard copy could provide. The Internet offers information from abundant sources and areas of the world, and the quality of information can vary greatly from page to page.

This consideration leads to another important difference with reading online: When searching the Internet, the pages that I might view and read would likely be different from the pages you would find—even when searching for the same piece of information. For example, imagine that we are both looking for information on a particular reading instructional strategy. We might start with the same search engine, but enter different keywords for the search (e.g., mental imagery versus visual imagery), and follow different links when the results were listed. My text selection would likely be very different from yours and be directed by what piques my interest, how well I comprehend the short blurbs with each entry, how strategic I am in using keywords for my search, and how well

I combine scanning and careful reading to home in on the information sought. Suppose we both succeed in finding information on the teaching strategy, but mine includes lesson plans and yours ends in a teaching video. If we had used a traditional text, we would also have scanned in some places and carefully read in others, but we'd have been more limited in what we could find in the time spent. Whereas the lesson plans might have been available in the traditional form, the video would certainly not have been.

Some Strategies Still Apply

The strategies for searching in conventional expository text continue to have online applications. We approach traditional text by looking at all options first, such as titles, pictures and diagrams, and sidebars. We can view these same items on a webpage, but clicking on the titles, diagrams, and sidebars leads to many other links, and this can be a risky business. Sometimes it is difficult to find your way back to the original page. However, students can be taught to "bookmark" important pages online, in the way they place slips of paper in a book to keep their place.

Just as we teach students to question the author when reading print, students need to be taught to evaluate the information they find on the Internet. We can control the quality of materials in our classrooms, but we face greater challenges online. For example, sites that have a *.gov* or *.edu* suffix have a different perspective than those with a *.org* or *.com* suffix. Official web sites merit a certain element of credibility when compared to unofficial webpages. Website suffixes are clues that can help students to evaluate who is maintaining the content and for what purposes. A tech-savvy middle school teacher I know routinely creates a website on the Internet and asks her students to view it. The website she creates is usually called something like Water is Dry and includes very official and scientific-looking articles that purport to explain how water is actually dry, although we perceive it as being wet. This she does in an attempt to demonstrate that anyone can post *anything* on the Internet—it need not be true. Her second purpose in exposing students to this temporary website is to highlight that *anyone* can post anything on the Internet—even students just like them!

It is important to emphasize security when going online to interact with other Internet users. Students need to be aware of the anonymity that is inherent in using the Internet and be given explicit instruction in protecting their identities. On the other hand, the Internet is a place where students can be freed by their anonymity. For example, when IMing, chatting, or blogging online, those with whom you interact don't need to know if you are male or female, popular or marginalized. Shy students may feel safe expressing opinions on the Internet that they would never express in person. The possibilities for using connected technology in the classroom are awesome and humbling, and they require thoughtful attention at every grade.

Implications for the Classroom

Teachers can ground their knowledge of Internet literacies by reading journal articles such as Coiro's *Exploring Literacy on the Internet* (2003), which provides essential background on reading comprehension in the digital world. The author explains the nature of the texts we use for instruction, the capabilities and motivations of students as readers of text, and the social contexts of these activities. Coiro's treatment of this topic provides an excellent theoretical framework for understanding classroom instruction in a digital format.

An article by Leu, Castek, Henry, Coiro, and McMullan (2004) offers inspiration and guidance in using the Internet as a resource for connecting students to children's literature. The article is chock-full of available resources (e.g., websites and print books) that can prepare teachers as they guide students to respond to literature and embrace diversity. Ideas for locating leveled books on a variety of topics and genres are highlighted, as are instructional techniques for enhancing comprehension and engagement in story experiences.

Innovative Approaches to Literacy Education: Using the Internet to Support New Literacies (Karchmer, Mallette, Kara-Soteriou, & Leu, 2005) contains chapter after chapter of classroom-tested ideas from award-winning teachers. Not only are student-centered projects described, but also advice and encouragement for teacher development and continued exploration are provided.

These resources, and others that are becoming available, can assist teachers as they endeavor to incorporate authentic and engaging reading and writing activities for students—activities that can be explored and enjoyed together. Our students may already surpass some of us in their facility with the Internet and its uses. There is much we can learn from them as we teach them the strategies and skills needed to navigate the digital world safely and meaningfully. As Toffler (1974) noted, if our image of the future is grossly inaccurate, our educational system will betray our youth. As educators, we need to commit to preparing students for their technological journey to the future. It is a journey toward literacies that grow and change more quickly than we can keep up with them. But by learning together, teachers and students can become fully literate in every sense of the word.

References

Coiro, J. (2003). Exploring literacy on the Internet. *The Reading Teacher, 56,* 458–464.

Karchmer, R.A., Mallette, M.H., Kara-Soteriou, J., & Leu, D. (Eds.) (2005). *Innovative approaches to literacy education: Using the Internet to support new literacies.* Newark, DE: International Reading Association.

Leu, D.J. Jr., Castek, J., Henry, L.A., Coiro, J., & McMullan, M. (2004). The lessons that children teach us: Integrating children's literature and the new literacies of the Internet. *The Reading Teacher, 57,* 496–503.

Toffler, A. (1974). The psychology of the future. In A. Toffler (Ed.), *Learning for tomorrow* (pp. 3–18). New York: Random House.

MALLOY is a doctoral student at Clemson University (G04-A Tillman Hall, Clemson, SC 29631, USA). E-mail jmalloy@clemson.edu. **GAMBRELL** is editor of the Issues and Trends in Literacy Department. She teaches at Clemson University.

Acting White

The social price paid by the best and brightest minority students

> "Go into any inner-city neighborhood, and folks will tell you that government alone can't teach kids to learn. They know that parents have to parent, that children can't achieve unless we raise their expectations and turn off the television sets and eradicate the slander that says a black youth with a book is acting white."
>
> —Barack Obama, Keynote Address, Democratic National Convention, 2004

ROLAND G. FRYER

A cting white was once a label used by scholars, writing in obscure journals, to characterize academically inclined, but allegedly snobbish, minority students who were shunned by their peers.

Now that it has entered the national consciousness—perhaps even its conscience—the term has become a slippery, contentious phrase that is used to refer to a variety of unsavory social practices and attitudes and whose meaning is open to many interpretations, especially as to who is the perpetrator, who the victim.

I cannot, in the research presented here, disentangle all the elements in the dispute, but I can sort out some of its thicker threads. I can also be precise about what I mean by acting white: a set of social interactions in which minority adolescents who get good grades in school enjoy less social popularity than white students who do well academically.

My analysis confirms that acting white is a vexing reality within a subset of American schools. It does not allow me to say whose fault this is, the studious youngster or others in his peer group. But I do find that the way schools are structured affects the incidence of the acting-white phenomenon. The evidence indicates that the social disease, whatever its cause, is most prevalent in racially integrated public schools. It's less of a problem in the private sector and in predominantly black public schools.

With findings as potentially controversial as these, one wants to be sure that they rest on a solid base. In this regard, I am fortunate that the National Longitudinal Study of Adolescent Health (Adhealth) provides information on the friendship patterns of a nationally representative sample of more than 90,000 students, from 175 schools in 80 communities, who entered grades 7 through 12 in the 1994 school year. With this database, it is possible to move beyond both the more narrowly focused ethnographic studies and the potentially misleading national studies based on self-reported indicators of popularity that have so far guided the discussion of acting white.

The Meaning of the Phrase

Though not all scholars define acting white in precisely the same way, most definitions include a reference to situations where some minority adolescents ridicule their minority peers for engaging in behaviors perceived to be characteristic of whites. For example, when psychologist Angela Neal-Barnett in 1999 asked some focus-group students to identify acting-white behavior, they listed actions that ranged from speaking standard English and enrolling in an Advanced Placement or honors class to wearing clothes from the Gap or Abercrombie & Fitch (instead of Tommy Hilfiger or FUBU) and wearing shorts in winter!

Only some of these behaviors have a direct connection to academic engagement. However, as the remarks of Barack Obama, who would later win a seat in the United States Senate, suggest, it is the fact that reading a book or getting good grades might be perceived as acting white that makes the topic a matter of national concern. Indeed, negative peer-group pressure has emerged as a common explanation for the black-white achievement gap, a gap that cannot be explained away by differences in demographic characteristics alone. If minority students today deliberately underachieve in order to avoid social sanctions, that by itself could explain why the academic performance of 17-year-old African Americans, as measured by the National Assessment of Educational Progress (NAEP), has deteriorated since the late 1980s, even while that of nine-year-olds has been improving. It may also help us understand the shortage of minority students in most elite colleges and universities.

Ethnography vs. Statistics

But is this well-publicized aspect of African American peer-culture reality or urban legend? Most ethnographers who examine school life in specific locations present acting white as a pervasive fact of high-school life for black adolescents. But the only two quantitative studies that analyze data from nationally representative samples of high-school students dismiss it altogether as cultural lore. My findings confirm the existence of acting white among blacks as well as among Hispanics, but offer important qualifications about its pervasiveness.

Although they did not coin the term (its origins are obscure), it was an ethnographic study by anthropologists Signithia Fordham and John Ogbu, published in the *Urban Journal* in 1986, that did the most to bring it to the attention of their fellow academics. Their "Capitol High," a pseudonym for a predominantly black high school in a low-income area of Washington, D.C., had what the researchers said was an "oppositional culture" in which black youth dismissed academically oriented behavior as "white."

In the late 1990s, Harvard University economist, Ron Ferguson, found much the same thing in quite another setting, an upper-class suburb of Cleveland, Ohio, called Shaker Heights. Although that city had been integrated for generations, large racial disparities in achievement persisted. When Ferguson detected an anti-intellectual culture among blacks in the local high school, Shaker Heights became virtually synonymous with the problem of acting white.

Fordham and Ogbu traced the roots of the "oppositional culture" to institutionalized racism within American society, which they contend led blacks to define academic achievement as the prerogative of whites and to invest themselves instead in alternative pursuits. Other observers, however, place the blame for acting white squarely on the shoulders of blacks. The Manhattan Institute's John McWhorter, for example, contrasts African American youth culture with that of immigrants (including blacks from the Caribbean and Africa) who "haven't sabotaged themselves through victimology." These two theories, the former blaming acting white on a racist society, the latter on self-imposed cultural sabotage, have emerged as the predominant explanations for acting white among American blacks.

In fact, however, shunning the academic is hardly the exclusive prerogative of contemporary African American culture. James Coleman's classic work *The Adolescent Society*, published in 1955, identified members of the sports teams and cheerleaders, not those on the honor role, as the most popular students in public schools. The former bring honor to the entire school, reasoned the University of Chicago sociologist; the latter, only to themselves. Since Coleman, ethnographers have found similar tensions between self-advancement and community integration. Indeed, variants on acting white have been spotted by ethnographers among the Buraku outcasts of Japan, Italian immigrants in Boston's West End, the Maori of New Zealand, and the British working class, among others.

Even so, the question remains whether the tension that Coleman identified is more severe in some cultural contexts than others. On this topic, two sets of scholars weighed in with quantitative studies based on nationally representative surveys. Writing in 1998 in the *American Sociological Review*, James Ainsworth-Darnell of Georgia State University and Douglas Downey of Ohio State University reported that anti-intellectualism is no more severe a problem among black or Hispanic adolescents than it is among whites. Meanwhile, in a 1997 study, economists Phillip Cook of Duke and Jens Ludwig of George-

town found that high-achieving black students are, if anything, even more popular relative to low-achieving peers than are high-achieving whites.

Of course, it is possible that the social rewards for achievement do not vary among ethnic groups in the United States. But both studies, each of which is based on data from the National Educational Longitudinal Study (NELS), have a common shortcoming in that they depend solely on a self-reported measure of personal popularity. The NELS contains a question that asks if the student "thinks others see him/her as popular." The answer choices are: very, somewhat, or not at all. Unfortunately, when students are asked to judge their own popularity, they can be expected to provide a rosier scenario than is warranted.

New Data and Methods

Fortunately, the Adhealth data I used in this study allow me to measure popularity in a more subtle way. All the students surveyed were asked to list their closest male and female friends, up to five of each sex. I first counted how often each student's name appeared on peers' lists. I then adjusted these raw counts to reflect the fact that some friends count more than others. The more frequently a peer is listed by others, the more weight I assign to showing up on his or her list.

The advantage of this research strategy is that one never has to ask a student about his or her own popularity. Students' natural tendency to brag, in this case by listing popular students as their friends, only gives us a more accurate picture of the school's most desirable friends. Students listed as a friend by many peers who are themselves popular, rise to the top of the social hierarchy. Those who are listed by only a few peers, who in turn have few admitted friends, stand out as the marginal members of the community.

Armed with an objective measure of social status, I could examine more systematically whether or not the ethnographers were correct in identifying a distinctive acting-white phenomenon within African American communities. Do high-achieving minority students have fewer, less-popular friends than lower-achieving peers? How does this compare with the experience of white students?

I first report my findings using a measure of each student's popularity within his or her own ethnic group, as that is the most direct test of the acting-white hypothesis. But as I explain below, I obtain the same set of results when I analyze the data without regard to the friends' ethnicity.

For black and Hispanic students who attend private school, I find no evidence of a trade-off between popularity and achievement.

I measure student achievement with a composite of grade-point average (GPA) based on student self-reports of their most recent grades in English, math, history/social studies, and science. When comparing the popularity of high- and low-achieving students, I compare students only with students who attend

Pressure to Be Average (Figure1)

The popularity of white students increases as their grades increase. For black and hispanic students, there is a dropoff in popularity for those with higher GPAs.

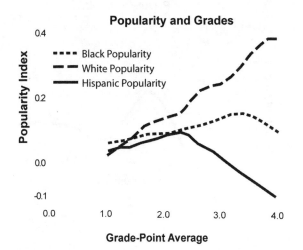

Popularity and Grades

- - - - Black Popularity
- - - White Popularity
—— Hispanic Popularity

Note: A grade of 1.0=D; 4.0=A

SOURCE: Author's calculations from National Longitudinal Study of Adolescent Health data

the same school, ensuring that the results are not skewed by unmeasured characteristics of specific schools. Even then, I take into account a number of factors, measured by the survey, that could affect popularity differently for students from different ethnic backgrounds. These factors include parental education and occupation and participation in various school activities, such as varsity sports, student government, and cheerleading.

Finally, to subject my findings to the strongest possible test, I adjust students' popularity to reflect variation in self-reported effort in school. Recall that some types of acting-white theory say that students are penalized only for trying hard, not for achievement per se. The bright kid who can't help but get good grades is not subjected to scorn. It's the plodding rate busters with books constantly in their faces who are annoying. By adjusting for the effort students are putting into their studies, I do my best to separate the social consequences of achievement from those of effort to achieve.

New Evidence of Acting White

Even after taking into account many factors that affect student popularity, evidence remains strong that acting white is a genuine issue and worthy of Senator Obama's attention. Figure 1, which plots the underlying relationship between popularity and achievement, shows large differences among whites, blacks, and Hispanics. At low GPAs, there is little difference among ethnic groups in the relationship between grades and popularity, and high-achieving blacks are actually more popular within their ethnic group than high-achieving whites are within theirs. But when a student achieves a 2.5 GPA (an even mix of Bs and Cs), clear differences start to emerge.

As grades improve beyond this level, Hispanic students lose popularity at an alarming rate. Although African Americans

with GPAs as high as 3.5 continue to have more friends than those with lower grades, the rate of increase is no longer as great as among white students.

The experience of black and white students diverges as GPAs climb above 3.5. As the GPAs of black students increase beyond this level, they tend to have fewer and fewer friends. A black student with a 4.0 has, on average, 1.5 fewer friends of the same ethnicity than a white student with the same GPA. Put differently, a black student with straight As is no more popular than a black student with a 2.9 GPA, but high-achieving whites are at the top of the popularity pyramid.

My findings with respect to Hispanics are even more discouraging. A Hispanic student with a 4.0 GPA is the least popular of all Hispanic students, and Hispanic-white differences among high achievers are the most extreme.

The social costs of a high GPA are most pronounced for adolescent males. Popularity begins to decrease at lower GPAs for young black men than young black women (3.25 GPA compared with a 3.5), and the rate at which males lose friends after this point is far greater. As a result, black male high achievers have notably fewer friends than do female ones. I observe a similar pattern among Hispanics, with males beginning to lose friends at lower GPAs and at a faster clip, though the male-female differences are not statistically significant.

Potential Objections

Could high-achieving minority students be more socially isolated simply because there are so few of them? The number of high-achieving minority students in the average school is fewer than the number of high-achieving white students. To see whether this disparity could explain my findings, I adjusted the data to eliminate the effect of differences in the number of students at each school with similar GPAs. This adjustment, however, did little to temper the effect of acting white.

It might also be hypothesized that high-achieving minority students are able to cultivate friendships with students of other ethnic groups. If so, I should obtain quite different results when I examine popularity among students of all ethnic groups. While one finds some evidence that high-achieving students are more popular among students of other ethnicities, the increment is not enough to offset the decline in popularity within their own ethnic group—a predictable finding, given that black and white students have only, on average, one friend of another ethnicity, and Hispanics just one and a half.

Indeed, when minority students reach the very highest levels of academic performance, even the number of cross-ethnic friendships declines. Black and Hispanic students with a GPA above 3.5 actually have fewer cross-ethnic friendships than those with lower grades, a finding that seems particularly troubling.

Finally, I examined whether high-achieving blacks and Hispanics can shield themselves from the costs of acting white by taking up extracurricular activities. There are many opportunities in schools for students to self-select into activities, including organized sports, cheerleading, student government, band, and the National Honor Society, that should put them in contact with students with similar interests.

The Private-School Advantage (Figure 2)

For black and hispanic students, the adverse effect of good grades on popularity disappears in private schools.

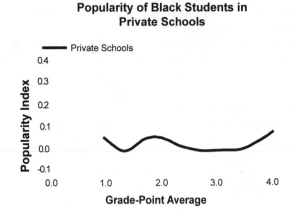

Popularity of Black Students in Private Schools

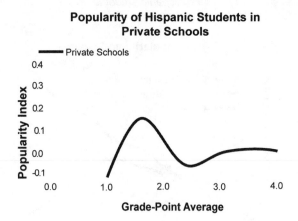

Popularity of Hispanic Students in Private Schools

Note: A grade of 1.0=D; 4.0=A

SOURCE: Author's calculations from National Longitudinal Study of Adolescent Health data

Unfortunately, when I look separately at minority students who participate in each of these activities, I find only one within which ethnic differences are eliminated: the National Honor Society. Among students involved in every other activity, new friends made outside the classroom do not make up for the social penalties imposed for acting white.

A Private-School Edge

The patterns described thus far essentially characterize social dynamics of public-school students, who constitute 94 percent of the students in the Adhealth sample. For the small percentage of black and Hispanic students who attend private school, however, I find no evidence of a trade-off between popularity and achievement (see Figure 2). Surprisingly, white private-school students with the highest grades are not as popular as their lower-achieving peers. The most-popular white students in private schools have a GPA of roughly 2.0, a C average.

These data may help to explain one of the more puzzling findings in the research on the relative advantages of public and private schools. Most studies of academic achievement find little or no benefit of attending a private school for white students, but quite large benefits for African Americans. It may be that blacks attending private schools have quite a different peer group.

The Segregated School: Is It an Advantage?

I also find that acting white is unique to those schools where black students comprise less than 80 percent of the student population. In predominantly black schools, I find no evidence at all that getting good grades adversely affects students' popularity.

But perhaps this changes when school desegregation leads to cross-ethnic friendships within the school. To see how the degree of internal integration within a school affects acting-white patterns, I calculated the difference from what I would expect in the total number of cross-ethnic friends in a school based on the ethnic make-up of the student body. Schools with a greater percentage of cross-ethnic friendships than expected are considered to be internally integrated. I divide schools into two groups of equal size: those with higher and lower degrees of internal integration.

Unfortunately, internal integration only aggravates the problem. Blacks in less-integrated schools (places with fewer than expected cross-ethnic friendships) encounter less of a trade-off between popularity and achievement. In fact, the effect of acting white on popularity appears to be twice as large in the more-integrated (racially mixed) schools as in the less-integrated ones. Among the highest achievers (3.5 GPA or higher), the differences are even more stark, with the effect of acting white almost five times as great in settings with more cross-ethnic friendships than expected. Black males in such schools fare the worst, penalized seven times as harshly as my estimate of the average effect of acting white on all black students!

This finding, along with the fact that I find no evidence of acting white in predominantly black schools, adds to the evidence of a "Shaker Heights" syndrome, in which racially integrated settings only reinforce pressures to toe the ethnic line.

In Search of an Answer

That acting white is more prevalent in schools with more interethnic contact hardly passes the test of political correctness. It nonetheless provides a clue to what is going on. Anthropologists have long observed that social groups seek to preserve their identity, an activity that accelerates when threats to internal cohesion intensify. Within a group, the more successful individuals can be expected to enhance the power and cohesion of the group as long as their loyalty is not in question. But if the group risks losing its most successful members to outsiders, hen the group will seek to prevent the outflow. Cohesive yet threatened groups—the Amish, for example—are known for limiting their children's education for fear that too much contact with the outside world risks the community's survival.

In an achievement-based society where two groups, for historical reasons, achieve at noticeably different levels, the group with lower achievement levels is at risk of losing its most successful members, especially in situations where successful individuals have opportunities to establish contacts with outsiders. Over the long run, the group faces the danger that its most successful members will no longer identify with its interests, and group identity will itself erode. To forestall such erosion, groups may try to reinforce their identity by penalizing members for differentiating themselves from the group. The penalties are likely to increase whenever the threats to group cohesion intensify.

Applying this model of behavior to minority and white students yields two important predictions: A positive relationship between academic achievement and peer-group acceptance (popularity) will erode and turn negative, whenever the group as a whole has lower levels of achievement. And that erosion will be exacerbated in contexts that foster more interethnic contact. This, of course, is exactly what I found with regard to acting white.

The effect of acting white on popularity appears to be twice as large in the more-integrated schools as in the less-integrated ones.

Understanding acting white in this way places the concept within a broader conceptual framework that transcends specific cultural contexts and lifts the topic beyond pointless ideological exchanges. There is necessarily a trade-off between doing well and rejection by your peers when you come from a traditionally low-achieving group, especially when that group comes into contact with more outsiders.

Alternative Explanations

Such a conceptualization is preferable to both of the two theories that have so far dominated discussions of acting white: the notion of oppositional culture and the allegation of cultural self-sabotage.

The oppositional culture theory, developed by Fordham and Ogbu in the wake of their experiences at "Capitol High," accounts for the observed differences between blacks and whites as follows: (1) white people provide blacks with inferior schooling and treat them differently in school; (2) by imposing a job ceiling, white people fail to reward blacks adequately for their

academic achievement in adult life; and (3) black Americans develop coping devices which, in turn, further limit their striving for academic success. Fordham and Ogbu suggest the problem arose partly because white Americans traditionally refused to acknowledge that black Americans were capable of intellectual achievement and partly because black Americans subsequently began to doubt their own intellectual ability, began to define academic success as white people's prerogative, and began to discourage their peers, perhaps unconsciously, from emulating white people in striving for academic success.

However plausible it sounds, the oppositional culture theory cannot explain why the acting-white problem is greatest in integrated settings. If Fordham and Ogbu were correct, the social sanctions for acting white should be most severe in places like the segregated school, where opportunities are most limited. The results of my studies, of course, point in precisely the opposite direction.

The notion that acting white is simply attributable to self-sabotage is even less persuasive. According to its proponents, black and Hispanic cultures are dysfunctional, punishing successful members of their group rather than rewarding their success. That theory is more a judgment than an explanation. A universal, it cannot explain the kinds of variations from one school setting to another that are so apparent in the data I have explored.

The Need for New Identities

How important are these social pressures? Although that story has yet to be fully told, in my view, the prevalence of acting white in schools with racially mixed student bodies suggests that social pressures could go a long way toward explaining the large racial and ethnic gaps in SAT scores, the underperformance of minorities in suburban schools, and the lack of adequate representation of blacks and Hispanics in elite colleges and universities.

Minority communities in the United States have yet to generate a large cadre of high achievers, a situation as discouraging as the high incarceration rates among minorities who never finish high school. In fact, the two patterns may be linked. As long as distressed communities provide minorities with their identities, the social costs of breaking free will remain high. To increase the likelihood that more can do so, society must find ways for these high achievers to thrive in settings where adverse social pressures are less intense. The integrated school, by itself, apparently cannot achieve that end.

ROLAND G. FRYER is assistant professor of economics, Harvard University and a faculty research fellow, the National Bureau of Economic Research.

Article 39

How Are the Boys Doing?

How Boys Learn

To respect that fury or those giddy high spirits or a body that seems perpetually mobile is to respect nature, much as one respects the strength of a hurricane, the rush of a waterfall.

—Sara Ruddick, author and mother

MICHAEL GURIAN AND KATHY STEVENS

I. The Mismatch between Boys and Conventional Education

The image of a schoolchild as someone sitting and reading has become the poster image for education, especially in the past fifty years. This is not a bad image, but it is an incomplete match with the way the minds of many of our boys work. Perhaps you have seen the mismatch in your own homes and schools: boys struggling to learn in the ways provided for them, teachers and families becoming frustrated, boys being labeled "difficult" or "failures" and becoming morose with self-doubt.

In a recent Gurian Institute workshop, material on "boy energy" and the male brain led to a spirited discussion about the issues our sons face. A teacher raised a key question—a question that is raised in nearly every setting in which the nature-based material is presented: "Should we keep trying to change the boys and their energy, or should we change the educational system they find themselves in?" Another teacher asked, "Is this just a pedagogical issue, or are we now facing a moral one?"

Those are questions each of us must now answer, armed as we are with scientific information about the nature of our sons. The authors believe that every time a teacher wonders why boys are "trouble in the classroom," he or she is asking a moral question. Every time the faculty lounge becomes a place of conversation about why boys are bringing down standardized test scores, the teachers are asking the same question. When a mother and father agonize over whether to put their son on medication, they are asking the question. Among our children themselves, the question is silently resounding as the kids who are having trouble learning their lessons look at others who learn so very well.

Should we keep trying to change our boys, or should we change the educational system in which they are now taught? The answer to that question will require parents, teachers, and schools to decide what parts of nature, nurture, and culture can and should be changed, and what parts can't and shouldn't. It tacitly—or directly—raises these questions:

- Is male nature—the male brain—plastic enough to be changed to fit today's classrooms?

- If it is, how do we better effect change than we are now doing, so that boys no longer get most of the failing grades?
- If it is not, how can our educational system change to accommodate the male brain so that we can gain the positive results we all want for our sons?

II. How Gender *Really* Happens in the Brain

Human nature hardwires gender into our brains in three biological stages. The first stage has been clarified by genetics research, the second by endocrinological research, and the third by psychosocial research.[1]

Stage 1. Chromosome markers for gender are included in the genomes of girls and boys at the time of conception. Researchers at UCLA have identified chromosome markers—built into the fetal brain—for the development of a male and female.

Stage 2. Those chromosome markers compel surges of male and female hormones in the womb that format XX brains to be female and XY brains to be male. In-utero bombardment of hormones into the brain occurs with intense frequency between the second and fifth months of gestation. Researchers at various universities around the world, including the University of London, McMaster University in Canada, UCLA, and the University of Pennsylvania, can now trace the development of gender in the fetal brain via bombardments of testosterone and other hormones.

Stage 3. The child is born a boy or girl, sending nonverbal and then verbal cues to parents, the nurturing community, and the larger culture. These cues are biological—based in the child's genetics and hardwiring. Mom, Dad, and extended family, then teachers, schools, and community members like you, like us, read the male and female signals, cues, and characteristics. These signals and readings are now being visually traced through SPECT and PET scan research in attachment theory, conducted in many parts of the world, including the University of Denver and Harvard University.

Did You Know?

- As of four days of age, girls tend to spend twice as much time as boys maintaining eye contact with adults. Bonding chemistry and the visual cortex of boys and girls already differ at four days old.
- By four months of age, boys are less likely than girls to distinguish between a known individual and a stranger. Memory centers as well as spatial-mechanical pathways already work differently in boys and girls. Male babies are in general more inclined than female babies to spend more time during a day looking at objects moving in space—for instance, mobiles hung from a ceiling. Girls, in contrast, are more likely to turn their gaze immediately to their caregivers.
- Infant girls also pay closer attention to the words of caregivers. Verbal centers are developing in the female brain more quickly than in the male.
- Little boys, when given dolls to play with, more often than girls pull the heads off, hit them against a table, throw them in the air, or generally engage in some kind of physical, kinesthetic, or spatial play with the dolls. Girls, in contrast, from very early in life, begin to use words with the doll. Given how much earlier the female centers for verbal communication develop in the brain, this comes as no surprise. Because of higher levels of oxytocin, girls form bonds with objects that boys merely use as physical learning tools.[2]

It's important to remember that none of these researchers is involved in a nature-*versus* nurture framework. All this research recognizes the *vast interplay* between genetic, hormonal, neural, and social forces. All the researchers also recognize that maleness and femaleness are things we start out with: we are born with them. Although it was popular thirty years ago to believe otherwise, scientific research in our era has put to rest the idea that gender is completely a matter of nurture. Gender is inborn and then it becomes socialized by cultures.

Why is the human genome, brain, and bonding system set up to be male and female by nature? No researcher can be completely sure. People with a religious base for understanding human nature say, "This is how God created us." The more science-based work in evolutionary biology suggests that the most probable cause for our male-female brain difference lies in the millions of years of human evolution, during which humans primarily hunted and gathered.

Because males mainly hunted, they needed to develop a more spatial-mechanical brain. They needed to see well, but did not need fine detail sensory awareness as much as did females, who cared for offspring. The male brain was wired, therefore, for more physical movement—with more blood flow in the brain stem than the female brain has—but for less verbal input and output. (Words weren't needed much during the hunt.)

Whether you choose a religious or scientific explanation, the new brain technologies allow us to see the differences for ourselves between male and female in the brain. And even if you don't have PET scan equipment in your living room—none of us does!—you can still see what the geneticists, biologists, and sociologists are getting at.

III. Ending the Myth of Gender Plasticity and Supporting the Way Boys *Actually* Learn

Given the biological and social evidence of male-female brain difference, can a nurturing community, a school, a family, a culture make a boy change the gender of his brain? Can a typical mom, by just talking to or reading to an average little boy, force his verbal centers to be like an average girl's? Should a school compel a boy to become the kind of learner it has decided will be "easiest to teach"?

The new sciences now challenge all of us—moms, dads, grandparents, teachers, policymakers—to come to an informed conclusion about the relationship between a boy's nature, his nurtured life, and his cultural experience. We spend only a few years in a close, day-to-day supervisory relationship with our children: how do we want to spend those years? What kind of care do we want to give to their very human nature, their wonderful minds?

The new scientific research merits concluding that although all children are unique and individual, and although everyone is constantly learning new skills and developing new modes of communication, *the gender of the human brain is not plastic, not a new skill to be learned, not a new mode of communication.* It is as hardwired into the brain as a person's genetic personality. In the same way that you cannot change a shy person into an extrovert, you cannot change the brain of a boy into the brain of a girl.

The idea that not all elements of the brain—especially not gender—are plastic is very important to our dialogue about the state of boyhood in education. Our educational system has bought into the idea of "overall neural plasticity." Because of this mythical concept of the brain as a magical, changing device, very few academic institutions train teachers in the neural sciences of gender. This aspect of human development is ignored, and young teachers, like young parents, are taught that being a "boy" or a "girl" is culturally insignificant in education, that basically all kids learn the same way and can be educated in a way that ensures gender-exclusive, predictable results.

Research from the new gender and brain sciences begs us to move beyond this myth. The move constitutes a second major step toward solving the crisis of male education. As step two finds its way into schools of education, young teachers will be shown PET scans, SPECT scans, and MRIs of the male and female brain and be trained to understand the gender reality we all experience.

You as an individual—and your school as a collective—can become a leader in making this happen. Because our biological sciences are now able to use PET scans, MRIs, and other tests, we can now discern how gender is marked into our genomes from millions of years of human development and still lights up the individual brains of boys and girls. You can bring this information to homes, schools, social policies, and universities and colleges. You can help your community notice how tough the myth of gender plasticity is making life for our sons. When you notice males in educational distress, you can point out that we are creating for our sons an educational system not well suited to certain aspects of their brains; a system that claims they are defective, disordered, or incorrigible because they can't learn; a system that insists that they should be able to change—even further, that their inability to change is yet another flaw in their character as males, one that supposedly requires medication.

If our civilization continues to buy into the myth of gender plasticity, larger numbers of our sons will continue to do poorly in school. They will emerge from years of waste and failure without the normal development and skills we've all assumed for years that they would acquire, and, during this entire struggle and conflict, *they* will continue to frustrate us by "not changing."

IV. A Boy-Friendly Model for Protecting the Minds of Boys

If you agree with our argument that the current educational system often fails to accommodate the hardwiring of boys' brains and does not provide them with an appropriate system of learning, and if you agree that our homes and schools should do less to try to change our boys and more to help them learn naturally, then you can become an ambassador for boys, a protector of their minds. As an ambassador you'll join us, not in trying to alter the nature of boys or girls, but instead in working toward two goals:

1. Expression and development of the natural self of the child. The child's genetic self is most important to his or her learning, and those who aid the child are charged with helping that self become fully expressive and developed within the frameworks of a humane society.

2. Compensation for areas of inherent disadvantage or fragility. These areas of disadvantage emerge for any child because of particular genetic or environmentally caused weaknesses in his or her learning brain or because the child as an individual carries learning characteristics that don't fit the mass.

Our suggestions detailed in other sections of *The Minds of Boys* avoid joining with any ideologies that measure success of the child's education by *measuring significant alteration* of the child's mind, whatever part of the gender-brain continuum the child is on. We believe that to base a child's education on the hope of altering a brain's inherent method of self-development is an affront to freedom and ultimately leads to suppression or disengagement of the child's true self and potential for success.

A child who expresses himself and learns to compensate for weaknesses is following one of the most natural instincts of our species: to *adapt*. We as adults protect the minds of children when we help the children adapt, using their own natural skills and talents, to

the needs of a society. We don't protect their minds by putting a generation of schoolboys on drugs or watching them gradually fail.

Breaking down the myth of gender plasticity is not necessarily a simple thing to accomplish. But our culture has, in a few decades, successfully confronted a great deal of the patriarchal, sexist, and industrial system that was hurting girls, and improved the lives of girls and women. There's still a way to go, but there has been substantial change. And in this process, our culture did not force girls' brains or nature to change in order for them to succeed in our educational system. All of us came together to change the system in order to fit girls.

Specifically, we brought more verbal functioning to our math and science classes, trained teachers to use more writing and group conversation in teaching those subjects, changed our testing of those subjects to include more explanative and discursive essay answers, and developed new ways to encourage our girls at home that fit their natural need for verbal encouragement.

The proof of our success with girls is measurable today: the industrialized world has closed the female-to-male math and science gaps in our schools. Girls now receive grades as good as and better than boys in these classes. In California, girls are now actually outperforming boys in math and science. As we noted earlier, girls are no longer shortchanged in many schools—they are high performers. The changes we made to our educational system worked!

Changing our educational system to help boys will admittedly be harder, because the changes that have been made to help our daughters will actually make boys' education more problematic. Furthermore, in our consideration of girls' needs, we never had to fight the myth of gender plasticity—we never said, "Our girls are defective." We always said, "The system is defective." Changing the system for our boys can be also accomplished—without hurting our girls—and it must be.

Notes

1. Dewing, Phoebe, Tao Shi, Steve Horvath, and Eric Vilain. 2003. "Sexually Dimorphic Gene Expression in Mouse Brain Precedes Gonadal Differentiation." *Molecular Brain Research* 118 (1-2): 82–90; Schore, Allan N. 2001. "Effects of a Secure Attachment Relationship on Right Brain Development, Affect Regulation, and Infant Mental Health." *Infant Mental Health* 22 (1-2): 7–66.

2. Rhoades, Steven E. 2004. *Taking Sex Differences Seriously.* San Francisco: Encounter Books.

MICHAEL GURIAN is the author of twenty books, among them *The Wonder of Boys* and *The Wonder of Girls*. He is the co-founder of the Gurian Institute in Colorado Springs, Colorado. **KATHY STEVENS** is the training director of the Gurian Institute.

Reprinted with permission of the authors from *Educational Horizons*, quarterly journal of Pi Lambda Theta Inc., International Honor Society and Professional Association in Education, P.O. Box 6626, Bloomington, IN 47401, Winter 2006, pp. 87–93.

The Overdominance of Computers

Our students need inner resources and real-life experiences to balance their high-tech lives.

Lowell W. Monke

The debate churns on over the effectiveness of computers as learning tools. Although there is a growing disillusionment with the promise of computers to revolutionize education, their position in schools is protected by the fear that without them students will not be prepared for the demands of a high-tech 21st century. This fallback argument ultimately trumps every criticism of educational computing, but it is rarely examined closely.

Lets start by accepting the premise of the argument: Schools need to prepare young people for a high-tech society. Does it automatically follow that children of all ages should use high-tech tools? Most people assume that it does, and that's the end of the argument. But we don't prepare children for an automobile-dependent society by finding ways for 10-year-olds to drive cars, or prepare people to use alcohol responsibly by teaching them how to drink when they are 6. My point is that preparation does not necessarily warrant early participation. Indeed, preparing young people quite often involves strengthening their inner resources—like self-discipline, moral judgment, and empathy—before giving them the opportunity to participate.

Great Power and Poor Preparation

The more powerful the tools—and computers are powerful—the more life experience and inner strength students must have to handle that power wisely. On the day my Advanced Computer Technology classroom got wired to the Internet, it struck me that I was about to give my high school students great power to harm a lot of people, and all at a safe distance. They could inflict emotional pain with a few keystrokes and never have to witness the tears shed. They could destroy hours of work accomplished by others who were not their enemies—just poorly protected network users whose files provided convenient bull's-eyes for youth flexing newfound technical muscles.

I also realized that it would take years to instill the ethical discipline needed to say *no* to flexing that technical power. Young people entering my course needed more firsthand experiences guided by adults. They needed more chances to directly connect their own actions with the consequences of those actions, and to reflect on the outcomes, before they started using tools that could trigger serious consequences on the other side of the world.

Students need more than just moral preparation. They also need authentic experiences. As more students grow up spending much of their time in environments dominated by computers, TV, and video games, their diminished experience with real, concrete things prevents them from developing a rich understanding of what they study on computers. The computer is a purely symbolic environment; users are always working with abstract representations of things, never with the things themselves. In a few months my students could learn to build complex relational databases and slick multimedia presentations. But unless they also had a deep knowledge of the physical world and community relationships, they would be unable to infuse depth and meaning into the information they were depicting and discussing.

Do Computers Help Achievement?

Educational technology researchers, who tend to suffer from a severe inability to see the forest for the trees, typically ignore the impact that saturating society with computers and other screen environments is having on children. University of Munich economists Thomas Fuchs and Ludger Woessmann recently examined data from a study of 174,000 15-year-olds in 31 nations who took the Programme for International Student Assessment tests. They found, after controlling for other possible influences, that the more access students had to computers in school and at home, the *lower* their overall test scores were (2004). The authors suggest that rather than inherently motivating young people or helping them learn, computers more likely distract them from their studies. But there may be other problems behind this phenomenon that point to inherent contradictions in the use of educational technology.

For example, although we know that computer programs can help small children learn to read, we also know that face-to-face interaction is one of the most important ingredients in reading readiness (Dodici, Draper, & Peterson, 2003). As a result of increased time spent with computers, video games, and TV the current generation of elementary students will experience an estimated 30 percent fewer face-to-face encounters than the previous generation (Hammel, 1999). Thus, teachers may be employing the very devices for remediating reading problems that helped cause the problems in the first place.

Nearly everything children do today involves technologies that distance them from direct contact with the living world.

The issue is not just balancing computer time with other activities in schools. Both inside and outside school, children's lives are dominated by technology. Nearly everything a child does today—from chatting with friends to listening to music to playing games—tends to involve the use of technologies that distance children from direct contact with the living world. If the task of schools is to produce men and women who live responsible, fulfilling lives—not just human cogs for the high-tech machinery of commerce—then we should not be intensifying children's high-tech existence but compensating for it. Indeed, as advanced technology increasingly draws us toward a mechanical way of thinking and acting, it becomes crucial that schools help students develop their distinctly human capacities. What we need from schools is not balance in using high technology, but an effort to balance children's machine-dominated lives.

To prepare children to challenge the cold logic of the spreadsheet-generated bottom line, we need to teach them to value what that spreadsheet cannot factor in: commitment, loyalty, and tradition. To prepare them to find meaning in the abstract text and images encountered through screens, we need to first engage them in physical realities that screen images can only symbolize. To fit students to live in an environment filled with human-made products, we need to first help them know and respect what cannot be manufactured: the natural, the living, the wild. To prepare students to live well-grounded lives in a world of constant technological change, we need to concentrate their early education on things that endure.

The Cost of Failing to Compensate

Anyone who has spent time in schools knows that what is keeping today's youth from succeeding academically has nothing to do with a lack of technical skills or access to computers. Rather, it is the lack of qualities like hope, compassion, trust, respect, a sense of belonging, moral judgment, stability, community support, parental care, and teacher competence and enthusiasm that keeps so many students imprisoned in ignorance.

Ironically, what students will most need to meet the serious demands of the 21st century is the wisdom that grows out of these inner human capacities and that is developed by community involvement. If the 20th century taught us anything at all, it should have been that technology can be a very mixed blessing. Children entering elementary schools today will eventually have to wrestle with the mess that their elders have left them because of our own lack of wisdom about technology's downside: global warming, increasingly lethal weapons, nuclear waste,

overdependence on automobiles, overuse of pesticides and antibiotics, and the general despoiling of our planet. They will also have to take on ethical conundrums posed by advanced technology, such as what to do about cloning, which decisions are off-limits to artificial intelligence devices, and whether or not parents should be allowed to "enhance" the genetic makeup of their offspring (only the wealthy need apply).

Those decisions should not be left to technicians in labs, CEOs in boardrooms, or politicians in debt to those who stand to profit from the technology. Our children should be at the decision tables as adults, and we want them to be able to stand apart from high technology and soberly judge its benefits and detriments to the entire human race.

How can young people develop the wisdom to judge high technology if they are told from the moment they enter school, implicitly if not explicitly, that they need high-tech tools to learn, to communicate, to think? Having been indoctrinated early with the message that their capacity to deal with the world depends not on their own internal resources but on their use of powerful external machines, how can students even imagine a world in which human beings impose limits on technological development or use?

Where to Go From Here

Keep to Essentials in the Early Years

So how, specifically, should educators make decisions and policies about the appropriateness of digital technologies for students of different ages?

One approach to tackling this dilemma comes from the Alliance for Childhood. During the last eight years, the Alliance (whose board of directors I serve on) has engaged educators, children's health professionals, researchers, and technology experts in developing guidelines for structuring a healthy learning environment for children, and has developed a list of essential conditions. Educators should ask themselves to what extent heavy use of computers and the Internet provides children in the lower grades with these essential school experiences:

- Close, lining relationships with responsible adults.
- Outdoor activity, nature exploration, gardening, and other encounters with nature.
- Time for unstructured play as part of the core curriculum.
- Music, drama, puppetry, dance, painting, and the other arts, both as separate classes and as a catalyst to bring other academic subjects to life.
- Hands-on lessons, handicrafts, and other physically engaging activities that provide effective first lessons for young children in the sciences, mathematics, and technology.
- Conversation with important adults, as well as poetry, storytelling, and hearing books read aloud.

This vision places a high priority on a child's direct encounters with the world and with other living beings, but it does not reject technology. On the contrary, tools are an important part of the vision. But at the elementary level, the tools should be simple, putting less distance between the student and the world and calling forth the students own internal resources.

Schools must also be patient with children's development. It would strike anyone as silly to give the smallest student in a 2nd grade class a scooter so that the child could get around the track as fast as the other kids his or her age. But our society shows decreasing willingness to wait for the natural emergence of students' varying mental and emotional capacities. We label students quickly and display an almost pathological eagerness to apply external technical fixes (including medications) to students who often simply aren't ready for the abstract, academic, and sedentary environment of today's early elementary classrooms. Our tendency to turn to external tools to help children cope with demands that are out of line with their tactile and physically energetic nature reflects the impact that decades of placing faith in technical solutions has had on how we treat children.

Study Technology in Depth After Elementary School

After children have had years to engage in direct, firsthand experiences, and as their abstract thinking capacities emerge more fully, it makes sense to gradually introduce computers and other complex, symbolic environments. Computer hardware and software should also become the focus of classroom investigation. A student in a technological society surrounded by black boxes whose fundamental principles he or she does not understand is as functionally illiterate as a student in a world filled with books that he or she can't read. The only thing worse would be to make technology "invisible," preventing children from even being aware of their ignorance.

By high school, digital technologies should take a prominent place in students' studies, both as tools of learning and as tools to learn about. During the last two years of high school, teachers should spend considerable time outfitting students with the high-tech skills they will need when they graduate. This "just-in-time" approach to teaching technical skills is far more efficient—instructionally and financially—than continually retraining younger students in technical skills soon to be obsolete. In addition, students at all education levels should consciously examine technology's role in human affairs.

I am not suggesting that we indiscriminately throw computers out of classrooms. But I do believe it's time to rethink the past decision to indiscriminately throw them in. The result of that rethinking would be, I hope, some much-needed technological modesty, both in school and eventually in society in general. By compensating for the dominance of technology in students' everyday lives, schools might help restore the balance we need to create a more humane society

---

TECHNO-BYTE

Percentage of U.S. students who used computers in school in 2003:

- 97 percent of high school students.
- 95 percent of middle school students.
- 91 percent of students in grades 1–5.
- 80 percent of kindergarten students.
- 67 percent of nursery school students.

—National Center for Education Statistics, 2005

The irony of postmodern education is that preparing children for a high-tech future requires us to focus our attention more than ever before on the task of understanding what it means to be human, to be alive, to be part of both social and biological communities—a quest for which technology is increasingly becoming not the solution but the problem.

References

Dodici, B. J., Draper, D. C., & Peterson, C. A. (2003). Early parent-child interactions and early literacy development. *Topics in Early Childhood Special Education, 23*(3), 124–136.

Fuchs, T., & Woessmann, L. (2004, November). *Computers and student learning: Bivariate and multivariate evidence on the availability and use of computers at home and at school.* CESifo Working Paper Series (#1321). Available: **www.cesifo.de/~DocCIDL/1321.pdf**

Hammel, S. (1999, Nov. 29). Generation of loners? Living their lives online. *US. News and World Report*, p. 79.

Author's note: The Alliance for Childhood has produced two publications to help parents and educators guide children toward a healthier relationship with technology: *Fool's Gold: A Critical Look at Computers in Childhood*, and *Tech Tonic: Towards a New Literacy of Technology* (both available online at **www.allianceforchildhood.org**).

LOWELL W. MONKE is Assistant Professor at Wittenberg University in Springfield, Ohio; 937-342-8648; lmonke@wittenberg.edu.

Morality, Medicine, and Meaning: Toward an Integrated Justification of Physical Education

What are the values of physical education (PE)? What is its meaning and possible significance to the individual and society? Should PE be part of a standard curriculum in the education of the young? If so, why? These questions are calls for a justification of PE, which is a socio-cultural construction created by people for people and on the basis of particular human goals and values. Reflection over such views is the topic of this paper. More specifically, the paper presents a critical review of what can be considered three ideal-typical justifications of PE: the justifications from morality, health, and meaning. In a final section, a proposal is made for an integrated justification restating and relating these justifications into a consistent whole.

SIGMUND LOLAND

W hat are the values of physical education (PE)? What is its meaning and possible significance to the individual and society? Should PE be part of a standard curriculum in the education of children and youth? If so, why? These are all calls for a justification of PE; for its *raison d'etre* so to speak. Although human physicality is a biological fact and movement is a biological necessity, deliberate education into the physical is neither. PE is a socio-cultural construction created by people for people and on the basis of particular human goals and values. Hence, views of the meaning and value of PE are as old as PE itself. It is precisely such views, or justifications, that will be the topic of this paper.

This is of course an extensive topic, and it can be addressed in many ways and from many perspectives. From psychological, sociological, and pedagogical points of view, PE is often seen as a significant sphere for the socialization of the young. From physiological and medical points of view, PE is considered a potentially significant contributor to overall health and well-being. My perspective will be limited primarily to philosophical considerations. More specifically, I will engage in a critical review of what I consider to be three ideal-typical justifications of PE and then try to reconstruct an integrated justification that I believe can be of relevance today.

Ideal-typical justifications are not precise empirical descriptions of the many and diverse views of PE actually found in persons, groups, and societies but internally consistent elaborations of core elements of such views. For instance, one traditional view is that PE is to serve the moral development of the individual. An alternative, perhaps more modern, view is that the primary concern of PE is to serve individual and public health. Although most people will sympathize with both, in an ideal-typical discussion, these views are defined as substantially different and treated separately. This approach helps clarify basic value tensions and ethical dilemmas in the field and makes possible examination of whether some arguments seem better founded and stronger than others. Through critical reviews and comparisons, then, possibilities for integrated and more extensive justifications can be explored.

Moralism

Historically speaking, a primary justification of PE is the moralist one. I understand "morality" as an actual scheme of norms and values held by a person, a given group or a given society defining what is right and wrong and good or bad for this person, group, or society (Beauchamp, 1991). Morality can be empirically described. Ethics is the systematic and critical philosophical examination of morality (Beauchamp, 1991). Ethical questions do not have simple empirical answers but require normative reasoning and justification through arguments. Moralism, then, can be understood as the nonreflective mixing of morality and ethics in taking for granted that a particular morality of a person, a group, or a society is the only right and true one. Often, moralists are absolutists and see as their mission to reproduce to the full and without questioning the actual norms and values in which they believe. To the moralist, education in general and PE in particular are instruments only to reach these goals. PE, or for that matter other subjects in school, have no particular meaning and value in themselves but are tools in the larger socialization' into a particular morality. The history of PE provides a long series of examples. Let me give you two.

The construction of PE in Western Europe from the 18th century onward was based on socialization concerns. The British sport historian Tony Mangan has described the Victorian development of an educational ideology called "Muscular Christianity" with among others the headmaster of Rugby, Thomas Arnold (1795–1842) as a key figure (Mangan, 1981). PE was given a key role. Through sports such as rugby and boxing, young men from the socio-economic elite were thought to develop the necessary sense of community and toughness to defend and expand the British Empire all over the world. Another, and to you a more exotic, example comes from my own country, Norway. The Norwegian humanist, polar explorer, Nobel laureate and skiing enthusiast Fridtjof Nansen (1860–1930) had only disgust for competitive sport and doubted seriously its value. In his view, sport *a la* the English had no cultivating force but could only be understood as an expression of the superficiality, stress, and unease of the modern condition. Noncompetitive skiing, on the other hand, combined with survival skills in a harsh climate, taught young men (and women) discipline, courage, and moderation and should be required curriculum for all (Repp, 2001).

The examples are not meant as historical claims on Arnold and Nansen being nonreflective moralists and absolutists. Presumably, both were probably reflective and for their time, independent thinkers with nuanced views. The point is that their statements on PE and sport can be interpreted and has been used in ideal-typical moralist ways. Their views are radically different in substance but share a strong flavor of viewing PE as a mere instrument to reach what are considered moral goals outside of PE itself. This moralist justification is no stranger to modern society, either. Although sociologists such as Anthony Giddens holds that Western societies are in a stage of reflexive late modernity (Giddens, 1991), pure instrumentalist views of PE have an amazingly strong position. The *doxa,* or the hidden premise that guides practice, seems to be that PE is basically an efficient school into morality. In a much quoted statement, existentialist philosopher and author Albert Camus claimed that all he had learned about ethics he had learned from sports (Simon, 2003). PE (and sport) teaches character.

There is, however, a growing body of literature that challenges the moralist justification of PE. The challenges take several forms. I will concentrate on one ethical and one empirical point. The ethical point is that a moralist position is ethically irresponsible. Without hesitation, moralists take the step from what they believe are statements of fact (these *are* the only true values) to normative conclusions (therefore this is how PE *ought to be* practiced). Moralists commit what philosophers call the naturalist fallacy, that is, a logical mistake in which more is put into the conclusions (norms) than what is found in the premises (statements of fact). Mary Midgley dissects this way of thinking in her attack on what she calls the "Hobbesian myth" (Midgley, 1985, 1993). Hobbes portrays human beings as being by nature egoist and competitive. The normative deduction is that society should be structured accordingly. As an alternative to an individualist "state of nature," in which life was "brutish, nasty and short," Hobbes deduced the idea of a social contract based on rational self-interest. Others have to a larger extent viewed self interest and competitiveness as positive human dispositions and argued in favor of stimulating them both in society and in schools and PE.

According to Midgley, these deductions fail as the premise is wrong. She argues convincingly that human nature (if there is such a thing) is a complex matter and includes multiple predispositions. We seem to have just as strong predispositions for empathy and cooperation as for egoism and competition. The implication for education is that students tend to develop the predispositions that are emphasized and cultivated in the educational settings in which they take part. In the moralist's taking for granted that their own morality is the only true one, and in their often one-dimensional claims on human nature, they miss this point. Their nonreflective premises make their educational philosophies ethically irresponsible.

Secondly, the modern moralist *doxa* of PE and sport as building character is a problematic one for empirical reasons. For moral development to occur, pedagogical competence and the establishing of the right socio-psychological and motivational climate are of key importance (Roberts et al., 2001). One activity, such as boxing, can give radically different outcomes depending on the way it is taught. On the one hand, it can be practiced in socially responsible ways. Imagine the rule in sparring that one party has to stop when the other party expresses discomfort or pain. Under this rule, students can develop empathy and sensitivity for another's well-being. On the other hand, if being taught with emphasis on dominance and the aggressive infliction of pain, boxing seems to lead to anti-social conduct both inside and outside of the ring (Endresen & Olweus, in press). The "bracketed morality" (Bredemeier & Shields, 1995) of sport in which conduct is allowed that is otherwise banned, expanding. In fact, the brackets seem to fall off. Aggression is internalized and constitutes a disposition for action in all spheres of life.

I am not rejecting the possibility of justifying PE with references to socialization and moral development. On the contrary, as I intend to argue later, such references are key elements in an integrated justification of PE. However, the moralist justification gets it wrong. The uncritical instrumental use of PE to serve whatever morality a person, a group, or a society takes for granted is ethically unacceptable.

Health

An alternative justification that has increased in significance in the last few decades is the justification from health. However, as with the moralist justification, views on connections between PE and health have long traditions. In ancient medical philosophy and practice, such as in Hippocrates, moderate gymnastics is prescribed as a means toward a balanced and good life. The origins of current health justifications are to be found in the development of modern natural science. Seventeenth century philosopher Renee Descartes' dualistic anthropology distinguished the body from the mind and viewed the body as a mechanism and in principle fully explainable by chains of cause-effect relationships. This was a landmark in the understanding of the human organism and lead to a series of new hypotheses. According to Wachter (1985), the idea of a causal connection between physical activity and health was first presented to a broader public in one of the 35 volumes of the French *Encylopedie,* published in the latter half of the 18th century. In a main article dealing with health, the covering image was that of a golf player!

The general public acknowledgement of PE as an efficient means toward public health belongs to the 20th century. Perhaps the first systematically developed health justification is to be found first in the so-called workers' sport movement of the European 1920s and 1930s (Kruger & Riordan, 1996). Although the movement was ideologically diverse, it shared a positive evaluation of PE and sport as a means to enhance public health. Health was seen not a goal *per se* but as an instrument in the strengthening of the working classes in the struggle with what was considered the hegemonic power structures of the time. Interestingly, at the same period of time the argument from public health was made from another and very different political point of view. Baron Pierre de Coubertin, the founding father of the modern Olympic Movement, argued strongly in favor of local public *gymnasia* in which people could exercise their physical abilities and skills and (according to Coubertin) thus develop physically, socially, and morally (MacAloon, 1981).

The emphasis on PE as a means toward health is even more intense today. But the premises have changed. Since the early 20th century there has been a gradual transition from openly ideological justifications toward epidemiology. Ainsworth (2005) provides a clear and informative portrayal of the epidemiological perspective. Due to the technologization of society and automation of working processes, the percentage of the population engaged in manual labor is dramatically reduced. Urbanization, or rather suburbanization, and the development of public and private transportation to and from work, has reduced everyday movement activities. In 2004, 74% of the U.S. population did not meet recommended activity levels, 23.1% reported no exercise at all, and 22.1% were characterized as obese (Ainsworth, 2005). There is solid evidence that physical inactivity is related to all-cause morbidity, and that an increase in public activity levels can improve public health. Probably associated with increasing inactivity, there has been a radical increase in the percentage of overweight and obese people in Western societies (Hardman & Morris, 2003). Actually, obesity and its associated health risks are defined by some as a global epidemic (Gard & Wright, 2005), and in the medical literature, dramatic new concepts can be found such as that of the Sedentary Death Syndrome (SDS).

These trends have given force to arguments for increased PE in school. In many educational institutions, the field has gotten a new name: Physical Education and Health (PEH; Evans, Davies, & Wright, 2004). Although the scientific evidence of the health benefits of regular exercise are overwhelming, and although the health risks associated with inactivity and overweight/obesity are obvious, there are good reasons to reflect critically over this justification.

One line of critique is based on an understanding of the body (and health) as a socio-cultural construction (Hepworth & Turner, 1991; Schilling, 1993; Turner, 1984). Conceptions of health and its role in human life change with social and cultural contexts. Waddington (2000) discussed Zola's ideas of the medicalization of modern life. This is a social process in which conceptions of illness, medication, and health take on an increasingly important role in the individual's life. Improved health seems to become the goal toward which everything else is means. Critics see this as a repressive process in which individual and public attention is led astray. Health is not an end value but a means in the quest for a meaningful and good life. The justification becomes instrumentally open ended. Moreover, in a visual, Western culture health is idealized not only as a bio-medical condition, but as an image, a "look." Health has become a social symbol (Synnott, 1993). The healthy image with the sporting body as the paradigmatic expression is cultivated almost to the extreme (Wachter, 1985). One problem is that to most people, these are virtually unattainable health and body ideals. The cult of health and fitness creates what Johansson terms "a logic of discontent" ("misnoyets logic"; Johansson, 1998). Surveys from a series of Western countries show that a majority of the adult population is dissatisfied with their own weight and body image (Loland, 1999; Sault, 1994). There is always an extra kilo to be taken off or an extra inch to be added and there always seems to be a new pharmaceutical product or technology with the promise of even more efficiency than the previous ones. In terms of bio-medical manipulation of the body, it seems as if enough is never enough (Elliot, 2003).

Hence, we have here a justification that offers knowledge of efficient means to reach another means but with no clear idea of the goal these means are supposed to serve. As the discussion above is meant to illustrate, the nonreflective and openended instrumentalism makes the health justification ethically irresponsible as well. As with the justification from morality, I do not claim that health is an irrelevant element in a justification of PE. On the contrary, I firmly believe that PE can be a counterforce to repressive medicalization processes and obsessions with unattainable body ideals. If this is to be achieved, however, health has to be integrated into a more extensive normative framework with articulation of the end values of a good education (Evans, 2003). It is to such a more philosophically sophisticated scheme I now turn.

Meaning

A third ideal-typical justification departs from particular characteristics in PE in itself. The justification is linked to what is often called the humanist tradition (Bullock, 1985). Simply put, the key premise is that human beings are meaning-searching and meaning-constructing beings with the potential of becoming free and responsible moral agents. Education, or more precisely, a liberal education, is considered decisive in the realization of human potential.

The humanist tradition has deep roots. In ancient Greek culture, gymnastics and PE were considered key elements m the upbringing of the young. In the Republic, Plato emphasizes that two arts must have been given to mankind by some god for the harmonious adjustment of body and soul: music and gymnastics. Key figures in Western thought such as Goethe, Schiller, Kant, Mill, and William James have upheld and explored further the ideals of a liberal education. In the context of PE, scholars such as Metheny (1968), Arnold (1988), Siedentop. (1994), and Kretchmar (2005) have delivered important insights. These justifications focus not on mere instrumental functions of the activity but on how the particular values of PE are interwoven with more general values of the good life and the good society. The interest is not so much in outcome as in "meaning in movement." These are rather abstract ideas. What more precisely does this mean in practice?

Let me exemplify in a rather sketchy way. In the study of the particular meanings and values of PE, the methodological tool is often that of phenomenology and qualitative inquiry. Phenomenologists attempt to grasp the phenomenon under study in its immediacy and the way it is given to us directly through experience; they study the life-world (Lebenswelt) to use a well known phenomenological term. In PE, students run and jump, throw and hit, kick and swing, they move in indoor and outdoor environments, on concrete, on grass, in water, and on snow and ice, in flat terrain, uphill and downhill. They experience the joy of free movement, the challenges of strictly defined motor skills, the discomforts of anaerobic exercise, the joys of a steady state aerobic activity, and cooperation and conflicts in team games. All these experiences have strong, nonverbal, embodied aspects. We can say that the typical PE experience is an immediate and sensual exploration of the possibilities and limitations of embodied movement.

However, a thin description of the experiential qualities of PE is no justification. A further step must be taken. Are these experiences good or bad? What are their values in the larger scheme of things? Can they be justified as meaningful in the context of human life? Here, the link between phenomenology and existentialism becomes apparent. PE has a concrete existential dimension. In a competitive game, outcomes are immediate and clear. One party wins, others lose. In the execution of motor skills, there is immediate and direct feedback in terms of mastery or failure. The direct and embodied joys over wins and mastery or disappointments over losses and failures seem to have a particularly strong take on us. Anderson (2002) talks of PE and movement as "an exploration of our humanity." PE, it can be claimed, represents a particular concrete the matization of existential questions such as these: Who am I? What can I do? Who are we? and What can we achieve together?

According to the humanist argument, thematization of existential questions constitutes the very core of an all round liberal education into free and responsible moral agents. Various school subjects do this in various ways. English cultivates a sense of language, expression, and story-telling. History provides knowledge of the past and an improved understanding of the present. Mathematics challenges and develops skills of logical and stringent thinking. PE has its own particular role as an exploration of our possibilities and limitations of embodiment and movement.

The humanist interpretation of PE has many strong aspects. As compared to the moralist and health justification, the humanist justification is nonreductionist in scope. It attempts to overcome the body-mind dualisms of the moralist and health justifications and presents a more credible account of human embodiment. Moreover, it represents a transition from instru-

mentalism to relationalism. PE is seen to have its own particular norms and values that at the same time are expressions of more general ideals. It connects PE to existential end values such as well-being and happiness.

However, the humanist justification is exposed to criticism as well. One key critique points to its idealism. PE is a human, historical, and socio-cultural construction. As social scientists keenly point out, the norms and values of PE usually reflect the predominant morality of the time (Evans et al., 2004). Even if there are strong experiential qualities in PE, they are not phenomenologically pure but shaped by socialization. A boy experiencing anxiety before his first dive and still carries it through is driven not primarily by a quest for excitement but by a learned inclination to impress, to demonstrate courage and individuality, and to attract admiration. A girl's gracious movements in the dance class are not just expressions of her aesthetic sense but of historical and cultural constructions of gender. Socialization shapes experience, sociology overruns phenomenology. Critics hold that the humanist justification is a-contextual, a-historical, and sociologically naive.

An extension of this critique points to the lack of pragmatic-political force. In the struggle over scarce resources and a role in a curriculum, there is a need for demonstration of concrete effects. References must be made not just to values in PE in itself but to its role in solving the immediate and concrete challenges, for instance in terms of public health problems. Although most educationalists at least in the Western world would agree on humanist educational ideals, PE easily loses impact if it cannot demonstrate short term utility. There is a need to modify and modernize the humanist justification.

An Integrated Justification

I have outlined three justifications of PE. The outlines are not empirical descriptions of views held by actual individuals, groups, or societies but cultivation of core elements of such views. The intent has been to clarify arguments around PE and to compare in more systematic and critical ways their strengths and weaknesses. Do some of these justifications seem stronger than others, and if so, in what way? Can any of the justifications be combined? Can they complement each other? Do the strengths of one justification outweigh the weakness of another?

From what is said above, in their ideal-typical versions, moralist and health arguments become instrumental and reductionist and build on vague or no conceptions at all of what PE is all about. The consequence of instrumentalism is that if there are other and better ways of reaching moralist or health goals, so be it. Then there is no more need for PE. Reductionism implies a view of PE as concerned only with a part of a human being, never the whole. To the moralist, the center of attention is the mind. The health justification is concerned with the body. In these respects, the humanist justification seems more promising. A view of PE is offered and grounded in a relational way to more general ideals of all round human education. In addition, the humanist justification builds on nondualist anthropology. more than the two others, the humanist justification offers a full normative theory of PE. Still, the critique of its idealist aspects and lack of pragmatic-political force has to be taken seriously. Two steps can be taken in this respect.

First, the understanding of the existential dimensions of PE can be and should be contextualized. Such a contextualization is found in its programmatic form in communitarian ethics, in particular in the neo-Aristotelian virtue ethics of Alastair MacIntyre (1984). MacIntyre's theory has inspired several works on sport and PE (McNamee, 1995, 2003; Morgan, 1994; Siedentop, 2002). I will give a brief sketch of its perspectives.

According to MacIntyre, moral virtues may develop through social interaction in what is referred to as social practices. One definitional element of a social practice is that it has standards of excellence shaped through historical and socio-cultural processes. In tennis, one standard of excellence is related to solid ground strokes with enough length and top spin to keep the opponent at a distance and under control. To the PE teacher, one standard of excellence is the teaching of motor skills through individualized didactic approaches. When these standards are realized in successful ways, the internal goods of tennis and PE come through. One such internal good in both tennis and PE is the experience of joy and mastery. The important point is that internal goods can only be realized in practice. The third step in the MacIntyrean scheme is to evaluate whether striving toward the standards of excellence and internal goods of a practice can be said to be of moral worth. Does such striving develop virtues of significance to a good life and a good society? Are they worthy goals for the socialization of the young? I cannot follow up with a full fledged analysis here but only hint at a conclusion. If PE is practiced according to its standards of excellence, its internal goods are the posing and tentative answering of existential questions as exemplified above. In good PE students are given the chance to explore their humanity in a particularly direct, embodied, and sensual way. Here, then, virtues can develop that probably can be defended on a more general basis as being of meaning and value to human life and society.

This is a reflection of a typical Aristotelian thought. One becomes good by becoming a good chooser and doer. Becoming good is accomplished not just by choosing or doing right actions but by doing them in the right way. Aristotelian ethics builds on what is sometimes referred to as a holistic-teleological frame of thought. In the good life, each particular action reflects the whole and the whole is reflected in its parts (Cooper, 1975). PE contributes with its own qualities in this more general picture that at the same time are interwoven with more general educational ideals.

The other line of critique pointed to the political-pragmatic impotency of the humanist interpretation. The neo-Aristotelian contextualization of PE offers an important response in this respect. Let me begin with the moralist justification. It was criticized for being pre-reflective and instrumental. It can now be viewed in new light. The neo-Aristotelian twist makes possible the transition from a moralist Justification to a reflective, ethical one. By walking carefully back and forth between PE's standards of excellence, its internal goods, and moral virtues, I have argued that PE has a necessary role to play in the education of the young into free and responsible moral agents. This is a reflexive and critical restatement of PE as an arena for socialization without the absolutist flavor of moralism. In PE, pupils learn to pose existential questions in immediate, direct, and sensual ways, not to accept pregiven answers. PE is no longer a means to an external, narrowly defined morality, but a sphere for the cultivation of our moral sense.

A similar inclusion can be done with the health argument. The need for increased physical activity in the population and the blessings of regular exercise in terms of improved health are indisputable facts; however, facts do not become good justifications until they are handled normatively within a framework of end values. Again, it is important to abandon simplistic instrumentalism in favor of relationism. Good health gives well-being and energy and increases the possibilities of living a meaningful life. Good health is something we strive for and something we enjoy as a value in itself. PE is no longer a means to an external, narrowly defined health condition, but a sphere both for the experience of good health and fitness in action, so to speak, and for the developing good health and fitness as a means in the larger quest for a good life (Kretchmar, 2005).

Concluding Comments

I have presented an updated version of the humanist justification with the inclusion of a restatement of the justifications from morality and health. I am talking here of an integrated, robust approach that gives flexibility and room for pragmatism without having to compromise on basic values. Being challenged on short term benefits, PE proponents can point to moral development and/or health. Upon further challenge and in the long run, a relational value scheme and humanist educational ideals lie ready at hand and give direction and stability.

In today's struggle for legitimacy, I believe the humanist framework is of crucial significance. If we are to believe the contributors in Evans et al. (2004) volume on PEH, the health discourse seems to acquire a hegemonic status. This is not necessarily problematic in itself. A strengthening of PE can be an invaluable response to the challenges of inactivity. However, if we do not hold fresh the humanist framework, we may end up with problems as described in discussion of the ideal-typical justification from health. Perhaps a worst case scenario is the reduction of PE to PA (physical activity). In the eagerness to solve public health challenges, educational ideals may slip out of focus. The understanding emerges that any movement and physical activity is as good as another. Then there will be no longer need for the particular competence of the physical educator. This really means to abandon the very old and important idea of education into the physical as a whole.

References

Ainsworth, B.E. (2005). Movement, mobility and public health. *Quest,* **57,** 12–23.

Anderson, D. (2002). The humanity of movement or "It's net just a gym class." *Quest, 54,* 87–96.

Arnold, P. (1988). *Education, movement and the curriculum.* New York: Falmer.

Beauchamp T.L. (1991). *Philosophical ethics: An introduction to moral philosophy* (2nd ed.). New York: McGraw-Hill.

Bredemeier, B.J.L., & Shields, D.L. (1995). *Character development and physical activity.* Champaign, IL: Human Kinetics.

Bullock, A. (1985). *The humanist tradition of the west.* New York: W. W. Norton.

Cooper, J. M. (1975). *Reason and human good in Aristotle.* Cambridge: Harvard University.

Elliot, C. (2003). *Better than well. American medicine meets the American dream.* New York: WW Norton.

Endresen, I., & Olweus, D. (in press). Participation in power sports and antisocial involvement in preadolescent and adolescent boys. *Journal of Child Psychology and Psychiatry.*

Evans, J. (2003). Physical education or health. A polemic or 'let them eat cake!'. *European Physical Education Review,* **9**(1), 87–101.

Evans, J., Davies, B., & Wright, J. (Eds.). (2004). *Body knowledge and control—studies in the sociology of physical education and health.* London: Routledge.

Hepworth, M., & Turner, B.S. (Eds.). (1991). *The body social process and cultural theory.* London: Sage.

Gard, M., & Wright, J. (2005). *The obesity epidemic. Science, morality and ideology.* London: Routledge.

Giddens, A. (1991): *Modernity and self-identity.* Cambridge: Polity.

Hardman, A.E., & Morris, J.N. (2003). *Physical activity and health—the evidence explained.* London: Routledge.

Johansson, T. (1998). *Den skulpterade kroppen. Gymkultur, friskvlård och estetik.* [The sculptured body: Fitness health and aesthetics.] Stockholm: Carlsson.

Kretchmar, R.S. (2005). *Practical philosophy of sport and physical activity* (2nd ed.). Champaign, IL: Human Kinetics.

Kruger, A., & Riordan, J. (Eds.). (1996). *The story of worker sport.* Champaign, IL: Human Kinetics.

Loland, N.W. (1999). *Body image and physical activity.* Unpublished PhD thesis. Norwegian University of Sport and Physical Education, Oslo, Norway.

MacAloon, J.J. (1981). *This great symbol. Pierre de coubertin and the origins of the modern olympic games.* Chicago: University of Chicago.

MacIntyre, A. (1984). *After virtue: A study in moral theory.* Notre Dame, IN: University of Notre Dame.

Mangan, J. A. (1981). *Athleticism in the Victorian and Edwardian public school: The emergence and consolidation of an educational ideology.* Cambridge: Cambridge University.

McNamee, M. (1995). Sporting practices, institutions, and virtues: A critique and restatement. *Journal of the Philosophy of Sport,* **XXII,** 61–82.

McNamee, M. & Jones, C. & Duda, J.L. (2003). Psychology, ethics and sports: Back to an Aristotelian 'museum of normalcy'. *International Journal of Sport and Health Science* **1**(1), 15–29.

Metheny, E. (1968). *Movement and meaning.* New York: McGraw-Hill.

Midgley, M. (1985). *Evolution as a religion,* London and New York: Methuen.

Midgley, M. (1993). The origin of ethics. In P. Singer (Ed.), *A companion to ethics.* Oxford: Blackwell.

Morgan W.J. (1994). *Leftist theories of sport: A critique and reconstruction.* Urbana: University of Illinois.

Repp, G. (2001). Verdiar og ideal for dagens friluftsliv: Nansen som foredome? [Values and ideals for today's outdoor activities: Nansen as a role model.] Unpublished PhD thesis. Norwegian University of Sport and Physical Education, Oslo, Norway.

Roberts, G. (Ed.). (2001). *Advances in motivation in sport and exercise.* Champaign, IL: Human Kinetics.

Sault, N. (Ed.). (1994). *Many Mirrors. Body image and social relations.* Rutgers, NJ: Rutgers University.

Schilling, C. (1993). *The body and social theory.* London: Sage.

Siedentop, D. (1994). *Sport education: Quality PE through positive sport experiences.* Champaign, IL: Human Kinetics.

Siedentop, D. (2002). Junior sport and the evolution of sport cultures. *Journal of Teaching in Physical Education,* **21,** 392–401.

Simon, R.L. (2003). Sports, relativism, and moral education. In J. Boxill (Ed.), *Sports ethics: An anthology* (pp. 14–28). Malden: Blackwell.

Synnott, A. (1993): *The body social. Symbolism, self, and society.* London. Routledge.

Turner, B.S. (1984). *The body and society. Explorations in social theory.* London: Blackwell.

Wachter, F.D. (1985). The symbolism of the healthy body. *Journal of the Philosophy of Sport,* **XI,** 56–62.

Waddington, I. (2000). *Sport, Health, and drugs—A critical, sociological perspective.* London: E & FN Spon.

Author Note: This paper was presented as the C. Lynn Vendien Lecture at the 75th Anniversary meeting of the AAKPE.

The author (AAKPE International Fellow) is with The Norwegian School of Sport Sciences, Oslo, Norway. E-mail: sigmund.loland@nih.no.

From *Quest,* vol. 58, pp. 60-70, National Association for Kinesiology & Physical Education in Higher Education - NAKPEHE. Reprinted by permission.

187

UNIT 8

The Profession of Teaching Today

Unit Selections

Key Points to Consider

- What is "expertise" in teaching? Be specific and use examples.

- Describe the learning needs of new teachers in terms of curriculum, instruction, assessment, management, school culture, and the larger community. How important is maintaining order?

- How would a teacher education program that is based on the premise of developing novice teachers as "transformative" urban educators place student teachers in urban classrooms?

- Why do teachers leave the profession? What can be done to solve schools' staffing problems?

Student Website

www.mhcls.com/online

Internet References

Further information regarding these websites may be found in this book's preface or online.

Canada's SchoolNet Staff Room
http://www.schoolnet.ca/home/e/

Teachers Helping Teachers
http://www.pacificnet.net/~mandel/

The Teachers' Network
http://www.teachers.net

Teaching with Electronic Technology
http://www.wam.umd.edu/~mlhall/teaching.html

The task of helping teachers to grow in their levels of expertise in the classroom falls heavily on those educators who provide professional staff development training in the schools. Meaningful staff development training is extremely important. Several professional concerns are very real in the early career development of teachers. Level of job security or tenure is still an issue, as are the concerns of first-year teachers and teacher educators. How teachers interact with students is a concern to all conscientious, thoughtful teachers.

We continue the dialogue over what makes a teacher "good." There are numerous external pressures on the teaching profession today from a variety of public interest groups. The profession continues to develop its knowledge base on effective teaching through ethnographic and empirical inquiry about classroom practice and teachers' behavior in elementary and secondary classrooms across the nation. Concern continues about how best to teach to enhance insightful, reflective student interaction with the content of instruction. We continue to consider alternative visions of literacy and the roles of teachers in fostering a desire for learning within their students.

All of us who live the life of a teacher are aware of those features that we associate with the concept of a good teacher. In addition, we do well to remember that the teacher/student relationship is both a tacit and an explicit one—one in which teachers' attitudes and emotional outreach are as important as students' responses to our instructional effort. The teacher/student bond in the teaching/learning process cannot be overemphasized. We must maintain an emotional link in the teacher/student relationship that will compel students to want to accept instruction and attain optimal learning. What then constitutes those most defensible standards for assessing good teaching?

The past decade has yielded much in-depth research on the various levels of expertise in the practice of teaching. We know much more now about specific teaching competencies and how they are acquired. Expert teachers do differ from novices and experienced teachers in terms of their capacity to exhibit accurate, integrated, and holistic perceptions and analyses of what goes on when students try to learn in classroom settings. We can now pinpoint some of these qualitative differences.

As the knowledge base of our professional practice continues to expand, we will be able to certify with greater precision what constitutes acceptable ranges of teacher performance based on more clearly defined procedures of practice, as we have, for example, in medicine and dentistry. Medicine is, after all, a practical art as well as a science—and so is teaching. The analogy in terms of setting standards of professional practice is a strong one. Yet the emotional pressure on teachers that theirs is also a performing art, and that clear standards of practice can be applied to that art, is a bitter pill to swallow for many. Hence, the intense reaction of many teachers against external competency testing and any rigorous classroom observation standards. The writing, however, is on the wall: The profession cannot hide behind the tradition that teaching is a special art, unlike all others, which cannot be subjected to objective observational standards, to aesthetic critique, or to a standard knowledge base. The public demands the same levels of demonstrable professional standards of practice as are demanded of those in the medical arts.

Likewise, we have identified certain approaches to working with students in the classroom that have been effective. Classroom practices such as cooperative learning strategies have won widespread support for inclusion in the knowledge base on teaching. The knowledge base of the social psychology of life in classrooms has been significantly expanded by collaborative research between classroom teachers and various specialists in psychology and teacher education. This has been accomplished by using anthropological field research techniques to ground theory of classroom practice into demonstrable phenomenological perspectives. Many issues have been raised—and answers found—by basic ethnographic field observations, interviews, and anecdotal record-keeping techniques to understand more precisely how teachers and students interact in the classroom. A rich dialectic is developing among teachers regarding the description of ideal classroom environments. The methodological insight from this research into the day-to-day realities of life in schools is transforming what we know about teaching as a professional activity and how to best advance our knowledge of effective teaching strategies.

Creative, insightful persons who become teachers will usually find ways to network their interests and concerns with other teachers and will make their own opportunities for creative teaching in spite of external assessment procedures. They acknowledge that the science of teaching involves the observation and measurement of teaching behaviors but that the art of teaching involves the humanistic dimensions of instructional activities, an alertness to the details of what is taught, and an equal alertness to how students receive it. Creative, insightful teachers guide class processes and formulate questions according to their perceptions of how students are responding to the material.

To build their aspirations, as well as their self-confidence, teachers must be motivated to an even greater effort for professional growth in the midst of these fundamental revisions. Teachers need support, appreciation, and respect. Simply criticizing them while refusing to alter social and economic conditions that affect the quality of their work will not solve their problems, nor will it lead to excellence in education. Not only must teachers work to improve their public image and the public's confidence in them, but the public must confront its own misunderstandings of the level of commitment required to achieve teacher excellence. Teachers need to know that the public cares about and respects them enough to fund their professional improvement in a primary recognition that they are an all-important force in the life of this nation. The articles in this unit consider the quality of education and the status of the teaching profession today.

Starting with the Soul

How can we nurture teachers for the long haul?
Stop putting subsistence strategies ahead of deeper needs.

SAM M. INTRATOR AND ROBERT KUNZMAN

When it comes to professional development for teachers, we think Abraham Maslow had it wrong.

We make this claim partly because it has rhetorical flourish, but more because we believe that professional development practices in our schools adhere to a philosophical orientation resembling Maslow's famous hierarchy of needs. Maslow (1943) posited that people are motivated by a certain order of needs: Our needs at the bottom of the pyramid, such as for food and safety, must be satisfied before we can pursue the higher needs of love, self-esteem, and self-actualization.

A similar logic holds sway in designing professional development. We assume that to he prepared for the reality of the classroom, teachers must first be trained in such subsistence strategies and techniques as classroom management, guided reading models, cooperative learning, and process writing. Once teachers learn these basic skills, we can address their higher needs by helping them reflect on their deeper purposes as educators. Yet as professional development workshops continue to emphasize content matter, technical skills, and pedagogical theory, many teachers are responding to these offerings with skepticism, impatience, and an underlying lack of enthusiasm (Farkas, Johnson, & Duffett, 2003).

We believe that effective professional development and the powerful teaching it can cultivate require an inversion of Maslow's pyramid. We need to begin with the soul of the enterprise, the passion and purpose that animate teachers' ongoing commitment to students and learning. Too many of our conversations about effective teaching focus on content, teaching methods, and learning outcomes. We neglect teachers themselves, the individuals who step in front of students each day committed to engaging them in the unpredictable and challenging process of learning.

The way to truly increase teachers' capacities and skills is to engage their souls.

Teachers yearn for professional development experiences that not only advance their skills and knowledge base but also simultaneously probe their sense of purpose and invite deliberation about what matters most in good teaching. Evoking the inner life of our teachers—that is, engaging teachers in activities that cultivate their capacity to teach with greater consciousness, self-awareness, and integrity—is a necessary condition for successful professional development.

Sustaining Growth for the Long Haul

Teaching day after day can exact a formidable toll on idealism, energy, and presence. No amount of professional development focused merely on technical proficiency will matter to teachers who are feeling overwhelmed, adrift in their mission, or disconnected from like-minded colleagues. You can be a lone ranger for only so long. Many teachers we work with describe their frustrations at professional development experiences focused on yet another curricular program, pedagogical innovation, or assessment tool. These teachers struggle most profoundly with how to keep learning and growing, and how to rekindle the sense of passion and purpose essential for maintaining such growth over the long haul. Schools need to better appreciate the role of professional development in sustaining teachers for the long term.

Models of Successful Growth

If we step back from our focus on schools and look at how any successful organization envisions professional development, it's not a stretch to say that groups who sustain their workers *do* turn Maslow's pyramid upside down.

Peter Senge's influential book *Schools That Learn* (2000) contends that if schools are to be successful in an increasingly competitive world—and if educators are to help students overcome systemic inequities—then schools must become organizations staffed byindividuals who know how to learn and grow. Senge lays out the Five disciplines of an organization that learns: personal mastery, shared vision, mental models, team learning, and systems thinking.

Senge asserts that instead of emphasizing the cultivation of technical skills or strategies, professional guidance should begin by helping each individual articulate a coherent personal vision. The primary challenge is to help people develop a set of practices that "keep their dreams whole while cultivating an awareness of the current reality around them" (p. 59). Effective reform and personal growth begin when individuals work to develop a deep understanding of their own thinking and when an organization comes together to foster a sense of shared purpose.

Two organizational researchers from Stanford (Collins & Porras, 1994) who examined what distinguishes an organization that is merely "good" from one that has achieved enduring success discovered that collective passion and mission were at the core of the latter kind of organization. Their findings dramatically support our contention. Organizations that flourish tend to be guided by what Collins and Porras call a "core ideology" that is infused among group members. The emergence of this ideology is not left to chance; the organization intentionally cultivates it by making it the centerpiece of regular professional development activities. This core ideology serves as the driving purpose and inspiration behind decision making, employee development, and resource allocation.

We have witnessed how effective professional development can be when it puts focus on teachers' inner life and reflection.

Andy Hargreaves and Michael Fullan (1998) speak more specifically about reforming the profession of teaching. They argue that education policymakers and administrators typically overlook the role that a teachers sense of purpose plays in education change. Educators will not change their practice, adopt new methods, or rethink their approach if they do not believe in the goals of the reform. Hargreaves and Fullan advocate going deeper, leading teachers into

> hard thinking and soul searching about the fundamental value and purpose of what we do as educators.... Going deeper, in other words, involves purpose, passion and hope. (p. 29)

Professional Development for Inner Reflection

Weaving a focus on purpose, passion, and hope into professional development is no small feat, particularly in the face of such constraints as lack of time, slashed budgets, and the pressures of standardized tests. The cumulative effect of these pressures creates a sense of short-term urgency that often pushes those responsible for professional development toward one-shot training sessions in an effort to support teachers. We have witnessed how much more effective professional development can be when it puts equal focus on teachers' inner life and reflection. The following two models foster this balance.

Courage to Teach

One professional development program that focuses on the "person in the profession" is Courage to Teach. This program seeks to renew and deepen an educators sense of purpose and to invite each teacher to explore what is important about his or her work. Parker Palmer piloted the program in 1994 with a group of Michigan teachers, and in 1997 the Fetzer Institute established the Center for Teacher Formation to develop and expand Courage to Teach. In this model, 20–30 teachers gather for a three-day retreat every academic quarter over a one- or two-year timespan. In groups and singly, participants explore what is at the heart of teaching for each of them, using personal stories, reflections on classroom practice, and insights from literature and various wisdom traditions. Consider a typical Courage to Teach group session:

> Twenty-five teachers and administrators sit in a circle, giving their full attention as an elementary teacher speaks passionately, and poignantly, about her love for her students and her commitment to reach each and every one of them. She goes on to tearfully describe the personal toll this is taking on her own lifecreeping guilt at not having enough time or emotional energy to give to her own family, hone-deep exhaustion, nonstop worrying about the safety of some of her students, the weariness of facing an always burgeoning mountain of papers and projects to grade, a sense of increasing isolation from friends and colleagues because there is simply no more to give. The listeners sit quietly, respectfully, as she finishes, each reflecting on their own version of her story....

> The next person to speak, a newly appointed principal, describes her recent attempts to mediate an explosive situation between a student, his parents, and a teacher. In the midst of helping the parties work through their threats and misunderstandings, she has become aware of the heavy burden of responsibility she carries, Yet in the telling of her story, she also is recognizing a growing confidence and inner sense of authority, grounded not in her role as a new principal hut in her personal integrity. And on around the circle it goes—each person relating stories and examples of how their complex journey as teachers and leaders has unfolded since the last time they were together a few months ago. (Jackson & Jackson, 2002)

As this vignette illustrates. Courage to Teach retreats do not focus on pedagogical methods or content knowledge, but rather on exploring personal and professional beliefs and how these beliefs affect our teaching. Facilitators also encourage participants to continue to reflect privately and with their colleagues during the school year. This inner exploration by teachers builds the foundation they need to engage with ongoing activities at the other end of Maslow's hierarchy—pedagogy, content, and policy.

Multi-Level Learning

Dutch researcher Fred Korthagen (2004) and his colleague Angelo Vasalos (Korthagen & Vasalos, 2005) have developed an approach to professional development that uses insights drawn from psychotherapy and research on human consciousness to support intensive reflection on teaching practice. This approach, which they call *Multi-level Learning,* invites teachers to think about specific events in their teaching and to engage in a process called *core reflection.* The idea behind core reflection is that a teacher's core personality—including his or her identity and mission—profoundly influences the way that teacher practices. Teachers reflect on their core qualities by exploring such questions as. Why did you become a teacher? and What do you see as your calling in the world?

Multi-level Learning also aims to help teachers develop specific coaching behaviors that support their colleagues as well as their students. Because mastering such behaviors requires practice, Multi-level Learning is not taught through a retreat, but through courses of about three days each spread out over two to three months. Participating teachers practice specific interventions for learning how inner realities influence their teaching behavior and apply these guidelines to their own learning and problem solving. Between course days, teachers practice using what they have learned with their students and also with their teaching colleagues. The approach is currently used to enhance teaching throughout the Netherlands, and there are plans to offer Multi-level Learning courses in the United States.

Improving Teaching

Programs like Courage to Teach and Multi-level Learning reconfigure the cycle that now dominates the landscape of professional development in education, ensuring that professional development begins by addressing those issues at the pinnacle of a teacher's professional life. Once teachers' purposes are clarified, their emotional resources rejuvenated, and their spirits nurtured, they will more effectively engage with their students, their colleagues, and their methods.

Teachers who took part in teacher renewal programs devoted more attention to framing good questions and listening to students.

Poutiatine (2005) reviewed the empirical research studies that have been conducted on teacher renewal programs and concluded that participation in such programs results in significant personal and professional growth. Teachers who took part in experiences like Courage to Teach or Multi-level Learning

- Articulated a renewed sense of passion for their work.
- Focused more on creating hospitable learning environments for students.
- Devoted more attention to framing good questions and listening to students.

- Clarified and renewed core beliefs about students and teaching.
- Committed to taking on leadership roles at their school sites.
- Deepened their appreciation for collegial relationships.

The process of telling about and reflecting on one's teaching life not only invites attitudinal change but also can stimulate changes in teaching behavior and classroom procedures. Professional development with this focus brings to the fore individuals' inner directives about teaching. With greater awareness of how those inner directives play out in their professional practice, teachers can make more discerning judgments on what's worth fighting for, letting go, or attending to in their daily teaching practice and in their long-term professional lives. As one Courage to Teach participant said.

> After I turned inward and asked myself what was really important in my teaching, 1 began altering the basic structure of my classroom. First I found myself asking more questions and really listening to what my students said. Then 1 started to alter the physical arrangement of the classroom, so that students were facing each other and engaging in more reflective exercises about the literature they read.

Working from the Inside Out

In a climate of standardized tests, prescribed curricular strategies, and high-stakes accountability, it is understandable that many administrators and policymakers might construe a focus on teachers' inner lives as a luxury, or at least as secondary to such issues as pedagogical technique and curriculum development.

But if we are right about needing to invert Maslow's pyramid, then professional guidance focused on rekindling teachers' sense of purpose is no luxury. Rather, it is the foundation that enables teachers to engage in deliberation on student learning and effective schools. Without laying the groundwork that creates purposeful, resilient teachers, any benefits of training centered around new procedures, techniques, and strategies will eventually fade. Overloaded teachers who work in isolation will not retain what it takes to do their most inspired teaching.

As one veteran kindergarten teacher said, comparing programs that focus on the inner life with more conventional forms of professional development,

> This approach did not offer a prepackaged right answer, technique, or style. There was not "something" that one could bring back to the classroom for Monday morning In a tangible way. Yet I would bring more of myself to the classroom each time.... Therefore, I was a better teacher. (Intrator &r Scribner, 1998, p. 33)

As it turns out, Maslow had it right. It is human nature to feel compelled to attend to our concrete, immediate needs before we aim higher. Efficient, programmatic professional development that focuses on content or classroom survival skills may appeal to schools because such programs seem to represent the education equivalent of food and safety But such programs alone don't ultimately answer teachers' deepest needs. If we want schools to sustain and develop effective teachers for the long term, and to foster both teacher growth and student learning, then we must recognize that the way to truly increase teachers' capacities and skills is to engage their souls.

References

Collins, J. C., & Porras, J. I. (1994). *Built to last: Successful habits of visionary companies.* New York: Harper Business.

Farkas, S., Johnson, J., & Duffett, A. (2003). *Stand by me: What teachers say about unions, merit pay and other professional matters.* New York: Public Agenda.

Hargreaves, A., & Fullan, M. (1998), *What's worth fighting for out there?* New York: Teachers College Press.

Intrator, S. M., & Scnbner, M. (1998). *An evaluation of the Courage to Teach program.* Kalamazoo, MI: Fetzer Institute.

Jackson, M., & Jackson, R. (2002). Courage to Teach: A retreat program of personal and professional renewal for educators. In S. M. Intrator (Ed.), *Stories of the Courage to Teach: Honoring the teacher's heart* (pp. 282–307). San Francisco: Jossey-Bass.

Konhagen, F. (2004). In search of the essence of a good teacher. *Teaching and Teacher Education, 20*(1), 77–97.

Kortbagen, F., & Vasalos, A. (2005). Levels in reflection: Core reflection as a means to enhance professional growth. Teachers and Teaching: *Theory and Practice, 11*(1), 47–71.

Maslow, A. (1943). A theory of human motivation. *Psychological Review, 50,* 370–396.

Poutiatine, M. (2005). *Finding common threads: Summary of the research on teacher formation and the Courage to Teach.* Bainbridge Island, WA: Center for Courage and Renewal.

Senge, P. M. (2000). *Schools that learn.* New York: Doubleday.

SAM M. INTRATOR is Assistant Professor of Education and Child Study in the Program in Urban Studies, Smith College, Northampton, Massachusetts; 413-585-3242; sintrato@email.smith.edu. **ROBERT KUNZMAN** is Professor of Curriculum and Instruction at Indiana University, Bloomington, Indiana; 812-856-8100; rkunzman@indiana.edu.

The Satisfactions of Teaching

How we teach is ultimately a reflection of why we teach.

Elliot Eisner

Each year, thousands of new teachers enter the field. Almost all seek deep satisfaction from the processes of teaching. Among the many satisfactions that exist, I would like to describe six.

Great Ideas

The first satisfaction pertains to the opportunity to introduce students to ideas that they can chew on for the rest of their lives. Great leaching traffics in enduring puzzlements, persistent dilemmas, complex conundrums, enigmatic paradoxes. On the other hand, certainty is closed, and closed streets don't interest the mind. Great ideas have legs. They take you somewhere.

Ideas can also provide a natural high. With them, you can raise questions that can't be answered. These unanswerable questions should be a source of comfort. They ensure that you will always have something to think about! But why do puzzlements provide satisfaction? Because they invite the most precious of human abilities to take wing. I speak of imagination, the neglected stepchild of American education.

Questions invite you in. They stimulate possibilities. They give you a ride. And the best ones are those that tickle the intellect and resist resolution.

Immortality

Second, teaching provides opportunities to reach out to students in ways that ensure our own immortality. The images of teachers past populate our minds and memories. Those teachers past sit on our shoulders, ready to identify infractions and offer praise for work well done. Their lives live in ours, and our lives live in theirs.

The immortality I speak of is private, rather than the public immortality that is garnered by only a few. You don't have to be a Mahatma Gandhi to be remembered or loved. Living in the memories of our students is no meager accomplishment.

The Performance

Third, teaching makes it possible to play your own cello. Despite the beliefs of some well-intended technocrats, there are no recipes for performance, no teacher-proof scripts to follow. Teaching well requires improvisation within constraints. Constraints there will always be, but in the end, teaching is a custom job.

We cannot separate what is learned from the manner in which it is taught. The arts teach us that form and content cannot be divided; how something is described affects what is described. Curriculum once enacted cannot be separated from the way it was taught because how it was taught influences how it is learned.

Artistry

Fourth, teaching provides ample opportunities for both artistry and memorable forms of aesthetic experience. After 40 years in the classroom, I still have vivid recollections of my sophomore high school art class in which I taught 35 adolescents—some eager and some not so eager. Those memories, in many ways, are among the most aesthetically satisfying and vivid I own.

Artistry is not restricted to the fine arts. Teaching well also depends on artistry. Artistry is the ability to craft a performance, influence its pace, shape its rhythms and tone so its parts merge into a coherent whole. Artistry in teaching depends on embodied knowledge. The body plays a central role; it tunes you in to what's going on. You come to feel a process that often exceeds the capacity of language to describe.

Why are these memories so vivid? The nature of long-term memory might have something to do with it, but I think there is more to it. The occasions we remember are those that were most meaningful to us. I still remember my 3rd grade teacher, Miss Eva Smith, calling my name from one end of the classroom to the other to tell me, in a voice that the whole class could hear, "Elliot, your work is getting better!" Oh, how I needed to hear that! I did not do well in school. Or Miss Purtle, who displayed my paintings on the walls of her classroom in a one-person show when I was in 4th grade. As a 9-year-old boy, I did not realize that I would carry these memories for the rest of my life.

A Passion for Learning

Fifth, teaching provides the occasions to share with others your deep affection for what you teach. When your eyes twinkle with

Mamie Till Mobley

"Miz Mobley" was my 5th grade teacher—and the mother of Emmett Till, who had been brutally murdered years before in Mississippi for whistling at a white woman. At the time of his death in 1955, the Chicago teenager was only 14 years old. Mamie Till Mobley took the brutal slaying of her son and turned it into a mission to end the ignorance that caused his death. Her son lives on in every one of her students.

Miz Mobley was more than just a teacher. She knew me before I knew myself. She showed me who I could be. Demanded that I be the best I could be. Made it impossible to do otherwise on her watch.

I remember how history came alive in her animated face. She loved teaching and learning and believed that the truth would indeed set us free. I watched, rapt, as she paced the front of the classroom, reading to us, questioning us, challenging us—loving us. I can still hear her voice, see her there in front of us, gesturing with glee as she led us to the promised land of intellectual enlightenment. Her plump brown face reflected our excitement back to us, magnified it a thousand times, creating an irresistible force.

I read ahead in textbooks, just imagining what she would sound like telling us these stories, showing us how to solve the problems, explaining how to read between the lines. I wanted her to shine on me the way she always did when she saw that I was trying, really listening.

You wanted to sit up close. You wanted to stand next to the fire. And most of all, when you left her, you wanted to take that light out into the world and shine it on everyone and everything. So the whole world could see and know and want to do better.

—Cynthia Dagnal Myron
Assistant Principal
Pistor Middle School
Tucson, Arizona

delight at the prospect of introducing students to what you love, you create a sense of contagion and convey your love of what you teach. Your passion for your subject is the sincerest and most powerful invitation you can extend.

Making a Difference

Finally, teaching provides the opportunity to discover that something you once said in class made a difference to a former student whom you happen to encounter 20 years later. Students you taught in years past recall to you an idea or a throw-away line you used so long ago that you can no longer remember it. Teaching is filled with such surprises. They reassure us that our contributions sometimes exceed those we can recall.

But the satisfactions, of teaching extend beyond the academic. Indeed, the most lasting contributions corne from saving lives, rescuing a child from despair, restoring a sense of hope, soothing discomfort. We remember these occasions longest because they matter. These occasions transcend academic interests. They address the human needs that all of us share.

The images of teachers past populate our minds and memories.

The Child Made Whole

At a time when schools are buffeted by performance standards and high-stakes testing, we must remember that the student is a whole person who has an emotional and social life, not just an intellectual one. And this is as true for graduate students in the grandest citadels of higher education as it is for students in elementary school. We teachers need to be more nurturing. The more we stress only what we can measure in school, the more we need to remember that not everything that is measurable matters, and not everything that matters is measurable. We need to pay attention to the whole child and address the whole child in our teaching practices. How we teach is related to achieving the deep satisfactions of teaching.

I have had the moments that I have described—and new teachers just starting out will have them, too. I envy them the journey. Oh, to be able to begin that journey once again today!

No such luck!

ELLIOT EISNER is Lee L. Jacks Professor of Education and Professor of Art at Stanford University, 485 Lasuen Mall, Stanford, CA 94305; eisner@stanford.edu.

Mayhem in the Middle: Why We Should Shift to K–8

Middle schools are increasingly switching to the K–8 model to improve student achievement. Ten strategies can help ease the transition.

CHERI PIERSON YECKE

In early 2005, the National Governors Association convened an education summit to address the dismal state of U.S. high schools. Nearly one-third of students eventually drop out, which annually costs the U.S. economy an estimated $16 billion in lost productivity. Although well intended, the solutions that many governors offered at the summit misidentified the cause of "high school" problems. Abundant evidence indicates that the seeds that produce high school failure are sown in grades 5–8 (National Center for Education Statistics, 2000). In far too many cases, U.S. middle schools are where student academic achievement goes to die.

As measured by international comparisons, such as the Trends in International Mathematics and Science Study (TIMSS), the achievement of U.S. students begins to plummet in middle school. And, as countless teachers and parents will attest, contemporary middle schools have become places where discipline is often lax and intermittent. Too many educators view middle school as an environment in which little is expected of students, either academically or behaviorally, on the assumption that students must place self-discipline and high academic expectations on hold until the hormone-driven storms of early adolescence have passed.

But if surging hormones truly drive middle school students' supposed lack of capacity to focus on academics, why does this phenomenon strike only in the United States? Other countries don't experience a similar decline in achievement at these grades. Something else is driving this precipitous drop in achievement. I propose that it is the anti-intellectualism inherent to the middle school concept.

To understand, we need to differentiate between middle schools and the middle school concept. Middle schools are simply organizational groupings, generally containing grades 6, 7, and 8. The middle school concept, on the other hand, is the belief that the purpose of these schools is to create students who are imbued with egalitarian principles; who are in touch with their political, social, and psychological selves; and who eschew competition and individual achievement to focus on identity development and perceived societal needs (Gallagher, 1991; Sicola, 1990; Toepfer, 1992). Although many U.S. middle schools are flourishing with strong and rigorous academic programs, the middle school concept—the notion that middle schools should be havens of socialization and not academies of knowledge—has wrought havoc on the intellectual development of many middle school students.

As any reform-minded superintendent or courageous middle school principal may tell you, reclaiming middle-grades schools from the clutches of the middle school concept has not been an easy task. In fact, this goal has been so elusive in some districts that the only alternative has been to eliminate the middle school grade configuration altogether, returning instead to the K–8 model.

Several urban school districts, such as Baltimore, Maryland, and Philadelphia, Pennsylvania, are now abandoning both the middle school concept and middle schools. By 2008, the number of K–8 schools in Philadelphia will have increased from 61 to 130. Baltimore has opened 30 K–8 schools in the last few years. Districts like Brookline, Massachusetts, and Cincinnati, Ohio, are now exclusively K–8. The goal for these districts is the same: to increase academic achievement and create an atmosphere more conducive to learning (Chaker, 2005).

Why K–8?

Although many U.S. educators embraced the middle school concept during the 1970s, 1980s, and 1990s, some educators refused to jump on the bandwagon. As a result, parents, teachers, and administrators at many schools that remained K–8 discovered anecdotally that their students demonstrated fewer behavioral problems and higher academic achievement than many students enrolled in middle schools.

School district leaders in Milwaukee, Wisconsin, Baltimore, and Philadelphia wanted to determine whether they could verify these anecdotal observations through research. The studies they undertook convinced them to accelerate a shift to the K–8 model in their districts.

The Milwaukee Study

Researchers in Milwaukee conducted a longitudinal analysis of 924 Milwaukee students who either attended K–8 schools or attended K–6 elementary schools and then proceeded to a middle school for 7th and 8th grade (Simmons & Blyth, 1987). The study controlled for race, ethnicity, teacher-student ratios, and levels of teacher education.

The researchers found that the students in the K–8 schools had higher academic achievement as measured by both grade point averages and standardized test scores, especially in math. These students also participated more in extracurricular activities, demonstrated greater leadership skills, and were less likely to be bullied than those following the elementary/middle school track. The authors concluded that the intimacy of the K–8 environment and the delay of the transition to a new school until students were more mature may have accounted for the discrepancy.

The Baltimore Study

In Baltimore, researchers undertook a longitudinal study of two cohorts of students: 2,464 students who attended K–5 schools and then went on to middle schools, and 407 students who attended K–8 schools (Baltimore City Schools, 2001). After controlling for baseline achievement, the researchers found that the students in the K–8 schools scored much higher than their middle school counterparts on standardized achievement measures in reading, language arts, and math. The students in the K–8 schools were also more likely to pass the required state tests in math. Further, more than 70 percent of the K–8 students were admitted into Baltimore's most competitive high schools, compared with only 54 percent of students from the middle schools (Baltimore City Schools, 2001).

The Philadelphia Study

Philadelphia carried its examination of the achievement of students progressing through either K–8 or middle schools into high school to determine whether academic gains or losses from either model were sustained over time. After controlling for student background, researchers analyzed achievement data from approximately 40 K–8 schools and 40 middle schools.

The analysis showed that the students in the K–8 schools had higher academic achievement than those in the middle schools and that their academic gains surpassed those of the middle school students in reading and science, with statistically higher gains in math (Offenberg, 2001).

Eleven percent more students from the K–8 schools were accepted into the most challenging high schools. Moreover, once in high school, the grade point averages of students who had attended K–8 schools were higher than those of former middle school students. Offenberg concluded, "As a group, K–8 schools are more effective than middle-grades schools serving similar communities" (2001, p. 28).

The study noted that one factor possibly contributing to these differences is the number of students at a specific grade level.

Although a K–8 school and a middle school might have the same total number of students, they are spread over more grades in the K–8 school, reducing the number of students in each grade. Offenberg's report suggests that as the number of students in a given grade increases, performance gains decrease.

Ten Strategies for Transition

I conducted site visits in all three school districts—Milwaukee, Baltimore, and Philadelphia—to see how the K–8 model was working and to gather advice for those interested in making the transition to the K–8 model. I selected one school in each district to visit on the basis of the school's ethnic diversity. The schools serve low-income urban students; each school faces its own demographic challenges. All three schools came to the K–8 model by a different route.

Contemporary middle schools have become places where discipline is often lax and intermittent.

Humboldt Park K–8 School in Milwaukee shifted from K–5 to K–8 a few years ago. Its student population is notably diverse: Approximately 35 percent of students are Hmong, 30 percent are white, 15 percent are Hispanic, and 15 percent are black. Hamilton Elementary/Middle School in Baltimore has been a K–8 school for more than 20 years; its student body is 75 percent black. The Julia de Burgos School in Philadelphia, originally a 6–8 middle school, expanded downward to add grades K–5; its student body is 89 percent Hispanic.

In all three schools, staff and administrators were committed to meeting the needs of underprivileged students and believed that they could best accomplish this in a K–8 setting. Their advice, along with feedback from students and parents, suggests 10 strategies that can ease the transition to a K–8 model.

Strategy 1: Include parents in the process.

To ensure the success of the K–8 model, parents should participate in all aspects of the planning process. Policy decisions concerning such varied issues as curriculum, dress code, and behavioral expectations call for parental input. The most academically successful school that I visited, Humboldt Park K–8 School in Milwaukee, also has the most active and organized parents. Parents initiated the move to transition Humboldt Park into a charter school because they were concerned that district policies might undermine the schools academic program. This high level of engagement was not a reflection of higher socioeconomic status: 70 percent of students at Humboldt Park come from low-income homes.

Strategy 2: Add higher rather than lower grades.

Incrementally adding higher grades to shift an elementary school to a K–8 school appears to be a smoother process than adding lower grades to a middle school. This approach seems to minimize grade-level imbalances and necessitate fewer building modifications. Faculty members at Humboldt Park unanimously agreed that when adding grades 6, 7, and 8, schools should add only one grade each year. This gives time for students, faculty, support staff, and administration to adjust.

Strategy 3: Ensure grade-level balance.

Attaining demographic balance among the various grade levels should be a priority. Having too many older or younger students means that the needs of the dominant group can drive school policies and set the school tone. For example, one schoolwide policy limited bathroom passes because some of the middle-grades students used them to roam the halls. However, because younger students tend to use the bathroom more frequently than older students do, lower-grades teachers challenged this policy

If transition logistics require a temporary imbalance, schools should ensure that staff members are aware of the undue weight that the overrepresented grades might bring to a school and remind them that the imbalance is only temporary.

Strategy 4: Make 6th grade a transition year.

Moving from the elementary to the upper-grades section of the school requires students to become familiar with a different location and learn rules that often give them greater freedom. Because this change usually occurs in 6th grade, it would be helpful to provide flexibility as students make the transition. Retaining some elements of the elementary school—such as recess, classroom learning centers, or walking in lines during classroom changes—may help 6th grade function as a bridge between the elementary and middle grades.

Strategy 5: Establish a strict transfer policy.

District officials need to acknowledge the challenges that transfer students bring to schools. Involuntary transfers are harder for schools to deal with and typically occur when the district administration decides to relocate students who have had difficulties elsewhere. Philadelphia wisely handles this issue through an alternative program that accommodates students with the most serious discipline problems. Baltimore has no such program in place, leaving staff members and faculty frustrated as they struggle to balance teaching students who do not have serious behavior problems with rehabilitating those who do.

Twenty-five percent of children in 4th through 8th grade care for themselves regularly either before or after school.

—America's Children:
Key National Indicators of Well-Being, 2005

Voluntary transfers present other challenges. Students who arrive from schools that have less structure and lower academic standards might find the transition to a challenging K–8 setting difficult. Humboldt Park addresses this issue by requiring mandatory after-school lessons to help transfer students catch up.

Schools can also provide an opportunity for students to receive remediation in the summer before the school year starts. Either way, schools should establish a policy that helps transfer students adjust to the level of work required.

Strategy 6: Modify facilities.

A school transitioning into a K–8 structure may need to make certain physical modifications to adapt its facility to students of various ages. For example, elementary schools adding middle grades will need to add computers in the library and include books appropriate for middle-grades students. If the library has limited space, the school may need to create a separate computer lab. The school might also consider adding lockers for older students or building a more advanced science lab. For any newly K–8 school, the cafeteria will most likely require scheduling changes and menu revisions to adapt to an influx of older or younger students. Moreover, making the transition from a middle school to a K–8 school entails creating centers and "nooks" in primary classrooms and modifying restrooms by lowering toilets and sinks.

In addition, designating a separate building wing for the upper grades provides older students with some time on their own and reduces unsupervised interactions with younger students. Humboldt Park in Milwaukee does a good job of this. In contrast, Philadelphia's Julia de Burgos School, which of the three schools observed had the least separation among its students, reported the most challenges with interactions between older and younger students.

Strategy 7: Have high expectations for both academics and behavior.

High academic achievement rarely happens in an undisciplined environment. Of the schools I visited, Baltimore's Hamilton had the most behavior problems. This was also the only school in which student achievement declined in the upper grades. In contrast, Milwaukee's Humboldt Park had the strictest discipline policy. There, 75 percent of students leave kindergarten reading at the 2nd grade level.

Policies establishing academic and behavioral norms—such as consistent expectations regarding homework or dress code—will set the K–8 school's tone for years to come, and parents should be involved in drafting them. Behavioral expectations don't need to be uniform throughout the school. Schools should provide some flexibility for upper-grades students, giving them greater freedom and responsibility as they prepare to transition to high school. For example, most K–8 schools allow upper-grades students to change classes independently as opposed to walking in lines.

Strategy 8: Decide on the academic approach.

The schools that I visited in Baltimore and Milwaukee organize their upper-grades teachers by academic department. The teachers at Julia de Burgos School in Philadelphia initially sought that structure but now prefer the self-contained approach.

The self-contained model, in which students stay with the same teacher for the core subjects of reading, math, science, and social studies, appears to foster better teacher-student relationships and a more nurturing environment. But it also means that teachers must prepare for four subjects instead of one, and it may force them into unfamiliar fields in which they have received no specialized training. The departmentalized setting, in which each teacher is a specialist in one or more areas, is more likely to produce higher academic achievement but provides fewer opportunities to counsel and mentor students.

It is fairly well established that strong subject-area knowledge in teachers correlates with higher student achievement (Whitehurst, 2002). It is therefore unfortunate that in 2004, half of Philadelphia's middle-level teachers failed exams assessing their content knowledge (Snyder & Mezzacappa, 2004). Although colleges of education might bear some of the blame, these gaps might also reflect a shift away from academics that has characterized much of the middle school movement's troubled history.

U.S. middle-level teachers with subject-specific certificates appear to be a dying breed. In 1980, 80 percent of middle-level teachers held subject-specific certificates, but that number had dropped to 52 percent by 2000 (Clark, Petzko, Lucas, & Valentine, 2001). One study shows that during the 1999–2000 school year, alarming percentages of middle-grades teachers lacked a college major or certification in the areas in which they taught: 58 percent lacked a major or certification in English, 57 percent in science, 69 percent in math, 71 percent in history, and 93 percent in physical science (National Center for Education Statistics, 2002). Another recent study found that only 22 percent of middle school math teachers surveyed indicated that they had majored in math, and fewer than half had a teaching certificate in that subject (Loveless, 2004).

K–8 planners need to find the right balance. A truly compassionate education cannot allow the desire for a nurturing environment to trump access to a rigorous, well-taught curriculum.

Strategy 9: Provide greater access to advanced courses and electives.

Because the upper grades have fewer students, K–8 schools have difficulty offering advanced subjects—such as foreign language classes or advanced math—that can enrich a curriculum. However, schools should not deny challenging academic opportunities to their students because of their particular grade configuration. One solution is to work collaboratively with other K–8 schools in the district, or even with the local high school, to have itinerant teachers come to the school to offer such classes. This may require some flexibility in scheduling. Another option might involve distance learning.

A truly compassionate education cannot allow the desire for a nurturing environment to trump access to a rigorous, well-taught curriculum.

Above all, students need access to higher levels of math. A study from the U.S. Department of Education found that the academic intensity and quality of a students high school curriculum were the most important factors in determining whether students completed a bachelors degree (Adelman, 1999). Students cannot take rigorous courses in high school—especially advanced math courses—if they have not prepared themselves for this challenging work in their middle grades.

Strategy 10: Provide greater access to extracurricular opportunities.

With a larger student body in a given age group, middle schools can offer band, choir, and sports activities to a degree that K–8 schools cannot. However, several K–8 schools working together might field a team or create a band or choir. Schools could also coordinate extracurricular activities after school for all students in grades 6, 7, and 8, regardless of whether they attend a K–8 school or a middle school.

A number of districts—even those on the cutting edge of the K–8 movement—are guilty of lumping K–8 schools with elementary schools in various administrative funding classifications. This practice often rules out funding for extracurricular activities.

Moving Forward

The K–8 model is no silver bullet for middle school reform, but it deserves consideration. In this era of flexible education options, K–8 schools and middle schools can coexist—provided that middle schools embrace standards and accountability.

C. S. Lewis once wrote,

> If you are on the wrong road, progress means doing an about-turn and walking back to the right road; and in that case, the man who turns back soonest is the most progressive man. Going back is the quickest way on. (1943)

This summarizes the key strategy for undoing the damage that the middle school concept has done to U.S. education: We must *go back* to find scientifically based research that reveals the strengths or weaknesses of specific education practices, go back to proven methodologies, and go back to parents and empathetically listen to their concerns.

The key to renewing middle-grades education in the United States is to treat it as education rather than as personal adjustment. That means having high academic standards, a coherent curriculum, effective instruction, strong leadership, results-based accountability, and sound discipline. That formula has begun to pay off in the primary grades. It can pay off in the middle grades as well.

References

Adelman, C. (1999). *Answers in the toolbox: Academic intensity, attendance patterns, and bachelor's degree attainment.* Washington, DC: U.S. Department of Education.

Baltimore City Schools, Division of Research, Evaluation, and Accountability. (2001). *An examination of K–5, 6–8 versus K–8 grade configurations.* Baltimore: Author.

Chaker, A. M. (2005, April 6). Middle school goes out of fashion. *The Wall Street Journal*.

Clark, D., Petzko, V., Lucas, S., & Valentine, J. (2001, Nov. 1). *Research findings from the 2000 National Study of Leadership in Middle Level Schools*. Paper presented at the National Middle School Association annual conference, Washington, DC.

Gallagher, J. J. (1991). Education reform, values, and gifted students. *Gifted Child Quarterly, 35*(1).

Lewis, C. S. (2001). *Mere Christianity* (Book One, Chapter Five) (Rev. ed.). New York: HarperCollins.

Loveless, T. (2004, November). *The 2004 Brown Center Report on American Education: How well are American students learning?* Washington, DC: The Brookings Institution.

National Center for Education Statistics. (2000). *Mathematics and science education in the eighth grade: Findings from the Third international Mathematics and Science Study*. Washington, DC: Author.

National Center for Education Statistics. (2002). *Qualifications of the public school teacher workforce: Prevalence of out-of-field teaching 1987–88 to 1999–2000*. Washington, DC: Author.

Offenberg, R. M. (2001). The efficacy of Philadelphia's K-to-8 schools compared to middle grades schools. *Middle School Journal, 32*(4), 23–29.

Sicola, P. K. (1990). Where do gifted students fit? *Journal for the Education of the Gifted, 14*(1).

Simmons, R., & Blyth, D. (1987). *Moving into adolescence: The impact of pubertal change and school context*. New York: Aldine de Gruyter.

Snyder, S., & Mezzacappa, D. (2004, March 23). Teachers come up short in testing. *Philadelphia Inquirer*.

Toepfer, C. F. (1992). Middle level school curriculum: Defining the elusive. In J. L. Irvin (Ed.), *Transforming middle-level education; Perspectives and possibilities*. Needham Heights, MA: Allyn and Bacon.

Whitehurst, G. J. (2002, March 5*). Research on teacher preparation and professional development*. Speech presented at the White House Conference on Preparing Tomorrow's Teachers. Available: **www.ed.gov/admins/tchrqual/learn/preparing teachersconference/whitehurst.html**

CHERI PIERSON YECKE (chancellor@fldoe.org) is Chancellor of K–12 Public Schools for the Florida Department of Education and author of two studies on the need for middle school reform: *The War Against Excellence: The Rising Tide of Mediocrity in America's Middle Schools* (Praeger, 2003) and *Mayhem in the Middle*: *How Middle Schools Have Failed America—And How to Make Them Work* (Thomas B. Fordham Institute, 2005).

Guess Again: Will Changing the Grades Save Middle-Level Education?

Educators need to look beyond grade configuration to the real problems plaguing middle schools.

JAMES BEANE AND RICHARD LIPKA

Judging by some recent newspaper headlines, middle schools in the United States are once again under attack: "Mayhem in the Middle," "Are Middle Schools Bad for Kids?," and "Muddle in the Middle," we read. Middle schools have been accused of everything from stunting students' academic growth to ruining their self-esteem. What's going on here?

Policymakers and the public have always had an uneasy relationship with middle schools, just as they have had with young adolescents themselves. No one seems to know quite what to do with either one. No wonder, then, that the history of middle schools has been a roller coaster of reform. In the latest dip, school officials in several large urban areas, such as Baltimore, Maryland, and Philadelphia, Pennsylvania, beleaguered by poor test scores and unmanageable student behavior, have decided to abandon 5–8 and 6–8 grade arrangements and return to K–8 schools. As a result, the media and middle school critics have gleefully declared middle schools a failure. That obituary comes as something of a surprise to many middle-level educators who thought their work was headed in a healthier direction. Could they have been so wrong?

The Middle School Concept

In the midst of all these ups and downs, middle-level education has been the subject of considerable research. Between 1991 and 2003, more than 3,700 studies related to middle schools were published (Hough, 2003). Out of these and earlier studies, a set of principles and practices generally known as the *middle school concept* emerged. Most middle-level advocates turn to two sources for a definition of the concept: the Carnegie Council on Adolescent Developments *Turning Points: Preparing American Youth for the 21st Century* (1989) and the National Middle School Associations recently updated policy statement, *This We Believe: Successful Schools for Young Adolescents* (2003). According to these two sources, high-quality middle-level schools should

- Improve academic achievement for all students.
- Understand young adolescence.
- Provide a challenging and integrative curriculum.
- Create supportive and safe environments through such structures as small teaching teams.
- Ensure better teacher preparation for the middle grades.
- Improve relationships with families and communities.

Interestingly, virtually all iterations of the middle school concept recognize that high-quality schools for young adolescents exist within a variety of grade configurations, including 5–8, 6–8, 7-8, K–8, 7–12, and K–12. And obviously, most of the components of the middle school concept are appropriate for any grade level. Why, then, would advocates of the concept specifically tie it to the middle grades? Quite simply, because they intended to implement it as an alternative to the impersonal, inequitable, and irrelevant structures and curriculums that characterized many junior high schools (and still, today, many middle schools).

Advocates of the middle school concept usually argue their case on the grounds that this approach is developmentally responsive to young adolescents. For example, they link small teaching teams to young adolescents' need for a sense of belonging and security; improved family relationships to their need for a support system through puberty's ups and downs; an integrative curriculum to their need for meaningful contexts for learning; and more appropriate teacher preparation to the many ways in which young adolescents differ from younger children and older adolescents.

Meanwhile, some studies have looked at what happens when schools actually implement the components of the middle school concept as a complete set, over time and with high fidelity (Anfara & Lipka, 2003; DePascale, 1997; Felner et al, 1997). The results? Increases in academic achievement and decreases in behavior problems, including among students who typically struggle with both. Moreover, various practices promoted by the middle school concept have independently shown considerable promise for improving achievement, engagement, and relationships: small teaching teams, authentic instruction, integrative curriculum, service learning, and affective mentorship (Beane & Brodhagen, 2001; Juvonen, Le, Kaganoff, Augustine, & Constant, 2004; National Middle School Association Research Committee, 2003).

But therein lies the real problem with the middle school concept: On the whole, its components have *not* been well implemented over time and rarely as a complete set of principles and practices. Most often, the title of "middle school" has had less to do with implementing the concept and more to do with changing the name on the front of the building.

In the unlikely event that the media and critics retract their obituary for the middle school concept, they might well title their correction "Sorry, Mistaken Identity." For they have indeed mistaken the practices found in too many middle schools for the middle school concept itself. But then, so have many middle-level educators, who thought that simply putting grades 5–8 or 6–8 together without implementing the middle school concept would ensure a better education for young adolescents. Both groups were wrong.

What Research Really Shows

The 5–8 and 6–8 grade configurations most widely associated with middle schools emerged mainly as a result of two trends that took place in the 1960s and 1970s. First, as baby boomers poured into elementary schools, school districts found that moving the 5th and/or 6th grades to a "middle school" was more cost-efficient than building extra elementary schools. Second, in many northern cities and southern states, the new configuration helped move students out of segregated neighborhood K–8 schools into more integrated middle or intermediate schools (George, 1988). Advocates of reform at the middle level argued for aspects of the middle school concept from the start, but those arguments would not have produced the large-scale move to middle schools without the presence of such factors as overcrowding and desegregation.

Given the relatively poor record of full implementation of the middle school concept and the enormous difficulties facing urban schools, it is not surprising that urban school officials would envision returning grades 6–8 to the elementary school. Moreover, some evidence seems to support the K–8 model with regard to enhancing academic achievement, encouraging parental involvement, and reducing affective difficulties for students in this age group (Abella, 2005; Baltimore City Schools, 2001; Juvonen et al., 2004; Offenberg, 2001; Simmons & Blyth, 1987).

At the same time, however, the research comparing K–8 and middle school configurations includes important caveats. First, although achievement test results for students in large urban districts may favor K–8 arrangements, such scores still fall short of state and national averages (Balfanz, Spiridakis, & Neild, 2002), and the K–8 advantage seems to disappear in the 9th grade (Abella, 2005). Second, the key difference between K–8 schools and middle schools seems to be the smaller size of the former, enabling teachers, students, and families to build better relationships. Third, virtually all of the studies caution that the middle schools involved have not done a good job of imple-

menting aspects of the middle school concept. Fourth, K–8 schools do not necessarily outperform middle schools when both serve high-poverty students (Balfanz et al., 2002).

We are left with two key points. First, the advantages of K–8 schools over middle schools in urban areas reside largely in smaller class and school size, which enable these schools to support better relationships with all of their constituencies. K–8 schools remove the transition from elementary to middle school, which for unexplained reasons seems to coincide with decreasing parental involvement both in school and in the lives of their children. Second, however much improved achievement test scores appear in urban K–8 schools, such scores still do not rise to state and national averages for this age group. This is not difficult to understand when we remember that a schools poverty index is the strongest correlate and best predictor of achievement test scores (Bracey, 1997). And no matter how much the media and middle school critics want us to believe otherwise, school grade configuration is not a remedy for the rising tide of poverty in our nation's urban centers.

The Fuss Over Grade Levels

Proponents of the middle school concept have long cautioned against equating the concept with grade configurations. Almost 20 years ago, Paul George (1988) suggested that

> slavish adherence to one grade configuration or another continues to obscure the need for substantive change and draws our attention away from potentially viable alternatives, such as K–8 and K–12. (p. 17)

In the early 1990s, Lounsbury and Clark (1991), two widely known middle school advocates, reported that 8th graders in K–8 schools reported more favorable experiences than their counterparts in 6–8 schools. *Middle School Journal* published Offenbergs Philadelphia study showing higher achievement in K–8 schools than in middle schools (2001). And the September 2005 issue of that journal focused almost entirely on research and policy questions related to K–8 schools.

No matter which grade configuration school districts choose, the most important decision is what kind of education they will offer young adolescents. Research on both middle schools and K–8 schools clearly suggests the importance of creating small learning communities, high-quality relationships, and strong transition supports. It may well be that attaching grades 6–8 to the elementary side of schooling proves more effective in implementing these principles and practices than does treating these grades as a junior version of high school. In this case, moving to K–8 schools might actually save the middle school concept from the more dangerous trend toward inflicting on middle schools the kind of structures more usually associated with junior high school setups, such as tracking and strict subject departmentalization.

Those considering K–8 schools must understand, however, that this configuration comes with its own set of potential problems. For example, resource reductions accompanying smaller middle-grades enrollments would likely reduce the number of specialized electives, services, accelerated courses, and extracurricular activities that some parents want for their children. And creating neighborhood K–8 schools may actually add to the resegregation of urban schools already in progress. Finally, there is certainly no guarantee that the middle grades placed within a K–8 school will implement all or any aspects of the middle school concept shown to work well with young adolescents (McEwin, Dickinson, & Jacobson, 2005).

Looking Beyond Configuration

The large urban school districts at the center of the move toward K–8 schools are complicated systems. Their sheer size may well work against creating the smaller school communities that the middle school concept promotes. Moreover, diminishing state and federal resources make school success more difficult for urban students, many of whom already suffer the injustice of having to live in poverty (Kozol, 2005). And the moves to punish struggling schools and students, sterilize the curriculum, and demand unattainable test results come down especially hard on large urban districts.

School grade configuration is not a remedy for the rising tide of poverty in our nation's urban centers.

It is misleading for middle school critics to suggest that poor achievement and difficult conditions in our urban schools result from a particular school configuration. This sleight-of-hand rhetoric does a disservice to young adolescents and their schools by diverting attention from the powerful effects of poverty and the unsavory resegregation of our nations communities and schools (Kozol, 2005).

Rather than debate which grade configuration is best for the middle grades, we would be better off expending our energy creating a curriculum that intellectually engages and inspires young adolescents, pushing for organizing structures that support high-quality relationships, and finding better ways to reach out to families and communities. If we really want to do something worthwhile for young adolescents, we should work to overcome the poverty and prejudice that relentlessly work against many of these students' chances for success inside school and for a decent life outside it.

References

Abella, R, (2005). The effects of small K–8 centers compared to large 6–8 schools on student performance. *Middle School Journal, 37*(1), 29–35.

Anfara, V., & Lipka, R. (2003). Relating the middle school concept to school achievement. *Middle School Journal, 35*(1), 24–32.

Balfanz, R., Spiridakis, K., & Neild, R. (2002). *Will converting high-poverty middle schools, facilitate achievement gains?* Philadelphia: Philadelphia Education Fund.

Baltimore City Schools, Division of Research, Evaluation, and Accountability. (2001). *An examination of K–5, 6–8 versus K–8 grade configurations.* Baltimore; Author.

Beane, J., & Brodhagen, B. (2001). Teaching in middle schools. In V. Henderson (Ed.), *Handbook of research on teaching* (4th ed.) (pp. 1157–1174). Washington, DC: American Educational Research Association,

Bracey, G. (1997). *Selling the record straight; Responses to misconceptions about public education in the United States.* Alexandria, VA: ASCD.

Carnegie Council on Adolescent Development. (1989). *Turning points: Preparing American youth for the 21st century.* New York: Author.

DePascale, C. (1997*). Education reform restructuring network: Impact documentation report.* Cambridge, MA: Data Analysis and Testing Associates.

Felner, R. D., Jackson, A. W., Kasak, D., Mulhall, P., Brand, S., & Flowers, N. (1997). The impact of school reform for the middle years. *Phi Delia Kappan, 78*(7), 528–550.

George, P. (1988, September). Education 2000: Which way the middle school? *The Clearing House, 62,* 17.

Hough, D. (2003). *R3 = Research, rhetoric, and reality: A study of studies addressing NMSA's 21st Century Research Agenda and This We Believe.* Westerville, OH: National Middle School Association.

Juvonen, J., Le, Y., Kaganoff, T., Augustine, C., & Constant, L. (2004). *Focus on the wonder years: Challenges facing the American middle school.* Santa Monica, CA: RAND Corporation.

Kozol, J. (2005). *The shame of a nation: The restoration of apartheid schooling in America.* New York: Random House.

Lounsbury, J., & Clark, D. (1991). *Inside eighth grade: From apathy to excitement.* Reston, VA: National Association of Secondary School Principals.

McEwin, K., Dickinson, T., & Jacobson, M. (2005). How effective are K–8 schools for young adolescents? *Middle School Journal, 37*(1), 24–28.

National Middle School Association, (2003). *This we believe: Successful schools for young adolescents.* Westerville, OH: Author.

National Middle School Association Research Committee. (2003). *Research and resources in support of This We Believe.* Westerville, OH: National Middle School Association.

Offenberg, R. M. (2001). The efficacy of Philadelphia's K-to-8 school compared to middle grades schools. *Middle School Journal, 32*(4), 23–29.

Simmons, R., & Blyth, D. (1987). *Moving into adolescence: The impact of pubertal change and school context.* New York; Aldine de Gruyter.

JAMES BEANE (jbeane@nl.edu) is Professor in the Department of Interdisciplinary Studies in Curriculum at National-Louis University, Milwaukee, Wisconsin, campus, and author of *A Reason to Teach* (Heinemann, 2005).

RICHARD LIPKA is Professor in the Department of Special Services and Leadership Studies at Pittsburg State University, Pittsburg, Kansas.

From *Educational Leadership,* April 2006, pp. 26-30. Reprinted by permission of the Association for Supervision and Curriculum Development. Copyright © 2006 by ASCD. All rights reserved. The Association for Supervision and Curriculum Development is a worldwide community of educators advocating sound policies and sharing best practices to achieve the success of each learner. To learn more, visit ASCD at www.ascd.org

Developing Social Justice Educators

**In a teacher inquiry group, educators collectively examine
how to teach for social justice.**

Jeffrey M. R. Duncan-Andrade

Although many teachers in high-poverty urban schools struggle to meet the needs of their students, some gifted educators achieve consistent success. What enables some teachers to effectively reach the same students whom other teachers can't seem to reach? Three highly effective teachers recently articulated their teaching philosophies as they participated in a teacher inquiry group at Power Elementary School[1] in South Central Los Angeles.

As these effective teachers shared the philosophies guiding their instructional practices, curriculum designs, and relationships with students, they made it clear that the strength of their teaching came from a focus on student-empowering social justice pedagogy. The inquiry group shed light on two questions: "How can a focus on teaching for social justice energize teaching and learning in an urban school?" and How can urban schools create a formal space for teachers to investigate and question their philosophies and beliefs and learn from colleagues who provide relevant, socially transformative instruction?"

A Social Justice Philosophy

I proposed the teacher inquiry group at Power Elementary as a three-year program. Its purpose was to support the development of student-empowering social justice themes in teachers' practice. Seven teachers signed up to participate. All were fairly new to teaching when we began; the most senior had six years of experience. At the outset of the program, their students' test scores covered the schools achievement span: Three of their classes consistently scored in the top quartile of the school, two were in the middle, and two were in the bottom quartile.

How can a focus on teaching for social justice energize teaching and learning in an urban school?

Ms. Grant, Ms. Kim, and Mr. Truong, the teachers with the highest student test scores in the group, all subscribe to Paulo Freire's idea that effective education for marginalized groups must employ a *liberatory pedagogy*—that is, one that aims to help students become critical change agents who feel capable of and responsible for addressing social injustices in their communities (Freire, 1970). Ms. Grant, a 4th grade teacher, explains.

> Racial, cultural, ethnic, and socioeconomic status has no effect on students' abilities to acquire knowledge. Schools should provide students with the fundamental skills and ideas necessary to develop within the system while also preparing them to transform the system.

Mr. Truong, a 5th grade teacher, cites a series of problems with the institutional culture of urban schools:

> The first tiling I wonder about urban schools is, Where is the love? Even a surface-level analysis of our school reveals that students dislike the school; they are unengaged und exhibit resistance. The environment is not child-centered. This is reflected in the scripted or mandated programming ... a set of decontextualized academic exercises, an overemphasis on basic skills. Students have become machines; they are not allowed to question the relevance of what they are learning. They are forced to perform for the sake of the task at hand. In short, our schools reflect a prison system mentality, a lot like the conditions in urban communities.

Mr. Truong believes that he can best care for his students by giving them the academic and critical skills to act as change agents in their communities. He teaches his students using what he calls the "4Es" of emancipator)'pedagogy:

- *Engage.* Provide culturally responsive teaching that validates students' funds of knowledge.
- *Experience.* Expose students to various possible realities by presenting narratives that show the perspectives of those often unheard in society.
- *Empower.* Use a critical and transformative pedagogy to give students a sense of agency, both individual and collective, to act on the conditions in their lives.

- *Enact.* Create opportunities for students to act out their growing sense of agency, learning from and reflecting on their successes and struggles.

Ms. Kim also develops traditional academic skills by paying attention to students' cultures, critical thinking, and agency:

> My practice begins with the recognition of the students' cultural capital: language, culture, family, interests, and so on.… My goal is to offer counter-discourse to the traditional curriculum and to incorporate this in a fluid, meaningful, and empowering way. It is important that my pedagogy identity' forms of oppression—and not ambiguously, either, or else students feel like things cannot change.

These three successful teachers are keenly aware of the dire conditions in which many of their students live. They believe that they should not ignore these conditions, but instead should talk about them in the classroom. They design their pedagogy to empower students with tools for recognizing, naming, analyzing, and confronting the most acute social conditions facing them: poverty, racism, violence, and inequality.

To these teachers, success means both raising students' test scores and developing students' ability to think critically and act constructively. They insist that one without the other is unlikely to reduce the opportunity gap for urban students. They do not accept urban poverty as an excuse for underachievement by either teachers or students. Instead, they see unequal material conditions as a set of constraints that students can and should transform.

The philosophies of social justice embraced by these educators go beyond the traditional narrative, which sees education as a vehicle to escape financially impoverished communities. These teachers view education as a vehicle to invest in that can improve conditions in urban areas. They want their students to become college graduates who will come back and transform their urban communities. Less successful urban teachers tend to have more modest ambitions, such as wanting their students to study for tests, behave well in class, and persist in school.

Social Justice Teachers in Action

Ms. Grant

Although Ms. Grant does not approve of the school district s scripted reading program (Open Court), she rejects the arguments of those teachers who claim that they are pedagogically handcuffed by it. She develops social justice-oriented units that incorporate media and critical literacy into the scripted Open court themes.

For example, as her class worked with the program's "Mysteries of Medicine" unit, she had students view the popular film *John Q,* discuss inequities in the health care system, and follow up with writing assignments and poster projects examining s how these issues affected their own lives and the lives of other people in their community. In these assignments, students developed individual and collective policy positions on health care issues.

After the class participated in these learning activities, class members significantly raised their scores in three of the reading program's measured areas: applications, strategies, and conventions. But Ms. Grant is especially proud of her students' transformative thinking about their own community, A typical student, D.T., not only made notable academic gains but also connected what he learned to local conditions. He wrote,

> I went to Ralph's and I seen strikers. One striker's son had a broken arm, and they was on strike because they didn't have enough health care. And it made me think about *John Q,* when his son didn't have enough money to get a new heart. It made me feel bad because a lot of people have more health care than the people who are on strike.

Ms. Kim and Mr. Truong

Ms. Kim is only in her third year as a teacher, but her students have some of the highest math and literacy test scores in the school. She attributes this success to three things: her social justice pedagogy, her collaboration with colleagues, and the fact that she was able to stay with the same students through 2nd and 3rd grades.

Mr. Truong's 5th grade students also show exceptional growth on standards-based testing—an amazing achievement considering the inexcusable working conditions he has experienced. Because of Mr. Truong's reputation for being effective with students other teachers could not reach, the school administration shuffled several "challenging" students into his class and collapsed an undersized 5th grade class into his room, leaving him with 38 students and no additional support. At the beginning of the year, fewer than 50 percent of the students in this class were scoring at or above proficiency in spelling, vocabulary, and proofreading. By February, however, class proficiency in these skills had risen to 83, 88, and 92 percent respectively. In the same time frame, the class average in reading fluency jumped by 20 words, exceeding the district fluency benchmark, and the percentage of students at benchmark in reading comprehension tripled. Mr. Truong's students showed similar gains in math.

Both Ms. Kim and Mr. Truong contend that their students' success is a result of instructional strategies that enable students to apply what they learn in the classroom to real issues in their lives. An example is their collaborative response when the school disciplined several students for having toy guns on campus—guns that the students had purchased from an ice cream truck in front of the school.

As part of their letter-writing unit, Ms. Kim's students wrote to the ice cream truck vendor, telling him that toy guns were creating a negative environment in their school and asking that he stop selling them. Mr. Truong's class wrote to toy manufacturing companies expressing similar concerns during their persuasive writing unit. When neither party responded, students from the two classes got together to organize an official protest. Under the supervision of teachers, parents, and the principal, students boycotted the ice cream truck. They held signs that read "No More Toy Guns and Don't Sell Guns Here" while chanting, "What do we want? No more toy guns at Power Elementary. When do we want it? Now!"

The ice cream truck left after several minutes of the protest, and it did not return. Although a rethinking of the school policy of letting a vendor sell toy guns near school property would have represented a greater victory, Ms. Kim and Mr. Truong emphasize the importance of letting students come to conclusions about their effectiveness on their own. They believe the real victory here is that students felt empowered to apply the lessons they learned in school to challenge the immediate conditions of their lives.

Teachers Teaching Teachers

It is not news that exceptional urban teachers like Ms. Grant, Ms. Kim, and Mr. Truong exist. To help the majority of teachers attain such success, however, urban schools must rethink their approach to teacher development. A promising approach is to create opportunities for successful teachers to reflect on their practice and share with less successful colleagues.

"This community of professionals is going to help everyone get better and keep people in teaching longer."

At Power Elementary, this strategy has proven effective and mutually beneficial for all the participants. The seven teachers in the inquiry group meet once a week for two hours in a four-week cycle of activities guided by the following themes.

Intellectual Development

During the first week of each cycle, the teachers discuss their written reflections on a reading chosen by one of the participants. Each reflection includes a classroom action plan for addressing issues raised by the reading. Group members who are already effectively addressing the issue use this time to share their practice with the other teachers. Those who are having less success can prepare an action plan informed by their colleagues' successes.

For example, Ms. Kim used her reflections on Henry Giroux's introductory chapter in *Literacy: Reading the Word and the World* (Freire & Macedo, 1987) to share with the group an activity she finds effective for implementing Giroux's emphasis on "naming and transforming" negative ideological and social conditions (p. 5). In her class, she explained, she uses periods of open dialogue to encourage students to identify and critique nondemocratic structures in their lives. She used the 2004 presidential elections, for instance, to develop dialogue about democracy. As students expressed their strong opinions about the candidates, Ms. Kim observed, they were empowered to "be dynamic, intellectual, and critical of what is going on."

Ms. Kim detailed how she charts student discussions on a Concept/Question Board in the classroom, which is used to continue previous dialogue and to display the students' various opinions. These discussions also enable her to assess students' functional and critical literacy skills. She uses these assessments to develop additional support structures in basic phonics for struggling readers and more advanced literacy techniques for those students who are ready.

Other teachers in the inquiry group were able to use Ms. Kim's ideas to address challenges in their own classrooms. Mr. Ballesteros, for example, began using similar student discussions to identify individual student needs and provide skill development appropriate to those needs in his math instruction. He started to decrease his use of whole-class instruction, adding more individual and small-group instruction tailored to his students' performance levels. As a result, he reported, 'I'm now seeing progress in the student work; they are showing greater understanding and they are getting it."

Professional Development

During the second week of the cycle, teachers pair up and observe their partners' classroom practice, debriefing afterward one-on-one to learn from their partner s reflections and feedback. When the entire group meets later in the week, each teacher reports on what he or she saw and learned from the observation. At these meetings, teachers use dialogue, questions, and suggestions to build a culture of teaching and learning.

Participants use the second hour of this meeting to discuss student work. Each teacher brings work samples from specific students (one high, one middle, and one low performer) whose progress they are following over the year. They draw from the samples to highlight challenges and successes and to get critical feedback from their colleagues. This activity allows for concrete support. It also develops accountability among colleagues because of the expectation that all the students will show academic progress.

Ms. O'Leary, for example, brought to the group her concerns about keeping her lowest performing students on task. She was welcomed to observe in Ms. Grant's class to generate more effective strategies. After the visit, Ms. O'Leary reported to the group,

> I recently tried something I never wanted to do because it seemed time-wasteful, but it worked well when I saw it in Ms. Grant's room. She had kids line up to check work with her, rather than stay seated and do something else when finished. My kids got one another distracted when I let them stay at their seats when finished with writing as I saw kids one at a time. So I tried Ms. Grant's method and it seems to work well. The kids worked harder and made more significant changes when I did the writing conferences this way.

Community Development

During the third week of each cycle, the teachers collaboratively develop out-of-classroom projects, such as after-school sports and game clubs, academic support systems, and parent and community partnership plans that the teachers want to implement or improve. With each new cycle, teachers evaluate the progress of their projects and discuss issues with the group to keep the projects moving forward.

Holistic Growth

During the final meeting, teachers review their reflections from the first week. They prepare new reflections detailing their progress on the issues they addressed in week one, discuss their growth, and ask for additional support in areas in which they would like better results.

The opportunity for teachers to articulate newfound feelings of motivation, professionalism, and commitment is central to the development of a positive professional climate. As Ms. O'Leary, one of the improving teachers, explains,

> This group makes me feel like things are gonna change. I'm gonna need to change because it makes me always want to get better, and I want to offer what I have. As long as this group is available, I'll feel professional. In fact, this is the first time I've felt like a professional. I no longer feel replaceable or like the goal of professional development is to make all teachers the same. This community of professionals is going to help everyone get better and keep people [in teaching] longer.

The holistic growth meeting also enables highly effective teachers, such as Mr. Truong, to improve their practice and model an enduring commitment to professional growth:

> Thinking back to my goals and previous reflections, I am reminded that I am not where I want to be with my goals.... I am not satisfied that I have fully taken advantage of potential literacy moments in science.... By the next reflection, or sooner, I will come back to this and see if I have ironed out the wrinkles.

The opportunity to be reflective ensures that all inquiry group participants, not just the struggling teachers, have the opportunity to identify themselves as achievers and learners.

Toward Better Teaching in Urban Schools

Urban schools face sizeable challenges. Two components that can help urban school leaders meet these challenges are (1) developing a better understanding of effective urban teachers' philosophies and practices, and (2) putting a system in place to support the professional growth of all teachers. School leaders can develop these supportive systems of professional development if they use successful practitioners as resources.

Power Elementary School's inquiry group enables highly effective teachers who espouse a pedagogy of social transformation to share their philosophy and practice with colleagues. The structure of the group balances high expectations with teacher autonomy, support, and collaboration. Such professional development communities hold great promise for helping urban schools improve professional practice and student achievement.

Note

1. School and teacher names are pseudonyms.

References

Freire, P. (1970). *Pedagogy of the oppressed.* New York: Continuum.

Freire, P., & Maccdo, D. (1987). *Literacy: Reading the word and the world.* South Hadley, MA: Bergin and Garvey.

JEFFREY M. R. DUNCAN-ANDRADE holds a joint appointment as Director of Urban Teacher Development, Institute for Democracy, Education and Access, University of California–Los Angeles (310-267-5432; jdandrade@gseis.ucla.edu) and Assistant Professor of Raza Studies and Education and Codirector of the Educational Equity Initiative, Cesar Chavez Institute, San Francisco State University (415-522-5020; jandrade©sfsu.edu).

The Boss in the Classroom

Louis P. Masur

On a warm spring day near the end of the last academic year, I found myself in class dancing with a freshman girl to Bruce Springsteen's "Born to Run."

I am not known as a particularly reserved professor. In teaching students that ideas matter, I try to bring passion to my courses in American cultural history: I do not mask my affection for such figures as Ben Franklin, Dorothea Lange, or Jackie Robinson; I've taken joy in reciting parts of Jonathan Edwards's "Sinners in the Hands of an Angry God" and imitating Marlon Brando's speech to his brother from *On the Waterfront.* But until that day, I had never discussed Springsteen in class. And I certainly had never thrown off my blazer and spun a student around the lectern.

The scene developed this way: For an introduction to the cultural rebellions of the 1950s, my students had read Glenn C. Altschuler's *All Shook Up: How Rock 'n Roll Changed America* (Oxford University Press, 2003). To facilitate discussion, I burned a CD that included classics like Chuck Berry's "Johnny B. Goode," Buddy Holly's "That'll Be the Day," and Elvis Presley's "Hound Dog." I added Bob Dylan's "Like a Rolling Stone," which, in 1965, marked a seismic shift in the history of rock. Altschuler ends his book with a brief discussion of Springsteen, so I decided to bring the class to a close by playing "Born to Run," the song that, 10 years after Dylan's masterpiece, marked another milestone in the history of rock 'n roll.

It had also been a benchmark in my personal history, though, of course, my students had no way of knowing that. I turned 18 in 1975, and *Born to Run,* the song and album, captured my teenage sense of longing, dreams of escape, and search for connection and love. I was not alone. The romance and tragedy of the characters, the symphonic music, and Springsteen's breathless vocals made him a national icon who appeared that fall on the covers of *Time* and *Newsweek.* I may have missed Presley and Dylan because I was too young, but Springsteen was a rock savior I could call my own.

That was 30 years ago, and Bruce and I have been together ever since. I first saw him in concert before the release of *Born to Run,* and I have gone back again and again. Like other early fans, I have grown old with him. As he has matured artistically and personally, so have we. Or at least that is the hope.

Until that day, however, my students had no idea of my passion and the meaning of Springsteen's music in my life. But as the opening beats of "Born to Run" blared into the lecture room, I started singing and annotating: "In the day we sweat it out in the streets of a runaway American dream" (the underside of making it in America, I told my students); "Baby this town rips the bones from your back" (the feeling of being cut off from community); "We gotta get out while we're young" (the need to hit the road to find oneself).

I was scampering up and down the aisles, singing, yelling, and performing before 50 students. And then I was dancing. I reached out my hand, and, to my surprise, a girl in the second row came forward and stepped onto the stage. Everyone was clapping and howling. We were all smiling. The song ended. I applauded the student and the class, and we all bopped off into the late afternoon.

That evening I received multiple e-mail messages from students who said that the class had been one of the best they had ever taken. I tried to keep the discussion going online, asking students to look closely at the album cover and examine the lyrics of other songs on it. Those were texts that had to be unpacked, just as the class had learned to analyze works by Melville and Twain earlier in the semester. Indeed, and here the scholar in me pushed aside the entertainer, I suggested that the cover of Bruce and his saxophonist Clarence Clemons, who is black, evoked nothing less than the biracial journeys of such literary figures as Ishmael and Queequeg, and Huck and Jim. My students were skeptical, but at least I did have them making connections and thinking more broadly about the material.

Then some of them suggested I teach a course on Springsteen, and I considered how I would frame it. I recalled an insight the singer himself had once made about Presley and Dylan. The one, he said, freed our bodies, the other our minds. He, I thought, freed our souls. In the next year or two, I plan to offer a seminar on "Body, Mind, Soul: the Cultural Meaning of Elvis Presley, Bob Dylan, and Bruce Springsteen." I think I will have to limit the enrollment.

But that was only the beginning of my newfound pedagogical and scholarly interest in Springsteen. A week or two after my classroom experience, a professional colleague who shares my passion for Springsteen sent me an online link to a call for papers for a conference, "Glory Days: a Bruce Springsteen Symposium." The conference, organized by scholars at Pennsylvania State University at University Park and to be held t Monmouth University, will bring together scores of scholars and writers in a variety of panels like "Bruce Springsteen and the Creation of Community," "Bruce Springsteen and Storytelling," and "Bruce Springsteen and Catholicism."

I may have missed Presley and Dylan because I was too young, but Springsteen was a rock savior I could call my own.

Clearly work on Springsteen and American culture has reached a critical mass. In addition to the conference, last year Penguin Books published *Racing in the Street: The Bruce Springsteen Reader,* edited by the journalist June Skinner Sawyers: The bibliography is more than 15 pages long. Last July the cover article of *The New York Times Book Review* surveyed a few of the more analytical Springsteen books, including the historian Jim Cullen's *Born in the U.S.A.: Bruce Springsteen and the American Tradition* (Harper Collins, 1997), the psychologist Robert Coles's *Bruce Springsteen's America: The People Listening, a Poet Singing* (Random House, 2003), and the music critic Jimmy Guterman's *Runaway American Dream: Listening to Bruce Springsteen* (Da Capo Press, 2005). The list of books featured might have been further expanded to include the historian Daniel Cavicchi's *Tramps Like Us: Music & Meaning Among Springsteen Fans* (Oxford University Press, 1998) and

the journalist Eric Alterman's *It Ain't No Sin to Be Glad You're Alive: The Promise of Bruce Springsteen* (Little, Brown, 1999).

At the conference, I'll be presenting a paper on "The Geography of 'Born to Run,'" exploring the competing geographies of place and time that inform the album and contribute to its power. Others have examined the importance of place in Springsteen's work (after all, he named his first album *Greetings From Asbury Park, N.J.*), but I'll be discussing temporal geography—time of life (youth), time of year (summer), and time of day (night).

My students were thrilled when they heard about the conference, and my paper. Some of them plan to attend. I've since learned that so many professors teach courses on Springsteen and use him to illustrate central themes in American cultural history that the conference will be holding a special session on Springsteen in the classroom.

Just months ago, I would not have believed that I could find a way to incorporate my passion for Springsteen into my teaching and writing, that Springsteen, of all subjects, would revitalize my scholarly interests. But playing "Born to Run" that spring day in class invigorated me. I'm listening to Springsteen with fresh ears, I'm reading widely in rock 'n roll history, I'm writing material that fuses the personal with the academic, and I'm thinking about teaching in new ways. Oh yes, I'm also practicing my steps, so that I'll be ready the next time I dance in class.

LOUIS P. MASUR is a professor of American studies at Trinity College, in Connecticut.

UNIT 9

For Vision and Hope: Alternative Visions of Reality

Unit Selections

Key Points to Consider

- What might be the shape of school curricula by the year 2020?

- What changes in society are most likely to affect educational change?

- How can schools prepare students to live and work in an uncertain future? What knowledge bases are most important? What skills are most important?

- What should be the philosophical ideals for American schools in the twenty-first century?

Student Website

www.mhcls.com/online

Internet References

Further information regarding these websites may be found in this book's preface or online.

Goals 2000: A Progress Report
http://www.ed.gov/pubs/goals/progrpt/index.html

Mighty Media
http://www.mightymedia.com

Online Internet Institute
http://www.oii.org

There are competing visions as to how persons should develop and learn. Yet there is great hope in this competition among alternative dreams and specific curriculum paths that we may choose to traverse. In this, all conscientious persons are asked to consider carefully how we may make more livable futures for ourselves and others. This is really an eternal challenge for us all. We will often disagree and debate our differences as we struggle toward what we become as persons and as cultures.

Which education philosophy is most appropriate for our schools? This is a complex question, and we will, as a free people, come up with alternative visions of what it will be. Let us explore what might be possible as more students go on the Internet and the wonder of the cyberspace revolution opens to teachers and students. What challenges can we expect in using the technology of the cyberspace revolution in our schools? What blessings can we hope for? What sorts of changes need to occur in how people go to schools as well as in what they do when they get there?

The breakthroughs that are developing in new learning and communications technologies are really quite impressive. They will definitely affect how human beings learn in the very near-term future. While we look forward with considerable optimism and confidence to these educational developments, there are still many controversial issues to be debated in the early years of the twenty-first century; the "school choice" issue is one. Some very interesting new proposals for new forms of schooling, both in public schools and private schools, are under development. We can expect to see at least a few of these proposals actually tried.

Some of the demographic changes and challenges involving young people in the United States are staggering. Ten percent of all American teenage girls will become pregnant each year, the highest rate in the developed world. At least 100,000 American elementary school children get drunk once a week. Incidence of venereal disease has tripled among adolescents in the United States since 1995. The actual school dropout rate in the United States stands at 30 percent.

The student populations of North America reflect vital social and cultural forces at work to destroy our progress. In the United States, a massive secondary school dropout problem has been developing steadily through the past decade. The next decade will reveal how public school systems will address this and other unresolved problems brought about by dramatic upheavals in demographics. In the immediate future, we will be able to see if emergency or alternative certification measures adopted by states affect achievement of the objectives of our reforms.

At any given moment in a people's history, several alternative future directions are open to them. North American educational systems have been subjected to one wave after another of recommendations for programmatic change. Is it any wonder that change is a sensitive watchword for persons in teacher education on this continent? What specific directions it will take in the immediate future depend on which recommendations of the reform agenda are implemented, which agencies of government (local, state/provincial, and federal) will pay for the very high costs of reform, and which shifts in perceived national educational priorities by the public will occur that will affect fundamental realignments of our educational goals.

Basic changes in society's career patterns should also be considered. It is estimated that in the United States the average nonagricultural worker now makes a major job change about five times in his or her career. The schools will surely be affected, indirectly or directly, by this major social phenomenon. Changes in the social structure due to divorce, unemployment, and job retraining efforts will also have an impact. Educational systems are integral parts of the broader social systems that created them; if the larger social system experiences fundamental change, this is reflected in the educational system.

In the area of information science and computer technologies applicable for use in educational systems, the development of new products is so rapid that we cannot predict what technolog-

ical capacities may be available to schools 20 years from now. We are in a period of human history when knowledgeable people can control far greater information (and have immediate access to it) than at any previous time. As new information-command systems evolve, this phenomenon will become more and more meaningful to all of us.

The future of education will be determined by the current debate concerning what constitutes a just, national response to human needs in a period of technological change. The history of technological change in all human societies since the beginning of industrial development clearly demonstrates that major advances in technology and breakthroughs in the basic sciences lead to more rapid rates of social change. Society is on the verge of discoveries that will lead to the creation of entirely new technologies in the dawning years of the twenty-first century. All of the social, economic, and educational institutions globally will be affected by these scientific breakthroughs. The basic issue is not whether schools can remain aloof from the needs of industry or the economic demands of society but how they can emphasize the noblest ideals of free persons in the face of inevitable technological and economic changes. Another concern is how to let go of predetermined visions of the future that limit our possibilities as free people. The schools, of course, will be called upon to face these issues. We need the most enlightened, insightful, and compassionate teachers ever educated by North American universities to prepare the youth of the future in a manner that will humanize the high-tech world in which they live.

All of the articles in this unit can be related to discussions on the goals of education, the future of education, or curriculum development.

The New WWW: Whatever, Whenever, Wherever

In an age of instant media gratification, learning must be real, rich, and relevant.

Tom March

A new world of personalized, device-delivered digital content and functionality hovers just over the broadband horizon. The New WWW—offering us *whatever* we want, *whenever* and *wherever* we want it—may seem like just an extension of our already-technology-enhanced contemporary life. In some ways, it is. But such a wireless stream of media gratification is actually a radical departure from typical human experience. And as tantalizing as this ready access to our hearts' desires may be, it creates great challenges for our children. To counteract the New WWW's potentially harmful impact on youth, educators must use technology to create learning experiences that are real, rich, and relevant.

What Is the New WWW?

From Personal Computers to Personal Handheld Devices

Around the world, companies are rolling out a new kind of service that brings broadband power to mobile personal devices. Commonly known as *3rd Generation*, or *3G*, this upgrade in cellular networks means that any media will be able to stream easily to our devices in full motion, including all manner of television programs, movies, videoconferencing, music, and multi-user games. Next will come 4G, in which data rates are expected to be 100 times faster than those in this first 3G wave. As the delivery platform of broadband content and functionality shifts from computer to personal device, we will be surrounded by a multimedia aura that accompanies us wherever we go. In this way, the New WWW is unlike anything humans have yet experienced.

From Mass Production to Niche Market

The last economic revolution began when the assembly line enabled common folk to afford their very own interchangeable Ford Model T in "any color, so long as it's black." Visit the Ford Web site today, and you'll find an interactive vehicle showroom that allows you to specify your preferred price range, body style, miles per gallon, and seating capacity and to select from such colors as Dark Stone, Estate Green, and Medium Wedgewood Blue. Point your browser to any Web portal, and you're likely to encounter the pervasive *my-ification* of our age. My Yahoo! offers you the power to "customize the Internet!" ("You choose it—My Yahoo! brings it together!") At Excite, you'll find MyWeather, MyMovies, MyTV, MySign, MyLottery, MyPortfolio, and MyScores. Even real-world license plates advertise the name of the official Web portal of the state of Florida: **"MYFlorida.com."**

The New WWW may put assembly-line education out of its misery.

Why this emphasis on serving the individual? According to Fiona Harvey (2000),

> Businesses everywhere see the potential of the technology; connected consumers will be big, mobile wallets. The plan is that you'll use your phone to spend money everywhere, all the time.

In the age of the New WWW, every instant of our waking lives becomes an opportunity to impulse-buy. See a chance for good seats at a concert if you act fast? Do it! Just remembered a film you've always wanted to see? Why not view it right now, as you sit stuck in rush-hour traffic? Unlike the buckshot approach of broadcast television (before TiVo), the New WWW knows what you want—and wants you to have it. Cheap. Right now.

Children and teens with mobile media devices are like kids in a candy shop. What choices do we expect them to make if their pockets are loaded with cash and the shelves bulge with penny candy—especially when there's no parent in sight? The choice won't be between *yes* and *no*, but between *what kind?* and *what next?* Maybe someone needs to watch over this New WWW.

The Pursuit of Happiness

What's *really* wrong with this picture? Our concern is more than the hell-in-a-handbasket grumblings of the older generation; it has everything to do with loving children and wanting them to be happy. Children believe that getting whatever they want will make them happy. As adults, we know otherwise.

The Real "Whatever"

Research conducted by Martin Seligman (2002) reveals that people typically use three strategies to chase happiness: pursuing pleasure, engaging in personally meaningful actions, and performing service to something larger than themselves. Only two work. Seligman has found that pursuing pleasure yields no statistically significant difference in subjects' levels of happiness. Chasing after what we want doesn't make us happy.

Need further proof? Look at the many high-profile examples of child actors and pop stars who *do* get everything they want: the best toys, coolest clothes, and most attractive companions. Sound great? Yet how many of these young people are happy, and how many are in rehab?

The New WWW can help us shift students from consumption to action and creativity.

More than a century ago, William James provided a simple formula that suggests why having high expectations doesn't necessarily lead to happiness. He said that self-esteem can be measured by the ratio between our *pretensions*, or expectations about what we will achieve, and our actual success (1890). When children and teenagers are full of MTV dreams and bombarded with Pixar peak experiences, their expectations of life sparkle with the extraordinary. Everyone's going to be a pop star, a professional athlete, or at least a millionaire. Such unrealistic expectations can lead to a long downward spiral.

Who hasn't heard that wrenching response so common among young people, the verbal shrug of complete apathy: "Whatever." The premature disillusionment expressed by that word is the real *whatever* that comes from getting whatever we want, whenever and wherever we want it.

Driving Students to Distraction

Here's a prediction: Within the next decade, a school district will be sued by the bereaved parents of a teenager who committed suicide. The parents will charge that school killed their child. Picture the heartbroken mother on the 6 o'clock news: "Joey was fine when he went to kindergarten. But over the years, the life went out of him. School bored him to death."

Just like adults, young people who are stressed or bored frequently choose distraction over real life. The clinical manager of an addiction treatment service said, "The desire to escape the routine or stress of life is a reason people become addicted to the Internet" (Hall, 2003). Could the assembly-line approach so dominant in education actually "drive students to distraction"?

The point is not to blame parents or schools, but to sound a wake-up call: Unlimited, ubiquitous, personalized media gratification is unlike anything we've ever had to contend with, and just letting it happen isn't a good idea. Envision the horror and glory of getting whatever we want, whenever and wherever we want it. Online gambling, panda cams, cam girls, hate groups, online fantasy role-playing games, the Worldwide Association of Seaweed Processors—it's all there. All we have to do is choose.

A Better Approach for Education

Schools will have to make choices as well. Some will ban 3G devices in an attempt to avoid change. But we can and must do better. In fact, as educators, we are just the people who can help.

If we acknowledge that boredom and stress are leading our young people to get lost in the New WWW, we must also acknowledge that schools have too much of both. But the joy of learning has neither! One of the most powerful definitions of teaching I know comes from Maria Harris: "Teaching is the creation of a situation in which subjects, human subjects, are handed over to themselves" (1991, p. 33). No virtual stimulus can accomplish this. Listening to MP3s doesn't compare with playing your own music. Watching a DVD isn't the same as producing your own film. Playing a video game pales in comparison to designing your own software. And let's be honest—downloading pornography doesn't stand a chance against a shy kiss.

How do educators help our students make truly satisfying choices? We can start by taking our cues from Seligman, James, and Harvey. We can "hand students over to themselves." We can engage them in the joys of learning, of making meaning, of being part of something larger than themselves, of testing themselves against authentic challenges. We can shift them from passivity and consumption to action and creativity. And believe it or not, the New WWW can help us.

Just as the Web has empowered students to undermine pointless, rote "research assignments" through copy-and-paste masterpieces, the New WWW shifts learning power to the students themselves. When the world of information explodes beyond what one head can hold, who decides what gets into that head? When students can demonstrate their learning in a persuasive essay, a sardonic blog, a moving short film, a robust wiki entry, or a humorous podcast, why would we demand deadening conformity? The New WWW may do us all a favor and put assembly-line education out of its misery.

Techno-Byte

On a typical day at the end of 2004, 70 million adults in the United States went online (up from 52 million in 2000).

—Pew Internet & American Life Project, 2005

A Strategy for All Teachers in All Schools

Ten years ago, as a classroom teacher attempting to make learning real for students, I found that the Web transformed what was possible. To support rich integration of the Web into learning, I have worked since 1995 to develop the WebQuest as one consistent process to scaffold advanced learning (March, 2003–2004). Typical WebQuests might challenge students to evaluate the most promising combination of alternative energy sources, use online tools to reapportion the U.S. budget in line with their ideal national goals, or distinguish between terrorist acts and fights for freedom in a quest to reach a definition of terrorism that can apply cross-culturally.

Unfortunately, few schools or school systems have integrated the Web into schools in a way that makes real changes in teaching and learning. Experience working with teachers and school systems has revealed that using WebQuests—or the many other good strategies that are available to leverage the medium for authentic learning—is a stretch for most educators and learners.

Without widespread institutional support, the Web has been slow to make its way into most classrooms. Some Web-savvy teachers make it a practice to incorporate links to Web resources into their instructional units. Others go beyond that and design goal-based authentic learning activities involving research with the Internet. A few engage their students in great WebQuests.

But to foster change in every classroom, every day, teachers need to find formats that are easier for every Web-connected teacher to integrate into the classroom. More and more teachers are venturing into one such format: They are creating class Web sites that go beyond homework lists and Web links to gather and share information about a topic of special interest to them.

I call this kind of Web site a *ClassAct Portal: Class* because the site involves a whole class of students; *Act* because it supports authentic, active learning; *ClassAct* because it provides a real-world forum for students to exercise their best efforts; and *Portal* because the site serves as a window to resources, information, activities, and communities.

A ClassAct Portal is a Web presence for each teacher's group of students. It focuses on one topic, which can fall under a traditional curriculum area—such as geography or mathematics—or explore a wide range of other areas, such as hobbies, world events, and popular culture. Environmental causes are a popular topic. The only requirement is that the teacher is passionately interested in the subject; such enthusiasm is contagious and a great model for students. Savvy teachers will also select topics that engage their students. Choosing a topic of all-consuming interest to many students—hip-hop music, Harry Potter, cartooning—is a great way to illustrate that all subjects are related and that sophisticated learning can evolve from deep immersion in any topic. The best thing about a ClassAct Portal is that it's flexible and will change with the interests of the class and the nature of the topic.

A classic example of a great ClassAct Portal is *Child Slave Labor News* (www.geocities.com/cslnews), created by students in Joann Fantina's U.S. History course at Immaculata High School in Somerville, New Jersey. As 1999 graduate Brett Peterson wrote on the site,

> The students and faculty of Immaculata High School are very concerned about the problem of child slave labor. Each year, the senior U.S. History II Honors class, taught by Miss Joann Fantina, publishes numerous newsletters throughout the year covering many aspects of child slave labor. A new group of students takes over the project each year as the previous class graduates. It is a common interest among the students and is continued enthusiastically year after year.

In addition to a hefty archive of student-written articles—including "Slavery and the Link to Chocolate," "250 Million Slaves and Counting," "How Fair Is NAFTA?", and "Wal-Mart in China"—the site provides links to organizations opposing slave labor and invites visitors to provide guest commentary. To support their research and develop their expertise, the students maintain contact with dozens of groups and individuals fighting child labor.

The *Child Slave Labor News* site has been online since 1998. As of this writing, it was the first hit in a Google search for "child slave labor." How's that for real, rich, and relevant learning that enables students to participate in meaningful action toward a higher good?

How to Build a ClassAct Portal

After you have chosen a topic based on your own passionate interests or on interests you share with your students, it's time to decide where your ClassAct Portal will live. A quick route is to begin with one of the free online blogs, such as Blogger or WordPress. Although such sites provide an easy way to get started, if you want to grow the site later by adding a wiki or a photo gallery, you may have to start all over again. I advocate setting up your own Web space instead; then you'll have more flexibility to make your ClassAct Portal an extension of your lesson plans, bulletin boards, and classroom persona.

Unlimited media gratification is unlike anything we've ever had to contend with, and just letting it happen isn't a good idea.

Thanks to the sophistication of open source software and competition among Web hosts, anyone can set up a powerful Web site for $60 per year—one that includes all the great tools that are now so easy to use. Just pick a buzzword: blog, wiki, forum, podcast, RSS (Really Simple Syndication), photo gallery, course management system, e-mail list, FAQ list—the possibilities are endless and are only getting better and easier. Simply search for a Web host that provides "cPanel" and "Fantastico" and follow a step-by-step tutorial to grow your Web presence (March, 2005).

To create content for your ClassAct Portal, you might start by gathering a hotlist of links on your chosen topic. See what

215

the World (Wide Web) has to say about the subject. As students' first contribution to the world of ideas on the Web, they can critique and annotate the links on the list. To build an online community, immerse students in the sites on your hotlist and have them send e-mails of appreciation to the people behind the most interesting sites.

To help students track the latest news and postings on the topic, subscribe to newsfeeds and podcasts through RSS. A search for these terms plus "tutorial" will provide step-by-step instructions to get you started. Use your Web site as the ultimate refrigerator on which to post exemplary student work on the topic. These days, such work can include audio podcasts and movies just as easily as written text and scanned drawings. You can also launch a blog on the site that features new and interesting thinking. Before long, you'll have a blogroll of like-minded people who are part of the online community interested in the topic. And guess what? Lots of them won't be students. Authentic learning reaches into the real world.

Giving students an online presence can cause concern about student safety. A number of steps can help you ensure that your ClassAct Portal is safe for students. First, follow your school or school district's acceptable use policy regarding student names and images. In addition, use open source software that allows you, as the site administrator, to set permission levels for who can post articles and to monitor postings and comments. Monitoring all postings encourages students to post only their best efforts and also keeps inappropriate content off the site.

These ideas suggest the big picture. To inspire participation, I recently developed ClassActPortal.com, a resource and directory to foster and celebrate such sites. Although still new, this site's Idea Pools already feature more than 100 suggestions for ClassAct Portal topics, such as "Wild Weather," "How Big Is That?" (understanding huge numbers), "Bumperstickers & Sound Bites," "Box Office Blockbusters," "Child Soldiers," and "Global Warming & Its Impact." In addition, the site provides a range of resources, such as user-friendly tutorials on setting up your own blog or wiki. More important, it enables visitors to read articles and view examples of sites that successfully integrate the Web into daily classroom learning.

Real, Rich, Relevant— and Essential

The ClassAct Portal is one practical way in which we can use the New WWW to create learning experiences that are real, rich, and relevant. Educators have a responsibility to develop such strategies if we want to provide our students with meaningful education in the age of whatever, whenever, wherever. Self-awareness and the construction of a meaningful life aren't just good ideas. In a culture permeated by the New WWW, these traits will be essential to counterbalance the lure of self-absorption that leads to despair.

When we watch young children, we witness joy in the present and an innate love of learning. Keeping this joy alive—nurturing it in all students as an alternative to the temptation of easy distraction—is part of our new task as educators and parents.

References

Hall, E. (2003, Sept. 26). Internet addiction: A rising problem. *Kansas State Collegian*. Posted by *The Emory Wheel Online*. Available: **www.emorywheel.com/vnews/display.v/ART/2003/09/26/3f73aa7lafe05**

Harris, M. (1991). *Teaching, and religious imagination: An essay in the theology of teaching*. New York: HarperCollins.

Harvey, F. (2000, Oct. 20). The Internet in your hands. *Scientific American*, pp. 40–45.

James, W. (1890). *The principles of psychology, volume 1*. Mineola, NY: Dover Publications.

March, T. (2003–2004). The learning power of WebQuests. *Educational Leadership*, 61(4), 42–47.

March, T. (2005). *ClassAct Portals handbook*. Available: **http://ozline.com/drive_2005_portal.pdf**

Seligman, M. E. P. (2002). *Authentic happiness*. New York: Free Press.

TOM MARCH is a Web-based educator, author, and instructional designer. He can be reached at 44 Murchison St., Mittagong, NSW 2575, Australia; 011-61-2-4872-3023; tom@ozline.com.

Listen to the Natives

Schools are stuck in the 20th century. Students have rushed into the 21st. How can schools catch up and provide students with a relevant education?

MARC PRENSKY

School didn't teach me to read—I learned from my games.

—A student

Educators have slid into the 21st century—and into the digital age—still doing a great many things the old way It's time for education leaders to raise their heads above the daily grind and observe the new landscape that's emerging. Recognizing and analyzing its characteristics will help define the education leadership with which we should be providing our students, both now and in the coming decades.

Times have changed. So, too, have the students, the tools, and the requisite skills and knowledge. Let's take a look at some of the features of our 21st century landscape that will be of utmost importance to those entrusted with the stewardship of our children's 21st century education.

Digital Natives

Our students are no longer "little versions of us," as they may have been in the past. In fact, they are so different from us that we can no longer use either our 20th century knowledge or our training as a guide to what is best for them educationally.

I've coined the term *distal native* to refer to today's students (2001). They are native speakers of technology, fluent in the digital language of computers, video games, and the Internet. I refer to those of us who were not born into the digital world as *distal* immigrants. We have adopted many aspects of the technology, but just like those who learn another language later in life, we retain an "accent" because we still have one foot in the past. We will read a manual, for example, to understand a program before we think to let the program teach itself. Our accent from the predigital world often makes it difficult for us to effectively communicate with our students.

Our students, as digital natives, will continue to evolve and change so rapidly that we won't be able to keep up. This phenomenon renders traditional catch-up methods, such as inservice training, essentially useless. We need more radical solutions. For example, students could learn algebra far more quickly and effectively if instruction were available in game format. Students would need to beat the game to pass the course. They would be invested and engaged in the process.

We also need to select our teachers for their empathy and guidance abilities rather than exclusively for their subject-matter knowledge. We all remember best those teachers who cared about us as individuals and who cut us some slack when necessary. In today's rush to find teachers qualified in the curriculum, we rarely make empathy a priority.

Shifting Gears

As educators, we must take our cues from our students' 21st century innovations and behaviors, abandoning, in many cases, our own predigital instincts and comfort zones. Teachers must practice putting engagement before content when teaching. They need to laugh at their own digital immigrant accents, pay attention to how their students learn, and value and honor what their students know. They must remember that they are teaching in the 21st century This means encouraging decision making among students, involving students in designing instruction, and getting input from students about how *they* would teach. Teachers needn't master all the new technologies. They should continue doing what they do best: leading discussion in the classroom. But they must find ways to incorporate into those discussions the information and knowledge that their students acquire outside class in their digital lives.

Our schools should be teaching kids how to program, filter knowledge, and maximize the features and connectivity of their tools.

Our young people generally have a much better idea of what the future is bringing than we do. They're already busy adopting new systems for communicating (instant messaging), sharing (blogs), buying and selling (eBay), exchanging (peer-to-peer technology), creating (Flash), meeting (3D worlds), collecting (downloads), coordinating (wikis), evaluating (reputation systems), searching (Google), analyzing (SETI), reporting (camera phones), programming (modding), socializing (chat rooms), and even learning (Web surfing).

We need to help all our students take advantage of these new tools and systems to educate themselves. I know this is especially hard when we're the ones floundering, but teachers can certainly ask students, "Does anyone do anything on the Web that is relevant to what we're discussing?" or "Can you think of any examples of this problem in your computer games?" Teachers can also help students figure out who has the best access to technology outside school and encourage students to form study groups so that more students benefit from this access. Teachers can learn what technological equipment they need in their classrooms simply by asking students, and they can lobby to get these items installed in school computer labs and libraries.

Student Engagement

More and more of our students lack the true prerequisites for learning—engagement and motivation—at least in terms of what we offer them in our schools. Our kids *do* know what engagement is: Outside school, they are fully engaged by their 21st century digital lives.

If educators want to have relevance in this century, it is crucial that we find ways to engage students in school. Because common sense tells us that we will never have enough truly great teachers to engage these students in the old ways—through compelling lectures from those rare, charismatic teachers, for example—we must engage them in the 21st century way: electronically. Not through expensive graphics or multimedia, but through what the kids call "gameplay." We need to incorporate into our classrooms the same combination of desirable goals, interesting choices, immediate and useful feedback, and opportunities to "level up" (that is, to see yourself improve) that engage kids in their favorite complex computer games. One elementary school in Colorado, for example, takes its students on a virtual journey to a distant planet in a spaceship powered by knowledge. If the students don't have enough knowledge to move the ship, they need to find it—in one another.

Collaborating with Students

As 21st century educators, we can no longer decide for our students; we must decide *with* them, as strange as that may feel to many of us. We need to include our students in everything we do in the classroom, involving them in discussions about curriculum development, teaching methods, school organization, discipline, and assignments. Faculty or administration meetings can no longer be effective without student representation in equal numbers. Our brightest students, trusted with responsibility, will surprise us all with their contributions.

This may sound like the inmates are running the asylum. But it's only by listening to and valuing the ideas of our 21st century students that we will find solutions to many of our thorniest education problems. For example, putting a Webcam in every classroom is a digital native way to show administrators and

parents what really goes on. Teachers could also volunteer for this activity to document and share best practices.

Digital tools are like extensions of students' brains.

Students could quite feasibly invent technological solutions to streamline homework submission and correction, freeing up teachers for more meaningful work. Encouraged to share their expertise, students can be a teacher's best resource for suggesting better access to technology, defining the kinds of technology that teachers should be using in the classroom, and showing teachers how they can use specific hardware and software tools to teach more effectively

Flexible Organization

In this century, we *must* find alternatives to our primary method of education organization—what I call *herding*. Herding is students' involuntary assignment to specific classes or groups, not for their benefit but for ours. Nobody likes to be herded, and nobody learns best in that environment. As educators become "teacherds" rather than teachers, we all lose. And creating smaller schools or classrooms is no solution if the result is simply moving around smaller herds.

There are two effective 21st century alternatives to herding. The first is one-to-one personalized instruction, continually adapted to each student as he or she learns. This practice has become next to impossible with growing class sizes, but it is still doable. Modem computer and video games have already figured out how to adapt every moment of an experience to a player's precise capabilities and skills. So has computerized adaptive testing. Classrooms need to capitalize on students' individual capabilities and skills in the same way.

How can we make our instruction more adaptive and, as a result, far more effective? Just ask the students; they'll know. Adaptivity, along with connectivity, is where digital technology will have its greatest impact on education.

The second alternative to herding is having all learning groups self-select. Kids love working with their friends, especially virtually. I'm not saying, of course, that students should join *any* group in this context, but that they should be able to choose their own learning partners rather than having teachers assign them. Optimally and under proper supervision, a 4th grader in one school could choose a learning partner in any 4th grade class in the world. Teachers could also guide students in selecting an approved adult expert to partner with.

If we let our students choose all the groups they want to be part of—without forcing them into any one group—we will all be better off. One great advantage of virtual groups over herds is that nobody gets left out. Everybody can find *someone* in the world to work with. Teachers and administrators must be willing to set this up, provide the necessary vetting, and let it happen.

Digital Tools

Today's students have mastered a large variety of tools that we will never master with the same level of skill. From computers to calculators to MP3 players to camera phones, these tools are like extensions of their brains. Educating or evaluating students without these tools makes no more sense to them than educating or evaluating a plumber without his or her wrench.

One of the most important tools for 21st century students is not the computer that we educators are trying so hard to integrate, but the cell phone that so many of our schools currently ban. "Cell Phones Catapult Rural Africa to 21st Century," blared a recent front-page *New York Times* headline (LaFraniere, 2005). They can catapult our students into the future as well.

Cell phones have enormous capabilities these days: voice, short messaging service (SMS), graphics, user-controlled operating systems, down-loadables, browsers, camera functions (still and video), and geopositioning. Some have sensors, fingerprint readers, and voice recognition. Thumb keyboards and styluses as well as plugin screens and headphones turn cell phones into both input and output mechanisms.

The voice capabilities of the cell phone can help users access language or vocabulary training or narrate a guided tour. Teachers could deliver interactive lessons over a cell phone and use short messaging service to quiz or tutor students. Students could access animations in such subjects as anatomy and forensics. Students will soon be able to download programs into their cell phones, opening up new worlds of learning.

In Europe, China, Japan, and the Philippines, the public is already using mobile phones as learning tools. We in the United States need to join them and overcome objections that students are "using them for cheating" (so make the tests open book!) or for "inappropriate picture taking" (so instill some responsibility!). In the United Kingdom, teachers are evaluating student projects over mobile phones. The student describes the project, and the teacher analyzes the student's voiceprint for authentication.

Programming is perhaps *the* key skill necessary for 21st century literacy.

Let's admit that the *real* reason we ban cell phones is that, given the opportunity to use them, students would "vote with their attention," just as adults "vote with their feet" by leaving the room when a presentation is not compelling. Why shouldn't our students have the same option with their education when educators fail to deliver compelling content?

Programming

The single most important differentiator between 20th century analog and 21st century digital technology is programmability Programming is perhaps *the* key skill necessary for 21st century literacy in this arena, teachers and schools are stuck in ancient times. If you wanted to get something written back then, you had to find a scribe; today, you need a programmer.

All 21st century kids are programmers to some degree. Every time they download a song or ring tone, conduct a Google search, or use any software, they are, in fact, programming. To prepare kids for their 21st century lives, we must help them maximize their tools by extending their programming abilities. Many students are already proficient enough in programs like Flash to submit their assignments in this medium. Schools should actively teach students this technology and encourage them to use it.

Of course, extending this literacy with our current teaching corps is problematic. A number of teachers I know have taken matters into their own hands, creating programming courses—especially in popular game programming—for students during the summer months, after school, and even in class. We need to capture these approaches and curriculums and make them available over the Web for all to use. Teachers can also arrange for certain students to teach these classes to their peers. In addition, outside experts are often willing to volunteer their services.

Legacy Versus Future Learning

Currently, the curriculums of the past—the "legacy" part of our kids' learning—are interfering with and cutting into the "future" curriculum—the skills and knowledge that students need for the 21st century. We need to consolidate and concentrate important legacy knowledge and make room in school for 21st century learning. Our schools should be teaching kids bow to program, filter knowledge, and maximize the features and connectivity of their tools. Students should be learning 21st century subject matter, such as nanotechnology, bioethics, genetic medicine, and neuroscience.

This is a great place for involving guest teachers from professions doing cutting-edge work in these emerging fields. If every district or school found just one expert willing to contribute his or her expertise; set up and videotaped a meaningful series of Q&A exchanges with students; and put those videos on the Web, enhancing them with additional relevant materials, we'd soon have a 21st century curriculum.

Students want and deserve to receive this content through 21st century tools that are powerful, programmable, and customizable—through tools that belong to them. We could offer this content to them on their cell phones, for example. A big part of our problem is figuring out how to provide this before the end of the 21st century.

School Versus After School

Pragmatically, our 21st century kids' education is quickly bifurcating. The formal half, "school," is becoming an increasingly moribund and irrelevant institution. Its only function for many students is to provide them with a credential that their parents say they need. The informal, exciting half of kids' education occurs "after school." This is the place where 21st century students learn about their world and prepare themselves for their 21st century lives. It is revealing that one of the most prevalent student demands regarding technology is to keep their schools' computer labs open until midnight (and for us to stay out of their

TECHNO-BYTE

U.S. teachers who say that computer technology has affected the way they teach:

- To some extent—86 percent.
- A great deal—55.6 percent.

—eSchool News, 2005

way while they are there). It is equally telling that so many software and Web programs aimed at enhancing kids' education are designed for after-school rather than in-school use.

If our schools in the 21st century are to be anything more than holding pens for students while their parents work, we desperately need to find ways to help teachers integrate kids' technology-rich after-school lives with their lives in school. It doesn't help if, in the words of Henry Kelly, president of the Federation of American Scientists, "the cookies on my daughter's computer know more about her interests than her teachers do," It helps even less that a great many of our teachers and administrators have no idea what a *cookie* or a *blog* or a *wiki* even is.

Student Voice

Our students, who are empowered in so many ways outside their schools today, have no meaningful voice at all in their own education. Their parents' voices, which up until now have been their proxies, are no longer any more closely aligned with students' real education needs than their teachers' voices are. In the 21st century, this lack of any voice on the part of the customer will soon be unacceptable.

Some organizations are trying to change this. For example, NetDay (www.netday.org) conducts an annual online student survey of technology use through its Speak Up Days. All school districts should participate in this survey. Then, instead of hearing from just the 200,000 students who responded in the last survey, we would know what 50 million of them are thinking. Districts would receive valuable input from their students that they could apply to improving instruction.

As we educators stick our heads up and get the lay of the 21st century land, we would be wise to remember this: If we don't stop and listen to the kids we serve, value their opinions, and make major changes on the basis of the valid suggestions they offer, we will be left in the 21st century with school buildings to administer—but with students who are physically or mentally somewhere else.

References

LaFraniere, S, (2005, Aug, 25), Cell phones catapult rural Africa to 21st century. New *York Times on the Web.* Available: **http://msn-cnet.com.com/Cell+phones+catapult+rural+Africa+to+21st+century/2100-1039_3-5842901.html**

Prensky, M. (2001). Digital natives, digital immigrants. *On the Horizon,* 9(5), 1–2. Available: **www.marcprensky.com/writing/Prensky%20-%20Digital%20Natives,%20Digital-%20Immigrants%20-%20Partl.pdf**

MARC PRENSKY (marc@games2train.com) is a speaker, writer, consultant, and game designer in education and learning. He is author of *Digital Game-Based Learning* (McGraw-Hill, 2001) and *Don't Bother Me, Mom, I'm Learning* (Paragon, 2005).

The Future of Education: Four Scenarios

ROBERT SANBORN, ADOLFO SANTOS, ALEXANDRA L. MONTGOMERY, AND JAMES B. CARUTHERS

Many forces will act powerfully upon the course of public education in the future. Trends engendered by new technologies, immigration, school choice, and alternative education methods carry with them the muscle to re-shape the form, content, and methods of education. Every competing interest wants time or money to solve the problem of education, and each is usually justified by some political, social, economic, moral, and/or philosophical reasoning. With so many forces at work, it seems unlikely that there is a single, predictable future for public education.

We believe, however, that it is possible to conceive of a number of realities that might exist at different points in the future. The following four futures for public education are alternative scenarios that might take place sometime in the next 20 years. Each future is independent within a broad spectrum of possible outcomes, making up a nonconsecutive timeline containing four separate scenarios based on our understanding of public education today as being volatile and in desperate need of change.

Scenario 1 (2012): Direct Education

By 2012, we can expect to see technology at every level of public education. Technological innovations such as implanted nodes will be attached to our brains through advances in noninvasive nanotechnology. Using Wi-Fi or Wi-Max, the nodes will access information from an advanced World Wide Web, and implants will be quite useful (sometimes essential) to learning. High-tech devices will offer school efficiency and transparency like never before. In this scenario, we have harnessed technology to enable students and teachers to make giant leaps in education and information access. Technology not only encompasses computers and multimedia presentations, but also the very essence of how we educate, learn, and access information that we might have once considered too varied, weighty, and difficult to manage. This view of personal access to learning and education is called Direct Education and consists of the following components.

- Continuous Accountability (CA) is a proven manner of showing students' success in taking advantage of these technological marvels and really learning. In Direct

Education schools, there is no need for regularly scheduled tests; through CA, students are tested randomly at levels suitable to what they have studied. Educators know on a consistent basis how well students are doing and where to emphasize new learning. Parents are also updated electronically on students' progress and given suggestions on how to help students progress and overcome challenges.

Implanted Nodes

- The primary accessory of Direct Education is implanted information nodes. Direct Education offers a line of direct information visors for those with a less-organic feel for technology, although most of Direct Education schools are well adapted to the information society. Either way, learning is merely a thought away, as information flows from wireless networks directly into students' consciousness. Direct Education is for those districts adventurous enough to truly prepare students for the future.

- The actual classroom is different for every age and for every student. Virtual classrooms can be joined wirelessly from home and enable access to and complete hands-on experiential education for every imaginable subject. Direct Education core classes available in 2012 include building your own best friend in a cyborg workshop, undersea welding, virtual tattoo and body art, Native American ritual dance, conversing with Freud and Jung, working inside an operating theater, firsthand experience of animal culture and pack mentality, and exploring America with Lewis and Clark.

Scenario 2 (2014): Homeschooling

In 2014, K–12 education will no longer be confined to four walls and a classroom. Education will take place in a variety of settings, including cyberspace and virtual reality.

In this scenario, everything in the home is automated (for those living in smart homes, of course), so homeschooling is just another modern convenience to keep children where they can be safe and secure. Everyday computers suffice as classrooms, and software takes care of all menial grading and record keeping.

Homeschooling grew in popularity as college-educated moms came to believe that public-school students were just test-takers and numbers for a head-count. For these moms, the official ways of measuring student intelligence and progress have long been debunked. Homeschool moms are adamant about one thing: They are far too informed to allow their children to participate in the manipulation of numbers as they relate to school performance and funding.

Parents are also concerned about special-needs children, another segment of the student population whose parents feel betrayed by false promises of equality in education. Upper-class moms of children with behavioral, developmental, or psychological challenges seem to prefer their own inexperienced but loving at-home care and instruction to the cold and impersonal shuffling their children received in public schools. The voucher and private school systems have failed, too, since taxpayer-funded vouchers did not accommodate the extra expense of special-needs programs. For the cost of private-school tuition, many parents turn instead to homeschooling, where they can bring in professional tutors, experts on their children's conditions, and consultants whose mastery exceeded anything public schools could offer.

In many ways, homeschooling in 2014 has become a status symbol: Mothers who homeschool their children are thought of (and think of themselves) as highly sophisticated and well connected. A homeschool educator tends to rank high on levels of education attainment (master's degree or better) and household income (well into the upper brackets). Many well-to-do mothers revel in the feeling of staying home with children. Savvy domestic skills, maturity, and intelligence are the ideal of contemporary motherhood, something no mother who works outside the home could accomplish.

There is an extreme polarity between the homeschooled and public-schooled. While personal, loving attention is bestowed upon one group, the other is reduced to being a test score in a government-monitored database. Homeschooled children are well rounded and have refined interests; public-school graduates have been stifled and processed through an impersonal and degrading system. Colleges and society accept both types, though there is a noticeable difference in the values and work styles of each.

The same society that lavishes worship on mothers who homeschool resents those who don't. While there may be a different type of liberation in the homeschool revolution (one that reveres mothers), there is a backlash against parenting that is not seen as selfless, particularly when it comes to educating one's child.

Moreover, nontraditional families and poor families are considered inadequate for the whole enrichment of a child. Though fathers play minor parts in the homeschool phenomena, their presence is mandatory. Homeschool moms consider it their life's work, but there is no financial reward. It is truly a labor of love—and a signal of certain elevated social status.

Scenario 3 (2020): Generations Left Behind

A poor, uneducated workforce—made up of new immigrants, dropouts from immigrant families, and the urban poor of all ethnicities—will become trapped in low-paying, menial jobs with no real opportunity for advancement. In 2020, there will be two distinctly disparate social segments: college-educated information pushers who work in the top and middle corporate echelons and manual laborers with corresponding demarcations in race and status. In other words, a class system based on education levels will have developed.

In this scenario, the United States has become helplessly polarized, and other segments of society (such as middle- and upper-class Angloand African-Americans) have grown resentful of the amount of national resources being used to improve the prospects for first-generation Americans.

Among immigrant populations, a sense of alienation pervades, and social assimilation levels continue to decline. In tandem, the quality of public education in urban areas continues to drop, and though mighty efforts have been made to get high-school graduates from poor-performing sectors into college, they lack the academic skills to survive once they arrive there.

Since the beginning of the twenty-first century, larger family households and lower incomes have compelled too many first-generation Americans to put less emphasis on education and more on sending youth into the workforce as soon as possible. Add up the variables two decades later, and that is how the United States in 2020 has created a Third-World workforce.

Scenario 4 (2025): Experiential Schools

By 2025, a combination of nontraditional and tried-and-true techniques will generate a new kind of expertise in the classroom. Research shows that experiential education—focusing on enriching social skills and interpersonal relationships—works best for student satisfaction, interest, engagement, and retention. In 2025, students at a typical experiential school will place in the top percentage nationally, with nearly all graduates either going directly to college or entering the workforce as skilled workers.

Master Teacher

In this scenario, all experiential-school students receive the fundamentals required of high-school graduates at the beginning of the century, including language skills, math, sciences, and history. But in 2025, these basics are now delivered by an entirely new approach to instruction and with a great deal more effectiveness. One way is through a "master teacher" program, where distinguished experts in every field come to the classroom, bringing their years of education and experience to work teaching the basics. A retired statistician from a prestigious research firm, say, might teach math, outlining course material, giving broad concepts, and explaining theory. After she's finished lecturing, the class divides into smaller groups, tended by teaching staff circulating around the room to help students assimilate and apply what they've just learned.

A nutritionist with a degree in sports medicine might be the master teacher in the physical education department. Students learn healthy lifestyles as well as enjoy an exercise program designed to keep them active and interested in maintaining good health. Thanks to legislation relaxing teacher certification guidelines, experiential schools are able to bring in people from the community with degrees specifically related to the fields they teach and considerable "real world" experience. Furthermore, through these sessions, students who grasp the material more quickly are encouraged to assist their peers.

At the experiential school, community involvement is paramount. A separate board, composed of parents, has considerable input in school decisions. A trained mediator is also on staff to help all branches of school government interact smoothly. Political firestorms are circumvented because the schools emphasize a solid foundation in key subject areas without interference from political agenda pushers.

For those students interested in careers in business, technology, or the liberal arts, specific learning paths emphasizing business skills, technology, or general college preparation are available. Local corporations and businesses help provide special facilities on campus, including a business department (complete with a student-run store and an office suite) and a technology department overseen by former techies who like the stability of teaching. In the business department, corporate volunteers guide students as they learn the ins and outs of running a small business, corporate and personal finance, and business etiquette. A similar setup in the technology department provides graduates of the program with certifications in technology, Web design, and software applications, giving them a competitive advantage when they are ready to join the workforce. It should be stressed however, that students from all learning paths graduate with the skills and credentials to pursue a degree in higher learning, and school officials do their utmost to extol the value of a college degree. Every year, the school's administrators hold a signing day on campus for seniors to announce which college they will attend to inspire younger students to work hard to achieve the same success.

Students from the experiential school tend to outperform their contemporaries in college. Those on the college-bound learning path are assessed for their mastery of fundamentals in their sophomore year. The on-campus guidance counselor and the experiential-school faculty work with students to conceptualize their future and help them discover the path to their dreams.

A vision is the future that we would most like to see take place. Our vision reflects the values we wish to convey to the rest of the world—how we think the future should be. Alternative futures can be visions, but they can be strategic, too. As our priorities and resources change, so will our perception of public education.

The Future Taking Shape

Amidst the agendas, politics, and funding battles over public education, the future is somewhere taking shape right now. Perhaps the rebirth of public education will come through experiential schools. Given the time and context in which we write, experiential schools might be a good strategic plan toward better schools. On the other hand, the solution might exist elsewhere, such as teacher-education restructuring, or smaller schools, or any of the other reforms and innovations that are taking shape right now. Perhaps the key is not a shared vision, but using our shared values as the catalyst to separate resources and ideas for improving public education

ROBERT SANBORN, former dean of Hampshire College, is the executive director of the Education Foundation of Harris County (Texas) and columnist on education and career topics for the *Houston Post*. E-mail **sanborn@hcde-texas.org**.

ADOLFO SANTOS is professor of political science at the University of Houston–Downtown and is involved in evaluating education policy. E-mail **santosA@uhd.edu.**

ALEXANDRA L. MONTGOMERY is a graduate of the master's program in futures studies at the University of Houston–Clear Lake. She serves as a program coordinator for the Education Foundation of Harris County. E-mail **alexandramontgomery@yahoo.com.**

JAMES B. CARUTHERS is the communications coordinator for the Education Foundation of Harris County. He is currently working on a book on public education. E-mail **jcaruthers@hcde-texas.org** or **madkinggoll@sbcglobal.net**.

Originally published in the January/February 2005, issue of *The Futurist,* Copyright © 2005 by World Future Society, 7910 Woodmont Avenue, Suite 450, Bethesda, MD 20814. Telephone: 301/656-8274; Fax: 301/951-0394; **http://www.wfs.org**. Used with permission from the World Future Society.

Déjà Vu All Over Again?

Schools will operate in the future as they do now

HENRY LEVIN

My vision of where education will be—and where it must be—overlaps with Chris Whittle's to some extent. But it also differs in significant ways. Whittle's essay, drawn from his cheerful book (*Crash Course*), tells us that most of our education troubles will be over in just a quarter century. I disagree. His assumptions often differ markedly from the available evidence on what works and ignore the complexity of the witches' brew of politics, unions, bureaucracies, immigration, economics, and the social sciences. He implies that his vision is inexorable when it is merely wishful.

Chris Whittle's projection for 2030 is an elaborated echo of the 1990s, when for-profit education-management organizations (EMOs) proposed a mission and rationale for transforming American education. The standard fare promoted by those EMOs and their venture-capital sources was that the education industry was the next big opportunity for private capital, following the profitable example of the earlier HMO transformation of health care.

The lead financial actor at the beginning of that EMO era was Merrill Lynch, advisor to Whittle's company, Edison Schools. Merrill Lynch published *The Book of Knowledge*, a 193-page report on the $740 billion education and training market. Distributed widely to potential investors, *The Book* identified five "Big Ideas" that would transform the education and training industry over the next decade. But the book's story begins with the ostensible failure of public education and its rapidly rising costs, mediocre student achievement results, poor high-school graduation rates, and limp international rankings. The reason given for this miserable showing was the inefficiency of government.

Business enterprise efficiency would rescue the schools through organizational improvements; selection, training, assessing, and rewarding of principals and teachers on the basis of performance; and adoption of promising education technologies. Sophisticated business projections were conjured to assure potential investors that these enterprises would be highly profitable (doing well) while serving society (doing good).

The Wrong Assumptions

Not all has gone well, and Edison is a good case study, having lost more than six hundred million dollars of its investors' funding. Edison has one of the most complete models among the EMOs. It has truly attempted to deliver a quality school, but the evidence on raising student achievement shows no revolution in results. According to a recent evaluation by the RAND Corporation and comparisons in Philadelphia and Baltimore, Edison's record is not very different from that of similar public schools, though it has received greater funding than its public counterparts.

Somehow, in projecting to the future, Whittle posits a large number of changes in the basic institutions for delivering education, education research, and education personnel, based on the "success" of the EMOs, especially Edison. And despite the financial losses and mediocre achievement results, he believes that schools should be turned over to large businesses—with "economies of scale." Teachers' salaries would be double those of today to obtain the best professional talent; new training institutions for principals would arise through collaborative efforts of top business and education schools to churn out exemplary leadership; and government would increase funding for education research by a factor of ten or more.

The Whittle scenario also assumes that school districts would retain only a tiny percentage of federal, state, and local revenues, perhaps 1 percent, and limit themselves to "monitoring and quality-control" oversight of schools; private contractors would receive the other 99 percent. National and international education firms will compete for these contracts, and their retention by the district will depend on their performance. Teachers will be chosen by contracted schools, but will be employees of both districts and contractors (opening up districts to liability for personnel whom they neither select nor supervise). Teachers' salaries will reach numbers like $130,000 (adjusted for inflation) at the highest ranks. Principals will earn up to $250,000 with a base of 60 percent of this amount and the remainder in bonuses.

Back to the Future

The complete shift of schools to for-profit contractors seems to be based on the old business claims of the 1990s and Whittle's selective interpretation of Edison's record. It is also based on the argument that the contracting firms will benefit from econ-

Figure 1 The Labor of Public Education

Despite a rush of technological advances over the past 35 years, the number of public school employees per pupil has grown by more than 50 percent.

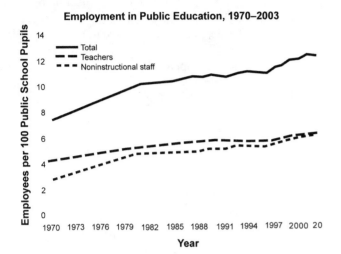

Employment in Public Education, 1970–2003

Note: Noninstructional staff comprises all school and district employees who are not teachers.

SOURCE: National Center for Education Statistics

omies of scale that are unavailable to the average school district in the United States. This is a strange and stubborn argument for Edison, which persistently claimed that annual losses in the tens of millions of dollars were due to insufficient numbers of schools. Subsequent expansions led only to larger losses.

Research has shown that beyond very small schools and school districts, there are few opportunities for economies of scale in education because most of the costs increase with enrollments and are not fixed costs that decline with additional clients. In fact, the number of teachers and other employees per student has increased in recent decades (see Figure 1). Further, size tends to depersonalize education. As a consequence, the leading edge of school reform is the promotion of smaller rather than larger units.

Whittle supports his assertion on scale economies with a table (page 180 in his book) that contrives the appearance of economies of scale by comparing a school district spending $28 million in 2030 with a hypothetical contractor receiving $25 billion in revenues. The table purports to show where contractors would experience scale economies and how they would yield a profit of 10 percent of revenues. As Yogi Berra would say, It's *déjà vu* all over again. It hasn't worked in the past; there's no reason to believe it will work in 2030.

Even more puzzling is how schools would prosper with half the teaching personnel. According to Whittle, this would be done largely through replacing teachers with student labor. Educators have long argued for greater participation of students in the education process, but not as a way of reducing costs. Four decades ago, noted economist William Baumol argued that the idea of reducing costs in education and similar labor-intensive

industries by substituting capital for labor or less-skilled labor for higher-paid professionals was impractical, at best. According to Baumol, education, by its very nature and its intransigence to change (whether public or private), is a teacher-intensive activity and so cannot benefit from standard approaches to increasing productivity. Equally, it is not possible to eliminate half of the opera singers in a classical opera or to replace two members of a string quartet with music synthesizers as a cost-effective way of improving quality. To this point no one has succeeded in disproving Baumol's thesis, nor has anyone discovered methods of providing the same education with half the number of teachers.

What Else Won't Work

Whittle's prime example of assigning students to peer tutoring is already used widely in public schools. I don't know a single situation where this method has reduced teachers' responsibilities. It is a form of supplementary instruction for selected students who are far behind other students (particularly for those with learning disabilities), not a substitute for regular teachers. And peer tutoring is not "free." The cost of effective peer tutoring is higher than alternatives, such as computer-assisted instruction or smaller class sizes or longer school days, because of the needs for adult personnel to coordinate, train, and monitor the student tutors. If peer tutoring has the capability of replacing half of our teachers, why wait until 2030?

Whittle suggests that charters and EMOs would do well to establish demonstration schools to show how we can use student chores to reduce the teachers by half. But it is remarkable that at present he can promise a sweeping future based on this phenomenon without dredging up even a single example as a proof of its existence.

We cannot count on technology. Of course, even as astute an observer as Bertrand Russell got this wrong in predicting in 1933 that instruction by motion pictures would require only large auditoriums with low-paid classroom monitors.

Whittle also assumes (in his book) that the "wireless revolution" will contribute to independent learning and a reduction in the need for teachers. But even if this claim were supported by evidence, the record shows that technology did not reduce teacher cost significantly enough to make Edison profitable or to create superior student achievement. Larry Cuban's history of the overblown promises of education technology (in his 2001 book *Oversold and Underused: Computers in the Classroom*) provides a concrete picture of why we cannot count on technology. Of course, even as astute an observer as Bertrand Russell got this wrong in predicting in 1933 that instruction by motion pictures would require only large auditoriums with low-paid classroom monitors. Whittle is in good company in his zeal for a strategy that has always generated more vision than reality.

In his infomercial on behalf of for-profit education enterprises, there is a technological determinism that assumes no opposition from or conflict with special interests such as teacher unions, administrators, and education bureaucracies. Every projected change is in the interest of all groups, a harmonious solution to what ails the schools. Even teacher organizations that would lose half of their membership and half of their collegial help at the school site will capitulate to the siren song of higher salaries. And new approaches to teacher training will enable them to get better results with half of the labor force and student assistance.

What Can and Should Be Done?

Whittle's assertion of the dominant role of for-profit firms in 2030 and the feasibility of halving the teaching force are not demonstrated to be feasible or desirable. Of course, the education system will be pressed to improve, especially on behalf of children from families in poverty, minorities, and immigrants, who will eventually compose a key component of the labor force. We will also need to find ways to ensure that all students master basic skills and that a substantial portion master the thinking skills and collaborative methods that will ensure a productive polity and prosperous economy. It should be noted that there has never been a golden age in education in which these goals were met, and the future will represent a struggle of incremental reforms in a system designed to "conserve" rather than transform society.

What types of reforms?

I agree completely with Whittle that we must improve the selection and training of teachers and principals, and increase funding for education research. Raising teachers' salaries is absolutely necessary to get the best talent into teaching. At the same time, the system needs better career ladders for teachers and far more effective approaches to selection, mentoring, and evaluation in order to enlist such talent productively. Teacher turnover, a high-cost item, must be reduced. Almost half of the teachers in Ohio's charter schools quit their schools in the four-year period between 2000 and 2004, in comparison with about 8 percent in conventional public schools and 12 percent in high-poverty, urban public schools, suggesting that new organizations are not a magic formula for school stability. Although technology is unlikely to replace many teachers, it is still a powerful tool for raising education quality by providing a vehicle for topic enrichment, student research, more challenging student projects, and greater student engagement. At the same time, the education community must be open to new forms of enterprise wherever it can make a contribution, such as contracting of specific instructional services, teacher cooperatives, and information technologies that enhance evaluation of students' knowledge and capabilities.

If present evidence is to be used, two potent contributions to raising student achievement will be widespread: effective preschool programs for all children and intensive interventions that build capacities of families to support the education of their children. I believe that both of these will be prevalent by 2030 because they show evidence of great promise even today. If I had my druthers, I would also add that education of at-risk students will shift from remediation and "drill and kill" to enrichment and acceleration, as we have tried to accomplish with the Accelerated Schools Project over the past two decades. The instructional approaches used in the best gifted and talented programs, with their emphasis on engagement, depth, and real-world applications, reinforce both basic skill development and more advanced learning. And the implementation of powerful and widespread approaches to building parents' capacity to support out-of-school learning will gain support from community organizations.

The future will represent a struggle of incremental reforms in a system designed to "conserve" rather than transform society.

Where will the money come from? By recouping funds that are "lost" to society because of poor education we can easily fund the improvements. Recent work by economists and other academic researchers—some of it presented at a recent symposium at Columbia University ("The Social Costs of Inadequate Education")—concluded that such investments have large payoffs in raising national income and tax revenues and reducing the cost of public services. For example, improvements in the availability and quality of preschool education would save large expenditures on special education and grade retention and improve high-school graduation rates and college attendance, especially among the poor, minorities, and immigrants. Just the loss in state and federal tax revenues from the 23 million high-school dropouts has been estimated at $50 billion a year. High-school dropouts pay about one-half the taxes of high-school graduates, and about one-third the taxes of those with more than a high-school diploma. Public health costs for the estimated 600,000 high-school dropouts in 2004 totaled about $58 billion. Some $10 billion could be saved each year in public assistance through universal high-school graduation; a mere 10 percent increase in the high-school completion rate would shave about $14 billion from the cost of crime. By investing in more productive educational practices, we can recoup magnitudes of investment that can easily fund the improvements set out above. And we don't have to wait until 2030.

HENRY LEVIN is professor of economics and education at Teachers College, Columbia University.

An Emerging Culture

RUDOLF STEINER'S CONTINUING IMPACT IN THE WORLD

CHRISTOPHER BAMFORD AND ERIC UTNE

Beginning at the end of the 19th century, a relatively unknown Austrian philosopher and teacher began to sow the seeds of what he hoped would blossom into a new culture. The seeds were his ideas, which he sowed through extensive writings, lectures, and countless private consultations. The seeds germinated and took root in the hearts and minds of his students, among whom were individuals who would later become some of the best known and most influential figures of the 20th century. Since the teacher's death in 1925, a quiet but steadily growing movement, unknown and unseen by most people, has been spreading over the world, bringing practical solutions to the problems of our global, technological civilization. The seeds are now coming to flower in the form of thousands of projects infused with human values. The teacher, called by some "the best kept secret of the 20th century," was Rudolf Steiner.

Steiner, a truly "Renaissance man," developed a way of thinking that he applied to different aspects of what it means to be human. Over a period of 40 years, he formulated and taught a path of inner development or spiritual research he called "anthroposophy." From what he learned, he gave practical indications for nearly every field of human endeavor. Art, architecture, drama, science, medicine, economics, religion, care of the dying, social organization—there is almost no field he did not touch.

> "My meeting with Rudolf Steiner led me to occupy myself with him from that time forth and to remain always aware of his significance. We both felt the same obligation to lead man once again to true inner culture. I have rejoiced at the achievements his great personality and his profound humanity have brought about in the world."
>
> **Albert Schweitzer**

Today, wherever there is a human need you'll find groups of people working out of Steiner's ideas. There are an estimated ten thousand initiatives worldwide—the movement is a hotbed of entrepreneurial activity, social and political activism, artistic expression, scientific research, and community building. In this report we limit our investigation to a tiny, representative sampling of these initiatives, primarily from North America.

Waldorf Schools

EDUCATION FOR THE HEAD, HANDS, AND HEART

Waldorf education is probably the most widespread and mature of Steiner's many plantings. There are more than 150 Waldorf schools in North America and over 900 worldwide, double the number just a decade ago, making it possibly the fastest growing educational movement in the world. Steiner's interest in education was lifelong. As a young man, he earned a living as a tutor, starting at 14 helping fellow students. Then, from the age of 23 to 29, he lived in Vienna with the family of Ladislaus and Pauline Specht, undertaking the education of their four sons, one of whom, Otto, was hydrocephalic. At the age of 10, Otto could hardly read or write. His parents were uncertain whether he could be educated at all. Steiner took responsibility for him. Believing that, despite appearances, the boy had great intellectual capacities, Steiner saw his task as slowly waking the boy up and bringing him into his body. To do this, he knew he first had to gain the child's love. On this basis, he was able to awaken his dormant faculties. He was so successful that Otto went on to become a doctor.

Lao Tsu (604-531 BC) Tao Te Ching, Chapter 42

The Tao begot one.
One begot two.
Two begot three.
And three begot
the ten thousand
things.

Dear Reader,

Over the last 30 years I've encountered Rudolf Steiner's ideas in a number of different venues: as an active parent of four Waldorf-educated boys; as a natural foods merchant distributing Biodynamic® foods (grown according to Steiner's indications); as a truth seeker, struggling unsuccessfully to understand Steiner's dense and, for me, impenetrable writings; as a former architecture student intrigued by Steiner's contributions to 20th-century art and architecture; and, more recently, as the seventh and then eighth grade class teacher at City of Lakes Waldorf School in Minneapolis.

Despite all this exposure to the manifestations of his philosophy, I didn't begin to fathom Steiner's own thinking until several years ago when I began reading his writings in earnest. His language suffered from translation, was often time- and culture-bound, and frequently filled with archaic and new-agey references. Yet, as I kept at it, his ideas soon became more accessible and increasingly meaningful to me. After I "graduated" with my class in June 2002, I decided to meet some actual people whose lives had been touched by Steiner's ideas. Last summer, my 17-year-old son Oliver and I traveled 2,500 miles around Europe, visiting centers of Steinerian activity. In Järna, Sweden, we participated in an international youth conference for some 200 Waldorf-educated 16- to 30-year-olds from every race and 40 countries. In Dornach, Switzerland, we met the leadership of the world-wide General Anthroposophic Society, founded by Steiner. In other places we met people who have been involved in various aspects of Steiner's work for two or three generations. Since returning, I've been taking similar people-meeting excursions to the East and West Coasts.

What I've found is fascinating and heartening to me, and I wanted to share it with you. So I went to see the folks at the Rudolf Steiner Foundation and asked them to underwrite the costs of researching, writing, and publishing a special section on the continuing legacy of Rudolf Steiner. They turned around and raised the funds from private donors. My co-author of this section is Christopher Bamford, who has written widely on a variety of topics, including the recently published *What Is Anthroposophy?* (Anthroposophic Press, Great Barrington, Massachusetts) and "An Endless Trace: The Passionate Pursuit of Wisdom in the West" (Codhill Press, New York).

As you read the section I think you'll agree that the people influenced by Steiner's ideas are at least as interesting as the ideas themselves. Like the rest of society, they are a diverse lot. Some are well-scrubbed and impressively accomplished, like the actresses Jennifer Aniston and Julianna Margulies, and American Express president and CEO Kenneth Chenault, all of whom are Waldorf educated. Others, like me, are rather wacky, basically inept, unreconstructed idealists and malcontents. But then, I never had a Waldorf education!

The people involved in Steiner's ideas that I find most compelling are working within the framework of communities, in Waldorf schools, Biodynamic® farms, anthroposophical medical clinics, Camphill Villages for the handicapped, early childhood and elder-care centers, and artistic collaboratives. They're not isolated and alienated, stuck in institutions inhospitable to their values. They're developing the social skills necessary to form real, viable communities. If they study anthroposophy, Steiner's non-religious path to self-knowledge, they're struggling to learn what we all sign on for in this human life—they're learning how to love.

There are an estimated ten thousand initiatives around the world that trace their lineage to Steiner and his ideas. These initiatives add up to an insurgent movement today that just may be the seedbed of a new, more just and humane emerging culture—the alternative that so many of us have been searching for all our lives. I believe these people, the heirs to Rudolf Steiner's legacy, are building, in our midst, a truly viable template for a greener and kinder world.

—Eric Utne

Waldorf students create their own "main lesson books" for each subject.

For Steiner, Otto was a learning experience. As he says in his *Autobiography:* "The educational methods I had to adopt gave me insight into the way that the human soul and spirit are connected with the body. It became my training in physiology and psychology. I came to realize that education and teaching must become an art, and must be based upon true knowledge of the human being."

As with everything Steiner did, his curriculum for Waldorf education began with a question. In 1919, in the chaos following the First World War, Emil Molt, director of the Waldorf Astoria Cigarette Company, asked Steiner to help with the creation of a school for his workers. Four months later, the first Independent Waldorf School opened in Stuttgart, Germany. From that spontaneous beginning arose the now worldwide Waldorf School Movement.

Waldorf Education: It's All in the Curriculum

Whenever he visited a Waldorf school, Rudolf Steiner's first question to the students was always, "Do you love your teacher?" Similarly, he would ask the teachers, "Do you love your students?" The class teacher accompanies the children from first grade through eighth grade, i.e., from childhood into the beginning of adolescence. Children and teacher grow together. Making and doing, creating beauty, and working with one's hands—knitting, crocheting, painting, drawing, and woodworking—are an integral part of the educational and developmental process. Besides teaching manual dexterity and training eye-hand coordination, the work with color, form, and different materials develops an aesthetic sense, which permeates all other activities. Coordinated physical movement, learning through the body, accompanies all stages of development. The practice of Eurythmy—Steiner's art of movement, which makes speech and music visible through action and gesture—allows the child to develop a sense of harmony and balance. Rhythm is an important component of all these activities. Rhythm (order or pattern in time) permeates the entire school day, as well as the school year, which unfolds around celebrating festivals drawn from different religions and cultures.

"I loved school. I hated being sick because I didn't want to miss anything. I felt teachers cared about me so much, it gave me confidence. Now I feel there's nothing I can't do."

Jessica Winer '80, artist

The curriculum is based upon an understanding of the developing child. From birth through ages six or seven, children absorb the world through their senses and respond primarily through imitation. As they enter the primary school years, they are centered more in feeling and imagination. Then, as they continue their journey into the middle school, rational, abstract thinking begins to emerge. The curriculum respects this developmental process and gives it substance. Based on the idea that "ontogeny recapitulates phylogeny," that a developing child goes through the phases of human cultural evolution, children at different ages study what is appropriate to their development. Thus they learn reading by first "becoming" the letters, through physical gesture. In their "main lesson" books that are their textbooks, crayoned pictures of mountains and trees metamorphose into the letters M and T, and form drawings of circles and polygons become numbers.

Most Waldorf kids actually like school and develop a real love of learning.

Movement, music, and language (including foreign languages) begin in first grade. They hear fables and stories of the holy ones of different cultures. They learn to knit and crochet and play the recorder. Leaving the "paradise" of the first two grades, they encounter the sacred teachings of their culture. For example, in North America, the stories of the Old Testament are taught. In Japan, ancient Shinto stories are told. Farming, gardening, house building, measurement, and grammar now enter the curriculum. They memorize poems and begin to play stringed instruments. With the fourth grade comes mythology, embroidery, zoology, geography, and geometric drawing. Mathematics and languages become more complex; art becomes more representational. In the fifth grade, history enters; they recite poems, begin botany, learn to knit with four needles, and start woodworking. And thus it continues, each grade providing more wonders.

Rather than pursuing several subjects at a time, the Waldorf curriculum unfolds in main lesson blocks of three or four weeks. The students create their own texts, or "main lesson books" for each subject. This enables students to live deeply into the subject. In this age of distraction, Waldorf children learn to be able to concentrate and focus.

Students learn the alphabet by first discovering the forms of the letters in nature

With high school, the mood changes in harmony with the tremendous developmental changes occurring at this time. Students no longer have a class teacher, but specialists in different fields who teach the various blocks and encourage dialog and discussion. Exact observation and reflection are prized. The aim is to engage students in the present and build on the confidence and ability to think for oneself that developed in the lower grades.

Waldorf Schools in North America

Waldorf education in America developed almost imperceptibly. The first school was founded in New York in 1928 and, over the next 20 years, only six more schools were founded. But something had germinated and slowly began to spread. Looking back, the growth was steady. The number of schools more or less doubled every decade. The reasons for this success are not hard to find. Waldorf schools appeals to parents seeking a truly holistic, child-centered, loving, artistic, practical, and wonder-filled education.

An Example: The Green Meadow Waldorf School

The Green Meadow Waldorf School in Spring Valley, New York, founded in 1950, is one of the oldest Waldorf schools in North America. As you approach the wooded suburban enclave you realize that this is a different kind of school. The several buildings are clustered around a courtyard, forming a little campus, which in turn is surrounded by mature oaks and white ash. Gardens, large climbing logs and stones, and sculpture abound. Each building has its own character and form, yet the entire assemblage works as a whole. The colors are warm and natural, not bright. There's no graffiti. The roofs are shingled and gently sloped. Many of the walls are set at softer, more oblique angles. Even many of the windows have their rectangular shapes softened with another edge, making them five- or six-sided instead of just four-sided.

There is something peaceful in the air. The impression intensifies as you enter. Warmth pervades the space. Your senses begin to dance. Beauty, color, and natural flowing forms surround you. Children's paintings adorn the walls. Muffled sounds filter through the classroom walls and doors as you walk down a corridor. You can hear musical instruments, singing, children reciting a poem, the calm voice of a class teacher. And the smells! Bread baking in the kindergarten, fragrant plants and nontoxic paints. When you enter a classroom, the impression is confirmed—this is what a school ought to be. The children are happy, they are learning, they seem to love their teachers and each other.

> **"My parents... felt that the Waldorf school would be a far more open environment for African Americans.... I think the end result of Waldorf education is to raise our consciousness.... It taught me how to think for myself, to be responsible for my decisions. Second, it made me a good listener, sensitive to the needs of others. And third, it helped (me) establish meaningful beliefs."**
>
> **Kenneth Chenault, President & CEO, American Express Corporation, Waldorf alumnus**

The Green Meadow School is home to a veritable United Nations of religious diversity. Of the 388 students (K–12) in Green Meadow, more than 60 are of Jewish descent, approximately 25 are the children of members of the nearby Jerrahi Islamic Mosque, and the rest come from Protestant, Catholic, Buddhist, agnostic, atheistic, and who-knows-what other religious traditions. Waldorf schools are sometimes assumed to be Eurocentric because of their European origins, yet the curriculum turns out to have universal appeal, adapting well in cultures as diverse as the *favelas* (slums) of Sao Paolo, Brazil, the black settlements of South Africa, rural Egypt and urban Israel, Eastern Europe, India, Southeast Asia, Australia, Japan, and the Pine Ridge Lakota Indian reservation in South Dakota.

Waldorf Graduates

Parents considering Waldorf want to know "What will become of my child?" According to Harm Paschen from the University of Bielefeld, Germany, studies of European Waldorf high school grads show that Waldorf graduates do very well indeed. Kids who go to Waldorf schools are as likely, or more likely, to attend college as students from public and other private schools. And after college, they are more likely to be employed than non-Waldorf grads. They are disproportionately well represented in teaching, the arts, business, medicine, and the social services professions. Similar research with North American grads is clearly needed.

On a recent college visit, Donna Badrig, associate director of undergraduate admissions for Columbia University, told one student, "We love Waldorf kids. We reject some students with 1600s on their SATs and accept others based on other factors, like the creative ability Waldorf students demonstrate." Similar enthusiasm for Waldorf grads was heard from admissions officers at Wesleyan University. City of Lakes Waldorf School (K–8) and Watershed High School (a new Waldorf charter school), both in Minneapolis, have seen their students go to such colleges at Sarah Lawrence, Juilliard, Wellesley, Hampshire, Wesleyan, and MIT, among others. But not all Waldorf grads go to college after high school. Many take a break from study to travel or do volunteer work before getting a job or going on to higher education.

> **Waldorf education is possibly the fastest growing educational movement in the world.**

From our own observations, Waldorf students seem to share certain common characteristics. They are often independent and self-confident self-starters. They have genuine optimism for the future. They also tend to be highly ethical and are compassionately intelligent. They keep their sense of wonder about learning and the interdisciplinary sense that everything is connected. They seem to have a very healthy measure of what author Daniel Goleman calls "emotional intelligence," a much more reliable predictor of "success" in life, by any definition, than IQ or SAT scores. Generally speaking, they are both artistic and practical. They seem to know intuitively how to do many things.

Waldorf grad Paul Asaro, an architect, says: "I still draw upon the problem-solving skills that were nurtured... during my adolescent years." Other graduates stress independent thinking, imagination, and the relationships they developed and enjoyed with faculty and fellow students. "That's what's so wonderful about Waldorf education," says actress Julianna Margulies. "You're exposed to all these different ideas, but you're never given one view of it. You're encouraged to think as an individual." Rachel Blackmer, a veterinarian, writes: "Waldorf education is learning in its purest form. It is learning to think, to feel, and to act appropriately and with conscience." Mosemare Boyd, president and CEO, American Women Presidents, adds: "At Waldorf, we were taught to see things from the perspective of others. We saw that doing things together... was always more fun.... We learned to love learning."

Behind the Scenes

According to the Association of Waldorf Schools of North America (AWSNA), in the United States there are currently 56 full member Waldorf Schools, 15 sponsored Waldorf Schools (on their way to full membership), 69 developing Waldorf Schools, and 29 Waldorf Initiatives affiliated with AWSNA. Besides this there are a number of Waldorf-inspired or Waldorf method charter schools, as well as other Waldorf-related initiatives in the public schools.

> "A Steiner education teaches you to think differently from the herd. I've found that independent ideas can be very valuable in the investment world."
>
> **David Nadel '87, managing director, Bear Stearns**

Trained, qualified Waldorf teachers are much sought after. In North America each year, schools hire a combined total of between 300 and 400 new teachers, yet the various teacher-training centers graduate less than half that number. Many of the teachers are parents making a mid-life career change, perhaps seeking new challenges or a way to contribute to society. Robert Amis, who sold a successful equipment leasing company and took early retirement at 46, found himself accepting an offer to become a class teacher at City of Lakes Waldorf School in Minneapolis. "It's the hardest work I've ever done," he says. "I feel like I'm in a crucible, much the same as my students; and we're all wondering what changes are being wrought."

> **Side by Side, a leadership development program of Sunbridge College, trains 17-to 23-year-old youth who then facilitate weeklong arts and environmental overnight camps for underserved children ages 8 to 12 in New York and Los Angeles.**

There are five full teacher-training centers: Rudolf Steiner College in Sacramento, California; Waldorf Institute of Southern California in Northridge, California; Center for Anthroposophy/Antioch Graduate School in Keene, New Hampshire; Sunbridge College in Spring Valley, New York; and Rudolf Steiner Center in Toronto, Ontario. In addition, there are two sponsored centers, one in Eugene, Oregon, and one in Detroit; and five developing centers—in Duncan, British Columbia; Sausalito, California; Honolulu; Chicago; and Seattle. And the Rudolf Steiner Institute, a summer school for adults and children, presently located at Thomas College in Waterville, Maine, provides a strong introduction to Waldorf education.

Waldorf in the Public Schools

According to George Hoffeker, former principal of the Yuba River Charter School in Nevada City, California, "Waldorf methods are so exciting and enlivening for all children that they shouldn't be reserved just for those who can afford it." Mary Goral, a professor at St. Mary College in Milwaukee and director of its early childhood education program, echoes this sentiment. She says, "I truly believe that what is needed in public schools is something much more like Waldorf, something that engages the whole child—body, soul, and spirit."

The first move in this direction began in September 1991 when the Milwaukee Urban Waldorf School opened—with 350 students, more that 90 percent of them African American—as part of the Milwaukee Public School System. Robert Peterkin, then superintendent of schools, had seen the need for a healthy education to serve the special needs of children in educationally deprived areas. Public school leaders, Waldorf educators, public school teachers, and scholars all worked together to found a school that would bring the integrated artistic, intellectual, and developmental Waldorf curriculum into the heart of an American city. Under the direction of Ann Pratt, an experienced Waldorf teacher, the experiment pioneered the development of an intensive teacher-training program for public school teachers. The result: reading scores increased and attendance stabilized. The school became a safe, quiet, well-ordered, attractive place to learn. A visitor recounted a telling anecdote. Waiting to see the principal, the visitor found himself seated opposite a student who was also waiting. According to the visitor, the student was, "threateningly large and had clearly committed some infraction. But there he sat outside the principal's office, quiet and self-composed, knitting."

Some publicly funded Waldorf schools are currently in transition. The Milwaukee experiment is still regrouping since losing founding principal Dorothy St. Charles to promotion. St. Charles' departure, combined with the school's move to "the worst zip code in Milwaukee," led to the loss of half its certified Waldorf teachers. The school, under the leadership of new principal Cheryl Colbert, is working with Cardinal Strich College to develop a teacher-training program to fill the need for certified Waldorf teachers. And the Sacramento school district, which operates a Waldorf-method magnet school, and the Twin Ridges Elementary School District of North San Juan, California, which operates seven Waldorf-inspired charter schools, including the first charter school in the United States to use Waldorf methods—the Yuba River Charter School—are in the midst of a court battle. The plaintiff's suit asserts that Waldorf education is religious in nature and that the two school districts are therefore in violation of the U.S. and California constitutional separation of church and state. The district court dismissed the suit, but on appeal, the circuit court gave the case new life, sending it back to district court.

> "Society tells you that there is only one way to do things. Steiner students learn to create their own initiative and to be can-do thinkers."
>
> **Deborah Winer '79, playwright**

Opponents of Waldorf education, which is based on Steiner's insights into child development, equate the curriculum with anthroposophy, which they claim to be a religion. Waldorf

231

advocates respond that Rudolf Steiner's anthroposophy is determinedly nonreligious and isn't taught in Waldorf schools anyway. The Waldorf curriculum stands on its own, they say, no matter what else Steiner taught or believed. "Anthroposophy is a founding philosophy, not a curriculum," says John Miller, a teacher at Watershed High School in Minneapolis. "Look at John Dewey, the educational reformer. Did anyone accuse his followers of teaching 'Deweyism'? No, because they just used a methodology he developed."

Critics also point to Steiner's early involvement in the Theosophical Society and to his more controversial views, such as his references to the lost continent of Atlantis. Several racist-sounding comments are often quoted to paint him as a racist. Waldorf's defenders say they reject racism out of hand. They say that Steiner was a person very much of his times, that his comments were made at the turn of the century, taken out of context, and are completely at odds with the vast preponderence of his statements having anything to do with race. They point out that many of Steiner's most reputable contemporaries shared beliefs with him that may appear today to be suspect or downright silly (Mahatma Gandhi was a member of the Theosophical Society, and Albert Einstein believed that Atlantis was a historical reality).

Despite the controversy, Waldorf-inspired charter schools are popping up all over the country. It is difficult to say just how many charter schools there are. Conservative estimates put the number at about 20 and growing. Though some fear a watering down of Steiner's principles, Donald Bufano, chairman of AWSNA, says, "Parents, and especially children at Waldorf or Waldorf-methods schools can enjoy the benefits of the education without commitment to its foundations just as one can enjoy Biodynamic® food or anthroposophic medicine whether or not they know how they work or where they come from."

Early Childhood Initiatives

The Waldorf approach to education is not limited to school-age kids. Recent students have pointed repeatedly to the critical importance of the nurturing children receive in early childhood, when infants and children are especially at risk. The combination of the breakdown of the family, the need for two working parents, and the growing number of single-parent families has left caregivers, whether at home or in daycare, uncertain how to care for children. Activities that were once natural and instinctive, like what to eat and how to bring up a baby, must now be learned consciously.

"Children," says Cynthia Aldinger, "are like sponges. They drink in everything and everyone around them." It is not only a question of the physical surroundings. What we say and do around a child, even how we think, is critical. A grassroots or-ganization growing out of the Waldorf Early Childhood Association, Life Ways is devoted to the deinstitutionalization of child care. Founded in 1998, Life Ways provides courses and training in parenting and child care and is expanding to establish child care homes, centers, and parenting programs throughout North America.

A related effort is Sophia's Hearth in Keene, New Hampshire. Taking its name from the ancient goddess of wisdom, Sophia's Hearth works with "the art of becoming a family." As founder Susan Weber puts it, "Our work supports families in creating an atmosphere of loving warmth, joy, and respect for their infants and young children, while at the same time nurturing each parent."

The Caldwell Early Life Center at Rudolf Steiner College acts as a center for these and similar initiatives. Only two years old, but with a prestigious advisory board including naturalist Jane Goodall, well-known authors and researchers Jane Healy and Joseph Chilton Pearce, and education and child advocate Sally Bickford, it is halfway through raising the $2.5 million needed to complete a building to house its activities. These will cover the full range of early childhood needs, from working to reduce stress and isolation for families in ethnically and economically diverse neighborhoods to the creation of a demonstration daycare component.

Another Example: The Wolakota Waldorf School

In the early 1990s a group of Lakota Sioux educators began to look for a better education for their children and discovered Waldorf education. They found that it paralleled their own wisdom traditions in many ways. Their hope was to create not only a school but also eventually a model community. In 1993 they created the Wolakota Waldorf Society as a nonprofit organization.

The Wolakota School is located on 80 acres of the Pine Ridge Reservation, near Oglala Lakota College, in Shannon County, South Dakota, the poorest county in the United States. Pine Ridge, the site of the Wounded Knee massacre, has been home to many famous Native American leaders, including Black Elk, Chief Red Cloud, and Fool Crow. The school serves 24 Lakota children. Among Waldorf schools it is unique, depending entirely on donations. There are only two teachers, Susan Bunting and Chris Young, who do everything from cooking breakfast and lunch to transporting children. If funds and space can be found, Edwin Around Him, Sr., will be hired next year as the school's third teacher. This year Edwin teaches Lakota and operates the van, when it's working.

Sponsored by Rudolf Steiner Foundation and Utne Magazine

Index

Index

Test Your Knowledge Form

We encourage you to photocopy and use this page as a tool to assess how the articles in *Annual Editions* expand on the information in your textbook. By reflecting on the articles you will gain enhanced text information. You can also access this useful form on a product's book support Web site at *http://www.mhcls.com/online/*.

NAME: _____   DATE: _____

TITLE AND NUMBER OF ARTICLE: _____

BRIEFLY STATE THE MAIN IDEA OF THIS ARTICLE:

_____

LIST THREE IMPORTANT FACTS THAT THE AUTHOR USES TO SUPPORT THE MAIN IDEA:

_____

WHAT INFORMATION OR IDEAS DISCUSSED IN THIS ARTICLE ARE ALSO DISCUSSED IN YOUR TEXTBOOK OR OTHER READINGS THAT YOU HAVE DONE? LIST THE TEXTBOOK CHAPTERS AND PAGE NUMBERS:

_____

LIST ANY EXAMPLES OF BIAS OR FAULTY REASONING THAT YOU FOUND IN THE ARTICLE:

_____

LIST ANY NEW TERMS/CONCEPTS THAT WERE DISCUSSED IN THE ARTICLE, AND WRITE A SHORT DEFINITION:

We Want Your Advice

ANNUAL EDITIONS revisions depend on two major opinion sources: one is our Advisory Board, listed in the front of this volume, which works with us in scanning the thousands of articles published in the public press each year; the other is you—the person actually using the book. Please help us and the users of the next edition by completing the prepaid article rating form on this page and returning it to us. Thank you for your help!

ANNUAL EDITIONS: Education 07/08

ARTICLE RATING FORM

Here is an opportunity for you to have direct input into the next revision of this volume.
We would like you to rate each of the articles listed below, using the following scale:

1. **Excellent: should definitely be retained**
2. **Above average: should probably be retained**
3. **Below average: should probably be deleted**
4. **Poor: should definitely be deleted**

Your ratings will play a vital part in the next revision.
Please mail this prepaid form to us as soon as possible.
Thanks for your help!

RATING	ARTICLE	RATING	ARTICLE
	1. The Biology of Risk Taking		28. Dealing with Rumors, Secrets, and Lies: Tools of Aggression for Middle School Girls
	2. Squeeze Play		29. The Heightened Significance of *Brown* v. *Board of Education* in Our Time
	3. Democracy's First Step		
	4. Social Science and the Citizen		30. The Role of Social Foundation in Preparing Teachers for Culturally Relevant Practice
	5. Parents Behaving Badly		
	6. Sobriety Tests Are Becoming Part of the School Day		31. Tolerance in Teacher Education
	7. The 37th Annual Phi Delta Kappa/Gallup Poll of the Public's Attitudes Toward the Public Schools		32. Dialogue Across Cultures: Teachers' Perceptions About Communication with Diverse Families
	8. Dancing Lessons for Elephants: Reforming Ed School Leadership Program		33. African American Boys and the Discipline Gap: Balancing Educator's Uneven Hand
	9. Textural Perceptions of School Time and Assessment		34. Grooming Great Urban Teachers
	10. The Father of Modern School Reform		35. Hearts and Minds: Military Recruitment and the High School Battlefield
	11. Friendly Competition		36. City's Pupils Get More Hype than Hope
	12. Urban and Rural Schools: Overcoming Lingering Obstacles		37. Approaching the Unavoidable: Literacy Instruction and the Internet
	13. Alternative Approaches to High-Stakes Testing		38. Acting White
	14. What Colleges Forget to Teach		39. How Boys Learn
	15. Boys at Risk: The Gender Achievement Gap		40. The Overdominance of Computers
	16. Standardized Students: The Problems with Writing for Tests Instead of People		41. Morality, Medicine, and Meaning: Toward an Integrated Justification of Physical Education
	17. Observer: A Little Ethics Left Behind		42. Starting with the Soul
	18. Keeping Score		43. The Satisfactions of Teaching
	19. Character and Academics: What Good Schools Do		44. Mayhem in the Middle: Why We Should Shift to K–8
	20. Patriotism and Education: An Introduction		45. Guess Again: Will Changing the Grades Save Middle-Level Education?
	21. Patriotism and Accountability: The Role of Educators in the War on Terrorism		46. Developing Social Justice Educators
	22. Should We Teach Patriotism?		47. The Boss in the Classroom
	23. Promoting Altruism in the Classroom		48. The New WWW: Whatever, Whenever, Wherever
	24. In the End You Are Sure to Succeed: Lincoln on Perseverance		49. Listen to the Natives
	25. Welcome to the House System		50. The Future of Education: Four Scenarios
	26. Discipline: Responding to Socioeconomic and Racial Differences		51. *Déjà Vu* All Over Again?
	27. Reach Them to Teach Them		52. An Emerging Culture

(Continued on next page)

BUSINESS REPLY MAIL
FIRST CLASS MAIL PERMIT NO. 551 DUBUQUE IA

POSTAGE WILL BE PAID BY ADDRESEE

McGraw-Hill Contemporary Learning Series
2460 KERPER BLVD
DUBUQUE, IA 52001-9902

NO POSTAGE
NECESSARY
IF MAILED
IN THE
UNITED STATES

ABOUT YOU

Name

Date

Are you a teacher? ❑   A student? ❑
Your school's name

Department

Address   City   State   Zip

School telephone #

YOUR COMMENTS ARE IMPORTANT TO US!

Please fill in the following information:
For which course did you use this book?

Did you use a text with this ANNUAL EDITION?   ❑ yes ❑   no
What was the title of the text?

What are your general reactions to the *Annual Editions* concept?

Have you read any pertinent articles recently that you think should be included in the next edition? Explain.

Are there any articles that you feel should be replaced in the next edition? Why?

Are there any World Wide Web sites that you feel should be included in the next edition? Please annotate.

May we contact you for editorial input?   ❑ yes ❑   no
May we quote your comments? ❑ yes ❑   no